In 1935 Professor Robert Newdick of Ohio State University wrote to Robert Frost—already America's most famous living poet—in order to suggest certain revisions in the arrangement of the poet's collected poems. The brief letter was to begin a relationship of nearly five years (ending only with Newdick's untimely death in 1939) in which Newdick assiduously gathered materials from a wide variety of sources for a projected (but not "authorized") Frost biography. Although only part (about 100 pages) of the biography was actually written, Newdick left behind him several files of factual data, as well as observations and comments by Frost and by many people who knew him. These materials have not heretofore been published, nor were they used in any subsequent biography.

In the present volume William A. Sutton brings together Newdick's partial biography with his various notes and letters, adding a narrative of the Frost-Newdick relationship which sheds new light on the poet and on the identity of poets. With Newdick, as with subsequent researchers, the fiction-making Frost was often playing a game of hide-and-seek so that he would never be completely "found out" as a mere empirical datum, although there is evidence that his candor with Newdick was at times greater than it would be in later years. Newdick, a perceptive admirer of Frost's poetry, had to struggle with his own realizations of such Frostian characteristics as secretiveness, ambivalence, and capriciousness, and so the book reveals a great poet who

gathered since 1969. Among h
*The Road to Winesburg, Sexua
Language*, and *Dear Bab: Lett
wood Anderson to a Friend*.

Edited by
William A.
Sutton

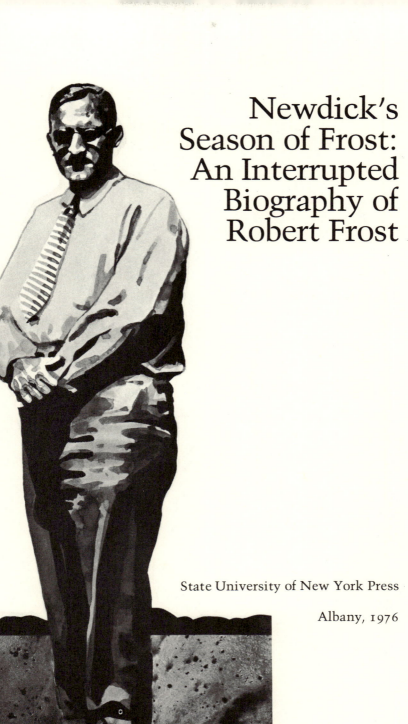

Newdick's Season of Frost: An Interrupted Biography of Robert Frost

State University of New York Press

Albany, 1976

First Edition

First published in 1976 by
State University of New York Press
99 Washington Avenue, Albany, New York 12210

Printed in the United States of America

Library of Congress Cataloging in Publication Data

Newdick, Robert Spangler.
  Newdick's Season of Frost.

  Includes index.
  1. Frost, Robert, 1874–1963—Biography. 2. Frost,
Robert, 1874–1963—Friends and associates. 3. Newdick,
Robert Spangler. I. Sutton, William Alfred, 1915–
II. Title. III. Title: Season of Frost.
PS3511.R94Z84 1976   811'.5'2 [B]   75-22009
ISBN 0–87395–316–9

Contents

Foreword

As I have often said, life is a series of circles within circles. It might be called Fate. Whatever it is, it often leads to an extraordinary sense of fulfillment: The feeling one has when dropping a crucial piece into a particularly difficult jigsaw puzzle—triumphant. This was what I felt when I learned that a manuscript, half-finished, half-completed, had been recovered from its oblivion of forty years.

It was in 1934, as a young professor at Ohio State University, that Dr. Robert Newdick had fallen in love with the poetry of Robert Frost. The correspondence that developed between the two men is particularly illuminating.

It was following the sudden death of Dr. Newdick in July of 1939 that everything in connection with the proposed biography somehow became "lost" in the archives of his widow. Apparently, no one was aware of how much valuable material in letters and articles (printed and unprinted) were available. I had visited the Newdicks in 1937 and, when a friend, Dr. William Sutton of Ball State University in Muncie, Indiana, was visiting me, he brought up the name of Robert Newdick. I wondered whether Mrs. Newdick had retained her husband's work on the contemplated biography. Opening an old address book, we found not only the address but the telephone number in Columbus, Ohio. She answered the phone! And, consequently, Dr. Sutton got in touch with her immediately on his return West. Mrs. Newdick's cooperation and interest were of the greatest benefit. As a result, *Newdick's Season of Frost* is herewith published.

Dr. Sutton is, indeed, fortunate in having added one more revealing insight into my father's complex life, particularly since it covers a period not so well known—that is, the years between 1934 and 1940.

Lesley Frost

Robert Newdick: An Appreciation

I am staring at a stack of "themes" (what a strange name to call the papers we wrote) composed for Professor Robert Newdick in a Derby Hall classroom at Ohio State University nearly forty years ago. His critical marginalia in a fluent handwriting were, and still are, perceptive, incisive, sometimes cutting, always designed to kick me in the literary pants, to strip me of affectation, to push me to my top potential. If my professional standards as a writer are high, Robert Newdick set the goals. He snatched me from a morass of freshmen, invited me to his house to see his treasured chessmen, to taste something I'd never eaten before, cheese rarebit (I had always thought it was actually made from rabbit!), and to read aloud some of my short plays, encouraging me, goading me, refining me.

Robert Newdick's dynamism as a teacher was matched only by his dedication as a scholar. He spoke often of his labors beyond the classroom. The last time I ever saw him, I asked him how his work was going, and he looked far off, and quoted his beloved Frost: "And miles to go before I sleep, and miles to go before I sleep."

Years later, I told that to Robert Frost, when I toasted him on his 77th birthday with this: "I think the American public, unlike the American refrigerator, will never be de-Frosted!" Frost, pleased and amused by that toast, grasped my shoulder: "Robert Newdick taught you, boy! The ripples a teacher makes in a life's pond never stop! It's a kind of immortality, isn't it? Writing. Yes, and teaching!"

Jerome Lawrence *

*Playwright/Author Jerome Lawrence's most recent work is the critically-hailed biography, *Actor: The Life and Times of Paul Muni* (Putnam's, 1974). His plays (in collaboration with Robert E. Lee), among them *Inherit the Wind* and *The Night Thoreau Spent in Jail*, have been acclaimed "contemporary theatre classics" and have been translated and performed in 31 languages.

Robert Frost & Robert S. Newdick

I. Newdick's Chapters on Frost

INTRODUCTION

These thirteen mini-chapters, evidently written in various parts of 1937 and 1938, were what Professor Robert S. Newdick, of the Department of English at the Ohio State University, was able to complete before he died suddenly of appendicitis in July 1939 at the age of 40. His friendship with Robert Frost, begun by correspondence in July 1934, had developed so that, by 1935, he was working on both a bibliography and a biography. From 1935 till his death both Newdick and Frost thought of Newdick as Frost's biographer.

Especially after Lesley Frost Ballantine read the Newdick manuscript in August 1972, with enthusiasm for the way she felt Newdick had caught the spirit of the father she knew, it has been thought that Newdick's work, though unfinished, should be published. It will be seen that Newdick had begun the process of assimilating much new (and heretofore unpublished) information, gained through dedicated research as well as through his interviews with his subject.

Part III, Newdick's Research Findings, contains the Frost material which Newdick did not have the opportunity to write into these chapters or to the others which would have covered Frost's life until 1939.

ACKNOWLEDGMENTS

The willingness of Mrs. Robert S. Newdick to allow the publication of her late husband's unfinished work and to allow the use of the materials he had accumulated and which became available after his death has made this book possible. Students of the work of Frost may be grateful to her for her curatorship in the face of much discouragement of the invaluable materials left by Professor Newdick.

The writer owes to the encouragement of Lesley Frost Ballantine, who was certain that further research concerning the life and work of her father was in order, his query to Mrs. Newdick which led to making these materials available.

The writer expresses gratitude to the Department of English at Ball State University for a general climate of interest and encouragement in this work as well as time and assistance rendered.

I. A Friendly Visit

M E for the hills!" Frost once exclaimed; and today in his early sixties, as yesterday in his boyhood, the hills and their life and lore furnish the setting in which he is most himself. Seek him in late June or July and you will find him on his farm near South Shaftsbury in a lovely old farmhouse facing the Taconic range in the hills of southern Vermont. Seek him in August or September and you will find him in a hillside cottage looking across the valley to Franconia Notch and beyond to the lofty Liberty range of New Hampshire's White Mountains. Seek him in his latest book of poems and you will find him absorbed in yet further ranges, for, as he writes in dedicating it to his wife, his subject matter went beyond the immediate and familiar, even to such subjects as government and religion, just as such ranges as the Andes and Himalayas were more distant than the White.[1]

Tall—nearly six foot; large-framed; a massive head and high brow, surmounted by a wealth of now white hair, parted roughly on the right and flaring rebelliously over the left of his forehead; large features, hewn out with bold strokes; high cheekbones; impudent nose; full, expressive mouth; deep-set blue-gray eyes, sometimes steely, flashing, and piercing, but oftener kindly and a-twinkle, — such is a thumbnail sketch of Robert Frost today.

Ordinarily, he stands neither rigidly erect nor with a slouch, but quite at ease, often with his hands in his pockets. He walks like one well used to following furrows and tramping over hills, with a long, free stride. Seated, he slides down comfortably in his chair, crosses his legs, now and again rumples his hair down

---

1. As will be the practice in this volume, Newdick's use of a Frost quotation, in this case from the dedication to *A Further Range*, is paraphrased.

over his eyes and back again, and frequently expresses the un-
wordable with gestures of his large, capable hands.

He greets a caller simply and cordially, and in but a moment
there is memorable talk, for Frost retains that quiet friendliness
characteristic of New England farm folk as he retains also his
pride in having been for years a New England farmer. Or, as he
has epitomized it in "A Time to Talk", he did not ask questions
or hesitate when some one called him from his hoeing for a
talk.[2] The reader can take that literally or figuratively, as he
chooses, and so he can take most of Frost's poems; but he will do
best to take it both ways, for, whatever the philosophical impli-
cations of their foliage, most of the poems send their roots down
firmly into the living earth.

On occasion, as on the lecture platform, Frost can talk at
some length in a half-soliloquizing monologue; but, provided
only that animated discussion never descends to profitless argument, he much prefers what Hazlitt called lively, sensible conversation tête-a-tête. If that opportunity offers he soon reveals
consummate mastery of the almost lost art of goodly converse,
though one is likely to become aware of that mastery only
afterwards. At the same time, too, with a skill too subtle to be
analyzed, he somehow stimulates his caller into thinking and
speaking better than he has ever spoken before.

In the endeavor, then, to present samples of the shrewdly-
shaped substance and unique flavor of Frost's talk, some of the
following account of his life will be given, directly and in asides,
in his own words, as well as in selections from the poems that,
having been published, are now among the permanent posses-
sions of all who read them.

2. Here Newdick quoted the entire ten lines of this poem, which he referred to
as "a poem."

Note: Various materials on this subject are found throughout Parts I and II and
Part III, especially Items 1, 2, 3, 4, 9, 21, and 30 of the latter.

II. Pride of Ancestry

I N their ancestral home in Fifeshire, Scotland, the Moodies were primarily a seafaring family, but Thomas Moodie, son of Thomas Moodie and Mary Gordon Nicoll Moodie, and grandson of John Nicoll and Christina Gordon Nicholl, was inclined toward the life of cities. During the year 1832–3 he studied Scots Law in the University of Edinburgh. About that time, too, he sat for his portrait to John Lawson, a cousin of his sweetheart Jane Ashwell, and afterwards a member of the Royal Academy.

Then Thomas Moodie heard the call of America. In 1836, he left his later home in Ayr and emigrated to the United States. Continuing westward over the Alleghenies, he descended the Ohio River to a point in Adams County, settled there for a while, and sent back to Scotland for his affianced bride. They were married in West Union on November 6, 1838 and shortly afterwards went on to Cincinnati. Then in 1840 they came north to settle permanently in Columbus. There Thomas Moodie gradually established himself as a respected member of the community—a prosperous banker, an elder in the Presbyterian church, and the father of nine children, four of whom, Euphemia, Jeanie, Frances, and Florence, grew to maturity.

Meanwhile, the sea had continued to take its toll of the Moodies in Scotland. One it had taken was Thomas Moodie's nephew, Thomas, only son of his widowed brother, John. Then in the middle fifties it took John himself, leaving his daughter, Isabelle an orphan. Born on September 16, 1844, Isabelle—or Belle, as she soon was called and called herself—was about twelve years old at this time. Her photographs show that she had her full share of the Moodies' high coloring and distinctive facial characteristics, many of which she was to transmit to her famous son, Robert—an oval face; a firm chin and a wide straight mouth; full lips; a long, sensitive nose: high cheekbones; deep-set blue eyes; a high forehead, and a wealth of very dark brown wavy hair.

Her uncle Thomas Moodie sent for her to become one of his family, and she came gladly, chaperoned on the long ocean voyage by her paternal grandmother. Her ship came up Delaware Bay, up narrowing Delaware River, and finally at Philadelphia into the Schuylkill, where her uncle met her at the pier. But, her son recalled, "she felt the spirit of America and became a part of it before she even set her foot off the boat. She used to tell me about it when I was a child. She was sitting on the deck of the boat waiting for orders to come ashore. Near her some workmen were loading Delaware peaches on the ship. One of them picked out one of them and dropped it into her lap. 'Here, take that.' he said. The way he said it and the spirit in which he gave it left an indelible impression on her mind. 'It was a bonnie peach.' she used to say, 'and I didn't eat it. I kept it to show my friends.'"

A spirited creature, soon winning her way into the heart of her uncle and his family, Belle grew up among her cousins like a sister. Her particular intimate was Jeanie, with whom she was nearest of an age, with whom she was graduated from Columbus High School in 1864, and for whom in after years she named her daughter. In the graduation exercises Belle's part was an essay on chemistry which, according to the local press, "was received with great favor by the audience, being [un]surpassed by any other effort of the evening."

Of the eight academic years between 1864 and 1872, Belle taught seven, omitting only 1865–6, in the Columbus public schools, and was steadily advanced in responsibility and rank. In 1864–5 she was a primary teacher in Middle Building. In 1866–7 she was an intermediate teacher in District No. 3. The two following years she was back in the Middle Building as second intermediate teacher. The next two years she taught in the high school. The last year, 1871–2, she returned to No. 3 as assistant principal.

In the autumn of 1872, she left the Columbus school system to take a position on the faculty of Lewistown Academy in Lewistown, Pennsylvania. There she met a fiery young New Englander six years her junior, William Prescott Frost, Jr., radical scion of an old and generally conservative family.

The name Frost is ultimately Scandinavian and Saxon. Among the Saxons, who invaded England in the fifth century

A.D., it was Forst, which could easily become Frost by the process known in philology as interchange. Among the Danes, who began their invasions in the eighth century, and among whom the name is still common, it was Frost. In either case, there were Frosts settled in England from three to six centuries before the Norman Conquest in 1066. And in 1135 one Henry Frost set up at Cambridge the Hospital of the Brothers of St. John the Evangelist, the establishment which in 1509 became St. John's College.

Henry's son Robert was an armiger, and certain charges on his coat of arms, even in strict heraldic description, may strike a modern reader as prophetic: "Argent. A chevron azure between two thistles slipped in chief, and a hind's head erased in base proper. Crest: a gray squirrel sejant, semée of estoilles sable, collared and chained or and holding between the paws a hazel branch fructed also proper."

Apropos of the Frost arms is an incident of 1928 that the Irish-American poet Padraic Colum liked to tell. "We were in Dublin, Robert and I. As the car swung into a courtyard, 'Where are we now?' he asked. 'In Dublin Castle.' 'What does one do in Dublin Castle?' 'If one is an American,' I said, 'one goes into that office and asks for a genealogy.' It was the office of the Ulster King-at-Arms. 'I'll do it,' Robert said. 'What name, sir?' asked the genealogical expert. 'Frost.' 'Lincolnshire Frosts or Somersetshire Frosts?' Robert did not know. 'What Christian name is usual in the family?' 'Robert.' 'Lincolnshire Frosts. There are tombstones. . .' He named the places. 'Then I want the genealogy of the Lincolnshire Frosts. . . Will you tell me what arms I get?' 'A grey squirrel and a pine tree, sir.'

The founder of Robert Frost's line in America was the Puritan, Nicholas Frost, who may have been on the lower coast of Maine as early as 1632, but who certainly landed with his Devonshire wife, Bertha Cadwalla Frost (b. 1610) and his two sons, John and Charles—from "ye Shipp Wulfrana. Alwin Wellborn, Master from Plimouth, Devon"—in June, 1634, at Little Harbor, now Rye, New Hampshire. After his daughter, Anna, was born there in April, 1636, Nicholas pushed up to the head of Sturgeon Creek, acquired a goodly acreage of land, and settled for life in what is now Eliot, Maine. Despite the fact that he was illiterate—he signed a petition to Oliver Cromwell with his mark, a combination of N and F—he served as one of old Kittery's first selectmen.

On July 4, 1650, his wife and daughter were captured by Indians according to Norman S. Frost, whose *Frost Genealogy in Five Families*, together with Everett A. Stackpole's *Old Kittery and Her Families*, is the authoritative work on the genealogy of the Frosts on this side of the Atlantic—"and taken to a camp at the mouth of Sturgeon Creek. Nicholas and his son, Charles, were at York at the time, and on their return, attempted to rescue them, but were unsuccessful; Charles, however, killed a chief and a brave. The next day Charles, his father, and some of the neighbors went back to the camp but were too late. The camp was deserted, only the bodies of Bertha and Anna were found there."

Nicholas died a natural death in 1663, but his son, Charles, who joined the regular colonial military forces and eventually became a major, fought the Indians through two wars and then met his death at their hands. Jeremy Belknap, the first historian of New Hampshire, gives this account of a notable incident that took place at Dover on September 6, 1676, at the close of King Philip's War: "[What was regarded as a] renewal of hostilities occasioned the sending of two companies to the eastward under Captain Joseph Syll [ancestor of Edward Rowland Sill], and Captain William Hathorne [forbear of Nathaniel Hawthorne]. In the course of their march, they came to Cocheco . . . where four hundred mixed Indians were met at the house of Major Waldron, with whom they had made the peace, and whom they considered as their friend and father. The two captains would have fallen upon them at once, having it in their orders to seize all Indians, who had been concerned in the war. The major dissuaded them from that purpose, and contrived the following stratagem. He proposed to the Indians, to have . . . a sham fight after the English mode; and summoning his own men, with those under Captain Frost of Kittery, they, in conjunction with the two companies, formed one party, and the Indians another. Having diverted them awhile in this manner, and caused the Indians to fire the first volley; by a peculiar dexterity, the whole body of them . . . were surrounded. . . They were immediately seized and disarmed. . . A separation was then made: Wonolanset, with the Panacook Indians, and others who had joined in making the peace the winter before, were peaceably dismissed; but the strange Indians [i.e., King Philip's men] . . . were made prisoners, to the number of two hundred; and being sent to Boston, seven or eight of them, who were known to have killed any Englishmen, were condemned and hanged; the rest were sold into slavery in foreign parts."

Though both the military and civil authorities meant to be discriminating, the Indians regarded those acts as treacherous and never forgave them. Twelve years later they had their revenge on Waldron, and twenty-one years later on Frost, killing him from ambush on July 4, 1697—the last English blood shed in New England in King William's War. "It hath pleased God to take a way," wrote Joseph Storer of Wells; "Major Frost, the Indians waylad him Last Sabbath as he was cominge whom from meeting at night; and killed him . . . it is a Great Loss to the Whole Province; and Espesely to his fameley . . . mistress Frost is very full of sorry; and all her Children."

Not content with that revenge, the Indians opened the major's grave, carried his body to the top of a hill, and suspended it on a stake. Then, according to his descendant Robert in an early and unpublished *jeu d'esprit* entitled "Genealogical," written in what he jokingly called "Whitmanese", his sons buried him securely under heavy stones. Wryly, he attributes to the fates of this glorious ancestor his continuing predilection for Indians.

A contemporary "poem" celebrated Major Frost as a chivalric New England martyr, along with Waldron and another officer. The curious may still climb Frost's Hill, read the inscription on Ambush Rock, or visit the Frost Garrison House erected thirty-six years later.

The next five generations of Frosts were relatively inconspicuous. Charles Frost's son, the Hon. John Frost, married the sister of Sir William Pepperell who captured Louisburg in 1745, and himself served His Majesty George III for a time as Commander of the man-of-war *Edward*. Later he became a merchant in Newcastle, New Hampshire, and a member of the Governor's Council. John's son William successfully carried on his father's business in Newcastle, but otherwise was undistinguished. William, Jr., however, was an officer in the Continental Army during the Revolutionary War, and died in Andover, Massachusetts. His son, Samuel Abbot Frost, lived most of his life in New Hampshire and was the father of four children. One of these was William Prescott Frost, who early in the 'fifties moved from Kingston, New Hampshire, to Lawrence, Massachusetts, and there became an overseer in a mill, working steadily, saving regularly, and otherwise achieving complete respectability.

Thus through seven generations the Frosts of Robert Frost's line had kept their roots within a radius of twenty-five miles from the point where the first of them landed in America. In times of necessity they had freely served as frontier fighters, as sailors, and as soldiers. In times of peace they had served as legislators and councilors. Their environment had gradually changed from colonial and agricultural to national and industrial, but they themselves were relatively constant as small property owners moderate in ambition and conservative in philosophy. Then in the eighth generation there came among them the brilliant and volcanic rebel who was to father a poet.

The young man in the poet's "The Generations of Men" half concludes his teasing his companion by asking her if she does not think too much is made of family ties. He says ancestral ideals, which will not bear investigation, are what matters. Newdick commented on Frost's use of "keeping still about" in this way: (That is, keeping quiet about—as well as—keeping still around!) Earlier he had questioned whether being proud of Yankee descent was not a kind of madness.

As far as William Prescott Frost was concerned, he hoped that his branch of the family would come along in what seemed to him to be the goodly patterns conventional with Frosts and New Englanders; but he soon realized that his only son, William Prescott Frost, Jr., was a problem. During the Civil War, for instance, before the boy was into his teens, Willie—as his parents called him, even on his tombstone—was a rabid copperhead who idolized General Robert E. Lee and who plotted means of escaping from the North and joining the Confederate Army. Sometime later he got into a blackmailing scrape, from which he was extricated only through the efforts of his politically influential uncle, Elihu W. Colcord.

In 1868, the first of his line to receive a college education, he entered Harvard, and in 1872 he was graduated *A. B. cum laude,* standing fifth in his Class and being elected to membership in Phi Beta Kappa. He was a splendid physical specimen—a good swimmer, and a walker who once with a handicap won a six-day race from Dan O'leary, afterwards his friend. He was also a fine looking young man, drily polite, and, as his father had been in his youth, something of a fop, sporting Dundreary whiskers and carrying a stick.

His father hoped he would now begin to read for the bar, but W. P. Frost, Jr., thirsted for a life of more vigorous action. No stodgy old New England for him while there was the virile and newly-opened Far West to go to. And since Lewistown on the Juniata River in mid-Pennsylvania was on the way in that general direction, he paused there for a year as principal in the freshly remodelled building of its sixty-eight-year-old academy. And there he met Belle Moodie, a Middle Westerner whose speech still held something of the burr she had brought with her from Scotland.

Drawn as strongly to her as she was to him, Will Frost courted Belle Moodie so openly and assiduously, especially after she had defied convention and nursed him through a siege of typhoid fever, that townsfolk and students enjoyed many a smile at their expense. On March 18, 1873, in the home of their friend George

Note: Because the Frost family had a record going back to New England in 16̣4, both Newdick and Thompson give (the latter particularly in his book of Frost's *Selected Letters* and then more sparingly in *The Early Years*) good information on the Frost lineage.

Problems relating to the Moodie family, that of Frost's mother, were more difficult. Newdick did get Isabelle Moodie's birth date and place right (September 16, 1844, in Alloa, Scotland, as opposed to Thompson's October 2, 1844, in Leith, Scotland). Neither of them, evidently, got a copy of her certificate of baptism, which states that event took place on October 13, 1844. Neither knew the maiden name of Emily Christie, Isabelle's mother. Both evidently accepted the idea that Emily deserted her child and that she became completely orphaned when her father, John, died at sea. New Zealand descendants of John and Emily, through Isabelle's brother, Thomas, actually lost at sea, understand that John and Emily Moodie were both victims of a cholera epidemic, died at approximately the same time, and are buried at Land's End, Cornwall.

Newdick did find and record in Columbus, Ohio, more than has ever otherwise been known of Isabelle Moodie's education and teaching career. It seems significant that Frost, during his visits to Scotland during his English residence, for example, did not attempt to find out more about his Scottish family.

Perhaps it will eventually be possible to determine on which ship and at what date Isabelle Moodie arrived in Philadelphia from Scotland. Newdick's identification of Philadelphia in the "bonnie peach" story, evidently unknown to Thompson, should be crucial in this regard. Both Newdick and Thompson say that Isabelle was twelve years old, though Mrs. Lesley Frost Ballantine, the poet's daughter, has said that, in hearing the "bonnie peach" story, she heard arrival ages ranging from six to twelve. A major cholera epidemic about 1850 suggests she would be no younger than six.

Newdick mentions an additional factor in the courtship of Isabelle Moodie by William Prescott Frost, Jr., that she nursed him through typhoid fever and that he thereupon intensified his ardor. Newdick was evidently not aware of the fact, becoming better-documented through discovery of additional Frost family papers, that Frost's father wanted to go to West Point and was not given the appointment. He had realized that the birth date Frost gave for nearly forty years, 1875, was erroneous.

W. Elder, they were married—by Dr. O. O. McClean, assisted by the Rev. Mr. J. H. Brown. Then at year's end the young husband resumed his westward trek, alone for the time being, and stopped only when he had reached the Golden Gate.

III. Gold in the Sunset Sky

Into May, 1885

"SAN FRANCISCO is a mad city," observed Rudyard Kipling in a newspaper account of his brief sojourn there in the 'eighties, "inhabited for the most part by perfectly insane people. . . Recklessness is in the air. I can't explain where it comes from, but there it is. The roaring winds off the Pacific make you drunk to begin with. The aggressive luxury on all sides helps out the intoxication, and you spin forever 'down the ringing grooves of change' (there is no small change, by the way, west of the Rockies) as long as money lasts."

Recklessness suited the radical young New Englander to a T. In August, 1873, he got a job on the *Bulletin*, a Democratic paper conducted along the scorching lines characteristic of partisan journalism in those days, and plunged zestfully into local controversy. In one letter back to his wife he recounted almost with glee how windows in the Clay Street editorial office had been shot out by someone disgruntled by an article questioning the worth of a certain stock issue.

As soon as he was established he sent for his wife, and there by the Pacific their first child was born on Thursday, March 26, 1874—a boy, who at his father's insistence was christened *Robert Lee* Frost, and who regularly used his middle name or its initial until he was thirty-two. His mother, however, and later his wife and intimate friends, always called him by the Scottish nickname Rob.

Following the joining of the Union Pacific and Central Pacific railroads at Promontory, Utah, in the spring of 1869, the early 'seventies in San Francisco had been years of abundant prosperity for others than the "Big Four" comprising Charles Crocker, Collis P. Huntington, Mark Hopkins, and Leland Stanford, but by the summer of 1875 the city was beginning to feel the effects of the depression which had begun in the East with the panic of 1873. During 1876, owing to the general failure of crops, the depression deepened, and by the summer of 1877 conditions were so bad that the recently naturalized and demagogic Irish teamster Dennis Kearney was so far able to threaten the peace and order of the community with his Workingmen's Party that United States naval vessels were anchored in the harbor and cleared for action. In May, 1878, there was happily a split in the ranks of the W. P. C., but Kearney's cry of "The Chinese must go!" resulted in the Exclusion Bill of 1879, and a number of his wiser adherents were active that same year in the Constitutional Convention.

Robert's own direct recollections, extraordinarily clear and accurate, began about the time of the adoption of the new Constitution on May 17, 1879, which was also the year his father lost heavily in California's last great stock market flurry. And of course he heard stories of the Spanish and English explorers who had coasted the land in the sixteenth century, of the Franciscan monks who had established missions there in the eighteenth century, of the acquisition of the territory by the United States in 1846–7 through war with Mexico, of the discovery of gold in 1848, of the subsequent rush of the forty-niners, and of the statehood granted in 1850.

Possibly his very earliest recollection is the typically Californian version of the familiar "peck of dirt", saying he recalled that the preoccupation in San Francisco with gold was such that children were told that was what they would eat, presumably instead of the plebeian dust mentioned to ordinary children in ordinary places.[1]

Like every other San Francisco boy, Robert was impressed by the showy mansions on Nob Hill and by the ornate splendor of the Palace Hotel, was awed by the vastness of Wade's Auditorium where Adelina Patti sang in 1884, and was fascinated by Lotta Crabtree's fountain with its four lions' heads and four chained brass drinking cups. It was more fun, though, to ride on the aquatic merry-go-round at Woodward's Gardens in the old mission district, or to focus a burning-glass on monkeys in the zoo there and to watch their pensive gestures suggestive of the human capacity to think.

Most fun were the annual picnics of the Caledonian Club at Cliff House. There at noon, while his parents enjoyed a hot bird and a cold bottle, he would look down at the seals playing on the rocks below, then in the afternoon run in the children's

---

1. This sentence paraphrases the entire twelve lines of the poem, "A Peck of Gold," which Newdick quoted.

races, and in the evening trail along the beach, sometimes watching his father and his father's friends Boyd and Adair draw their revolvers and amuse themselves by shooting at a corked bottle thrown far out into the waves. Memories of one evening on the beach when a sudden storm came up Frost afterwards packed into "Over by the Pacific", making of his recollection of the furious action of the water against the land a premonition of future violent action in the career of earth.[2]

Unlike his sister Jeanie Florence Frost, born July 10, 1876,[3] Robert disliked school, though after sixty years he could call off the names of his first principal and teachers—J. W. ("Cock-eyed") Anderson, and the Misses   ("Chocolate") Fisher,   Radford, and   Dudley. And despite the fact that she had taught hundreds of elementary children herself and there-fore knew their ruses, his mother was never proof against his tears of reluctance and rebellion: he had simply to turn them on to have her release him for a while from the regular discipline.

Then she would tell him stories of Scotland's heroes, Sir Wil-liam Wallace and King Robert Bruce, or read aloud to him, sometimes stories of her own composition, such as *The Land of Crystal, or, Christmas Days with the Fairies*, published in 1884. She much preferred such activity to housework, and about half the time the family lived at the Hotel Abbotsford. Occasionally she wrote reviews, usually of books of verse, for the newspapers, and Robert never forgot her delight in a beauti-ful new edition of Herrick's poems.

She may have realized that as a literary center San Francisco in 1875–1885 was not comparable with what it had been during the preceding quarter-century. Pennsylvania's then journalistic Bayard Taylor, New York's lucky Bret Harte, and Missouri's roguish Mark Twain had come and gone, the first to Germany, the second to Gotham, and the third to Europe and all America, while Joaquin Miller was still amusing Mayfair with his boots and red bandanna, and Frank Norris had not yet begun to pub-lish.

She was a deeply religious woman, too, and found in her

2. This paraphrase is of the entire sonnet, which Newdick quoted.
3. Newdick had written "*June* 26" above the typed *July* 10 and then added this longhand note in the left margin of the page: "July 10 is date in cemetery rec-ords. June 26 is H.U. [Harvard University] date in W.P.F.'s [word not decipher-able] Class of '72 Report."
4. Newdick left blank spaces where Frost could not supply first names.

church and children the consolation she needed because of her husband's absorption in journalism and politics. Born and brought up a Presbyterian,[5] in San Francisco she became first a Unitarian and then a Swedenborgian, the faith in which she died. Robert remembered being baptized in the Presbyterian church and then afterwards attending Unitarian and Swedenborgian Sunday schools.

Meanwhile Robert's father was conditioning him along other and usually contrary lines. More than irreligious, W. P. Frost, Jr., was one of those frontier hearties who could blaspheme and curse picturesquely for half an hour at a stretch without repeating himself. He was also merciless in his exactions. Robert remembered his grabbing hold of a careless office-boy and shaking him violently while holding him out of a window four stories above the sidewalk. And for the slightest infraction of discipline, such as a thoughtless discourtesy, he would whip Robert with anything at hand, not barring even a length of dog-chain.

His fits of temper and violence were unpredictable. Once when he was writing at home in his study he gave Robert a quarter to buy him a package of cigarettes. On the way to the store the boy let the coin slip from his hand, and it dropped through a crack in the board sidewalk. Try as he might, he could not recover it, and neither could sympathetic passersby. So he went on to the store and begged for the cigarettes on credit, but the storekeeper just laughed at him. Finally, in dejection, he returned home and explained his predicament to his mother. In those days women were deemed financially irresponsible, so she had no money to give him, but she knelt with him in prayer that his punishment might be less severe than usual. Then Robert went into the study and told his father what had happened. His father hardly looked up. "Never mind," he said, and went on writing.

In contrast to the elder Frost's frequent moods of fanatical violence or complete absorption were his occasional moods of exuberance and his general mood of intense earnestness. He liked to tease Robert when the lad was taking his bath, and when on Sunday mornings he was sleeping later than usual. On the Fourth of July he outdid the biggest boys in town in the wildness of his celebration with noisemaking and the upsetting of

5. Miss Isabella Moodie was received into membership in the First Presbyterian Church, Columbus, Ohio, on May 30, 1859, on examination, according to records of The Presbyterian Historical Society.

outhouses. All the while, too, he was indoctrinating Robert with his own concepts of post-war nullification and secession. Once he took the boy on his lap, spread out a map of the United States, and pointed out the boundaries of the five nations into which he believed the country would sometime break up.

In his personal friendships and political maneuvering he was both inconsistent and unscrupulous. On the one hand, in the seventies he was warm friends with idealistic Henry George, then writing *Progress and Poverty* and arguing for a single tax on land as the panacea for the economic ills of society. On the other hand, when he ran for the office of local Tax Collector in 1884 he was glad to have the support of the diabolically clever Chris Buckley, the "Blind White Devil" who bossed the city's Democratic machine throughout the 'eighties. Again, from September, 1875, until June 1, 1884, he was city editor of the *Daily Evening Post*, a staunchly Republican paper, but resigned to become city manager of Grover Cleveland's first campaign for the presidency.[6]

It was no fault of his, however, that that campaign, successful nationally, was locally a failure. Besides writing for the press he wrote a campaign pamphlet, *Sumptuary Laws*, made speeches, devised floats, and marched in torchlight parades. Moreover, he inducted Robert into all this hectic political activity, encouraging him to don costumes and ride on the floats, to trudge along in the parades until overcome by weariness, to sell papers on the streets, and to fasten campaign cards to the ceilings of saloons by tossing them up with silver dollars that drove the tacks home.

By the conflict between the lives and philosophies of his parents—his mother's gentleness and goodness, his father's violence and unscrupulousness — Robert was unconsciously but inevitably thrown out of balance physically, emotionally, and ethically. All of his boyhood cuts and bruises became infected. There were times when he had a strange feeling of thickness and bigness. For hours on end he would sit in a chair resolved on silence because he felt that inside him there was a voice that would mock him if he spoke, and of which there is a distant reminiscence in "The Demiurge's Laugh." Sometimes he was content to work alone on his small poultry "farm" in the back-

6. Newdick's marginal note, "1880 at Cin," indicates he intended to add information about W. P. Frost, Jr.'s, attendance at the Democratic National National Convention in Cincinnati in 1880.

yard. Sometimes with other boys he baited Chinamen, and once, having to jump from a shed roof to make his escape, he fell and drove his teeth through his lower lip. But normal forms of activity were not always enough for him, and for a while, probably to prove his courage and daring to himself, he joined a gang of juvenile thieves who repeatedly were guilty of breaking and entering.[7]

It would have gone harder with Robert if he had been caught in his boy gangsterism by his father than if he had been apprehended by the police, for gradually the elder Frost's fits of moodiness and violence intensified as his hard living caught up with him. After he had struck it rich, he said, he would take care of his cough by a trip to "the Islands" of Hawaii. He was always figuring that on his next plunge into the stock market he would strike it rich. Meanwhile, to alleviate his disease, he drank glasses of fresh warm blood at the packing house, and, to keep

---

7. Newdick crossed out of this line, after the word *thieves*, "including the notorious Seth Balser". Note Frost had not correctly given the name, which was really Balsa.

Note: A significant element of the consciousness of Professor Lawrance R. Thompson, Frost's biographer from 1939 until Frost's death in 1963 and his own death after completing two of three projected volumes, and of Mrs. Kathleen Morrison, Frost's secretary from 1938 to 1963, is that Frost told many versions of episodes of his life. The Newdick chapter gives exemplification of how his information differed from that given Thompson.

The account of Robert's being sent by his father to buy cigarettes in Paragraph 13 may be compared with the version on p. 25 of *The Early Years*. In the Thompson account it is the dime received in change from the purchase which rolls a considerable distance before falling through a crack. Two sticks were used in an effort to recover the lost money in the Thompson account. Instead of asking to have the cigarettes on credit, he asks the storekeeper for another dime. In both accounts the mother prays with her son, though Thompson does not say the prayer was for alleviation of punishment.

Newdick says Frost's teeth were driven through his upper lip when, while baiting Chinamen, he had to jump from a shed roof. Thompson heard that the lip was badly split during an initiation fight related to the Seth Balsa gang. These two items may be added to a wealth of evidence that his own life was a prime source of raw material for his fictional processes.

Newdick had two otherwise-unrecorded items which may be deemed significant. The reference to the small poultry "farm" in a San Francisco backyard may explain his later tentative efforts in chicken-raising. Too, his comment about the funeral of his father being, at the time, "life's darkest hour" must be considered along with all the evidence concerning his father, whom he evidently fictionalized according to need.

up his energy and spirits, the last of which he expended writing for the *Daily Report*, he consumed quantities of whiskey.

On May 5, 1885, in the middle of his thirty-fifth year, he died. When a playmate told Robert there was crepe on the door of his house at 1404 Leavenworth Street, Robert was crushed. "I thought America's greatest and grandest figure had passed," he recalled a half-century afterwards. "I could not see how the country could get along without my father. To me, the little funeral in San Francisco was life's darkest hour."

IV. Monarch of a Desert Land

May, 1885–September, 1888

IKE all San Francisco newspapermen in the 'seventies and 'eighties, W. P. Frost, Jr., had been well paid; but he was by nature a spender, not a saver; and his widow found to her dismay that even in the face of his illness his extravagance and improvidence had led him to allow his life insurance to lapse. With no bulwark of funds she shrank from the prospect of trying to support herself and the children in the wild community where she was, and after thirteen years away from her cousins she was reluctant to call on them for help or to go to them in Columbus. The best way out seemed to be to take her husband's body back to Lawrence for burial in the family plot in Bellevue Cemetery and to trust in some further assistance from the family.

One way in which ten-year-old Robert beguiled himself on the long railroad journey across the continent was by listening to the click of the wheels passing over the rail-joints, and there is a reminiscence of this in a poem he wrote twenty-seven years afterwards. After beholding "visions" and playfully recounting them to his new-found friend, the young man in "The Generations of Men" then announces to her that he will consult the "voices", a process he associated with evoking voices and music out of train-noise heard while riding in childhood.

Inevitably sorrowful to begin with, it soon appeared that the "homecoming" was disappointing all around. Still in his early sixties, W. P. Frost, Sr., had recently retired from business, though he continued occasionally to serve the community as a deputy sheriff in civil cases. Age had not mellowed him, however, and now his natural severity was intensified by his bitterness at the untimely death of his son. He thought it his duty, for example, to follow his grandson into the bathroom to see how much dirt he had wiped off on the towel, and he punished him for setting off firecrackers before the Fourth of July.

His wife Judith Colcord Frost was similarly dour. An early

feminist, in conversation she habitually kept shaking her head, as if in resentment against the ascendancy of the male. After his retirement she got her husband to enter into a curious agreement with her: turn and turn about, each of them performed the household tasks and services on alternate days, so that for each of them every other day was one of leisure. Like her husband, she rarely smiled, and Robert never heard either of them laugh. To a boy fresh from life among good-natured and high-spirited Californians, the atmosphere of his grandparents' home was cheerless and depressing.

A similar atmosphere prevailed in the homes of other of his relatives. Partly from slices of Andover and Methuen, but chiefly on the plain at the base of Tower, Prospect, and Clover hills, and with a strikingly beautiful Common at its center, Lawrence had been founded on the banks of the power-giving Merrimac River in the eighteen-forties, and by 1885 it was a thriving mill town. The Pacific Mill alone, then the largest in the United States and the second largest in the world, employed some five thousand hands, many of whom were foreign-born. Long afterwards Frost recalled the intolerance of his great-aunt Colcord:

> I had an aunt in New England who used to talk long and loud about the foreigners who were taking over the country. Across the way from her house stood a French Catholic Church which the new people of the village had put up. Every Sunday my aunt would stand at her window, behind the curtain, and watch the steady stream of men and women pouring into church. Her mouth would twist in the way peculiar to dried-up New Englanders and she would say, "My soul!" Just that. "My soul!" All the disapproval and indignation and disgust were concentrated in those two words. She could never see why I laughed at her, but it did strike me funny for her to be calling upon her soul for help when this mass of industrious people were going to church to save theirs.

It is no wonder that Frost was seventeen or eighteen before he came really to be fond of New Englanders. "At first," he said, "I disliked the Yankees. They were cold. They seemed narrow to me." And at the outset he found in the common copper penny a means to dramatize his scorn. First he would hold up a nickel and exult, "San Francisco!" Then he would hold up a penny and sneer, "Boston!"

Meanwhile Robert's mother was learning that her husband's people thoroughly disapproved of her. They disliked her free Western manner and speech, resented her Swedenborgian serenity, and condemned her for rearing her children under the rule of patience and affection instead of the rod and fear. They implied, too, that she was somehow responsible for Willie's death, and they refused to do anything to help her get along. For the next five years, then, she and the children lived in one or two rented rooms up near Salem, New Hampshire, where she supported the three of them by teaching thirty weeks a year at wages of nine dollars a week.

Robert and Jeanie, however, were put to school in Lawrence. The opposite of his sister as a student in the elementary grades, Robert was such an indolent and intractable young rogue that except for a Miss   Chase his teachers had no use for him. After a year and a half they informed his mother that he would probably be six more years in getting through the eighth grade.

At that point Belle Frost took matters into her own hands. Beginning in January, 1887, Robert sat in school in Salem as one of her pupils. She showed him no partiality; when he stuck a schoolmate with a pin, she yanked him out of his seat and whipped him before the class. And now that he was compelled to observe discipline and apply himself, he learned with surprising rapidity. In June, 1888, just after a year and a half under his mother's instruction, he passed the full set of high school entrance examinations—four and a half years sooner than his Lawrence teachers had predicted.

Often in the afternoon after school he would run himself out in a game of baseball, but sometimes he would go off by himself on long walks, following the banks of streams, climbing the hills, and otherwise learning external New England as afterwards he absorbed it spiritually. Then in the evening, after supper had been cleared away, he would either write, or listen while his mother read aloud to him and Jeanie. A book his mother liked for its "message" was Edward Bellamy's socialistic *Looking Backward*. His favorite book was Thomas Hughes' English story of life at Rugby, *Tom Brown's School Days*, but he could not bear the thought of its coming to an end and would never permit his mother to finish it.

If he wrote, it was usually to add to an endless serial that he had begun in San Francisco—a story about a tribe of Indians who lived in a far-off mountain canyon secure from the outside world. Sometimes after he was a grown man Frost would put himself to sleep by dreaming of those same strange Indians off by themselves in their mountain fastness. A reminiscence of those dreams forms a part of the minister's philosophizing in "The Black Cottage". The speaker wishes for an isolated, uncoveted place where ideas could be held and not assailed by aggressive intruders.

During the long summer vacations, Robert regularly found work. One job he undertook—the only one in all his life, he said, that evidently was not satisfactory to his employer—was that of carefully wrapping and packing shells for an architect whose hobby was conchology. Another, to which he returned several times, was that of nailing shanks in a shoe factory—three nails on each side, a piece-work job on which he could earn as much as a dollar and a half a day and still have time to slip off for good cool swims with his friend Charles Peabody.

Though at thirteen Robert could not have realized what was in the balance, his employment by a cabinetmaker during the summer of 1888 was fateful to a degree. All through his boyhood he had shown rather remarkable aptitudes in things mechanical, and therefore it seemed to his mother that woodworking might be just right for him as a regular occupation. She consulted with the cabinetmaker, but luckily for poetry he was in no need of an apprentice, (and Robert went on to high school.)[1]

Newdick understood that Belle Frost decided the best plan would be to take her husband's body back to Lawrence for burial. Thompson was told that her husband's last request before he died was that his body be taken back to New England.

Frost recalled setting off firecrackers before the Fourth of July, against specific orders. He told Newdick he was "punished." When he discussed the same matter with Thompson, he mentioned no words or actions but rather a cruel, reproachful look. Newdick adds a few details about Frost's grandparents and his great aunt Colcord, but the picture certainly has the same tone as Thompson's.

In this chapter, Newdick records Frost's recollection that his mother showed him no partiality in school, that she whipped him before the class. Because his mother "compelled him to observe discipline," he became a scholar and made up what he had missed. Thompson has a picture of the mother being indulgent, a matter of her being hopeful about a boy who was spoiled and unpromising.

Newdick deals with the same serial about a remote and friendly tribe of Indians as Thompson (pp. 37–8, *The Early Years*). Thompson was told Frost wrote out only the first chapters, but Newdick seems to have understood that, when he wrote, he wrote about the Indians.

1. Newdick drew parentheses around "and Robert went on to high school" and put "omit?" in the left margin beside that line.

V. The Future Rises
September, 1888–July, 1892

ARLY in September, 1888, half way through his four-teenth year,[1] Frost entered the Lawrence High School as a freshman. Shortly thereafter, at its first meeting, the Class of 1892 made the momentous decisions of choosing heliotrope for its color, red pinks for its flower, and *Vincit Qui Se Vincit* for its motto, a motto peculiarly appropriate in a Puritan New England community.

The high school offered two courses. One, known as the English course, was general in scope and was intended for students who did not plan to pursue education further. The other, known as the Latin course, concentrated on the classics and prepared students for entrance into college. Robert, like his precocious sister Jeanie, with whom he had at last caught up, chose the classical curriculum: one year of history (Greek, Roman, and English), two of mathematics (algebra and geometry), three of Greek, and four of Latin.

He was an apt student. Classmates recalled that he stuttered a bit when he read his translations before the class, but the translations themselves were remarkably faithful to the originals in both letter and spirit; and while he was reading Caesar's *De Bello Gallico* he constructed to scale a small wooden model of a Roman bridge. Greek, which he began to study the second year, engaged him even more than Latin, and he often said that his happiest hours as a high school student were those he spent reading the *Iliad* with Miss Ada Lear.

The second year encompassed one of his awakenings; then, for the first time, he began to read for himself, in books of his own choosing. The first of these was Jane Porter's internationally famous *The Scottish Chiefs*, a sentimental romance of William Wallace and Robert Bruce. Gradually he passed from such

---

1. Newdick did not get the opportunity to revise this after he freed himself from the idea that RF was born in 1875.

thin and casual reading to enjoying good books — Shelley and Keats, Poe, Bryant, and Sill, Emerson, Holmes, and Prescott. He was particularly attracted to Prescott's histories, in part because of the fascination all Indians exerted over him, and the *Conquest of Mexico* fairly possessed him.

Then one gusty day in March, 1890, while he was walking home from school swinging his books in a strap and thinking again of the stirring episodes he had been reading about, something that was going through his head suddenly took shape. He ran the rest of the way home and began to write:

> Anon the cry comes down the line,
> The portals wide are swung,
> A long dark line moves out the gate,
> And now the flight's begun.

So was born "La Noche Triste", his first poem.

The next day he showed it to the editor of the *High School Bulletin*, Ernest C. Jewell. Jewell accepted it, all twenty-five stanzas of it, for publication in April. "I knew that I would never do anything else after that," Frost confessed years later. "I was lost when I wrote that first poem."

In one sense, however, he was found. The first impression some of his classmates had formed of him, chiefly those who were enrolled in the general course and who therefore seldom or never sat in class with him, was that he was a grind. Now, in view of "La Noche Triste" and of "The Song of the Wave" in the May *Bulletin*, they began to revise their opinions. There was no denying Robert's shyness, but at the same time he was a pleasant boy, more than willing to be friendly, and quietly eager to participate in other extra-curricular activities. Near the end of his sophomore year he was proposed for membership in the Debating Union and elected.

During the next two years he took a notably active part in the "D. U.," and eventually became its president. The *Bulletin* reports of debates throw significant light on the liberal character of Frost's opinions at sixteen. Debating the Indian Bill he urged that certainly "some change should be made in the Indian's condition as it was very bad and growing worse." Though he drew a distinction between natural resources on the one hand and manufactured products on the other, he approved in principle the state control of municipal water works. On the proposal to construct a million-dollar highway from Lowell to the sea he argued that it would be far better "to buy a large tract of land and make parks for the people to enjoy."

Not infrequently the D. U. meetings grew tempestuous. When paper wads and pieces of chalk were not flying, epithets and strong words were. Publicly Frost deplored these breaches of parliamentary decorum, but in meetings he matched his opponents wad for wad and taunt for taunt. "I should expect," remarked one member in feigned surprise, "that a fellow with so much frost about him would be rather cool." Another member tried to tag him with the damning appellation of "professor." Apparently no one ventured to rib him with the epithet "poet", perhaps because it was known that he was someone to reckon with in a fist fight.

Yet he was writing verses steadily. Most of his work was of course derivative and unconsciously imitative. These, for example, are the opening lines of "A Dream of Julius Caesar," published in the *Bulletin* of May, 1891:

> A dreamy day; a gentle western breeze
> That murmurs softly 'midst the sylvan shades;
> Above, the fleecy clouds glide slowly on
> To sink from view . . .

Frost had written, in his introduction to a Dartmouth book of verse in 1925, that any poet must draw from the work of all poets ever encountered. He took it as axiomatic, however, that the poet must strike a unique note some time in that decade between the ages of fifteen and twenty-five. Frost began to strike his during the autumn of 1891 in "The Sachem of the Clouds," a Thanksgiving legend, read first at a Friday afternoon rhetorical in school, and on November 2 published in the Lawrence *Daily American*:

> When the sedge upon the meadows, crosses, falls, and
>   interweaves,
> Spent, the brook lies wrapt in silence on its bed of autumn
>   leaves;
> When the barren fields are moaning, where the autumn
>   winds rush by,
> And the leaves start up in eddies and are whirled athwart
>   the sky;
>
> On the lonely hillside, darkened by the over-hurrying
>   clouds,

> Ghostly, stand the withered corn-rows, in their waving
> moonlight shrouds . . .

There gleam several touches of faithful observation and felicitous expression, and the trochaic octameters, reminiscent of
Tennyson's, are remarkable for a schoolboy.

In the autumn of his senior year Frost cleared up completely
any lingering misconceptions there may have been that his
capacities were intellectual only. In the eighteen-nineties the
football teams of Lawrence High were loosely organized. There
was no general faculty supervision, no medical attendance, no
budget for equipment, no paid coach. The captain, in complete
authority in theory, in fact often had difficulty getting the players out for early season practice. The 1891 captain, afterwards
an official in the Pacific Mills, was Thomas L. Sullivan, and he
met the problem by dismissing laggard members of the squad
and filling their places with others. One to whom he offered a
place with but the faintest hope was Frost. Eager to play but
unwilling to ask, Frost accepted. His speed made him a natural
at right end, and he played in that position all season.

"I will never forget how dumbfounded we were when Bob
played his first game," Sullivan recalled in 1937. "He was like
some wild animal let loose. He charged, tackled and played like
a fighting bull. He had no fear. Right then and there he became
one of us." That was in the out-of-town game with Bradford
which Lawrence won, 4-0. "Coming home," chronicled the
Bulletin, "the boys took possession of the baggage car and
cheered themselves hoarse. Speeches were called for and received amidst great applause . . . On arrival home, the boys
formed in line and marched down Essex street to Page's, where
light refreshments were served." After that, yelling the school
yell,

> Chi hee, chee haa!
> Chi ha, ha, ha!
> Lawrence High School
> Rah, rah, rah!

shouting the score, waving banners of orange and blue, and
cheering for the members of the team individually, the crowd
staged another demonstration and then dispersed. The Lawrence team won all of its regular games that year, and at the
close of the season the members sat in a group for their photo-

graph. None of them ever suspected that after every game their quick-charging, fast-running, hard-hitting right end had gone home dizzy and ill.

It was shortly after the close of the football season that Frost showed he would not endure a prolonged trial of his patience. His classmates had chosen him editor-in-chief of the *Bulletin* in the preceding spring, and for a few months after the opening of school in the autumn all was well. The tone of the editorials in the September issue was cheerful and optimistic: in one he stated his two fundamental editorial principles to be complete frankness and personal caprice; in another he expressed gratification at "the increasing number in school who aim at a college education"; and in the last he announced a series of prizes for the best work published in the magazine during the year. In the October issue he recommended improvements in the school library. In November, however, besides making an appeal for verse ("serious or otherwise, and especially otherwise"), he declared that the response to the prize contest was "far from satisfactory." The December issue was his last. "I worried for half a year," he explained afterwards, "got mad one day, and wrote the whole issue myself as fast as I could supply the printer with copy. The next day I resigned in favor of a better worrier."

Steadily through the first three years Frost had led his class unchallenged, but in the last year he had to cope with a rival — black-eyed Elinor Miriam White, two years his senior. Daughter of Edwin White, formerly a Universalist minister but then a wood-turner living at 10 Valley Street, Elinor was descended both from Peregrine White of the *Mayflower* and from the Whites of Acton who fought at Concord. In high school she was accomplishing the work of four years in two and a half and with almost perfect marks.

She was also, Robert found, an extraordinarily attractive girl in her quiet way, and as the year slipped by she came to absorb his attention almost exclusively. During recess periods they used to walk up and down the sidewalk in front of the school building until the bell called them back to classes. After school he would stroll home with her and loiter with her there as long as she would permit. Long before the end of the year they were engaged to be married.

They played leading parts in the graduation exercises held in the City Hall on the rain-cooled afternoon of Juy 1, 1892. Eighteenth on the program was Elinor's essay, of valedictory rank, on "Conversation as a Force in Life." Two paragraphs from it may suffice to show some of the qualities which had won Robert's admiration:

> First of all, say nothing if there is nothing in you that imperatively demands a voice. If it becomes needful to look east and west, to search in the zenith or in the nadir for material for conversation, choose rather a sympathetic silence, for your words will be drowned by the ring of insincerity that resounds through whatever is said merely to fill the moments. To be of value your speech must be dictated by a spirit as unrestrained as an elastic gas . . .

> Beware of rehearsing the opinions of other people; it proves the poverty of your own thought. Follow the path that the polarity of your own mind traces for you. He whose judgment is instantly drawn from within, whose words bear centrality and conviction, is the law-giver.

Then came Robert's original declamation, "A Monument to Afterthought Unveiled." It is not to be wondered at that it went over the heads of most of the auditors, for it was as cryptic in style as it was compressed.

Frost's basic idea was that great action and great work are the result of long and careful re-examination of that which has gone before.[2] The close of his valediction seemed abrupt to some in the audience who failed to realize how it was pointed dramatically toward the last line of the class hymn:

> To all old school associations here we show our purposed way in one bell-toned Farewell!

Except for the benediction, the program was brought to a close with the singing of the class hymn. To Robert's words, printed in the Order of Exercises distributed to the audience, Elinor's mother had arranged the music from Beethoven:

> There is a nook among the alders
> Still sleeping to the cat-bird's "Hush";
> Below, a long stone-bridge is bending
> Above a runnel's silent rush.

2. This paraphrase is of paragraphs 8–11 of the nineteen found in the address, the whole of which is quoted on pp. 130–131 of Thompson's *The Early Years*.

A dreamer hither often wanders
And gathers many a snow-white stone;
   He weighs them, poised upon his fingers,
Divining each one's silvery tone.

   He drops them! When the stream makes music,
Fair visions with the vault-voice swell:
   And so, for us, the future rises
As thought-stones stir our hearts' "Farewell!"

As the new-fledged graduates made their way from the elaborately decorated hall (the galleries, for example, were "draped with lace, surmounted with a border of heliotrope") they were handed copies of the June issue of the *Bulletin* containing the graduation parts. There were thirty-five of the new alumni, hardly a third of the number who had entered together four years earlier.

Except for the fact that Jeanie was ill at home, it was a proud day for Robert's mother. Since 1890 she had made a home for herself and the children just north of Lawrence in Methuen where she was teaching. Seven years of widowhood and family responsibility had hastened the graying of her hair; but she always carried her head high, and, as other women never failed to observe, she usually managed to have a smart bonnet to wear. Despite her anxieties she was essentially an easy-going woman, serenely content in the Zion of her Swedenborgianism.

Frost looked back on his high school days as among the happiest in his life. Thirty-odd years after his graduation he replied to a schoolmate, the Rev. Mr. Harry E. Safford, who had written him reminding him of their fellowship in Lawrence and congratulating him on the winning of the Pulitzer prize with *New Hampshire*:

You call up some of the pleasantest memories. Weren't we all good children together in the old High School by the alley, McAllister, Andrews, Morrison, you and I and the girls we have since married? I know I was at my best as a school boy there. Both before and after that my teachers always found me, if I didn't always find my studies, difficult. But in those days I took everything exactly as it came, at odds with nothing and nobody. I liked Miss Lear and Miss Newall who were really all the teachers I ever saw in my restriction to Greek and Latin. I liked my schoolmates better than later at college. I liked to carry on in the "D. U." and write for *The Bulletin*. I almost never see anyone now to remind me of it all.

Note: Brief as it is, this chapter adds significant touches to the much more extended coverage of Thompson. Classmates remembered that Frost's uneasiness in class took the form of stuttering. His interest in Latin and his desire to please were sufficiently intense that he made a small wooden model of a Roman bridge while studying Caesar's *De Bello Gallico*. The enjoyment of his studies with Miss Lear, who gave him his "happiest hours as a high school student" is not mentioned elsewhere. Newdick collected important recollections of Frost's high school classmates. (See Item 12, Part III.)

VI. Scarce Dappled with the Snow
September–December, 1892

ETWEEN W. P. Frost, Sr., and his grandson there gradually came to be several bonds besides the tie of blood. Sometimes they sat down together for a friendly game of cribbage, which Robert usually lost. Frequently they talked of politics, for in their admiration for Grover Cleveland during his first administration they were in full agreement, approving particularly of his policies with regard to tariff, labor, and the recovery of public lands.

W. P. Frost, Sr., had been grievously disappointed in 1872 when his son, just graduated from Harvard, had decided to enter upon a career in teaching and journalism, for he had long hoped that the young man would choose to read for the bar. Then the son's untimely death in 1885 had embittered him. By 1892, however, he was taking pride in his grandson's prowess, and had transferred to him the ambition he had once cherished for his son. Robert would, he hoped, become a lawyer, and he made no secret of his hope, either to Robert or to his friends.

But Robert was little inclined to accept a plan of life drawn up for him by another, even when that other was a benevolent grandfather. Furthermore, Robert held the profession of the bar in no great esteem. His high school classmates realized the opposite pulls of grandfather and grandson in this matter, and the class historian remarked allusively, "Our curly-headed member says that he would be a lawyer, but that is impossible, for being a true follower of George Washington he would always be obliged to tell the truth."

Any detached observer might have noted that it would be forever impossible for the grandson and grandfather to see eye to eye on essentials. As the retired mill overseer sized up life, the best prizes of the world were to be won with the least difficulty by the urban, the industrial, and the professional; whereas all that the youthful high school graduate could see in it that he much cared for was the rural, the agricultural, and, in the best sense of the word, the amateur. He had already tried the mill and the factory. So far as earnings were concerned, he had tried them profitably. Otherwise he had found them wanting. Only as a hand on farms in Windham and Salem had he found work that was completely satisfying to him, labor that daily filled his mind and heart while it tired his body to exhaustion.

There was, of course, another way to fill the mind, if not the heart,—the traditional way of higher education. For law or for anything else, urged the grandfather, a college education was a highly desirable foundation. With this line of reasoning the grandson was readily inclined to agree. In 1891 he had taken and passed several of the entrance examinations for Harvard. Later, in a *Bulletin* editorial, he had noted with pride the excellent records Lawrence High graduates were making, usually without additional preparation, at Harvard, at the Massachusetts Institute of Technology, and elsewhere. And finally, in a way to resolve the question, Elinor had decided not to continue the study of music but to enter St. Lawrence University.

On September 8, 1892, not by examination but on the basis of his high school diploma and valedictorian honors, Frost matriculated in Dartmouth College at Hanover, New Hampshire, with the Class of 1896. He chose Dartmouth instead of Harvard because Dartmouth offered him a monitor's scholarship worth $70, a stipend which promised to defray about a third of his expenses inasmuch as tuition was then only $90 for the three terms, the best rooms rented for $25 a year, and good board could be had for $2.75 a week. Frost was monitor of the first division (the first half of the freshman class of 77 in alphabetical order), and his duties consisted chiefly in making record of his division's required attendance at weekday college classes and prayers, at Wednesday oratorical exercises, and at Sunday public worship and prayers.

Frost wrote in 1915 that he found much of his enjoyment at Dartmouth in living up to the idea that it was a school for Indians. He liked the interclass battles, particularly the one in which his class got "salted" by the sophomores after fighting it out in the Old Chapel; he actually thought the freshmen fought their enemies to a draw, spilling across pews and using cushions and footstools for weapons.

Louis S. Cox, a classmate of Frost, and subsequently justice of the Supreme Judicial Court of Massachusetts, clearly remembered the preliminary "salting" after forty-six years. It occurred, he wrote, "after we had been in Hanover but a matter of a week or so as freshmen. When the freshmen and sophomores were playing the customary fall games of baseball, some one in our class brought out a '96 banner. This was instantly resented by the sophomores who charged the freshmen. Clothes were torn as well as the banner, and the opposing forces surged back and forth upon the campus for some time until the sophomores had gained possession of the greater part of the banner and had retired to one side of the diamond. It was then that Frost rallied the freshmen, most of whom were unknown to one another, and with a remnant of the banner in his hand led the freshmen in a charge across the diamond and against the sophomores. I can see him now out in front of the huddled mob as he led them to the charge." Neither Cox nor any other of his classmates suspected that at this time Frost was really in questionable health, on a diet, and under the care of a physician.

Frost's room was No. 23 in Wentworth Hall—"top floor, rear, side next to Dartmouth," he once particularized. It had a door, he remembered, "that had the advantage of opening outward and so being hard for marauding sophomores to force from the outside. I had to force it once myself when I was nailed and screwed in. My very dear friend was Preston Shirley . . . and he had a door opening inward that was forced so often that it became what you might call *facile* and opened if you looked at it. The only way to secure it against violation was to brace it from behind with the door of the coal closet. I made common cause with Shirley and sometimes helped him hold the fort in his room until we fell out over a wooden washtub that we owned in partnership, but that I was inclined to keep for myself more than my share of the time. I may say that we made up afterward over kerosene. One of us ran out of oil after the stores were closed at night and so far sacrificed his pride as to ask to borrow of the other."

Like the other residents of Wentworth Hall, Frost was known as "a Wentworth Heller," and evidently he lived up to the appellations as if it were a personal responsibility. Shirley, an asthmatic who annoyingly spat often and anywhere, was also a mocking fellow given to long, loud declamation, and once Frost retaliated by smudging him out with a tube of newspaper wet on one end and burning at the other.

The best known of Frost's pranks, however, was the one perpetrated in connivance with Raymond D. Hazen, afterwards a prosperous bond salesman in New York, on Guy W. Richardson. The victim was naturally more comfortable in recalling the episode as "merely a phrenological reading. He examined my head very carefully, and made some comments that seem to have been justified by future developments," Richardson wrote soberly in 1938. But "Hair: A Farce in One Act" in the *Aegis* for 1893 bears out Judge Cox's recollection that, when Richardson remarked his two months' growth of hair ought to be cut, "Frost suggested that there was no reason for him to pay for the hair cut because he, Frost, and Hazen could give him one. Richardson assented to this and Frost sat him in a chair and proceeded to give him a hair cut, but instead of following the conventional method, he cut a strip about two inches wide down to the scalp from Richardson's forehead over the top of his head and down the back to the nape of the neck. He then cut a corresponding strip from one ear up over the head and down to the other ear. About this time Richardson realized that something was wrong and interrupted the barbering to look in the mirror." The upshot was that Richardson bolted from the room, packed his belongings, walked down the hill to the railroad station at Norwich, and left Dartmouth for good. There is some irony in the fact that he afterwards became editor of *Our Dumb Animals* and secretary of The Society for the Prevention of Cruelty to Animals.

Meanwhile Frost had undergone a number of the customary "chinning" sessions preliminary to fraternity bidding. At one of these sessions the rushees were provided with watermelon to eat while an especially talented member of the fraternity told stories. The diabolical object of the raconteur was to make the candidates lose their appetites—or to regurgitate what they had already eaten. Frost and Shirley managed to survive all such ordeals, and on October 21, 1893, after a banquet at the Wheelock, they were initiated into membership in Theta Delta Chi, a national brotherhood founded at Union College in Schenectady in 1847.

At this time Dartmouth offered two courses leading to the B. A. degree, the Latin-Science course and the Classical. Frost chose the latter. Normally, according to the catalogue, there were sixteen weekly exercises in the five required studies: Greek, Latin, Mathematics, Divinity (Hebrew History), and English (themes in English history). Frost was "getting past the point," he said years after, where he "could show any great interest in any task not self-imposed," but he showed proficiency in reading Latin with Charles H. Gould and Greek with George Dana Lord, the latter a notably conscientious and inspiring teacher who used to stride up and down the classroom with watch chain flopping and hair disheveled while he talked of Schliemann's diggings at Hissarlik. In a mild way, too, history repeated itself: Frost's classmates very soon perceived his marked ability and dubbed him "scholarly."

They thought him rather queer, too, because he liked to go off alone on exhaustingly long walks, sometimes with a book in his pocket. His favorite walks were over what he called "the Five Mile Round," just east of Hanover, and through the Vale of Tempe. On these walks, as on both earlier and later walks over countrysides in southern New Hampshire, he absorbed the scenes around him with the thoroughness of the poet he was coming to be.

"The memory of the past resolves itself into a few bright star-points set in darkness," Frost once remarked apropos of his days at Dartmouth. One bright memory was of a talk on reading by Professor Charles F. ("Clothespins") Richardson, who had known Emerson, who quoted, in a way to stimulate Frost, a line of Shelley's—
Where music and moonlight and fooling are one,
and who introduced Frost to Palgrave's *Golden Treasury*, to which the youth was soon devoting much time that strictly should have been given to his studies. Another bright memory was of B. A. Smalley's undergraduate poem "Lake Memphrama-gog in Winter" in the *Dartmouth Literary Monthly* for April, 1892. Still another was of Richard Hovey's "Seaward," an elegy on Thomas W. Parsons, friend of Longfellow and translator of Dante, in the New York *Independent* for November 17, 1892.

Such were the forces that combined to prompt Frost, if prompting were needed, to continue his own efforts to write while he was at Dartmouth. "I wrote while the ashes accumulated on the floor in front of my stove door and would have gone on accumulating to the room door if my mother hadn't sent a friend a hundred miles to shovel up and clean house for me," he recalled. There he wrote the elegy "My Butterfly" and the autumnal lyric "Now Close the Windows." "I still like as well as anything I ever wrote," he declared in 1915, "the eight lines in the former "beginning the gray grass" and comparing the flight of the butterfly to the waving of a wreath by fairies in a dance (lines 8–17). Incidentally, it is characteristic of Frost that he kept that Dartmouth-written elegy in his portfolio for a year and a half before he sent it out in the hope that it might find, as it did immediately, a friendly publisher.

In time Frost might have overcome his annoyance at being regarded as "scholarly" because he really enjoyed studying the classics and as "queer" because he liked to get off by himself to walk and read and write; but another disturbing factor proved decisive. He was not generally and habitually thoughtful of his mother, as she was of him, but his loyalty to family and friends was always intense, and he could always be counted on in an emergency. There was no hesitation, then, when he learned, perhaps from the friend who had come to Hanover to clean house for him, that his mother was having extraordinary difficulties, in the Methuen school where she was teaching, with a class of unusually big and unruly boys. Without so much as calling on a college administrative officer to explain the situation, Frost packed a few belongings and boarded a train for Lawrence. When he next stepped foot on the Dartmouth campus, on January 22, 1916, he was no longer an unknown from a turbulent Massachusetts mill town, but a poet internationally famous.

Note: Newdick reports a closeness to Frost's grandfather, by the end of his high school career in 1892, not otherwise recorded. Frost considered, but did not heed, his grandfather's ambition, the same one he had had for his son, to study law. Newdick was told that Frost, when at Dartmouth, was in questionable health, though the ailment was not specified.

Newdick understood that Frost was introduced to Palgrave's *Golden Treasury* by Professor Charles F. Richardson. Thompson was told Frost found the book, quite by accident, in a bookstore at Dartmouth.

Frost's leaving Dartmouth is interpreted differently by Newdick and Thompson. As Newdick understood it, Frost responded immediately when he learned of the difficulties his mother was having with unruly pupils. As Thompson understood it, going to help his mother was as good a reason as any to escape the "prison" at Dartmouth. His mother, unwittingly, provided him the excuse he needed.

The "Hair" episode is not reported elsewhere. (See Item 15, Part III, for the text of "Hair.")

VII. The Music of the Iron
December, 1892–March, 1894

ARRIVING at home, Frost found that his mother's problem was fully as difficult as he had sensed it to be. Thereupon he proposed to the school authorities that for the remainder of the year 1892–3 he be allowed to take over the troublesome class and that his mother be given a class of younger children. The proposal was accepted.

Whatever the swaggering bullies may or may not have learned from books under their young and inexperienced teacher, they soon learned who was master in the classroom. Frost never had the physique or the endurance of a really big fellow; but he had a reserve of strength he could draw on when he needed to, and both in high school football and in college rushes he had found how to use that strength to the utmost advantage. Promptly, then, and for the first and only time in his teaching experience, he resorted to corporal punishment, not switching the boys but soundly thrashing them.

One of the biggest of the boys, John Hare, finding himself outfought by the new teacher, menacingly drew a knife on him. Frost was equal to that too; he quickly disarmed Hare and took him before the principal. The principal thought charges ought to be preferred, but Frost refused to press the matter and was content simply to retain possession of the knife as a kind of grisly souvenir. Hare, in after years, became a selectman in his town.

Toward the close of the school year Frost saw in the Boston *Evening Transcript* an advertisement by a Portland dramatic reader who wished to engage the services of an impresario. Frost applied by letter, and by letter the arrangement was made, Frost undertaking to prepare a prospectus of the reader's offerings, to secure publicity for him, and to handle the business involved in booking him for engagements. Yet Frost was canny enough to proceed with caution. The reader had insisted that selections from Shakespeare were his special forte. Then for a really persuasive prospectus, suggested Frost, it would be desirable to get puffs from several recognized authorities. The reader agreed. Thereupon Frost made arrangements for a private performance in Boston, renting a hall for the purpose and inviting, among others, Henry Austin Clapp, dramatic critic of the *Transcript*, and William J. Rolfe, Shakespearian scholar of Cambridge. The performance was a complete failure, however, and Frost withdrew from his engagement.

One day about this time, while he was browsing through the new poetry in a Boston bookstore, Frost came upon a poem, in a volume entitled simply *Poems*, that galvanized him instantly. As he phrased the point years afterwards, the person who is equipped to appreciate a poem "will never get over it". The poem Frost had instantly recognized as one he could never forget was Francis Thompson's "The Hound of Heaven." Though he could hardly afford to, he bought the book then and there, and took it home with him, a "first" that always held an honored place in his library.

Elinor White had meanwhile come home from college, where she was maintaining the pace she had set for herself in high school, and now was summering with her mother and sister at Canobie Lake, just over the Massachusetts line in southern New Hampshire. So the rest of the summer Frost too spent at Canobie Lake, camping among the pines along the shore, taking what odd jobs he could find, reading, writing, loafing, and courting Elinor.

W. P. Frost, Sr., did in some measure realize what his grandson was bent upon, and did not utterly condemn it. "Go ahead and give poetry a try for a year," he suggested one day early in the autumn of 1893; "then, if you find it doesn't pay, why, there are many other honorable kinds of work you can choose from." Frost responded with an unconscious prophecy in the chant of an old-time auctioneer, "Give me *twenty*! Give me *twenty*! Give me *twenty*!"

Yet beginning in September, after Elinor had returned to St. Lawrence, Frost did take one last fling at the kind of employment his grandfather most approved. In one of the vast, sprawling Arlington mills he got a job as an electrician's helper, tending and trimming the carbons in the arc-lights that hung high over the looms.

There he discovered that human nature would somehow find playful expression even under the burdens of wages of ten cents

an hour, a ten-hour day, and a sixty-hour week. "I used to think
the mill people, scooting home in the dark, were sad," he once
recalled, "till I worked in the mill, and heard them singing and
laughing and throwing bobbins up at me as I stood up on a ladder
fixing the lights."

There too he broadened the base of his tolerance and democ-
racy until he could laugh without bitterness at their opposites.
Many of the mill employees were of foreign birth, as was his
own mother. To her, he knew, America had always meant
"something live and real and virile," and he saw that to these
frugal, industrious, and religious "foreigners" it meant the same
—a state in which they could work out their dreams and des-
tinies in their own ways. As he summed it up in an interview
in 1923:

> I had an aunt in New England who used to talk long and
> loud about the foreigners who were taking over the
> country. Across the way from her house stood a French
> Catholic Church which the new people of the village had
> put up. Every Sunday my aunt would stand at her window,
> behind the curtain, and watch the steady stream of men
> and women pouring into church. Her mouth would twist
> in the way peculiar to dried up New Englanders and she
> would say, "My Soul!" Just that. "My Soul!" All the disap-
> proval and indignation and disgust were concentrated in
> those two words. She never could see why I laughed at
> her, but it did strike me very funny for her to be calling
> upon her soul for help when this mass of industrious
> people were going to church to save theirs.[1]

Three of the light-trimmers made up a kind of triumvirate—
Frost, William Golden, who continued in the mill until his
death, and Edgar Gilbert, who eventually organized the Gilbert
Research Institute in Morristown, New Jersey. Early in the
mornings, late in the long afternoons, and almost continuously
on dark, cloudy days, these three were kept busy on their ladders
fixing the lights. On bright, clear days, however, much of their
time was free, and they usually passed it in boxing, wrestling,
and general horseplay. Sometimes, though, Frost would slip off
by himself and read, usually in a pocket Shakespeare in which

1. Newdick did not have the opportunity to remove this repetition of the quotation used in Chapter IV.

he was marking the lines to show precisely how they should be read in order to bring out their full significance.

Only in his later years did Frost reveal in a few published poems that he had observed as closely and as understandingly in the mill as he had on the farm and in the woods. Take, for example, the opening of "A Lone Striker", in which the intricacy of the spinning machines and the necessary deftness of the operator were described (lines 18-32). There was a rule of the mill that latecomers be locked out for half an hour and their pay docked accordingly. Frost, once caught so, made a day of it, going to a place in a woods where he could walk, drink from a spring, reflect on the things he loved, all of which represented for him a compelling form of action (lines 37-50). So always he was given to rebel against merely formal and institutional claims on him—never so much by the cold white light of reason and analysis as by the quick lightning-flash of intuition and impulse.

From time to time thenceforward Frost's manuscript portfolios contained a number of other poems embodying his observations, experience, and reflections as a mill worker. A very early one, typical of those full to heart's depth with compassion, is "The Mill City." Therein he described the workers going to and coming from their labors—

> Their passage in the morning like a dream
> In the arc-light's unnatural bluish beam,
> Then back again at night, like drowned men from the sea,
> Up from the mills and river hurriedly,
> In weeds of labor, to shrieks of steam . . .

Then he voiced his purpose really to know workers and to understand their problems—and his will to be

>   . . . resolute to cope
> With what thoughts they compelled who thronged the
>   street,
> Less to the sound of voices than of feet.

The ache of his own body and spirit, after long toil in the mill, found expression in another early poem:

> When the speed comes a-creeping overhead
> And belts begin to snap and shafts to creak,
> And the sound dies away of them that speak . . .

Then, he knew,

> Unwilling is the flesh, the spirit weak,
> All effort like arising from the dead.

> But the task ne'er could await the mood to come:
> The music of the iron is a law:

> a law that lay its heavy hand

> Upon the soul, still sore from yesterday.

Evidently Frost was a practicing American workers' poet before most of the noisy academic "proletarians" of the nineteen-thirties were out of rompers.

Perhaps even more notable than these early poems, inasmuch as it makes its survey and its thrust from a more general point of view, is "The Parlor Joke," a piece possibly begotten by the history of Gary, Indiana. Withheld from publication until 1920, and never collected, it is the angriest and bitterest poem Frost ever wrote; referring as it does to a process of building a city which should not have been and then working to populate it with people degraded by their employment.

That [meaning] ought to be unmistakably plain even to those who miss Frost's many oblique comments on his times all through his poems. Of the industrialism that dominated his day, he was conscious from his youth onwards, fully conscious, as only those who have known it at first hand can be. Steadily, too, though never exclusively and disproportionately, he wrote about it. And clearly and repeatedly, though always as an artist rather than as a propagandist, he pilloried its insatiable greed, its monstrous tyranny, and its manifold oppressions of free human spirit and effort.

Note: Newdick gained comment from Edgar Gilbert, who worked at the Arlington mill with Frost, but most of it was made after Newdick's death. (See Item 19, Part III.)

Newdick's realization of Frost's interest in the mill workers seems more intense than that of Thompson. Note the extensive use of poetry, much of it unpublished or uncollected, the result of Newdick's visit to the Huntington Library in 1937 to see the manuscripts there.

VIII. Only More Sure

April–June, 1894

B Y the end of the winter of 1893–4 Frost had had enough of mills to last him a lifetime. Then, and now of his own volition rather than of a necessity sprung from loyalty, he turned again to teaching, a profession from which he was to be free only at intervals during the rest of his life.

His mother had taught in the schools of Salem, New Hampshire, for five years after her husband's death. More recently, his sister Jeanie had taught in an outlying school under the jurisdiction of the same town. Now he himself undertook, at wages of $34 a month, the Spring Term of eleven weeks in Salem's District School No. 9 at Messer's Crossing, and gave instruction to twelve pupils in a curriculum comprising reading, spelling, grammar, composition, penmanship, history, arithmetic, and geography.

He had not yet become honestly interested in teaching, either as a science or as an art. As he wrote frankly to a friend, the work was so unpleasant for him that he found he was merely enduring it.

Yet there was much that was connected with teaching near Salem in which he did take pleasure. Nervous, and invariably distressed by noise, often to the point of illness, he liked the relative peace and quiet of the country day. He liked also his long morning and evening walks over the countryside and through the woods between his mother's home in Lawrence and his school at Messer's Crossing. He was always hoping, he said, "to feel really lost in the woods"; but, he added, "I never realized that hope. Somehow I would always run on to a path."

The walks, the trees, the thoughts that crowded upon him, and then the telling afterthought—why, there were the ingredients of a poem! So, while his pupils worked quietly at their desks in the schoolroom he sat by the window with his paper on the sill, looked out into the woods, and wrote. The result was the first sketch for what eventually became the sonnet-variant "Into My Own", containing as it does his statement of how he would submerge himself in nature and find strength to hold to the ideas and principles he had evolved. Which, with its Shakespearian echo and all, is a text on which half a dozen lectures on Robert Frost and his art could be based.

By this time Frost was sure enough of his poems to be sending them out to the periodicals. Usually, of course, they came back, accompanied only by formal rejection slips. But one day early in spring he experienced the unique thrill of receiving his first significant recognition as a poet: William Hayes Ward bought "My Butterfly" for the weekly New York *Independent*. More stimulating to Frost than the fifteen dollars was the personal interest Ward expressed in his letter of acceptance. Frost's reply is the earliest of his letters that is known. Writing on March 21, 1894, expressing his pleasure in having his poem accepted, he carelessly said it was the first of his to be published. He promised to send more poems when they were available, referred to his high school education and his few months at Dartmouth, remarked that "inflexible ambition" spurred his study of poetry, and suggested his desire to seek inspiration for better work in the future. Signing himself Robert Lee Frost, he authorized the use of his name with the poem.

Then Ward's sister and editorial assistant, Susan Hayes Ward, took up the correspondence, applauding Frost's achievement in "My Butterfly," nevertheless suggesting some revisions in it, and cordially inviting him to tell more about himself. His response, written on April 22, throwing light on his confidence, determination, reading, and study, so pleased Miss Ward that she preserved it, together with Frost's later letters and manuscripts. He told her that her discriminating criticism was just what he had been waiting for, confided that he read the novels of Henrik Sienkiewicz and Thomas Hardy, commented on a bond in Scotch romanticism which he felt with Walter Scott and Robert Louis Stevenson, mentioned his favorite poems were Keats' "Hyperion", Shelley's "Prometheus", Tennyson's "Morte d' Arthur", and Browning's "Saul"; that he liked everything in Palgrave's *Golden Treasury of English Verse*, that he did not know the work of Sidney Lanier, about whom the Wards were enthusiastic. He mentioned that the intent of his current study was to read French, for relaxation, and Greek, which he wanted to master, though he found Homer discouraging. He thought he could eventually do "everything but spell," his problems (lifelong) with which were exemplified by spelling the name of one of his favorite authors as Tenneson.

What? Ignorant of Sidney Lanier, so many of whose poems had been published in the *Independent* and whose ars poetica was at once revealing and final? Shocking! Forthwith Miss Ward dispatched to Frost a copy of the 1884 edition of the true master's *Poems*, edited by Mrs. Lanier and with a memorial by William Hayes Ward.

Frost was here very close to the chief turning-point in his career as an artist, very close indeed to what was for a long time to be the turning-back point; but at just this moment neither he nor the Wards quite realized what was at stake. Frost's letter of acknowledgment, dated June 10, 1894, expressed thanks and enthusiasm for a volume of Lanier's poems, which Mrs. Ward had evidently sent him. At first, that is, like many another critic then and an occasional one even today, Frost was swept away by the earnestness and eloquence with which Lanier insisted that the laws of music and verse are identical, that every foot represents a mathematically equal time interval, and therefore that length of interval, not accent, is the determining element in prosody.

Happily, however, Frost's enthusiasm was short-lived; and, in a kind of left-handed way, the Wards themselves were instrumental in his awakening. One of them wrote to their friend the Rev. Mr. William A. Wolcott, pastor of the Lawrence Street Congregational Church in Lawrence, suggesting that he look Frost up and cultivate him. Wolcott complied, and soon the two were talking poetry. Like the Wards, Wolcott was a Lanier enthusiast, and at the outset he expected that Frost was, too; but to his surprise he found Frost already dubious of Lanier's critical principles, and shortly he was amazed to see Frost manifest antagonism toward them. True, there was hardly a single point of Lanier's that Frost could controvert in reasoned exposition; yet he was somehow, one might say instinctively, distrustful of them all. And at the same time, though he was unable to define it, he felt the pervading want of an essential ingredient in the body of Lanier's poetry.

The Wards soon came to realize Frost's stubborn rejection of Lanier as the ideal American poet and critic. Wolcott's tentative report was more than confirmed by Frost's silence: never again did he even mention Lanier in his letters. Once, indeed, he spoke of the place of sound in poetry, but evidently then only in response to a direct question:

> Yes, I think sound is an element of poetry, one but for which imagination would become reason. I justify the use of dialect in this way; it contributes to the illusions (perhaps) and gives the artist the courage of his imaginings. Kipling says nearly all he says under the influence of sound.

And while the Wards were coming to some realizations, of no great moment to them, Frost was realizing some things for himself, of tremendous import to him. The Wards might not be able to establish a writer simply by their nod of approval, but unquestionably they could speed or retard his rise: they knew all the right literary people in New York and elsewhere, and they completely dominated a powerful literary periodical. So one of Frost's realizations was that, given discoverers as fixed in their ideal of poetry as were the Wards, he was almost deliberately cutting himself off from their further support in not embracing, or in not pretending to embrace, a similar ideal.

The other realization, even more vital, came with the suddenness of a tropical dawn. One day Wolcott, talking over Frost's poems with him, complained of their tone. It was, he said, too much like that of talk. To Frost that observation was like the crucial drop of acid that brings down the precipitate from a chemical solution. Without being quite conscious of it, the tone of talk was precisely what he had been striving for. Now he knew what he had taken the keenest delight in when, as in his pocket Shakespeare, he met them on the printed page: tones of voice. Now he knew, too, what had at length offended him in Lanier's theory and practice: the underlying concept of the essentially musical character of poetry, a concept resulting in verse in which, as Frost phrased it later, "all the tones of the human voice in natural speech are entirely eliminated, leaving the sound of sense without root in experience." And now, finally, he knew what had drawn him year after year to the farms and hamlets of southern New Hampshire: the fascination of the sound of sense in language whose roots drove far down into rocky, native soil.

With this ideal of his own, diametrically opposed to that of Lanier, of the Wards, of Wolcott, and of no matter how many others, why, reasoned Frost, should he play the hypocrite in any degree, pander to any editor, or sacrifice his integrity as man and artist? He did indeed wish to get on. Anyone as conscious of his own "inflexible ambition" as Frost was, yearns to get on. But he willed to get on only under his own colors and on his own terms. Elinor and his mother understood all this and agreed with him. So he stood his ground.

Yet there are no heroics to be written into the record either at this point or at any other point. The high moments in Frost's life, like those most characteristic of his poetry, are not so much of the senses as of the intellect and ultimately of the spirit. Frost never made his way by contest or argument. When obstacles were not to be overcome directly, he simply stepped back and around them. Neither did he ever strike Byronic poses or assume the role of martyr for a cause. Avoiding the flares of what in journalism pass as color, spectacle, and showmanship, Frost merely pursued his own way, quietly true to his own lights. Thus, preoccupied with the study and practice of "the sound of sense," and steadily gaining in knowledge, understanding, and command of that sound so difficult to capture and fix in language, Frost wrote on almost wholly neglected for the next nineteen years.

Note: Newdick's recording of Frost's attitude toward teaching, related to his personal problems, is unique: "Nervous, and invariably distressed by noise, often to the point of illness, he liked the relative peace and quiet of the country day."

IX. The Time When after Doubt
July, 1894–December, 1895

THE last half of 1894 was a period of storm and stress for Frost, but during the following year he moved steadily toward the most decisive single step in his life.

The trouble began when his mother rented the third floor of their home to the Parkers, a young married couple. One afternoon some difficulty arose, the wife flared and attacked Frost, and he was compelled in self-defence to hold her by the wrists until her rage subsided. Steadily, then, his own anger mounted; and that evening when he heard the husband come home, he went upstairs and thrashed him soundly. His satisfaction in that part of the business, said Frost, was worth the fine it later cost him in court for assault and battery.

But the fine was far from all. Now the scowls of censorious townsfolk deepened, and Frost felt himself openly regarded as a pariah. Acquaintances, old teachers, even some "friends", turned aside when he approached, or deliberately cut him. In some painful instances Frost could see himself fall and hit bottom in the estimation of an individual who had had some confidence in him. For instance, there was Sanborn, formerly a mill boss who had once employed him as a gatekeeper, but now a sea captain looking up likely young men for his crew. Sanborn either had not heard the town talk about Frost or else chose to ignore it, for he called at his home to sign him for a voyage; but when he found him loafing there in stocking feet and shiftlessly reading a book, he was patently disgusted and quickly took his leave without extending the offer he had come prepared to make.

When finally it seemed best to Frost to get out of town for a while, he went down to Boston and got a job as a blue-print boy in an architect's office. On August 22 he wrote to Miss Ward from 35 Cambridge Street that he was about to "declare for literature", wherever the decision might lead him.

It meant, he found, poverty unendurable. He stuck it out for a week or two, supplementing his starvation wages by drawing on his slender reserves; but when those were gone and he felt the gnawing of unsatisfied hunger, he walked the twenty-eight miles back to Lawrence by road, picking and eating berries on the way, and arriving home exhausted and ill.

His mother received him and cared for him as if nothing had happened. He could always depend on her. Never once did she chide him, Frost recalled, never once complain of him, during all the years of his "worthlessness." She knew, far better than anyone else, what he was intent on doing with his life, and her faith that someday he would achieve his purpose was as firm as it was serene.

But now she could only look on silently while he fought to keep his head up when Elinor White, to the relief and applause of her circle of friends, broke her engagement to him and almost immediately became engaged to another. That was the hardest blow he suffered in all his youth. It sent him reeling, sick in body and soul. For a while, indeed, it threatened to encompass his ruin. "We provincials," he had written in June, "affect Bohemianism—experience, give us experience!" Now he was getting experience with a vengeance, getting too much to endure. So he raised a little money, packed a bag, and headed for New York and the South, ostensibly in search of work but really in quest of distraction and self-orientation.

He sailed from New York for Norfolk on November 6, 1894. Up to this time, he sometimes told lecture audiences in after years, he used to think that everyone who could, wrote poetry, and that those who couldn't, went into some kind of business. He learned otherwise, he would add, from a middle-aged passenger on shipboard, a man of business who roundly declared that *he* approved of poetry because it was the solace of his ailing daughter.

From Norfolk Frost went on south to Elizabeth City, North Carolina, on a tramp steamer. On the way down he fell in with several men from Elizabeth City who took him across Albemarle Sound to Nag's Head on a drinking party one night and on a dizzy and dangerous duck-hunting expedition the next morning. A liquor dealer in the group, John B. Brocket, more or less adopted him for the time being, and, learning he was looking for work, introduced him to Enoch F. Lamb, a writer for the weekly *Economist* and one who knew all the local ropes. The latter, when he found Frost had been a teacher, arranged an interview for him with Samuel L. Sheep, organizer and principal of Elizabeth City Academy. Sheep, in turn, presented him to the students, and would have employed him to teach Greek and Latin in the academy, had not Frost backed out.

Then, his money exhausted, Frost gradually but quickly sank down among common laborers and panhandlers. For some days he worked in a lumber camp, sleeping with another white man in one end of an abandoned box car. Negro laborers slept in the other end. Years afterwards Frost recalled their songs around the stove at night—and their peculiar smell.

He became adept, too, at bumming his way on freight trains. On one he saw a Negro draw a gun on a member of the train crew and suffer a fearful beating in consequence. On another he was robbed of all his remaining kit by a hard-boiled brakeman who refused even his plea for his razor.

When at last he reached Baltimore he thought his worst experiences were over, for there, he remembered, lived the Rev. Mr. Hiram Vrooman, founder of the Union for Public Good, and a professional reformer whose article in the February, 1894, issue of the Boston *Arena* on "The Organization of Moral Forces" had so much interested his mother. But under the minister's long cold look of appraisal the youth was uncomfortable, and the necessity of having to scramble on the floor to pick up some of the change that Vrooman at length held out to him was a humiliation Frost never forgot or forgave.

Several days later, again suffering from hunger, he asked for work and food at the little grocery of James C. Williams at 303 West Saratoga Street. How nearly famished he was, Mrs. Williams saw for herself when he wolfed down six cups of coffee one right after another. The family, touched by his need, took him into their home. To earn his keep, Frost went from door to door throughout the neighborhood trying to secure new customers for his benefactor. As a solicitor, however, he was no great success, and eventually he wrote to his mother for train fare home.

Meanwhile, on November 8, "My Butterfly" had been printed in the *Independent*, and from Lawrence on December 4 Frost wrote self-analytically to Miss Ward that his recent "desperately absorbing" wanderings in Virginia, North Carolina, and Maryland had given him a new perspective from which to enjoy the publication of the poem. His sense of futility over the past eight months was assuaged.

But the greatest reason for his being "nothing morbid now" was that on his return he had overborne Elinor's misgivings and had persuaded her to break her engagement to his rival and again pledge herself to him. His experiences in the outer darkness, his early winter homecoming, and the conclusion of his vagabond thinking, may lie beneath his poem "Reluctance", which insists on one's allegiance to one's own desires. [Newdick here quoted the last of the four stanzas of the poem.] And unquestionably at the end of "A Line-Storm Song" there is an echo of his own time of "storm and rout", when love was renewed after a period of doubt. [Here Newdick quoted the last of the four stanzas of the poem.]

He celebrated his triumph by taking "My Butterfly" and four other poems to a newspaper office and having them printed as a booklet bound in brown pebbled leather and entitled *Twilight*. Only two copies were printed. One, which was subsequently destroyed, he gave as a Christmas gift to his mother. The other, from which the inscription-leaf was afterwards cut out, he gave to Elinor.

There was further stimulation in store for him. Again he was writing frequently to Miss Ward, sometimes enclosing poems for her to judge, sometimes thanking her especially for her encouragement. Meanwhile her brother had written to Maurice Thompson, genial Indiana author of *Alice of Old Vincennes* and regular contributor of prose and verse to the *Independent*, asking his frank opinion of "My Butterfly," and now she quoted to Frost what Thompson had said:

> [I]t has some secret of genius between the lines, an appeal to sympathy lying deep in one's sources of tenderness; and moreover its art is singular and biting, even where the faulty places are most obtruded. My wife read it aloud to me the other evening when my eyes ached after too hard a day's work; and it made me ashamed that I could feel discouraged when I thought of the probable disappointment in store for young Frost all his life long. If I had a chance to say to him I should tell him to forget that he ever made a poem and to never pen another rhyme.

To this Frost responded on January 30, 1895, that he appreciated being praised by a professional writer, that he had confidence in his capacities, that he would undertake a future as a poet. [Newdick here quoted two paragraphs from Frost's letter.] The letter carried the news that he had got a job on the Lawrence *Daily American*.

What he liked best on the paper was the opportunity the editor soon gave him of writing single-paragraph observations and essays run under the heading "The American About and Abroad." As he said in an interview with Gardner Jackson in 1924:

> It's amusing that I once had a column on the newspaper, before columnists were ever known. Of course, it wasn't like the present columns. I wrote about things I'd seen. Sort of prose poems. I remember one thing was about women I'd watched from my window picking up coal along the railroad tracks. Another was about an eagle that flew over Lawrence and alighted on the brass ball at the top of the flagpole on the Postoffice Building. An ardent hunter got out his gun and shot the eagle on his flagpole perch. That was worth writing about, wasn't it? It angered me, of course.

This is Frost's account of the coal pickers:

> I am going to betray a confidence and worse than that, a poor man's confidence, but only in the hope of compelling for him your natural if unrighteous sympathy.
>
> There are a lot of women and children that have let me see them looting coal in a yard near here. They come with buckets and gather it piece by piece under the coal cars. It is feverish work keeping warm, for such people. And the curious part of it is, they will not take the coal otherwise than from off the ground, which necessitates their twice handling it, once from the car to the ground, and again from the ground to the bucket. The moral strain attendant on such work must be excessive and one suffers to watch them skulking and stooping all day.

As for Frost's ability in objective reporting, Lawrence newspapermen were inclined to agree with his own estimate, given to James A. Batal in 1925: "I was as bad a newspaper reporter as I am a farmer." One anecdote that they repeatedly told of him was that once while he was taking notes on an address by a local minister he heard a fire alarm and hastily left the church to cover the fire. Then he wrote up both stories. The account of the fire was as straightforward and as factual as any editor could wish, but the report of the sermon was shocking: judging by the opening remarks that he had heard, Frost had ventured to outline the speaker's conclusion, but unfortunately his conjecture was the opposite of the truth!

Frost branded this tale as apocryphal, and thought that he did well enough with the routine of reporting sermons and church affairs and on such special assignments as writing up fires and suicides. But his tendency to comment, which was his strength as a columnist, was his weakness as a reporter, who ought never to editorialize. Besides, prone to reticence himself, he was unjournalistically inclined to respect the privacy of others, and was averse to nosing out news that rested on names.

So early in the spring he abandoned newspaper work and went to see Elinor in Canton, New York. There at Saint Lawrence University she was matching in college her achievement in high school, completing her scientific course and graduating B.S. in just two years and a half.

Frost made the trip to Canton again for Elinor's commencement exercises on June 26. Through the summer, too, until he went up into the Ossipee Mountains above Melvin Village for his health, and after he came back, he continued his assiduous courtship. One of the poems that mirrors these courting days is "Meeting and Passing," which records an early encounter of lovers-to-be. [Newdick quoted the first nine lines of the sonnet.]

Both of them taught school during the autumn, Elinor at ,[1] Robert at No. 9 again. Then, on December 28, after a courtship of nearly five full years, they went down to the home of the Rev. Mr. John A. Hayes, a Swedenborgian, in Salem, Massachusetts, and were married. Those before whom Robert chose to stand for public judgment were to remain skeptical during the next eighteen years of hardship and trial; but for him and Elinor personally the time of doubt was over.

---

1. Newdick had not learned that Elinor taught at Mrs. Frost's private school that fall.

Note: The juxtaposition of Newdick's Chapter IX and Thompson's Chapter XVI of *The Early Years* shows both how Frost could give variant versions of his experiences, real and imagined, and how important it is to realize the undependable nature of the statements he made about his life.

Newdick, it will be noted, understood that Frost's trip to the Dismal Swamp of Virginia and its environs, in November 1894, was in at least indirect response to what he recalled as Elinor's breaking of their engagement. His account shows no relationship to his two-copy edition of *Twilight*. In need of distraction and self-orientation, he used a cover of looking for employment for his travels. The route of the trip is the same in the accounts given to Newdick and Thompson; thus there seems little doubt that the trip actually happened. There are at least two accounts of how he came to do it. Thompson leaned to the idea, doubtless encouraged by the vivid account of the cool reception of *Twilight* by Elinor, that Frost wandered the swamp in a quasi-suicidal mood. No such desperate overtones are in the account recorded by Newdick.

The fact that, in Thompson, it was Ed Dozier, owner of a bar in Elizabeth City, N.C., who tried to get Frost a teaching job, is representative of incongruencies in the accounts, whatever caused them. In Newdick, it is John B. Brockett, a liquor dealer. In Thompson, both "a man named Lamb," who was editor of "the local paper" and "a man named Sheep" who "headed up the local academy" are willing to help Frost. Lamb introduces Frost to Sheep. They both offer him a job. He escapes without saying goodbye. In Newdick, Enoch F. Lamb, editor of the weekly *Economist* (a newspaper which did exist in 1894) in Elizabeth City, introduces him to Samuel L. Sheep, principal of the Elizabeth City Academy, who would have employed him to teach Greek and Latin. In this case, Frost merely backed out.

Both Newdick and Thompson agree that, at this point, Frost's money was exhausted. Substantially, the accounts agree, though that of Thompson is much fuller. Newdick says Frost recalled songs sung by the tramps; Thompson gives one of eight lines. Perhaps it is a warning that Frost told Thompson that, in reacting to the violence about him on a boxcar, he ran away, only recalling he had left his satchel behind when it was too late. He told Newdick, however, that a hard-boiled brakeman robbed him of his remaining kit, not even allowing him to keep his razor.

All this is minor compared to the problems of accounts of the publishing of *Twilight*. In Newdick, the five poems were printed in celebration of the appearance of "My Butterfly" in the *Independent* while he was on his travels. The fact of the poem's appearance while he was traveling is substantiated by a letter of December 4 to Miss Susan Hayes Ward, of the magazine staff. Newdick merely says that, of the two copies, one, which was subsequently destroyed, he gave to his mother as a Christmas present. The other he gave to Elinor; it is the one which has survived, with the inscription page cut out.

When he related the publication of *Twilight* to Thompson, Frost told him the poems were printed *before* he went to the Dismal Swamp. Taking her copy to her at St. Lawrence University only to be rebuffed *caused* him to go on his travels.

It is doubtless possible to use these deviations only as a reason not to use them as a basis for drawing conclusions concerning Frost's emotional state during his youth. What they do demonstrate is the way he felt when he told them. Probably it would be a suggestion that Thompson's manuscript record of all the conversations during the twenty-four years he was officially designated as Frost's biographer be published, something he could not do in a biography. This could throw light on the most significant fact of Frost's life, that he believed the events of his life were most importantly used as bases for the fictions found in his poetry.

X. The Call to Arms

January, 1896–Summer, 1897

D
URING the year and a half following his marriage
Frost spent most of his time teaching, giving up
the district school in Salem after the winter term
at the outset of 1896 and from then on working
again with his mother in her private school. Steadily, too, he
was trying to write; but the poetry was coming slowly, and he
was dissatisfied with what he did produce. On January 25, 1896,
after nearly a year's silence, he wrote Miss Ward in a very dif-
fident way about the poems he was enclosing, suggesting that
perhaps he was not a poet, expecting she would not find his
work what she wanted.

Evidently Miss Ward found three of the poems acceptable,
except for the last line of one of them, "Caesar's Lost Transport
Ships," and on July 8 Frost wrote her again. Because he had had
a good rest after the closing of school, he could bring himself to
write her, suggesting a changed last line for the poem:

And overhead the petrel, wafted wide.

On August 15, returning proof for "The Birds Do Thus," a
light reminiscence of summer courting days published in the
Independent on August 26, Frost remarked immediately, jokingly, that he was in danger of becoming more interested in
teaching than in writing poetry. Asking to be remembered to
Miss Ward's sister Hetta, he added, alluding to counsel the
sisters had joined in giving him as to the desirability of his
studying botany, that he is doing it whether he wants to or not,
having been presented with much to read about botanizing.

The enthusiast was Frost's slightly older friend Carl Burell,
afterwards state president of the Maine-New Hampshire-Ver-
mont branch of the Shut-in Society. Capitalizing on Frost's
naturally great fondness for the out-of-doors, and taking as basic
guides Mrs. Dana's *How to Know the Wild Flowers* (1893) and
Plants and Their Children (1896), Burell made Frost an ex-

cellent amateur botanist in short order—although Frost was
strangely long in learning that it was not from colds but from
hay fever he suffered every year when the rag weed dusted.

Attentive readers of his *Collected Poems* will have realized
for themselves that in the vegetable kingdom Frost began,
speaking generally, with flowers, moved on to trees and leaves
—his special stronghold being ferns and lichens. [Here Newdick quoted lines 3 and 4 of the third stanza of "Leaves Compared with Flowers".] As for the flowers, whether wild or of
gardens, he never obtruded his exact knowledge and intimate
observation of them, but both of these run through his poems
like nearly continuous threads of changing colors, from the "old
silver" of goldenrod at the very end of autumn to the "leaping
tongue of flame" of butterfly weed in the mowing field in June.
On the mountain, there is low-growing bloodroot, and snowberries are to be found on stream-side rocks. [Here Newdick
quoted lines 97–98 of "The Pauper Witch of Grafton".] On the
hillside could be found coral root, whose shade-loving leafless
plants produced spotted, hanging flowers. [Here Newdick
quoted lines 5–7 of "On Going Unnoticed".] In the deep woods,
carpets of hardhack and sweetfern, and fox-grapes clustering on
vines twined through a birch. Along the brook, moisture-loving
blue-bells and weak-foliaged jewel-weed. By the wayside, "pur-
ple-stemmed" wild raspberries, lupine "living on sand and
drouth," and, for a marvel, the rarity of a white, instead of blue,
heal-all, questioning what would cause a flower to be of one
color rather than another. [Here Newdick quoted lines 9–10 of
"Design."] In the dooryard, at morning, were sprays of dewy
honeysuckle [which Newdick documented by quoting lines
10–12 of "To Earthward"] and, at nightfall, the tight morning-
glory vines on strings against the house [supported by quoting
lines 107–108 of "The Death of the Hired Man"]. And time and
again, though most memorably in "The Self-Seeker," the native
New England orchids—the rare Calypso, the Ram's Horn, both
the yellow and the purple Lady's Slipper, and of rose pogonias
with the yellow and the purple "Lady's Slipper", and of spiked
rose pogonias in a jewel-like meadow, tinged with the colored
spears. [Newdick here quoted lines 1–2 and 13–16 of "Rose
Pogonias".] The Misses Susan and Hetta Ward, Mrs. William
Starr Dana, Carl Burell, "and I don't know who all," may have
combined to get Frost afield with his vasculum at the outset,

but transmuting "specimens" to poetry through the rest of his life was one of Frost's own achievements.

In September he went to teaching again, and on September 30, with the birth of his son Elliott, he became truly a pater-familias. It was three months after that event, however, before he realized that some printed sheets which he had meanwhile received from Miss Ward were proofs and ought to have been returned to her promptly. Chattily, he mentioned the birth of his son, for whatever *that* might be worth, even wishing her a Happy New Year and with it the discovery of a genius, even offering the rediscovery of himself, if he should make such beneficial changes as to be worthy. The poems were duly printed in the *Independent*—"Caesar's Lost Transport Ships" on January 14, 1897, and "Warning" the following September 8—but apparently Frost thought he had no occasion to write again to Miss Ward until 1901.

Yet he soon realized more than his wish that he were reporting again. Beginning early in 1897 he was employed for about six months as reporter-editor-manager of the weekly Lawrence *Sentinel*. Perhaps he thought something about following in his father's long journalistic stride, now that he was in a position to exercise some influence in moulding local public opinion and action. That his social, economic, and political views were temperately liberal, as suggested by his choice of sides in high school debates and also by his sympathies in paragraphs written for the *American*, becomes clear from his reference in 1896 to Bryanism and to the defeat of the champions of "free silver." But he could make little headway against the strong conserva-tive forces in Lawrence, and gradually his joy in potential edi-torial power gave way to weariness before the weekly battering of the deadline. No analyst, it may be added, can write other than generally of Frost's editorial work in 1897, because no file of the *Sentinel* for that year is known to survive; and, as Frost remarked when he was apprised of this fact, "Perhaps it is just as well or better."

Some time before his resignation from the *Sentinel* Frost had tried another door. He had observed that the literary department of the Boston *Transcript* was unusually strong for a newspaper. Even more remarkable, its editor was alert to poetry, and re-printed pieces not only by such widely popular poets as Bliss Carman and Richard Hovey, but also by such then little known writers as William Ellery Leonard and Edwin Arlington Robinson. Occasionally, too, the editor would print some of his own work, notably his metrical translations from Scandinavian verse.

So Frost went down to Boston to call on him. The *Transcript* building was on narrow Washington Street, near the Old South Meeting House, and diagonally across the street from the Old Corner Bookstore, formerly owned by George Ticknor, and with a back room where Lowell and Holmes and Longfellow used to meet and smoke to their mind's content. Frost climbed the three flights of wooden stairs to Charles Hurd's dusty and crowded little office on the top floor and handed him a small sheaf of manuscripts. When Hurd had looked them over he cocked his head and said, "How about something to eat? Let's go pick up a snack somewhere."

At lunch he told Frost how he himself had once had his heart set on a literary career, had hopefully come to Boston with a packet of stories and poems in his bag, but finally had been driven into journalism by sheer necessity. "There's no money in poetry," he concluded, echoing Maurice Thompson and many another disillusioned versifier. Yet he said he really liked Frost's poems, and would take one to print; but he could offer nothing in payment for it, and Frost would be wise not to take too much encouragement from the publication of any poem not paid for.

The poem Hurd chose was "Greece," and it appeared in the *Transcript* on April 30, 1897. It was Frost's almost immediate response to the outbreak of the Graeco-Turkish War. Frost appeals to the Greek to prove, as in ancient times, that a few valorous souls may be triumphant against many. [Newdick quoted all three of the four-line stanzas of the poem he had discovered in the *Boston Transcript*. Text may be found on p. 539 of Thompson's *The Early Years*.]

"Dreadful, dreadful," Frost wrote in the margin of a copy I sent him in 1936. "I was trying very hard to show sympathy with the people who made me learn Greek." But in 1897 Frost's interest in Greece and in the classics was indicative of one more good fight he was himself about to make.

XI. The Lines of a Good Helve
Autumn, 1897–Spring, 1899

F OR not quite two academic years, beginning in the
autumn of 1897 and extending into the spring of 1899,
Frost submitted himself for the second and last time to
the formal processes of higher education. During this
period the poet in him was for the most part quiescent; he wrote
but little. Instead, the scholar in him shone, and he absorbed far
more than he consciously realized either then or later. His approach to the experience, his spirit in carrying on, and his accomplishment, all of these were in contrast to their parallels in
his interlude at Dartmouth five years earlier; yet the outcome
was almost precisely the same in terms of his mental attitudes.

The impulse to return to college came to him one day while
he was reading in Tacitus, to whose style, compressed yet vital,
his own later manner bore clear resemblances. Elinor encouraged him when she learned what he was pondering, and so also
did his mother and his grandfather. Finally he determined upon
Harvard.

Ignoring his credits for the Harvard preliminary examinations
that he had taken in 1891, he went down to Cambridge in September and took History (Greek and Roman), and Physical Sci-
ences (Astronomy and Physics)—on four successive days. Then
he posted bond at the bursar's office, rented a room at 16 Rut-
land Street about ten minutes' walk up Massachusetts Avenue
from University Hall, and on September 30, just a quarter of a
century after the year of his father's graduation, attended his
first classes in Harvard College.

His programme for the freshman year comprised courses in
English, German, Latin, and Greek. German A, required of all
students who had not presented it for admission, was least to his
liking, even though Elinor studied it with him. She had come to
Cambridge with her parents when they took a house in Ellery
Street shortly after college opened, and for the remainder of the
year the two families lived together.

English A, likewise required of all freshmen who had not anticipated it by examination, was almost as distasteful to Frost as German. The text, Hill's *Principles of Rhetoric*, was tolerable; the assigned reading—in Shakespeare, Macaulay, Eliot, Thackeray, and Kipling—was worth while; and in Dean Briggs' genial "third-hour" talks to the group meetings of sections there was both wisdom and delight. But what writer ever really enjoyed, even though he might profit by, the Sisyphean labor of the daily themes and translations, the dozen fortnightly essays and papers, and the monthly conferences with his instructor in freshman English?

Frost's instructor, subsequently a well known educator but then an assistant teaching English A for the first time, was Alfred Dwight Sheffield, whose meticulous speech was marked by long pauses during which he would search for exactly the right word. Friendly toward his students, he invited them to call on him at his lodgings in 25 Holyoke Street, and Frost accepted the invitation notwithstanding the fact that Sheffield had given him a mark of only B on some of the poems he had submitted, poems in which he had a firm personal faith later justified by their popularity when they appeared in his books.

"Frost had already matured his own distinctive approach to writing," Sheffield wrote retrospectively in 1939. "I remember very congenial talks with him in which he effectively contrasted the potent element of 'sentence-tone' with the syntactic mechanisms in terms of which I tended to work for sentence-sense in the freshman group. I was myself at that time much influenced by Sidney Lanier, and by a discipline in the patterning of music which, I think, prevented me from appreciating the full importance of Frost's special sensitivity to the expressive cadences of speech. He was then, I recall, absorbed in reading the *Odyssey*, and his talk made it very evident that he was taking his own line as a writer, and could give any young teacher as good as he got."

Frost's "passion," as he himself called it, was for Latin and Greek. Like young Harold Wilson in "The Death of the Hired Man", who studied Latin because of his affinity for it. [Here Newdick quoted lines 79–80 of "The Death of the Hired Man".] He took a half-year course in Latin composition, and in Latin C, under the brilliant Oxonian Charles P. Parker, read in lyric, elegaic, and iambic poetry, and in Terence and Livy. Thinking of these days Frost wrote in the margin of Miss Sergeant's copy of his *Selected Poems*, "First heard the voice from a printed page in a Virgilian Eclogue and *Hamlet*." And again in the margin: "'Black Cottage,' 'The Housekeeper,' 'The Death of the Hired Man' date from 1905. Virgil's Eclogues may have had something to do with them."

Then, as both earlier and later, Frost's drive was inner and personal rather than outward and formal. Simply for his own gratification he committed to memory passage after passage that for one reason or another appealed to him when he encountered them in the classics. His method in memorizing such a passage was first to throw up a rough scaffolding of translation around it, next to work into it from the platforms of the scaffold, and then finally to kick away all external aids and to absorb it in its native idioms and melodies. Hence his realization of the impossibility of any completely satisfactory translation, and hence also an observation pertinent to his concern in poetry for "writing down the voice":

> Really to understand and catch all that is embodied in a foreign masterpiece, it must be read in the original because while the words may be brought over, the tone cannot be.

In Greek, Frost had two courses under Frank Cole Babbitt, a half-year course in composition and a full year course in Homer. The *Odyssey*, as Sheffield observed, quickly became one of his favorites, and it remained so throughout his life. In 1930, for instance, in his talk on "Education by Poetry," he made several references to it. In one passage, speaking of the virtue of "a gathering metaphor," he cited a boy's characterization of someone as "the kind that wounds with his shield," and then went on to discuss the use of metaphor in the *Odyssey*. He remarked on how great a figure Odysseus was. And in 1936, when he was asked the inevitable—to name ten indispensable books other than the Bible and Shakespeare—he placed the *Odyssey* at the very head of his list, remarking, "The *Odyssey* chooses itself, the first in time and rank of all romances."

Of all his courses he recalled those under Babbitt with the greatest fondness. Babbitt was a young man, and a wise one. His prime concern was not for a student's regularity in attending classes, nor for the effort he made, nor for any other incidental matter; it was exclusively for the quality of the student's finished work. And despite the handicap of numerous absences from class, usually caused by his own illness or by that of Elinor or the baby, Frost always got his work in sometime, and invariably, whether translation or composition, it was work of distinguished quality.

Apropos at this point is an anecdote Robert Hillyer tells: "When I was teaching at Trinity College in 1927, a student of modernistic tastes was arguing the case for 'untutored inspiration' and cited Robert Frost as an example of natural ability without classical background. Professor Frank Cole Babbitt, the Greek teacher, happened to be present, and with a slight smile excused himself from the company for a moment and returned with his record books from the days of his instructorship at Harvard. He turned the pages to Robert Frost's name and there, for at least one year, and possibly two stood an unbroken series of A's which Frost received in Greek."

As for the "student of modernistic tastes," one can only wonder how he had missed the classical allusions scattered effectively though not profusely through Frost's books. The handful of such references in *West-running Brook* (1928) and in *A Further Range* (1936), including that in "Build Soil" to Virgil's first Eclogue and that in "Iris by Night" to Lucretius' *De Rerum Natura*, were of course not available to the student of 1927; but what of the others? In *A Boy's Will* (1913), the relatively incidental one to Minerva and that to Pan in the modern world in the last line of "Pan With Us". In North of Boston (1914), the apt one to the *Odyssey*, referring to the adventure with Nausicaa. [Here Newdick quoted lines 155–6 of "The Generations of Men".] And in *New Hampshire* (1923), both the fractious one to Pegasus and that to Eurydice in "Wild Grapes". [Here Newdick quoted lines 11–13 of "Wild Grapes".] The young man cannot have been a very attentive reader.

At Harvard, in contrast to his life at Dartmouth, Frost took no part in informal athletics, dormitory escapades, or fraternity horseplay. To support his family and meet his college expenses, in which tuition alone was an item of a hundred and fifty dollars, it was imperative that he convert into cash all the time he could. So, aided by the recommendations given him by the school committee of Salem, he secured appointment for the year 1897–1898 as principal of the Shepard Evening School in North Cambridge.

The school term was from October 1 to April 1, and classes were held on Monday, Wednesday, and Friday evenings from seven-thirty to nine-thirty. Since there were a number of young men who registered just for the fun they expected from disrupting the order of the school, Frost's first task was to spot the playboys and to weed them out. Some of his staff would have preferred the easier way of ignoring discipline altogether, but Frost was firm in insisting upon at least enough to work with. One of his corps of teachers, subsequently principal of the local Sleeper School, was Elizabeth G. Nelligan, who by day was then still a school girl herself.

"I remember him very distinctly," she wrote in 1938, "for his kindly and courteous manner. . . He was really interested in the teachers' work and in the progress of the pupils." Regularly, she added, he dropped into each of the classrooms several times every evening, asking the pupils questions and keeping tab on their progress. Yet Frost himself did not regard his principalship as entirely successful, did not again undertake it, and thirteen years later declined the tender of a similar executive position in Pinkerton Academy.

Counting administrative officers and members of the instructional staff as well as University and College students, the academic community of Harvard then numbered about five thousand, and among students in the Graduate School were Percy Boynton, Charles Gestre, and Ashley Thorndike. Merely in the entering Class of 1901 there were four hundred and seventy-one, many of whom of course became distinguished in later years. The demands made on Frost's time were so many and so heavy, however, that he had little opportunity to mingle with his fellow students except during class periods or while crossing the Yard with his heavy green felt bag thrown over his shoulder in the customary manner. "One of the few friends I made at Harvard," he recalled, "was the man who translated the *Odyssey* next to me on a narrow bench in Sever Hall" — Waddill Catchings of Louisville, Kentucky, who had lodgings in 7 Wendell Street, and who afterwards became prominent as a financier in New York.

At the close of the year Frost was unutterably weary; to one who saw him frequently throughout the year he "always seemed rather tired." Yet he had the satisfaction of knowing that by awarding him a scholarship for the following year—a Sewall, worth two hundred dollars—the College formally recognized his freshman record as of "marked excellence." He had, moreover, placed a poem. A bit of religious juvenilia which he never allowed to be reprinted or collected, and the only one of his poems to be published while he was a student, "God's Garden" appeared in the Boston *Transcript* on June 28. A part of the third and last stanza is typical of the whole, insisting that looking to the stars will keep one free from error. [Here Newdick quoted lines 25–32 of "God's Garden".]

In his second year, after a summer's rest, Frost elected to continue his study of Greek, and Latin, and then, free from the incubi of the required courses in English and German, elected two courses and two half-year courses that brought him under some of Harvard's greatest teachers. The half-year course for the first semester was Geology 4 under Professor Nathaniel S. ("Uncle Nat") Shaler. Large-framed, tall, with rugged features, upstanding gray hair, and a Jove-like beard, Shaler at fifty-seven had enjoyed international fame as a productive field scientist for a quarter of a century, and through his impressive platform appearance and his ability to make geology fascinating year after year to classes of hundreds, was veritably a Harvard institution.

His spell caught Frost as it caught everyone else. His lectures, illuminated by a flood of apposite illustrations, seemed to one observer "spontaneous revelations of a long familiarity with his subject," but Frost saw their solid core of substance and delighted in their ingenious form. One, of which he long after recalled even the lecturer's analogies, was that on Earth Strains, in which Shaler explained the "explosions" of Kansas prairies as caused by adjustments in the earth's crust under the application of geologically sudden pressures. Frost listened raptly. This was what he liked best among the advantages of an institution of higher learning: "knowledge dumped," as he expressed it vigorously, "in great heaps, all around me, and on me."

And many were the uses to which he put his knowledge of geology in after years—in word, figure, concept, and speculation: In "A Drumlin Woodchuck," the sly nominal adjective in the title that sends an average reader to the dictionary (*"Geol.* An elongate or oval hill of glacial drift") and an enthusiast to the particular drumlin that rises to the right of The Gulley, Frost's second farmhouse near South Shaftsbury, Vermont. In "Geode" (*"Geol.* A nodule of stone having a cavity lined with crystals or mineral matter"), the title-key to a packed metaphysical exercise otherwise inaccessible. In "What Fifty Said," the general principle that the inflexible must give way to force, [Newdick quoted line 7 of "What Fifty Said".] which could easily have proceeded from everyday experience, but which is possibly reminiscent of Shaler's lectures on strains. In "In Time of Cloudburst," the dominant figure deals with how, as hills and valleys can be reversed, so despair can be turned into hope. [Newdick quoted lines 12–20 of "In Time of Cloudburst"] which may be a transmitted recollection from the text of Shaler's *Outlines of Earth's History* and more particularly of an illustration on p. 98 ("Diagram showing the effect of the position of the fulcrum point in the movement of land masses"). And, finally, in "A Star in a Stone-Boat," observations that may imply no more than the fusion of the poet's ordinary knowledge, personal thought, and individual expression, but that happen to be scientifically as well as poetically close and accurate, and as much so for astronomy at one end and for botany at the other as for geology in between, referring to how a rock-remnant of a starfall whirl becomes part of a decorative boat, containing flowers. [Here Newdick quoted lines 1–24 of "A Star in a Stone-Boat."]

Yet it was philosophy, rather than geology, that constituted Frost's second chief field of interest while he was in college, and during his sophomore year he studied philosophy as diligently as he continued to pursue the classics. The Harvard "school" of philosophy, America's first really great University group of philosophers, was then at the height of its strength, and included George Herbert Palmer, William James, Josiah Royce, George Santayana, and Hugo Münsterberg. By taking concurrently two basic courses, of which each half was offered by a different professor each semester, Frost came under all of these masters, except James, in the one year.

In the first half of the General Introduction to Philosophy, Palmer devoted most of the time to the study of logic. The Alford Professor of Natural Religion, Moral Philosophy, and Civil Polity had begun his career, like Le Baron Russell Briggs, as a tutor in Greek, and at fifty-six was a man of extraordinary range and balance in culture. Small and frail, with a heavy, drooping moustache and deep-set, kindly eyes, he sat while he discoursed; and his expositions, though apparently casual, were finely wrought. They were, moreover, informed throughout with his quiet faith. As he observed of a colleague, "Personally he fairly lived with the Eternal, the affairs of time being still counted worth while because in them too can be seen 'bright shoots of everlastingness.'"

In marked contrast to Palmer was the thirty-five-year-old
assistant professor who gave the first half-year's lectures on the
ancients in the course on the History of Philosophy. Santayana's philosophical dogma was straightforwardly mechanistic
and materialistic. Yet in all things, including religion, the aristocratic Harvard-educated Spaniard was primarily an aesthete,
and even hard-headed Münsterberg regarded his *The Sense of
Beauty* (1896) as an important contribution to formal aesthet-
ics. As for religion, Santayana professed to regard the old faith as
dead; but it is clear in his *Sonnets and Other Poems* (1894) that
he yearned nostalgically for the old faith and its ritual.

It is likely that Frost had looked into Santayana's poems. Certainly the sonnet "O World, thou choosest not the better part"
would have won his approbation, and likewise most of the
thought in the poem beginning "My heart rebels against my
generation"—perhaps all except the prayer that his friend be
"well-born, gentle." That last would strike a sour note to Frost's
democratic ear, for after forty years he recalled with still-
smouldering resentment:

> I was sitting in a class in college when I heard a man spend
> quite the best part of an hour making fun of the expression
> that we are all "free and equal." So easy to dismiss. Let's
> have a look at it:
> All men were created free and equally funny. Before you
> laugh too much at that, take another look at it:
> Four hundred years ago the only people who were funny
> were yokels; now, today, even kings are funny. We've
> come a long way.

In the second half-year the instructors in the two philosophy
courses were carefully paired to offset each other as they were in
the first. In those days, all good philosophers were psychologists
as well, and all competent psychologists were philosophers too.
So it was only nominally that the second half-year's work in the
General Introduction was given over exclusively to psychology
under Münsterberg, whose lectures were supplemented by
laboratory experiments and by readings in James's briefer *Psychology*. Tiring of the laboratory himself, James had called the
Wundt-trained but rebellious Münsterberg from Freiberg in
1892 in his twenty-ninth year, and by 1898, despite an intervening sojourn on the Continent, the tall, blue-eyed German

with his pince-nez and Kaiser-like moustache was firmly established at Harvard. Always of an honestly divided allegiance, Münsterberg dreamed and occasionally talked of bringing the Germanic countries together, particularly Germany and the United States; and it was possibly from this poetic side of "Hugo Terberg" that Frost received the initial impulse toward his own ultimate conviction that Germany and England are natural allies and someday would be politically so. Usually, however, Münsterberg's tone was that of a thoroughgoing empiricist.

Josiah Royce wound up the year's work in the History of Philosophy by lecturing part of the time with hair-splitting precision on modern thought and thinkers, and by rambling expansively the rest of the time on almost everything else, including his conception of God. Most of his students agreed with his own judgment that his homeliness was unparalleled except by that of Socrates, for there was no portion of his face unfreckled; his gigantic round head, sprinkled with red hair, was sunk in the shoulders of his stocky, short figure; and it was obvious that he never wasted a moment in thought of his personal appearance. But if they remained unaware of his prodigiously productive scholarship, most of the students were impressed by his vast erudition. "Perhaps his classes did not always follow the intricacy of his lectures," a colleague suggested kindly, "but they knew that something big was going on above them, and they were all duly elevated. Each gained his own vista into an unsuspected world, many having their minds and characters recreated in the process. . ."

Opposed to any kind of empiricism, whether that of James, Santayana, or Münsterberg, Royce maintained the supreme virtue of idealism. "In his all-embracing Absolute," wrote the likeminded Palmer, "Royce found room for our individual existence here and hereafter, for our sins, repentance, atonement, and salvation. Loyalty to this sovereign Person made him one of the most unshakably religious men I have ever known. From organized religion he held aloof, partly because it was his disposition to go his own way, partly, too, through reaction from certain rigidities of his boyhood." Frost's poem "God's Garden" indicates that he must have found numerous parallels, of course at a distance and with differences, between much of Royce's stalwart character and faith on the one hand, and, on the other, elements in his own make-up and spiritual conclusions at this time.

Frost said of the teachers under whom he studied philosophy, "Of course I enjoyed all four extremely, but I cannot say that any one of them had an outstandingly great influence on my mind." It was the policy of the department of philosophy carefully to maintain the clash between the older and stronger idealists and the numerically greater empiricists. Frost may have realized that and may have looked upon the conflict dispassionately as simply intellectual integrity in action. Or he may have judged that the earnest claims of the one group were cancelled out by the equally earnest counter-claims of the opposing group. In any event, his personal faith was not undermined. By the examples of the steadfast Palmer and Royce it may indeed have been fortified. And certainly, though never a formalist, he remained essentially a religious man all his life.

But if no one of the philosophers had "an outstandingly great influence on his mind," Frost was disturbed by the age-old fundamental questions. Many an evening, resolving them for himself, he tramped the city streets far into the night. And sometimes, returning, he would look up to the clock in the tower of Memorial Hall, and there find confirmation of his realistic conclusions concerning, for example, complaint about the rightness of the time in which one lives. [Here Newdick quoted the first three and the last four lines of "Acquainted with the Night."] One such conclusion, never altered, was that Platonic idealism, with its concept of divine archetypes, was not for him. As he expressed it forty years afterwards in a letter when Robert P. Tristram Coffin was preparing an analysis of him and Edwin Arlington Robinson, he could not be a Platonic idealist who could remain a bachelor for fear of defiling the perfect ideal.

The last of Frost's noteworthy courses, an elective he chose to complete his program for the second half-year, was that in Milton under George Lyman Kittredge, disciple and successor of Francis J. Child, and himself both a memorable scholar and one of the greatest teachers who ever strode before a class. Kittredge began the first hour by reading Milton's Horton poem beginning "Fly, envious Time, till thou run out thy race." First of all he read it entire as literature with evident enjoyment; and then expatiating upon it, he read it and illuminated it line by line so that all of its riches became apparent and the students' appreciation was deepened through complete understanding of its language, figures, and allusions. According to Frost's values, all of this was precisely as it should be. But when he looked around in the classroom he was dismayed. There sat row after row of undergraduates, most of them with heads bent over volumes of Milton thick with interleaves, slavishly writing down every point "Kitty" was scoring. If such meticulous learning was expected of him, thought Frost, he had better drop the course. And he did, after just the one class.

As the winter of 1899 wore on toward spring, Frost had no reason to doubt his standing in the eyes of the authorities. Had he not been summoned, just before the Christmas recess, to the customary ceremony in Sanders Theater and *pro insigni in studiis diligentia* been presented, as his father had been, with a detur—a copy of John Selden's *Table Talk*?

Yet he was increasingly uncomfortable in his situation. For one thing, he was living alone, at 61 Oxford Street, since the Whites had moved back to Lawrence, and Elinor, again with child, had gone with them. Now the family was together again only for too swift hours on those days when he went up to Lawrence by trolley to talk about the current books with an evening class of grown-ups. And as for Harvard, he disliked the endless talk among the younger undergraduates about "credits," and he resented the unrelenting pressure of classes that left him almost no time to think things over or to write.

He left college early in the spring, just before his daughter Lesley was born on April 28, and so was less than "half a Harvard man," as Edwin Arlington Robinson described himself when he left Harvard in 1893, the year his friend William Vaughn Moody was graduated. The business of his leave-taking, however, Frost handled much better than he had at Dartmouth. He called on the marvelously understanding Dean Briggs and explained what was bothering him and why he felt he had best withdraw. The dean talked with him kindly; more than that, he wrote him a letter as a kind of honorable discharge. The troubled sophomore never showed the letter around, but it pleased him to have it in his pocket as tangible evidence that he had left college without prejudice.

And to see his generous judgment of the young man visibly confirmed by results, the dean had only to wait the seventeen years until 1916 when Frost was called back to Harvard — to be initiated as an honorary member of Phi Beta Kappa, and to read for that society, most appropriately, "The Axe Helve," the curves of which came from the grain within rather than being imposed from without. [Newdick quoted lines 72–75 of "The Axe-Helve".]

Note: Newdick contributes to the view of the relationship between Frost and Sheffield the recollections of the teacher. He gives added dimensions to the figures of Frost's teachers, Professors Shaler, Palmer, James, Royce, Santayana, and Münsterberg.

Frost's principalship of the Shepard Evening School in North Cambridge in 1897–98 is described in more detail than is available elsewhere.

XII. In the Wayside Nook
September, 1899, through 1905

THE year and a half following his withdrawal from Harvard was a period of anxiety and heartache for Robert and Elinor. About the only bright thing in it was that in the *Independent* for September 28, 1899, in an article on "A Decade of Poetry, 1889–1899," Susan Ward commended his "My Butterfly" and quoted his saying that he composed it "when it first dawned upon him that poetry 'ought to sound well'." But what was that against the task of teaching the year with his mother in her school and the trial of seeing her hopelessly wasting away, lingering in pain until her death on November 2, 1900, at the age of fifty-six? Or what could anything avail, then, against the shock of the death of little Elliott, their firstborn, on July 8, 1900? Frost uses the bereaved mother in "Home Burial" to express furious resentment of the way people turn quickly from ceremonies for the dead to the more understandable pursuits of life. [Newdick quoted lines 107–117 of "Home Burial".] So, in "Home Burial," cries the bereaved and hysterical young mother to the husband trying desperately to understand and soothe her — lines in a dramatic dialogue, to be sure; but also hard truths that Robert and Elinor learned less from impartial observation than from their bitter personal experience.

Elinor, naturally the most deeply shaken, was yet the first to recover the power of unemotional thinking. Robert, she realized, would be no hand to continue with the school alone; and he ought, as he wished, to get away from Lawrence and the painful associations there. Why not, thought Elinor, go to a small farm? She recalled that he had told her of the "farm" he had wishfully created in the backyard when he was a little boy in San Francisco; and she knew his happiest recollections of later years were of summers on Charles Hall's New Hampshire farm near Windham. Accordingly, she begged grandfather Frost to buy them a thirty-acre place they knew to be for sale at $1,200 in Rockingham County, New Hampshire, about fifteen miles north of Lawrence. "That's as good a place to die as any," cheerfully concluded W. P. Frost, Sr.; and in September, 1900, while still a few peaches lay on the ground in the orchard, they moved out and took possession.

Frost was always receiving impressions, naturally and unconsciously, from the life he lived and lived in, and many of these showed up afterwards, either as flashes or as whole episodes, and as much to his surprise as anyone's, in his poems. Thus the piece significantly named "In the Home Stretch" is a pretty close account of his and Elinor's first hours on their farm, in their first home of their own; and at this point in the narrative it might well be inserted entire, rather than in tantalizing excerpts.

When the poem opens, the moving men are still unloading the van of its load of furniture and household goods, and the young mistress is standing near the sink. Husband and wife display through their raillery the way they both have wanted this place for each other; they immediately feel as much at home as the firelight which dances on the ceiling. Elinor, it may be remarked, appears either in the foreground or in the background of more of Frost's poems than she is absent from, and the characteristic tone of the exchanges between husband and wife, as in the selections above, [Newdick had quoted lines 13–21, 27–35, 165–176, and 202–205 of the poem.] is one of banter glancing lightly and playfully over depths of philosophical seriousness and unplumbed affection.[1]

The farm lay to the east of the Boston-Concord turnpike that passed it running northward over Cline's Hill to West Derry, afterwards simply Derry, a mile or two beyond. The two-story, white, frame farmhouse with cross-gabled roof was set back a hundred feet or so from the road, to which there was a view across the lawn either from the bay window or from the small stoop at the seldom used front door. Full length across the south side of the house, extending to the built-on shed that virtually connected the house to the door end of the barn, ran a porch screened from the sun by morning glory vines on strings. Just across the short drive from the road to the barn was the pump over a dug well. South of the house, along the road, was the orchard; southeast, the mowing field that ended at the brook and

---

1. These two passages Newdick had marked for expansion.

woods; and east, the upland pasture. The north line was marked by a low wall of loose stones fetched originally from the fields and set up without mortar, like those in Wales.

Grandfather Frost made several provisos when he bought the farm for Robert and Elinor. One was that it should not be sold for at least ten years. Another was that, given a cow, a horse, and a cart too big for the horse, Robert should shift for himself as to other equipment and tools. The third was that, since Robert seemed to lack enough gumption to get along by himself, they should take Robert's old school friend and amateur botany instructor, Carl Burell, to live with them as a kind of overseer and to look after the cow particularly. This last arrangement provoked difficulties, of course; and soon after the death of W. P. Frost, Sr., in his seventy-ninth year on July 10, 1901, Carl packed up his belongings and left.

Meanwhile, on January 15, 1901, Frost had written to Miss Ward, briefly and a little stiffly after his silence of nearly four years, enclosing a poem and speaking casually of a book he saw in the future; sending her poems taken from those he hoped would make a book, he indicated he would be pleased to have them in the *Independent*. Evidently Miss Ward found the poem acceptable, for "The Quest of the Orchis" was published in the *Independent* on June 27, 1901. Apparently, too, she told him that she was about to sever her connection with the magazine, and it was five years before he again submitted a manuscript to the *Independent* or published another poem anywhere.

Grandfather Frost had not been entirely wrong in his view of Robert. Some of the young man's lethargy was admittedly owing to the hay fever that annually struck him about the middle of August and left him choked and miserable until about Christmas, but some of it was undeniably owing to sheer laziness and to his inclination to put things off. It was six months, for example, before he put up the curtain fixtures in the farmhouse; and, though the well was hardly more than forty feet away, he never did dig a trench and lay pipe from it to the kitchen so that Elinor could have the convenience of a pump inside the house. Inevitably such shortcomings were noted audibly by members of Elinor's family when they came to visit her, but she herself never complained. Robert had not converted her to his way of life: she had simply surrendered to it when she gave in to him, and until her last few years the surrender was complete and final.

In dealing with women, one ameliorates one's manhood, ruefully observes the husband in "Home Burial." And in "Snow" another husband declares emphatically that "dishonest" pretense of gentility has made him ashamed of such healthy interests as watching two boys fight. [Newdick quoted lines 97–100 of "Snow".] Yet Robert made some of the adjustments necessary on both sides if a marriage is to be really successful.

Frost looked on love between man and woman as only an essential part of a full and normal life, never as an end romantically to be exalted out of all right proportion to the other essential parts. He had the integrity, too, unlike some of his flamboyant artist contemporaries, to be constant in his attachment to one woman, and his fervor matched his constancy. Well along in life he wrote, in "To Earthward", that joy and pain were always mixed and that he sought the spicy blend. [Newdick quoted lines 17–24 of the poem.] But at the dawn of manhood, he confessed, in the same poem, that sexual love had seemed sweet beyond endurance [lines 1–3]. And only a purblind prude can miss the mature physical intensity that is manifest in a number of his poems, such as, from one point of view, the sonnet "Putting in the Seed," and from another, the quatrain "Devotion," which uses the intimate figure of the repeated interaction of shore and ocean.

Within five years of their moving to the farm, when Lesley was a year and a half old, the Frost household had increased to six. Carol was born on May 22, 1902, Irma on June 26, 1903, and Marjorie on March 24, 1905.

They were a happy family, notwithstanding their difficulties, isolation, and neglect. True, the farm was unproductive; but the income from a trust fund which W. P. Frost, Sr., had set up in his will for Robert and his sister Jeanie was sufficient to guarantee them the bare necessities of existence for a while, though it was a steadily diminishing income. True, no neighbors came to call on them socially for eight years, and only twice in that time was Robert out after eight o'clock at night; but that left him and Elinor what leisure they could manage, to spend as they wished, and Robert spent his reading—whole poets at a sitting, many of them aloud while Elinor sewed, and sometimes as many as five in one day. And also true, Robert's granduncle Elihu W. Colcord, probably thought to punish him severely by ignoring him in his will and leaving all his money to build a dormitory for Sanborn Seminary at Kingston; but Robert showed his mettle and Elinor's by turning the intended rebuke into a poem! Entitled "In Neglect," it will ever stand guard for Frost against those who otherwise might be tempted to sentimentalize his nine years on the farm at Derry, stating the amusement of the couple at those who thought them forlorn in their isolation.

XIV. A Boy's Will
September, 1912–May, 1913

THE two and a half years Frost spent in Britain from September, 1912, to February, 1915, marked the turning-point in his career. Practically unknown when he sailed from America at thirty-eight, and utterly unknown in England, in those thirty months he was to publish two successful books, to make a host of personal and literary friends, and to return home acclaimed by both English and American critics of all schools and also by the poetry-reading public—just then an unusually alert and growing public.

Even before they left America the Frosts had decided where they wished to settle down in England: somewhere in the quiet of the country, not too far from London, in a small cottage with a thatched roof. (Mrs. Frost insisted on the roof of thatch.) But was such a place to be had? *T. P.'s Weekly*, Frost observed, contained a regular department devoted to country walks, so he went around to the office and enquired of the conductor of the department. The conductor, an ex-policeman to whom Frost took an immediate liking, recommended the undulating pastoral countryside of southern Buckinghamshire. And with little more ado than that the Frosts were soon established in The Bungalow, under a real thatched roof at last, yet just twenty-one and a half miles from Paddington Station via the Great Western.

Immediately Frost set about getting his lines up between Beaconsfield and America, and one of his first letters, dated September 15, 1912, was to Miss Ward. Noting he was writing from the precincts of Milton, Gray, and Chesterton, insignificant as he held mere locality to be, he asserted he felt he had demonstrated his practicality as a teacher and had thus earned a chance to prove himself as a poet. Noting his neglect by edi-

Note: There was no Chapter XIII.

tors, he expressed the hope he could still achieve the poetry he longed for.

But of course there *is* some virtue in location, just as there is in a particular kind of roof! Bucks, adjoining Middlesex on the northwest, and otherwise surrounded by the shires of Berks, Oxford, Northampton, Bedford, and Hertford, is roughly about ten miles wide from east to west and twenty-five miles long from north to south. In the southwest rise the chalky Chiltern Hills, and groves of beech trees everywhere interrupt the waves of rich pasture land. In High Wycombe, a town of twenty thousand, the largest in the county, chairs are made of the beechwood, and elsewhere some of the cottagers cling to their ancient craft of lace-making; but most of the shire's inhabitants are small farmers who tend their cattle by day and their kitchen gardens in the evenings.

In and around Beaconsfield, a village of twenty-five hundred in southeastern Bucks, cluster rich historical and literary associations. Thence Benjamin Disraeli, who lived at Hughenden Manor, not far from his father's home at Bradenham, took the name under which he was elevated to the peerage. Two miles off is the old Quaker meeting-house of Jordans, in whose burial-ground lie William Penn, his two wives, and five of his children. On the road to High Wycombe, seven miles away, are the prehistoric fortifications of Desborough Castle and the ruins of the twelfth-century Hospital of John the Baptist. Chalfont St. Giles and Stoke Poges, to which Frost alluded in writing to Miss Ward, are both within easy walking distance, and so too are Windsor, Eton, and Horton. Edmund Waller's tomb is in Beaconsfield's parish churchyard, and in the church itself Edmund Burke lies buried.

Yet even among these living folk whose ways he pretty well understood, and these celebrated dead whose accomplishments he knew so intimately, Frost felt his aloneness. He had come to England with not a friend there, not an acquaintance, not even a letter of introduction to a friend's friend. "At first the isolation so far from home and help scared me," he admitted afterwards; "but it stimulated me to work. I wrote!"

For a time he struggled to write the novel he had in mind, but it was no go; he could get no further than Chapter I. "I always meant to write that novel, honestly," he later told Paul Waitt, "but I always found myself writing poetry. I kept it in a stack, and every once in a while I would weed it out or add more to it."

Regarding that stack of manuscript about Christmas time in 1912, Frost asked himself, "What have I here and is it good for anything?" Then the thought of a book suddenly dawned on him.

> One day as I was looking over old papers dating back some of them twenty years, I saw in a flash that I had one book already written and all I had to do was throw it into shape to make it mean me. I had a kind of modesty in those days that I'm afraid rather reflected on my fellow men. I liked what I wrote, but I doubted if I could succeed with the public. I hadn't the shadow of a hope that I would find a publisher for a book in any country in many years. I couldn't afford to set my heart on getting published if I was going to be happy in my writing. Nevertheless, I resolved to have a shot or two at the publishers.

To throw the book into shape, Frost first selected the thirty-two poems that seemed to him most to belong together. Next he arranged them into a three-part series that revealed their outer and inner unity and continuity, and for a title put over them a phrase from Longfellow's "My Lost Youth"—*A Boy's Will*. Then, in listing them for the table of contents, he there provided all but two of them with a kind of gloss that further manifested the rising curve of their intellectual and spiritual sequence, providing for consideration of intelligibility, the soul, love, death, art, and science. The gloss, by the way, while retained in all subsequent separate editions of the book, was omitted from the 1930 edition of the *Collected Poems*; but it is of some permanent significance as evidence of the design which Frost always had in mind in ordering the poems in his books and always in one way or another strove to make clear to the close and thoughtful reader.

Two things remained to be done before the manuscript was ready for examination. One was to add a note acknowledging permission to reprint certain of the poems from *The Forum*, *The Independent*, and *The [Youth's] Companion*. (The omission of *The New England Magazine* was simply an oversight.) The other was to dedicate the book to E. M. F., his wife, to whom he dedicated also, with one exception, his five later volumes.

With the completed manuscript in his pocket he went down to London and consulted his friend at *T. P.'s Weekly*.

I asked him if he knew of some small respectable publisher who might buy my poems and not kick me out of the door. He said that no one published poems and that I would myself have to pay to have them printed. I never wanted to do that. Somehow I never liked the idea.

Among other publishers, the ex-bobbie happened to mention David Nutt. That name struck a responsive chord in Frost; he recalled that Nutt had been Henley's publisher; so forthwith he took his manuscript there. David Nutt, he was told, was not to be seen that day, but would receive him the next day.

Calling at the appointed hour the next day, Frost was shown into a private office for an interview with a lady dressed in black. She did not introduce herself to him, but simply said that she would speak *for* David Nutt. At the time this struck Frost as mysterious, for he was not yet aware that Mrs. Nutt was carrying on with her deceased husband's business; but he left his poems with her, and his address. In two days he had a letter from the firm of David Nutt, formally accepting *A Boy's Will* for publication and asking him to come in to sign a contract.

Thus within four months of beginning his rash adventure abroad Frost had taken the first long step toward the recognition so long withheld from him as an artist. And surely in the ear of his mind he heard his chanted response to his grandfather's proposal in the summer of 1892, "Give me *twenty*, give me *twenty*, give me *twenty!*"—This, however, was merely the beginning; and in all of it, Frost realized, there was "a great deal of luck."

Possibly it was luck that led him to walk by 34 Devonshire St., Theobald's Row, in London that evening in January, 1913, when Harold Munro was opening his Poetry Bookshop with a reception and reading; but it was of his own will that, although uninvited, he walked in with the guests and sat on the stairs during the program. Munro, just five years younger than Frost, was a Cambridge man with a remarkable zeal for activity and prominence in literary circles, especially among poets. He had published two volumes of his own verse, *Poems* (1906) and *Before Dawn* (1911). During the previous year he had been editor, under the aegis of the Poetry Society, of *The Poetry Review*; but his liberality toward experimental work in poetry was so much at variance with the policy of the Society generally that he resigned at the end of the year—and was succeeded by Stephen

Phillips. Now Munro was taking the road with a team of his own in hand—the Bookshop and a quarterly called *Poetry and Drama*, of which the first number was to be published in March.

Sitting below Frost on the stairs was a pleasant, round-faced bespectacled man in his middle twenties. "I see by your shoes you are an American," he remarked to Frost. It turned out that he was F(rancis) S(tewart) Flint, a self-made Londoner already the author of one book, *In the Net of the Stars* (1909), which he had come to disdain because of its echoes of nineteenth century poets, and just then absorbed in reading French Symbolist poetry and in experimenting with various "unrhymed cadences" instead of meters. When he learned that Frost too was a poet, he enquired whether Frost knew Ezra Pound; and when Frost confessed to never having heard of Pound, Flint emphatically advised him never under any circumstances to admit that fact to Pound himself.

What Pound heard of Frost from Flint aroused his curiosity, and he sent Frost a card bearing his name, address, and the notation "At home sometimes." So, a month or so later, on his way to Nutt's for proofsheets of *A Boy's Will*, and doubtless after he had read up in Pound's work, Frost called at Pound's lodging. At first, unaccustomed to be taken thus casually, Pound was cool toward his caller; for by this time, after little more than four years in London, Pound was looked upon by a number of the younger poets as their literary prophet and high priest.

Born in Idaho in 1885, Pound had been brought up in eastern Pennsylvania and at Hamilton College. In graduate studies he became something of a specialist in the Romance languages and literatures, travelled in Europe on a fellowship while concentrating on Lope de Vega, and took a master of arts degree. Then for a while he essayed college teaching; but when the authorities at Wabash College requested his resignation because they deemed him a misfit "Latin Quarter type," he abandoned America and its academic institutions to their fate without him, and early in 1908 sailed for Europe.

Landing at Gibraltar, he paused in Venice to have his first book printed, *A Lume Spento*; and then, drawn by his devotion to William Butler Yeats, made his way to England, where shortly his second book was printed, *A Quinzaine for This Yule*. The next spring he made a third book of his early poems, *Personae* (1909), which, according to Glenn Hughes, "created, within a limited circle, an impression which amounted to a sensation" and indeed "began the modern vogue of erudite poetry." Then Pound drove on with new work in *Exultations* (1909), *Provenca* (1910), *Canzoni* (1911), *Ripostes* (1912), and *Sonnets and Ballate of Guido Cavalcanti* (1912). Several of those titles themselves indicate Pound's continuing devotion to the Romance literatures; but no sketch can more than suggest either his avidity for any and all old materials reworked according to novel techniques, his habit of absorbing and re-presenting the suggestions and ideas of his friends and acquaintances, his power in fertilizing the minds and in energizing the methods of his more pliant disciples, or his bold assumption of absolute dictatorship in the whole art of poetry.

It was careless of Frost not to realize all this and be suitably deferential, but Pound generously forgave him and accompanied him to Nutt's for the proofsheets. When they were produced, however, Pound calmly tucked them under his own arm, steered Frost back home with him, and curtly directed him to entertain himself. Pound sat down at his desk with the proofsheets and began to read. Once he paused to look up and ask, with the royal *we* which he sometimes affected, "You don't mind if we like these, do you?" A moment later, when he came to "In Neglect," he began to chuckle. When he had finished reading he dismissed Frost peremptorily, saying he had a review to write but omitting to say that it was of *A Boy's Will* and that it would be sent to Chicago for Harriet Monroe's new poetry magazine of which he was the general European correspondent.

In the months that followed, Frost and the unpredictable Pound became good friends, dining out together, talking tête-a-tête of poets and poetry, and joining in group discussions. Once in a restaurant Pound gave a demonstration of jiu jitsu on Frost's person. On another occasion, when they were dining with two ladies, Pound became disgusted at the triviality of their patter, rose so angrily from his chair that he knocked it over, and took his leave with the disconcerting remark to Frost, "I leave these ladies to you!"

Frost recounted some other diverting recollections of Pound in his introduction to Edwin Arlington Robinson's posthumous *King Jasper*. When he first met Pound, in London in 1913, a bond developed because of their mutual amusement over the fourth thought in "Miniver Cheevy".

A slender book of sixty pages, bound in a pebbled dark bronze cloth stamped in gold, the first issue of *A Boy's Will* appeared

late in February and immediately received a good press. The
first notice in print was that in *The Athenaeum* for April 5. On
April 10 *The Times Literary Supplement*, while noting occasional obscurity in it, remarked the book's "agreeable indi-
viduality," its "vein of reflection," and the poet's capacity for
"complete absorption in the influence of nature." Pound's review, written immediately after he had read the proofsheets
that day, and published in the May issue of *Poetry: A Magazine
of Verse*, declared the book to be "a little raw" and with "a number of infelicities," but roundly asserted that "underneath them
it has the tang of the New Hampshire woods, and it has just this
utter sincerity."

In June, Katherine Tynan in *The Bookman* observed Frost's
"way of keeping one expectant" but judged the whole achievement of "no great matter"; in *Poetry and Drama* Flint noted
"faults of diction here and there, occasional inversion, and
lapses," but saluted the "direct observation of the object and immediate correlation with the emotion" and also Frost's subtle-
ty in the evocation of moods," his humor, and his "ear for silences"; and in *The English Review* Norman Douglas praised
the poems as images of "things really heard and seen" and as
sounding "that *inevitable* response to nature which is the hallmark of true lyric feeling."

The reviews continued into September. *The Nation* reviewer
felt that at times Frost attained "a really simple dignity." The
critic for *The Academy* waxed eloquent: "the poems combine,
with rare sufficiency, the essential qualities of inevitability and
surprise. We have read every line with that amazement and delight which are too seldom evoked by books of modern verse.
Without need of qualification or a trimming of epithets, it is un-
doubtedly the work of a true poet. . . One feels that this man has
seen and *felt*: seen with a revelatory, a creative vision; felt personally and intensely; and he simply writes down, without confusion or affectation, the results thereof. . . We have not the
slightest idea who Mr. Robert Frost may be, but we welcome
him unhesitatingly to the ranks of the poets born. . ." Writing
for *The Dial* in Chicago—the second review of Frost's book to
appear in his homeland—William Morton Payne defined Frost's
world as "a world in which passion has been stilled and the soul
grown quiet," and added: "His songs give us the sort of pleasure
that we have in those of the *Shropshire Lad* of Mr. Housman."

Clearly, among critics of widely different sympathies and schools, Frost had scored a remarkable *succes d'estime*. That encouraging fact was apparent to Frost himself as early as May 13, 1913, the date of his second letter to Miss Ward. He gave her information about how *A Boy's Will* came to be published, not omitting to mention that he believed she would know the poems in it were the natural result of his life. He speculated over whether the book might have been accepted by such an American publisher as Mosher of Portland, Maine, who had shown interest after the arrangements were made with David Nutt. Taking satisfaction in being under an agreement to submit his next book to Nutt, he, at once, suggests the tie he feels to England and that he and the rest of the family were longing for such places as Plymouth, Derry, and South Berwick, in New Hampshire, where the living was the best in the world.

And of life in just such small new England towns and villages, together with their outlying farms, Frost was already writing his second book.

Note: Both Newdick and Thompson note that Frost worked on a novel in this period, getting no further than Chapter I and then turning again to poetry. They both failed to indicate any realization that Frost's poetry was just as much fiction as a novel would be, that this work should be related to the "serial" story about Indians (written in the San Francisco period and later), and that he was constantly fictionalizing his own life, thus causing errors in biographical judgment.

Newdick also supplied added elements of the Frost-Pound relationship in this chapter.

II. On Further Finding Out

INTRODUCTION

This narrative of the relationship between Robert Frost and Robert S. Newdick, covering almost exactly five years, from July, 1934, to July, 1939, represents an outstanding record of the connection of Frost with an individual. Not as full in terms of his recorded comment as several to whom he wrote more letters, outstandingly Louis Untermeyer, it has the advantage of displaying both parts of the equation.

Too, it provides part of the material of what will be an important part of the understanding of Robert Frost, his attitude toward his biographers, who were, like the world he lived in, an attractive nuisance.

Writing a biography of Frost was like making a transit of the rapids of the Colorado River. The record Newdick kept makes it possible for those interested in Frost to know one aspect of the way the poet feared society. Also, Newdick, in his loving and dedicated effort to capture a valid record of the life out of which the poetry for which he had a near-idolatry had come, has provided posterity with much new information about his admired (and feared) subject.

Aside from the obvious debt due Robert S. Newdick by those who find new light on Frost in this account, Mrs. Marie Newdick must be thanked for keeping the papers of her husband nearly intact. Though she did sell the Frost letters, thereby allowing several of them to find their way into the hands of people who would not allow their use, in general she kept intact the file of the relationship between her devoted husband and his difficult subject.

Important material from the pen of Robert Frost is here reproduced through the courtesy of Mr. Alfred C. Edwards, executor of the Robert Frost Estate. Significant quotations are included through the permission of Mrs. Lawrance Thompson, Mrs. Theodore Morrison, and Mrs. Leonard Eyges (for John Holmes).

Part II: On Further Finding Out

W HEN Robert Frost received Robert S. Newdick's letter of July 30, 1934, at his home in
New Hampshire, he doubtless had never heard of
the member of the Department of English at the
Ohio State University.

His own experience as a teacher must have aided in his immediate response to the summer-preparation efforts of the man
who wrote to "My dear Mr. Frost":

> Beginning in October we shall use your *Selected Poems*
> (1928) in our classes in recent and contemporary literature,
> and therefore I am becoming more professional—and
> perhaps professorial—in my study of your poems.

Doubtless the natural playing with professional and profes-
sorial, just the kind of thing Frost was doing in all his writing
and speaking, appealed instantly. Further, he found the most
compelling evidence of what he always looked for, actual reading of and concern for his work: Newdick's letter contained in
its second paragraph:

> That, however, is not the immediate point. The imme-
> diate point is, Am I anywhere near rightness in my cyclic-
> seasonal regrouping of your *Selected Poems*? My object is,
> of course, to assist my students in knowing you and your
> work.

The three typed sheets attached to the letter were most convincing evidence that Frost was hearing from a capable and
devoted reader. The first page was entitled: A Suggested Regrouping of Frost's Selected Poems. Its text was a harbinger of
the way Newdick was to devote himself to the study of Frost
and his works for the next five years:

> Presumably it was Robert Frost himself who grouped

the poems in his volume of *Selected Poems* (1928) under
the nine numbered headings that appear there. The significance of these headings, however, is extremely enig-
matic, even after one has read and reread all of the poems
a number of times and over a period of years. Of course no
professor can satisfactorily explain all of Frost's enigmas
to college freshmen, or even, perhaps, to himself. But certainly, out of his knowledge of the poet's New England
background and multi-phased experience among the rural
Yankees, the teacher should be able to illuminate most
of the problems involved.

And with Frost's farm experience uppermost in mind,
I venture to suggest a five-season cycle and regrouping of
his poems,—one that, without much straining, will
enhance all the poems in the collection, and one that may
therefore be of great assistance in orienting the beginning
student. The cycle may be regarded as having a sort of
proem in Revelation (207), and having an epilogue in Bond
and Free (209), and as comprising a sweep of experience
and observation from early in one autumn (In the Home
Stretch, 135–217 [147]) to late in the following autumn
(Goodbye and Keep Cold, 99–100). Some of the lyrics, it
must be confessed, have to be brought in on an associational, rather than a seasonal, basis; but even here the tie-
up is, or can be made, closer than one would think offhand:
surely, for example, it is no far cry from Home Burial
(21–27) to Fire and Ice (13). Such lyrics are enclosed within
parentheses in the list. Again, the poems that rest more on
a basis of observation than on a basis of direct experience,
such as An Old Man's Winter Night (19), can be indicated
by indenting them in the list. Perhaps it should be added,
that the specially symbolic poems, such, for instance, as
The Road Not Taken (163), will of course require a deal
of additional exegesis.

The process represented by these comments and the actual
listing (reproduced in Appendix A) was familiar and congenial
to Frost. It was the one he had been using since he had first sat
down in the cottage in England with his poems about him to see
what order he could make out of what he had written and saved
to that date. Shortly thereafter the organized grouping became
A Boy's Will. He was probably no more pleased by this recog-

nition of his own seeking for system in his work than by the last paragraph of the letter:

> And will you not also accept my personal salute to you as a beauty-and-truth-revealing American poet?

The reply Newdick received, dated September 16, from Franconia, New Hampshire, and postmarked September 18, from Lisbon, N.H., was all that he could have hoped for:

Dear Mr. Newdick:

You may be sure I appreciate an interest that could carry you so far with my book. If you will accept it, I think you might like to have a copy of it from my hand for thanks. I never realized before how completely I could be summed up in the four seasons of the year; though I am not unaware of always having lived like a countryman in the day's weather. A friend of mine says the first thing he does when he comes out doors is to look at the sky, instead of at the doorsteps for safety. I'm the same. The state of the sky, direction of the wind, and temperature are my bearings in everything I do. I should hate to miss the least glow of northern lights that might be mistaken by a city person for a city below the horizon. Nothing flatters me more than having anyone take the trouble to find me out. Haven't I said in a very early poem that my reason for hiding is to be found out?

New selections from a book, rearrangement of a book are its best criticism. This "Selected Poems" is in a way self-criticism. I made it. And to any one who asked me point blank (for his thesis) what I thought of my own work I might reply. Perhaps you can infer from a comparison of my Selected Poems with my Collected Poems.

Sincerely yours

Added after the signature and date was the following: "I've been wondering if I could add a dozen poems from West-running Brook to the Selected without throwing it out of shape[.] RF."

As further evidence of his esteem, Frost sent an inscribed copy of the *Selected Poems*, the package, bearing an eleven-cent stamp, was insured; the stamp indicating the transaction was undertaken by the post office at Lisbon, N.H., on September 17. On the package, in Frost's hand, was the return address:

"From / Robert Frost / Amherst Mass." The book, the fourth printing of August, 1932, was inscribed: "To Robert S. Newdick / for having further found / me out / Robert Frost / Franconia New Hampshire / September 16, 1934."

There is no record of the immediate excitement which the receipt of the Frost letter/note and book brought to Newdick. Evidently the pleasure of Frost's response was leavened by personal sorrow and followed by the rush of opening days of an autumn quarter. Perhaps he spent some time mulling over the long answer dated October 14 and addressed to "Dear Mr. Frost":

> When I first wrote to you, enclosing my seasonal re-grouping of your Selected Poems and asking whether I was anywhere near rightness, I expected merely the tersest sort of reply. Then, to my surprise and great joy, came your letter and an inscribed copy of those *Selected Poems*. I thank you sincerely for both of them. And I think you will be pleased to know that they came at a time when my heart was as heavy as wet ashes, from a piece of black news concerning a member of my family, and that coming so, they were to me as that memorable dust of snow one day was to you.

In his next paragraph, heartened by the warmth of Frost's response, he reached out for a relationship which was to last five years and provide significant insights into the life of the poet for whom he already had great admiration:

> I know quite well that you are a busy man, and I have no intention of becoming a nuisance to you. And yet, because I turn from you[r] letter with a feeling of having been welcomed and not dismissed, I shall venture, this once at least, beyond the writing of my heart-deep "thank you."
>
> I turn from your poems with the same feeling—and I have read them all. That is, I have read all of those you have published: the individual volumes, the Collected Poems, and those, more recent, in periodicals. (I've made comparisons, too, and have wondered, for example, why you omitted the lovely Asking for Roses from the Collected Poems.) Then, too, I've read every thing that any one has ever publicly written about you. (That was *after*

I'd received and focused my own impressions!) And incidentally, in the course of the last adventure, I've looked upon very nearly every one of the photographs and drawings of you that have been published.

The results? Well, first of all, growth for me personally and individually in mind and spirit (I'm old-fashioned, still distinguishing these)—the basis of my personal salute to you. Next, and as an inevitable corollary, some wisdom, I hope and trust, in leading my students to know and understand you to the full of their several (literally, forty-five) capacities. And, finally, unless you specifically forbid it, a complete and critically anotated bibliography—a tool that will be useful to all following students of your accomplishment.

(For you[r] glance and amusement I'm making a few enclosures: our class schedule in Recent and Contemporary Literature; a list of topics prepared for discussion at a forum of the Department's professors; and the first page of a checklist of your published likenesses.)

And *so* it is that personally and professionally I have found you out to the very best of my ability.

The list of topics filled a whole typed page and bore the heading: "Some Essential Questions for the Student of the Poetry of Robert Frost." The full text may be seen in Appendix B. The main topics deal with Frost's life, his poetry related to farm life, comparison of rural and other bases for poems, realism, symbolism, philosophy, comparison of strength of his lyric, narrative and dramatic verse, speech-rhythms, vocabulary, subjects, comparison with Masefield, and classicism (specifically related to the Greek).

On the second page of his single-spaced, typed letter Newdick continued:

> And reading your poems with my students, upperclassmen for the most part, has been an experience both delightful and profound,—delightful, to be specific, in The Cow in Apple-Time, and profound in Home Burial. There is a two-generation gap between you and these midwestern youngsters, on the calendar; but, in their almost immediate and very intense response to your pieces, there is no gap whatsoever between you and them: another proof—if another were needed!—of the timelessness

and universality of your reading of life and the world about you.

The next paragraph refers to a query raised in the letter of September 18:

> You ask whether you could add to your Selected Poems, without throwing it out of balance, a dozen poems from West-Running Brook. I should say, *emphatically*, yes. And then I would hasten to add special pleas for Still Pools and a Passing Glimpse in particular.

The reference to "A Passing Glimpse," which is subtitled "To Ridgely Torrence / on Last Looking into His 'Hesperides,'" gave Newdick a chance to refer to a poet who had long been of interest to him and who, as he might have guessed, was a good friend of the Frost family:

> That tribute to Ridgely Torrence reminds me: Do you happen to know that that exquisite artist once "professored"? It was for somewhat more than half of the academic year of 1921–22, when he came to Miami University at Oxford, Ohio to take over the classes of Alfred H. Upham, who was leaving Miami to become president of the University of Idaho. I was a cub then, and probably swaggered a little with a brand new master's degree from Harvard; so I hardly got to know Torrence, who gave the impression of being rather shy—though he did invite me, when he left, to call upon him in New York. But I heard much of him from students who sat in his classes, and the sharp ones among those students got untold wealth from his lectures, especially the lectures on Shakespeare. That was the year that President Hughes prevailed upon Percy Mackaye to come and live in Oxford, and occasionally to write in a romantic shack specially built for him in the lower woods of the campus. Leonine Percy was then awriting on Dogtown Common. Students who were very, very good and very, very nice were sometimes invited to come to the shack of an evening and read pieces they had written. Perhaps that was good for them. But the fact remains that those same students got more from Torrence's revealing flashes in class than from the theatricality of Mackaye in his studio.

These shop-talk remarks would naturally have appealed to Frost, whose background as a teacher at Amherst and elsewhere along with his role as a poet would have made him interested in efforts to "teach" poetry elsewhere. Doubtless the idea that more was gained from Torrence than from Mackaye would have been congenial to Frost.

The next paragraph, inaugurating the idea of a visit by Frost to Ohio State, where Frost had appeared in 1922, is self-explanatory. It was the beginning of Newdick's becoming Frost's agent for lectures out of the New England area:

> Is there any chance of your coming out our way on a round of lectures or readings this year? If there is, I shall hasten to make arrangements with your manager (if you make arrangements through a manager), for the Department is eager to have you again. (Your last visit here was before my appointment, and I didn't know of your visit to Denison last year until days afterward.)

That letter was signed "Faithfully yours": Newdick was to work faithfully on the bibliography and wait five months before he heard further from Frost. It is doubtless representative of the impact of such a peripheral influence as Newdick was originally that Frost wrote, on April 16, 1935, to Richard Thornton, at Holt and Co., his publisher, "Will you give me the name in print of the Ohio professor who is at work on my bibliography [?] I have a letter from him with a difficult signature. Should you say it was Robert S. Newdick?" Then he added, "It will do no harm for both of us to write him gentle letters."

Because the Newdick files are meticulously complete, it may be assumed that Frost was preparing to respond to Newdick's letter of October 14. Both of Newdick's letters had had only a written signature. Frost had the name right when he sent the letter and book in September, but presumably he had lost the July letter and had, perhaps because of passage of time, become unsure of the name of the man who was carrying on a project congenial enough to be remembered.

It seems to be a coincidence that Newdick wrote Frost, on April 24, just as Frost was ascertaining his correspondent's right name. The letter explains why Frost considered Thornton one who would know the name:

> That "complete and critically annotated bib[l]iography"

with which I threatened you gently last October has been growing steadily. Late last month, indeed, I described it in general terms to your chief American publisher, Henry Holt and Company, and enquired whether that company would be interested in examining it with a view to publication. There followed a long silence. [Presumably Thornton had thought it wise to consult Frost about the matter.]

The week after he had mentioned the bibliography to Frost in October, Newdick made his first preliminary approach to Holt. A reply from B.A.B. of the Holt office, dated October 23, gives, in answer to his questions, the date of issuance of editions of *North of Boston* and *Mountain Interval* (September 28, 1922, and April 15, 1921, respectively) and, on returning an "old list" of Frost portraits, invites him to send his list when it is finished. Barbara Bliss then responded on November 27 to a further query and thanked him for a "Check List of Frost portraits."

By March 27, Newdick had prepared a letter for Holt and Company about his bibliography, addressed to Barbara Bliss, asking her to place it "in the proper hands, if those hands are not your own." In it Newdick explained:

> For nearly a year now I have been engaged assiduously in the preparation of a bibliography for Robert Frost through 1934, and the purpose of this letter is to describe that bibliography in general and to enquire whether Henry Holt and Company cares to examine it with a view to publication. It will constitute a book of no small size, though the arrangement of parts, as described below, is of course tentative.

In his two-page letter, offering to send a "nearly-but-not-quite-finally-prepared typescript," he indicated plans for a book with seven parts: (1) An annotated list of Frost's poems, 1894 to 1934; (2) Frost's separate publications through 1934; (3) Frost's contributions to joint publications; (4) Periodical contributions of Frost; (5) Biographical and critical material on Frost; (6) Published likenesses of Frost; (7) A chronology of Frost's life. (A complete text of this plan will be found in Appendix C.)

A letter of April 9 contained the unwelcome explanation from Richard H. Thornton at Holt that delay had been caused by the need to gain information about a Frost bibliography being prepared by the Library of Amherst College. He mentioned that Frost had visited Thornton on April 8, had indicated he knew of the Amherst work, and that "he thought we should look at yours, as it seems to have certain features not contained in the other." The letter concluded with an invitation to submit his work, in whole or in part, that it might be considered for publication.

Newdick wrote Thornton on April 11 that he was forwarding the bibliography by express. He added a note that he was making arrangements with European scholars to find "reviews, essays, and studies of Frost in their literatures." The chronology he was presenting was a "one-evening's beginning thereof" and should be expanded, he thought. He expressed his belief that the scope of his work was greater than that of the bibliography being prepared at Amherst.

Even though it was less than two weeks since he had sent the manuscript to Holt, Newdick was referring, in his April 24 letter to Frost, of "another silence." Assuming good communication between Frost and Thornton, he did not tell Frost he had sent the manuscript. He recognized Frost's help in this way:

> But whether the verdict is yes or no, I wish to thank you for your kindness in bespeaking a hearing for my work. It has been a labour of love, into which I have put hundreds of hours with unflagging zeal.

He concluded the letter by noting he would shortly have the pleasure of sending a reprint of "The Juvenilia of Robert Frost and Some of His Revisions" from the May *American Literature*. (See Appendix D for the text of this article.)

The next day Newdick wrote to the librarian of the Amherst College Library to learn about a bibliography which Richard Thornton of Holt had told him was in preparation there. Noting his own bibliographical work on Frost, which had been going on for a year, he asked for a description of the work. He received, typed on the bottom of his own letter, postmarked July 9, a note which said that no such work was in progress. But he received a letter written on April 29, from Professor George F. Whicher, of Amherst College, the information that Charles R. Green, of the Jones Library in Amherst, was working on a Frost bibliography with another man.

The disappointment of that discovery was softened by receipt of a present from Frost, for which thanks were sent on April 25:

Dear Mr. Frost,

I thank you cordially for the brochure of *Three Poems*. (It came through the mail unfolded and unharmed—in perfect condition.) It is indeed an "item", and a splendid piece of printing too; but to me its significance lies in personal values of which I hardly dare speak. And I need not add that I am particularly delighted with your note on the fly-leaf. [This inscribed pamphlet has not been found.]

Appreciatively yours,

On May 18, Newdick wrote to Thornton to ask if his manuscript had been received and to report that he had "turned up forty or fifty new items for the bibliography within the last month, and two corrections." This evoked an apology on May 21 from Thornton for not notifying him of the receipt of the manuscript and telling further that his work had been compared with "the Clymer bibliography which is nearly ready for publication." He pointed out the undesirability of having two bibliographies come out at the same time and suggested that Newdick "hold your manuscript for two or more years," at which time Holt would be willing to reconsider it.

Newdick's letter of May 24, two single-spaced, typed pages, expressed his disappointment and resistance, noting, "Perhaps Clymer has been as thoroughgoing in his research as I have been. My difficulty in believing so is the difficulty of believing that anyone else could have been so insanely diligent!" He also reviewed his relationship with Frost to that date:

I wrote to Mr. Frost, thanking him for bespeaking a hearing for my work; but before the thank-you letter was mailed I received from him an autographed copy, with a pleasant note on the fly-leaf, of the *Three Poems* from the old *Independent*. Then for this too I thanked him. But I have had no word concerning the bibliography. That's a bit curious, too, for I wrote him on October 14 of last year that I was preparing "a complete and critically annotated bibliography—a tool that will be useful to all following students of you and your accomplishment." But I've heard that Mr. Frost has not been in very good health this year, and doubtless he overlooked that sentence in the letter; surely, had he taken note of it he would long ago have dissuaded me, not from continuing my study of him but from duplicating the work of another, if indeed my bibliography is to be described as duplicating Mr. Clymer's.

He recognized that the above paragraph and the page which preceded it were "one long wail" but thought that was the "inevitable" result of his hoping and working "so strenuously to associate my name in some way with that of Frost." Recovering well, he suggested in the last paragraph of the letter the publication of "Frost's *prose*," an idea which was to be a consideration for many months to come.

Doubtless Thornton communicated Newdick's disappointment to Frost, whose longhand letter of June 10 was obviously meant as a kind of reparation to some one whose attention and following he valued:

Dear Mr. Newdick:

I want to tell you how sorry I am about your bad luck in finding Shubrick Clymer ahead of you with a bibliography. I'm not satisfied, however, that yours does not make a place for itself. You have gone into things that he hasnt. And you must have made discoveries all your own. I left judgement to Thornton and Melcher both of whom are much impressed with what you have done and inclined to think a year or two after Clymer you might well have a turn. Thornton asked me to tell you to wait.

Several of you now know more about me and my books than I do myself. The article in American Literature frightens me with the closeness with which it follows on my trail. I shall have to walk in water for a mile to see if I cant throw you off.

That about leaving out part of *The Youth's Companion's* name was a home one. The only thing you failed to notice was my tucking the acknowledgements away in the end of the book where I hoped no one would notice them. I hated to have to mention the damned magazines but was afraid to leave them out. I made them as inconspicuous and hard to identify as I could offhand.

Of course there was no deep plotting. There was no time for that—I found a publisher so suddenly and unexpectedly. I left the MS with the first publisher I thought of and within a few days I had been summoned in to sign a contract.

I believe I really forgot the poor old *New England Maga-zine*, as I forgot the extent of my obligations to *The Youth's Companion*. I should be very grateful to Mark Howe who was then poetry editor as I have since learned. I had carried the idea that Reluctance had first appeared in some maga-zine not named on my list. Neither Clymer nor Charles Green (Jones Library, Amherst) had been able to run it down for all their trouble. I couldnt help them much: All I recalled was that Thomas Mosher had used part of it in his Amphora and Reedy had quoted it in Mirror. It was news to me personally that October went into *The Youth's Companion*.

I'm glad you think my changes are improvements. Of course I never held that nothing could be done about a poem once it was written. When I am coordinating well (in good form mentally and physically) I notice I falter in the verse very little and get in my best strokes as I go. The Mountain for instance was all done in one sitting and stands today pretty exactly as I wrote it. I was saying in public the other night a poem discovers its subject in its writing. That is why when I feel a poem begin I dont let it develope unless I am where I can attend to its full devel-opement once for all. I stave it off till I am alone with it.

I suppose not many first drafts of any poems are in existance. Not many of mine are. It might amuse you to have a sworn-to first draft of one of my most recent. I suppose I shouldnt expose myself to your researching eye. But I am not afraid of anyone so friendly. Keep the piece as a memento of having made the most of it throw it away.

Sincerely yours / Robert Frost

Newdick had been restrained in the interim between letters from Frost by one of six handwritten pages from Mrs. Frost on February 21, from 367 Avocado Ave., Coconut Grove, Florida. She told him that they had arrived in Florida on December 24, that Robert had spent a week in New York because of a cold, that the cold had been made worse by the trip, that the weather in Florida was so cold that, in fact, Robert had not shaken off his cold for a month. She was disappointed that only three days of sunshine in three weeks had rewarded their leaving the com-forts of home. She mentioned the anticipation of going back to the cold to give the Norton lectures at Harvard in March, 1935, and the strain of preparing the manuscript for his new book, *A Further Range*. She asked his understanding about not answering letters and questions. She had forgotten the questions, which were in a letter buried under others.

Giving their Cambridge address as 56 Fayerweather St., making reference to plans for a Frost visit to Ohio State (which was eventually to occur in May, 1936), and noting that Eunice Tietjens had told the Frosts of correspondence with Newdick, she concluded by saying that Robert joined her in sending "warmest regards" to all and that he would write as soon as he could.

Taking a few days to savor the excitingly pleasant letter which had, at last, come, Newdick wrote on June 17:

Dear Mr. Frost:

Thank you sincerely for the first draft of Not Quite Social. "Throw it away?" Man, I'm going to frame it and *hang* it in the intimacy of my study at home!—I'd not think of "making the most of it" in any public way; but I have amused myself by attempting to transcribe it on the typewriter (I'm enclosing a carbon copy of that attempt [See Appendix E.], together with another of the probable appearance of the poem in print), and someday I shall write out, for just two pairs of eyes, a conjectural story of the composition process. —May I add that I like the poem as a poem? It has your characteristic compassion and tone, and the third stanza, particularly the third line, is especially rich in Frostian ore. I'm sorry, in a way, that you saw the article in *American Literature* before I got a copy into your hands; and, even though you have read it, I'm indulging my pride and vanity by enclosing a reprint to you. And of course I was pleased that I had indeed dug up a few facts that you had forgotten and that other researchers hadn't found.

Naturally I am deeply disappointed that Clymer had beaten me out with a bibliography, but I am consoled by the kind things that you and Mr. Thornton and Mr. Melcher have said about my work and by the prospect of publishing it in a year or two. (You see that, since you have added your word to that of Mr. Thornton, I have decided to try no other publisher.) Perhaps, too, I shall be able to place a review or two of Clymer's work, for certainly, so far as knowledge of the printed biographical and critical material goes, I am loaded for bear! —Of course I shall not be hypercritical: I too much admire Clymer's taste.

This summer, after a year of stress and heartbreak, (my father died a terrible death here in my home last month,) I'm taking my wife and small son on a camping tour. We're starting first for Washington, where I wish to work a few days in the Library of Congress; later, by way of Providence, New Haven, and Cambridge (more libraries!), we're coming up into your New England mountains again. May I then have the pleasure of calling on you?

On the same day he wrote that letter to Frost, Newdick wrote to his bibliographic rival, Shubrick Clymer, to congratulate him on the fact that he had, doubtless unknowing, "scooped me indeed with your bibliography of Robert Frost." Reiterating the quip he had sent Frost, he declared, "I cannot for the life of me feel vengeful: I too much admire your taste." He also asked Clymer to suggest his name to the publisher for a review copy.

The following two letters are self-explanatory in regard to the meeting of Newdick and Frost on August 29:

Dear Mr. Newdick:

Here we are at last where we mean to stay for several weeks. I had better say exactly how many and indeed give you my calendar for the summer so you can calculate your own chances of finding me. I shall be in South Shaftsbury, Vermont from now until July 24th, in Boulder, Colorado or on the train between here and there, from July 24th until August 5th, at Breadloaf August 8th and 9th (probably) and from then on till late in September at the Fobes Farm near Franconia New Hampshire. I have to take to the White Mountains for my hay fever, less fatal of late than it used to seem, but still to be considered.

I hope you will let me see you some time in your travels. I have to explain about our hospitality that on account of my wife's condition (since a loss in the family last year) [death of daughter, Marjorie, in childbirth, May, 1934] we are not entertaining any one in the house. When I want to have a good talk with anyone as I do with you I put him up at a small hotel near by so we can have a long evening together. We ought to feel well introduced and old friends, what with all the letters that have passed between us, and especially the description of you and your ways in the newspapers you sent. The hospitality, limited as it has to be, is cordially proferred. Do show up.

This later was dated July 8, 1935, from South Shaftsbury, Vermont.

Newdick's answering letter was dated August 11 and gives the place of its origin as simply "New York, N.Y.":

Dear Mr. Frost:

Mail addressed to me at the University has just caught up with me, and I am hastening to say Thank you: I'll be there! to your invitation to come up and talk with you. Indeed, had you said otherwise; I should have been a pilgrim forbidden his shrine, for I am a pilgrim this summer and wherever you are is Mecca.

After two weeks in Washington, much of it spent in the Library of Congress, and after two weeks near Virginia Beach, most of it spent in the ocean, I've had two pleasant and profitable weeks here in New York. With a word of introduction from Miss A. H. Lerch of the Rare Book Room in the Library of Congress, I called on Mr. and Mrs. Roland A. Wood of the Harbor Press and had a delightful talk with them. They gave me a note of introduction to Mr. Joseph Blumenthal of the Spiral Press, and the consequence was two more hours of good talk. Then your good and longtime friend Mr. Frederic Melcher very kindly invited me for dinner, the evening, and the night to his home in Montclair, but for that experience I lack words. Mr. Richard Thornton, too, was gracious and helpful; and I spent a whole day among Holt's file copies, clippings, etc. And after I rifle the libraries at Brown, Yale, and Harvard I ought to be loaded for bear. Yet, interesting as all this bibliographical investigation is, I do not, I trust, lose sight of the prime matter: the poems as poetry.

I shall wish to go to Amherst to meet Mr. Green and examine the Jones Library Collection, and so shall probably be coming to Franconia late this month or early in September. I quite understand what you speak of as the limitation of your hospitality and am grateful that in the circumstances you will receive me at all.

The first meeting of Frost and Newdick, on Thursday, August

29, 1935, at the Fobes Farm, Franconia, N.H., resulted in five pages of single-spaced, typed notes. As Newdick described the event:

> Stopped to enquire, about 3:15 [p.m.], whether F lived nearby and was at home, for Green had been fearful that F was suddenly gone to the coast. Frost himself opened the door. In travelling clothes, shirt soiled, beard unshaven, and clothes mussed from having slept in the car the night before, I was for a moment speechless. Finally I got it out: "I . . I'm Robert Newdick." With his left hand he swung back the door and extended his right: "Come in. We've been wondering whether you'd be along." About 7:15 I went out to the car and Jimmy and Tucky. "This," I remarked needlessly, "is where he lives, and he's at home!"

In 1972, Mrs. Newdick still remembered the four hours of waiting for her devoted husband. It was she who took down the following notes, which as her husband recorded, ". . . were dictated to Tucky between ten and twelve, after we'd dined at the Iron Mine Tavern and made camp in Mrs. Corey's large field across the road and stream." Newdick then, as always, respected RF's desires not to have notes taken while he was talking and always made his notes later, sometimes as late as three in the morning. (This potpourri of items will be found in Item 1 of Newdick's Research Findings, Part III of this book. Similarly, the notes for Friday, August 30, comprise Item 2.)

When Newdick left the sessions on August 30, he had in his possession a 1934 edition of *Selected Poems*, autographed "Robert Frost / For Robert S. Newdick / Franconia New Hampshire / August 30 1935." (The omission of punctuation on inscriptions and autographs is typical of Frost.) The fly leaf was inscribed with the third stanza of "Not Quite Social."

The word *leave* replaced *flea* of the published version in the first line. Similarly *lightly* was substituted for *loosely* in the second.

Perhaps acquired in this same period was the edition of *North of Boston* containing the James Chapin illustrations. This is simply autographed: "Robert Frost / to / Robert S. Newdick." The fly leaf has a longhand date: August 6, 1935. It is presumably Newdick's note, certainly not Frost's. It is possible to think of this book as erroneously dated, for no mention of the book was made in Newdick's letter of August 11 and the one by Frost of July 8. For want of a better explanation, it may be that the book came from this period of great openness by Frost and eager reception by Newdick. In any case, the inundation of information and comment continued on the third day, August 31, the result of which will be found in Item 3 of Part III. Similarly, on the last day, Sunday, September 1, the families participated in a lingering parting, again meticulously recorded. (See Item 4 of Part III.)

The day after Newdick left Frost at Franconia, he went to Amherst and conferred with Green at the Jones Library about the Clymer bibliography, which had been originally intended for publication in May. An agreement was made to split the work between the three men: "Each of us, I am sure, should have liked to do the job alone; but all of us, I am convinced, are happier in knowing that the three-man job will be best," Newdick wrote on September 12. After mentioning that the family had traveled four thousand miles (on the trail of Frost) and including snapshots he thought might be of interest to Frost (none of people), he concluded:

I still lack words to express our appreciation of and great joy in the abounding kindness of you and Mrs. Frost during our days in mountain-girt Franconia. I must and do trust that what I would say was clearly to be read otherwise.

And now we are looking forward to further happy hours with you in our home when you come out to talk at the University. (As soon as you let me know the date I shall proceed with the arrangement of details and inform you of them.)

Bibliographically, biographically, and sincerely. . . .

When Newdick typed a three-page, single-space letter to Clymer on September 17, he already had a copy of the manuscript prepared by his collaborator. (His annotations are in its pages as it remains in the files which survived him.) He stipulated his idea that, while the work had been partitioned, each participant "is to speak his mind fully on every point that engages his interest or attention." After a number of suggestions relating to procedure, he told Clymer he was "*accurate* as can be, and that's the greatest of all the virtues in any form of true scholarship; I am urging simply that in points of detail in form, you make a few changes."

In pursuing bibliographical information, Newdick wrote one

source on September 30, that, "I have already begun work, with the consent and approval of Mr. Frost, on a biography of the man . . . ." Newdick assessed his "delightful four day visit with Mr. Frost in Franconia" for Thornton in a letter of October 10:

> One result is this, that he has consented to my doing a full-length biography, now that the bibliographical tools are assembled and now that he has taken my measure in personal contact as to discernment, understanding, and so on. Such things as the bibliography and biography do not interest him a great deal, but he cooperated generously in supplying me with facts and views, and will do so hereafter. The biography is the goal I had in mind all along.

A paragraph later he closed the letter by giving his opinion on a matter strongly related to the biography: "I doubt that Mr. Frost can ever be induced to write his memoirs, but I hope that you persist in the effort to persuade him to do so."

By the beginning of October, Newdick had begun in earnest pursuing the leads he had found in his summer's work, with Frost and separate from him. On October 9, for example, he wrote Professor Sidney Cox, of Dartmouth, who had then known Frost for nearly a quarter century, telling of the collaborative bibliography and his own plans for a biography. In addition to requesting permission to question Cox, he outlined his more immediate plans and attitude:

> I am proposing to prepare a number of . . . papers, each one gathering, ordering, and presenting essential points on some one important aspect of the man and his work. From now on, too, I shall submit the papers to Mr. Frost for his nihil obstat, for I shall hardly be able to avoid inweaving material gleaned from our talks together and I should rather suffer paralysis than misquote him or give him pain in any way. Happily, I shall never need to compromise my own independence and integrity of interpretation, for I find absolutely nothing in the record, personal or printed, that is not at home in full sunlight. Nevertheless it is a fact that Mr. Frost retains undiminished the extreme sensitiveness that must surely have contributed to his art from the beginning.

Because Frost had mentioned the possibility that Louis Untermeyer had saved his letters, Newdick wrote to Untermeyer to inquire if they had been saved and if he might arrange to have access to them. He received a postcard (postmarked October 16, from Toledo, Ohio) saying the letters, "a hundred or more," were at his farm in the Adirondacks: "I hope to use them in some future analytical biography, but you can certainly glance at some of them." These were published in 1963.

On October 16, Newdick wrote to Frost, expressing the hope that he "disliked the record-making business at Columbia less than you thought you would" and more importantly outlining an article he wanted to do on "your theory and practice as an educator . . . on your methods and what you have had to say about the whole business at various times. Is it too much to ask that you glance at the chronology and questions on the enclosed sheet and make a few notes thereon for guidance? (I don't want my questions ever to become a nuisance to you, and I've tried to hit on a device to make them fairly painless.)" To make his letter more attractive he included a personal note: "Jimmy is playing cowboy with 'Mr. Frosht's rope' (though why you get the credit when it was Mrs. Frost's idea, I don't know) . . . ." The sheet of questions was headed: "Tentative and Preliminary Chronology / of / Robert Frost's Teaching Positions."

In response, Frost sent both a letter (of which only the postmarked envelope has survived in the Newdick papers) and a package, both postmarked 8 p.m., October 16, 1935, from Amherst. Newdick's letter of October 25 indicates the envelope contained at least the answers to the questions on the sheet: "Your notations on the memorandum of your teaching experience straightened me out almost finally on the factual matters I was uncertain of."

The package contained, on the one hand, a book: "And the Random House edition [1930] of your *Collected Poems* is a most satisfying piece of printing; I am delighted to possess it, and your inscription confers on it the vitality and warmth of your presence." Frost had written on the half-title page: "Robert Frost / to / Robert Newdick / in all friendship."

With the book was the most exciting gift thus far received, extremely strong evidence of Frost's acceptance of and confidence in Newdick:

But I am most deeply happy in the notebook of reflective jottings set down for the most part before 1912,—and I didn't miss your sideline observations of 1935. As I study these early notes and compare them with what you've said since, and in *both* making use of "ingenious inference," I find you utterly consistent with yourself, — only, as time has gone on, more sure of what you thought was true.

And I believe that what I'm about to say is quite true, or I wouldn't say it: Close study and exposition of your philosophy of exposition and practice as a teacher has recalled me to myself as a teacher; surrounded and beset by difficulties, I was slipping to the right.

The notebook for which Newdick wrote that he was grateful "For more reasons than you can know" was as noted on the first inside page, "For R.N. to keep and get what he can out of by ingenious reference / R.F. 1935." It contains entries in longhand on 27 ruled pages, 6½ inches wide by 8½ inches deep, concerning impressions, notes for classes and talks, and early drafts for poems or ideas for poems. On the front cover, Frost wrote, "Bring all under the influence of *great* books as under a *spell*. Teach all the satisfaction of successful speech. 1912." Below that is this explanation: "Most of this goes back to earlier than the above date. R.F. 1935."

The inside pages contain Frost's random notes on literature, poetry, teaching, sense impressions, and on many subjects often only a line at a time. On one page is the genesis of a poem, captioned by Frost, *The Waiting Spirit*. On another page, among his notes on writing and speech, Frost later pointed out, "I seem not to have hated the word thrill as much as I do now in 1935." At the back of the notebook, after many blank pages, appear notes, headed *The Waiting Spirit*, originally for a poem or essay, and on the last page are notes on *A Business Letter*, about which Frost has penned a later comment: "Somebody angered me by saying about as much as we can expect from them is a correct business letter. R.F., 1935." A few other random comments of Frost, to give some idea of the tenor of the notebook, are "The spirit won't stand waiting for years till the mechanics of learning are mastered. It must be enlisted from the first or it will fly away to other things"; "Education depends on the number of times you have stirred to a right feeling. Number of times the fine thrill has run your fibers"; "This rain is as dry as a sand storm"; "The writing and reading converge on the point of the conscious use of words, sentence forms, intonations and figures (marks of personality) in both pupils and authors"; "It is healthy and normal for things and objects to keep a child's mind off words (spoken or written) till he is well along in years"; "The mind must be induced to flow: to see there is a plenty to say on a thousand subjects"; "Things happen to you and things occur to you, the latter with as little help from you as the former"; "Every thing that is a thing is out there and there it stands waiting under your eye till some day you notice it"; "Reading for pleasure, reading for improvement, Families where the word improvement is never heard. Movies in the name of improvement." (The complete text of Frost's writing in this notebook will be found in Appendix F.)

Newdick thought he ought to clinch a Frost appearance—of which they had spoken during their summer meeting—at Ohio State that fall, and thus on October 25 he sent a business letter in reference to a reading and conducting of a writer's conference. He did add to the formal document "that Marie and I are looking forward and eagerly to entertaining you and Mrs. Frost in our home."

Evidently too preoccupied at Amherst, opening the Social Union series with a reading on November 21, for example, Frost was not ready to commit himself to travel as far away as Columbus. He did manage to put into an envelope, on November 13, a copy of "The Topographical Terms Interval and Intervale," by Albert Matthews, reprinted from the *Publications of The Colonial Society of Massachusetts*, vol. 6, 1901. It was sent without comment as an adjunct to comments during their summer meeting on the word as in *Mountain Interval*.

Because he was trying to act in cooperation with a campus organization, Chi Delta Phi, Newdick finally felt he had to do something. His file contains a longhand copy of the following night letter:

> Please forgive importunity of telegram but special problems at University make it imperative. Stop. Can you set date for lecture and reading within a week? Stop. Early January or mid-spring as satisfactory here as late November or very early December and preferable to mid-December or late December because of final examinations under four-quarter plan. Stop. Please telegraph reply collect. Kindest regards

The fact that Frost's reply is dated at 9:53 a.m. on November

21 seems to suggest the conclusion that Newdick had tele-graphed sometime on November 20. Frost's reply was

CAN YOU ARRANGE TO HAVE ME DECEMBER FIRST SECOND OR
THIRD PREFERABLY FIRST OR SECOND IF NOT WILL POSTPONE
VISIT UNTIL SPRING WILL YOU WIRE DECISION TODAY GREET-
INGS AND BEST WISHES FROM US BOTH

Newdick did not write his reply till November 24, allowing the time between Thursday and Sunday to go by, because he had been "too disappointed to venture to write sooner."

When your telegram came Thursday morning, I imme-diately turned to set the wheels in motion, but soon found that the young women of Chi Delta Phi had got us all into an impasse. Their representative, who called you by phone and talked with Mrs. Frost in your absence, tells me that Mrs. Frost was most gracious and kind, and set finally with them on some day in the first week of April of next year for your talk and reading. I hope this arrangement with you is really as satisfactory as the young women believe it to be.

His next paragraph suggests the annoyance at the students' interfering with arrangements: "The Department is indignant, however, at the light in which the organization was thrown in this instance." The girls are referred to as "regretful that they got themselves and us into a situation beyond their solving" but also sharing the "universal and eager enthusiasm" for the reading. Because "your coming is to be not simply another lec-ture but a great University event" and thus, in view of "no ade-quate auditorium being available on the campus for any of those dates . . . , it was best all around to countenance the postpone-ment."

His next paragraph suggests how much the relationship had come to mean and with what alarm any disturbance of it, how-ever innocent, might be greeted: "Yet I shall rest uneasily until I learn directly from you in some way that this postponement has thrown no shadow between us." He had also written to a colleague, adviser of Chi Delta Phi, on November 21, "I cannot possibly allow if I can possibly prevent it, any misunderstanding to arise between Robert Frost and myself." This extreme sen-sitivity may have caused Frost to see Newdick as much like himself and have strengthened the bond which already existed.

In closing the letter, Newdick reported that his house had undergone major refurbishing, "but Marie and I took extra pleasure in them in thinking that you and Mrs. Frost would be the first to honor them as guests. And now — " And he mentioned his hope that the Frosts could see a way of breaking their coming trip to Chicago and Rockford (where Lesley was a member of the college faculty) by a stopover in Columbus. "Do please give it a lot of thought."

Very possibly, Frost was relieved to have his schedule for December made less complicated, though it should be noticed he would have made the trip to Columbus. His letter of December 2 showed that Newdick had nothing to worry about:

> It was bad about our not being able to arrange it with you for a visit this fall; but it is not beyond remedy. Let's both try to survive the winter and see each other in the spring.
>
> In haste before setting out on our travels tomorrow I am packing and mailing to you all the letters of E.T. [Edward Thomas] I can seem to find. There should be more. I must have lost some. You were going to have one of your P.W.A. research boys make copies of them in type so it would be easier for us to read them. This is getting a good deal out of the New Deal. But nonsense aside I shall be very grateful to you for the favor. I have shrunk from handling the letters themselves. Perhaps I can face them better in copies. I know you will take care of the little parcel. [Sent by registered mail.] You keep them in a safe place till I come out. Keep the interval pamphlet till then too. [The pamphlet is still in the Frost-Newdick papers.]
>
> It looks as if we might be in Coconut Grove Florida for a few months. My best mailing address will remain Amherst for a while. This week Elinor and I will be with Lesley in Rockford Illinois.
>
> We were particularly sorry not to be in on your new paper and paint. Try to keep them fresh for us. Dont [sic] let the lamps smoke.
>
> Ever yours
> Robert Frost

Discussion of a cluster of Newdick letters to the Frosts (none of which, it appears, was answered immediately) will add to the picture of the developing work on Frost. On December 8, Frost was given a report that the work of transcribing the "sixty-odd" Thomas letters had begun. Several paragraphs of discussion of Frost's possibly writing to Professor Henry C. Morrison (see Item 7 of Part III) were also included in that letter. Mention was also made of a five-thousand-word paper on Frost as teacher and educator.

Feeling he needed advice from Mrs. Frost (and evidently feeling he could ask it of her) Newdick wrote her on December 9, a two-page, single-spaced, typed letter about the Frost manuscript collection at the Huntington Library at San Marino, California. Frost had told him (See notes of August 30, 1935, in Item 2, Part III) that the material there was not authentic. Having written to the Huntington, he had just received "a page-long checklist of poems and other items." The librarian had also reported that Frost had been at the library "some years ago and seemed somewhat vexed, to say the least, that those early poems of his were still in existence." Thus Newdick wrote:

> Evidently the Library officials maintain the letters to be genuine early work of Mr. Frost, while Mr. Frost maintains, unless I misunderstand him, that all of the papers there are, to put it bluntly, forgeries.

The next three paragraphs capture rather well the biographer's attitude toward his revered (and somewhat fearsome) subject:

> I should like very much to examine these papers directly, but, inasmuch as that is impossible, I should like to examine them in photostat copies. If there are forgeries, I venture that I can establish the fact and reinforce it with Mr. Frost's disclaimer. If they are not forgeries but papers that somehow got out of Mr. Frost's possession, knowledge of them ought to be in the hands not only of library visitors and neutral-minded librarians but also in the hands of his friends and champions. Much that Mr. Frost told me and said to me this last summer, I shall never make any public use of whatsoever: he said what he said in full faith of my good faith, and I shall never be unmindful of that. Yet all that he told me and said to me is valuable to me, whether it shows on the surface or not, because it helps me to sure, firm foundations of understanding. So with these papers, whatever they be.

On the other hand, if the matter of these papers still "vexes" Mr. Frost, as Mr. Bliss expressed it, perhaps the subject should not again be raised with him, and much less should I ask him to write a line out there on my behalf.

Will you not guide me with a word of counsel? You see my dilemma: I wish heartily to examine copies of the papers; yet I wish much more heartily not even to annoy Mr. Frost. My hope is that the problem will not appear to you to be so much of a dilemma as it appears to me to be. But whatever your advice I shall follow it.

On December 12, Newdick wrote to Frost, in care of his New York friend, Frederic G. Melcher, that he did not need him to write on his behalf to Professor Morrison but thoughtfully quoted Morrison's reference to him as a "valued friend and companion" and mentioned the probability that Morrison would be "pleased to have a line from you." He also mentioned his awareness that "This is the day you are hearing yourself from recordings in New York, and I wish the graph of my eardrum vibrations were paralleling yours."

"I must confess my crimes," he wrote Frost on December 16. He admitted collaborating on two textbooks and a monograph, part of his dissertation at Harvard: "I'm joyfully hastening to send one off to you." "Some points of my credo as a biographer show through on pp. 7, 11, 27." He concluded his letter with an account of a special project being carried on with students.

In a special longhand memorandum, Newdick recorded that "At Christmas, we sent to Mr. and Mrs. Frost a greeting comprised of two of our linoleum blocks,—the one of 1294 West First Avenue and the one of the locomotive (and the implied train) bearing Express Greetings,—addressed to Coconut Grove, Florida." He wrote Frost on December 29 that he was sending a revised draft of his article on Frost as a teacher. "And I do wish to say that you have given me your nihil obstat to its substance." He noted he would be going to the Modern Language Association meeting in Cincinnati, the first time in years he had found "enough courage to undergo the intellectual anaesthesia of the meetings." He noted, too, that "Mr. Melcher kindly sent me a copy of Neither Out Far Nor In Deep," the Frost Christmas greeting pamphlet for that year.

Newdick received, in a letter of December 26, insight and advice from Frederic Melcher:

I saw quite a little of Mr. Frost last week. He was unfortunately laid up in a hotel here with a bad cold and has now gone to Florida. I asked him the question about the banquet menu card [the encounter with T.S. Eliot] to which you referred in your recent letter, but he didn't preserve that memento. I think he was very tired when he left here, and if I were you I wouldn't follow him with many questions about his past in your search for records during the next few weeks. Both he and Mrs. Frost have a way of backing away from the responsibility of digging up material from the past. Perhaps you'll have to proceed rather slowly.

As a concluding scholarly item for the year, he received settlement, in a letter of December 30, of the matter of how the Frost manuscripts, bogus or not, got to the Huntington Library. Every one seemed to think that the story which had been told, of a lost brief case, was hardly creditable. The letter, from P. K. Foley, of Boston, recorded the fact that the Huntington papers had been purchased by Foley from the son of Dr. William Hayes Ward, editor of the *New York Independent*, who was liquidating his father's estate. "Previous to my arrival he had destroyed what he had pronounced worthless—and he had a second series of the holocaust almost ready for the devouring element. . . . So the 'Brief case' story is only froth and foam."

On January 3, Newdick responded to the advice Melcher had given him on December 26: "I am in truth an almost morbidly sensitive person, and had you made it bluntly I should have been deeply wounded. And had it come directly from Mr. Frost I am afraid I would have been crushed."

He added that Frost ". . . made it clear to me last summer that he did not wish what I was doing to be oppressive to him in any way, and I have tried strenuously not to be a nuisance." He then gave an accounting of what he considered a moderate series of requests. He concluded:

Evidently, however, I have produced the wrong impression, for you know and understand as I suppose no one else in the world, out of his ken, does; so I shall indeed proceed rather slowly, shall in fact not write again till I am written to. Meanwhile I shall pray that not too much damage has been done already, and shall be grateful if you can give me any assurance on this central point, for I can work *alone* with undiminished assiduity if only I have the sense that men work together whether they work together or apart.

Probably surprised at the intensity of the reaction to his advice, evidently given casually rather than as an indirect message from Frost, Melcher replied on January 9:

> You must not take too seriously my word of caution. I am so anxious that everything should go right about your plan that I did venture to pass on the caution, because of the fact that during the last few years when both Mr. and Mrs. Frost have been frail they have been more easily bothered about details and pressure than ever before. Mr. Frost writes few letters and Mrs. Frost always feels responsible, and she has been the frailer of the two. I hope my caution *won't* cramp your style, but you can take it for what it is worth.

Several weeks later, he took the opportunity Melcher gave him to ask for advice on Frost-related matters. In November, Newdick wrote Thornton about the bibliographic collaboration which had started during the previous summer, asserting that "I grow impatient to be off with the bibliography and on, under full steam, with the biography." Thus, on January 27, he discussed differences of opinion about bibliographical form for two single-spaced, typed pages. His attitude is captured by this sentence: "I concede that this devotion of amateurs is lovely and all that, but why, why should the bibliography of Robert Frost go forth looking like the work of amateurs?" Eventually, Newdick bowed out of the bibliography, which Clymer and Green produced in the spring of 1937. He had followed the advice given him on February 3 by Melcher: "It looks very much to me as tho collaboration on a Frost bibliography was not possible and that you had better work by yourself."

On March 2, Newdick wrote Mrs. Frost that "Your gracious letter of February 21 [not available] brought great joy to us, for I had been exceedingly anxious lest mine had become a bother." By that time Frost had delivered the manuscript of *A Further Range* and had returned to Harvard to deliver the Charles Eliot Norton lectures. Newdick wrote to Frost on March 11, "indulging myself in the luxury of a note," to observe:

Your triumphant return, through Baltimore and New
York, to Cambridge and Harvard and the Norton lectures,
I have followed as closely as possible with great joy. And
it seems almost too good to be true that within not too
long a time you will be coming out to us.

A few days earlier he had written Thornton that the lectures
at Harvard and the new book would cause "Frost again to take
that forefront place to which his genius entitles him . . . . I believe his lecture here will be another triumph, but at the same
time I am determined to do all I can to make it so."

As Newdick eagerly awaited the satisfaction and excitement
of Frost's visit to the Ohio State campus and to the Newdick
home, he took warranted satisfaction in the appearance of three
articles on his guest in May. "Robert Frost—Impressions and
Observations," appearing in *The Ohio Stater*, gave the Ohio
State family the benefit of Newdick's study of and acquaintance
with his subject and congratulated the university on its forthcoming opportunity to know Frost better (Appendix G). "Robert
Frost and the American College. . . ." appeared in the *Journal of
Higher Education*. Starting with the premise that Robert Frost
was recognized by college administrators as the "dean of America's living poets," the article records Newdick's view of Frost
as an educator, one whose central aim had been to help students
determine their personal philosophies. (Appendix H) An article
which appeared in the *Columbus Sunday Dispatch*, on May 17,
used the research Newdick had done in Columbus, about the
fact that Isabelle Moodie had lived and taught in that city before
going to Pennsylvania, where she met and married Frost's
father. (Appendix I).

Because he always refrained from taking notes while Frost
talked, he was probably astonished when he read in *The Ohio
State Lantern* on May 21, the day of the reading, that the poet
had told a reporter, "Don't worry about asking questions—I'll
just talk and you can take it down." He was doubtless pleased
to see how effectively this had put Frost's ambivalent attitude
toward education on record:

I've been thinking a lot lately about this problem of
educating future poets and writers. You know, when I was
young, there were no courses designed to give students an
appreciation of literature, or to encourage them in creative

writing. But today, you can go to college and be told how to write.

"I haven't decided which method produces the best writers," he said, referring to courses in which a volume of poetry could be written under supervision and those in which, after a general arts education, the student grappled with life and wrote poetry as an avocation. "He mentioned the views of his friends at Chicago, William Vaughn Moody and Robert Lovett, who used to say, not without humor, that literary students should be driven from the college in order to save the college and to save literature":

> It's hard to say whether or not genius can be taught, and whether poets really are helped by courses in creative writing. Back in the nineties, before there was any sign of the new attitude toward potential writers, we took our literary pleasures like stolen apples. All our writing was extra-curricular. And I think that the little magazines we put out in those days were just as good as those published by students today.

Frost pointed out that his own education consisted mainly of courses in Latin and Greek and commented on the economics of literature:

> Nowadays there seems to be the feeling that earning money is sordid, and that a poet should not have to be concerned with such matters. But several of my friends, who are bankers or secretaries, also manage to write poetry. And there was once a famous Greek poet who was a garbage collector. Well, it's a difficult problem. After all, literary creations are every man's private affair, and every case of real art is different.

Having been presented to the Ohio State audience (which filled University Chapel) by Newdick, who said, "To introduce the speaker of this evening to this large and brilliant company would be like introducing Saint Francis to the birds!" Frost proceeded to remark:

> Poetry is a way of speaking that you can count on to be understood only by those who know how to take you. I assume you know how to take me.

I used to think, when I began writing poetry at 15 and selling it at 18, that every one who could went into the arts, and that the others worked for money. Then I heard a man say that writing poetry is all right . . . if you're not well.

He added that poetry is not fancifulness or inaccuracy; it must declare something. Writing poetry, he said, is a perilous task—for the performer. The poet, however, sometimes enjoys his failures and makes an adventure of being misunderstood. But when he does make a virtue of being misunderstood, the public will scorn his poetry because he scorns it himself.

After reading "To a Thinker in Office" (a satirical reference to then-President Franklin D. Roosevelt), "The Road Not Taken" and "Stopping by Woods on a Snowy Evening," he announced:

I want to read you some poems about animals. When I get enough poems about animals, I am going to put them in a book. So far I've got several horses, a cow, a hen, and a woodchuck; it's going to be a book about farm life and I'm not sure that the woodchuck fits into the plans . . . but then I never like to plan a book until after I've written it.

After reciting "A Drumlin Woodchuck," "Desert Places," and "Departmental," he read "The Death of the Hired Man," pausing to criticize a dramatization of it which had made clod-hoppers of his characters: "I had to timidly but firmly inform the actors that their 'clodhoppers' had been to college."

Strangely, Newdick did not leave, and apparently did not take, any such notes in May, 1936 as are related to all the other times he met with Frost. Possibly he did not have time to sit down and talk/listen with him. The poet arrived in Columbus on the morning he was to speak, Thursday, May 21. A newspaper article which lists entertainment does not say anything about any event before the evening appearances. A luncheon at noon on Friday at the Faculty Club, guests to include members of the Ohio State English department, was the first announced event after the reading-with-commentary. Chi Delta Phi, the literary honorary which sponsored Frost's lecture, had a tea for him on Friday afternoon. Though Frost was the house-guest of the Newdicks, there is no record of just when he left on Friday or of anything he said.

The only record of what he did, in relation to Newdick, is in

the form of inscriptions in books. One of the autographs he left
is dated May 22, 1936, and this is certainly related to this visit.
It would have been eloquently reassuring to his host: "To
Robert Newdick / for all he has done / to find me out in / my
ways poetic / Robert Frost."

No doubt, the account written for *The Ohio State Lantern*
by one of Newdick's colleagues, Professor William L. Graves,
who recalled Frost's visit in 1922, gave Newdick a lot of satisfaction. He clipped it for his file:

> It was a heartening thing to people who have a liking for
> literature, and who think it ought to have a fair show along
> with science and politics, to see crowds clamoring for seats
> to listen to a poet talk and read, — actually so many people
> wanted to hear Robert Frost the other night that the room
> would not hold them, and many had to be turned away.
> Mr. Frost, who has come slowly and steadily into a great
> fame, is of course a very notable person; but then all the
> poets who have come our way have had big audiences and
> have roused deep interest, —Masefield, Stephens, Unter-
> meyer, —the whole lot. I believe it is actually true that
> these practitioners of the poet's art have drawn larger
> audiences than any other speakers we have welcomed to
> the campus, scientists included. Just what that may indi-
> cate I hardly know, but it is somehow very gratifying.
>
> Mr. Frost must have been a surprise to most of his young
> auditors. People have a way of imaging a poet as a person
> quite unlike what he really is. Every poet I have seen has
> contradicted my notion of him, made in ignorance, of
> course. We feel that we know how such men ought to
> look; and when we find they don't look that way, whatever
> way it is, we have to make a swift readjustment, which
> is sometimes a little bewildering. Certainly those of us
> who saw Frost fourteen years ago knew pretty well what
> to expect; but people to whom he was a stranger probably
> got the usual surprise. He is a rural type, not an urban sort
> at all. His stocky, strong body, his rather large, competent
> hands, his slightly weather-beaten countenance with the
> wavy hair above it all suggest outdoor life, physical labour,
> or at least the ability to do it, and every quality contra-
> dictory to anything like sentimentality, or affectation, or
> "preciousness," or conceit, — all traits poets have some-

times had, traits we are likely to attribute to them, as to most artists, rightly or wrongly. I suspect Mr. Frost would admit to some sort of pose, for he seems to think that all men must live by posing, in a sense; but a more intimate contact with him than that which comes from sitting before him as a part of an audience reveals a complete lack in him of any affectation, though he certainly exhibits a gentle egotism, tempered always by saving humor, —a willingness to laugh at himself, a drollery that one feels is a part of that New England love of fun, tinged with irony, that he is so fond of showing and telling of. The poet does not laugh much, but he smiles often, and on his winning, genial face there moves constantly a flitting whimsicality of expression that keeps one keenly expectant of every word he may say.

His speech is not fluent, often indeed it is halting, and he stops for long silences while he meditates the right words for an idea that is shaping itself in his mind. He loves to make new definitions of familiar terms. One sitting with him can fairly see first, as he insisted, the feeling developing, and then the thought following it out into words. With friends his talk is racy and at moments earthy, and he is capable of half a dozen memorable epigrams in an evening. He likes to tell stories of his country neighbors, or, on request, of his literary acquaintances, and though these tales are often extremely funny, and take people off spicily, they are never malicious. I think he is highly sensitive in nature, —indeed he must be, to have written as he does. He likes his own poems, and likes to read them. He probably likes praise, too, —as who doesn't? In a word, he is a natural, genuine, simple man with a big heart, a fine mind, a powerful imagination, a masterful use of ordinary words, in extraordinary ways. . . . What's a poet? Well, I don't exactly know, —but Robert Frost is one.

(May 26, 1936)

Two paragraphs written by Newdick on the day after Frost left for home give additional impressions. To Mrs. Frost he reported, "Of course the evening was a triumph, an unequivocal one, though for a matter of hours Mr. Frost was in doubt. His kindness in meeting afterwards with a group from the Department will be a precious and stimulating memory for them always." To Thornton of Holt he declared:

> Mr. Frost came, talked, read, and conquered utterly. A thousand packed the auditorium to hear him, and he generously talked and read for an hour and a half. And judging from the swarms of autograph hunters with new books his appearance helped the trade markedly.

Soon after the Frost visit to Ohio State, Newdick instituted an inquiry which brought him into acquaintance with his eventual successor, Prof. Lawrance R. Thompson, then of Wesleyan University in Middletown, Connecticut. Newdick had written the librarian at Wesleyan to ask for an opportunity to review the *Robert Frost: A Chronological Survey*, which had been published in April by the library. On June 8 he received a reply from Fremont Rider, the university librarian, that the 250 copies in the limited edition were already sold out. On June 17, Thompson, the compiler of the document, wrote from his home in Peterboro, New Hampshire, to offer one of the five he had bought and to offer to meet, "if you would care to spend an evening with someone who is as interested, albeit not as intelligent, concerning the subject of Frost bibliography . . . ." Though they corresponded that summer and attempted to meet, they did not, but, along with trading bits of Frost information, Thompson sent Newdick a copy of his survey, autographed, as of July 10. (Then Newdick had Frost add on the title page: "Robert Frost / to / Robert Newdick.") The time during which Newdick and Thompson might have met was in the period July 1 to August 18, when Newdick was teaching at the New York State College for Teachers at Albany.

Though any correspondence leading up to the next meeting of Frost and Newdick has not survived, arrangements seem to have been made after Newdick's arrival at Albany. Newdick's "Recollections from the Day with Robert Frost, July 26, 1936," at South Shaftsbury, Vermont, may be found in Item 9 of Part III.

The next day, Newdick wrote to Frost:

> I've just been reading Robert Hillyer's letter to you in the current *Atlantic*, and with great pleasure. I like particularly its whole-heartedness. And apropos of yesterday I am moved to echo, perhaps a bit turned to my own feelings, part of two lines of his:

> my few perfect moments seem
> Eternal,

for in friendly contact with you I find, as surely you must
know, unutterable joy. Now my summer is all golden.

With the day to think of and my treasures on the seat
beside me, the drive back in the moonlight was not
lonely. . . .

His letter of the following day was more business-like, correcting a couple of errors left over from the big day of conversation.
He included a list of 42 reviews of the 1913–1915 period, in response to the observation that "You seemed a bit interested in
the early reviews. . . ." His rampant enthusiasm made him conclude the letter with this information:

> We took time out to see the movie of *The Green Pas-
> tures* tonight. I don't know quite what I expected, but I
> found it disappointing. But another session with *A Further
> Range* restored me. With no effort to memorize, I now
> have most of it by heart.

He designated himself, in closing: Ever yours.

As has been seen, a basic aspect of Newdick's attempt to realize as fully as possible the nature and significance of Frost's
artistic product was a collection of authentic and complete bibliographic information. Two letters of August 9, 1936, throw
light on successes and failures in Newdick's effort.

Attempting to find out what Frost had published in Derry,
Newdick wrote to Raymond C. Fisher, editor of the Derry
News. He asked for a copy of "A Lost Faith" as it appeared in
the *News* for March 1, 1907, wanting the "signature or by-line
exactly" and the exact page and column in which it appeared.
He also wrote: "If you ever happen to run across any other of
Mr. Frost's early poems in the News, 1900–1911, will you not
let me know about them? (I'd give three dollars for one called
"A Tuft of Flowers," I believe in 1907, though I couldn't spot
it. . . .)"

In an undated response, Fisher reported that "The Lost Faith"
was read by Rev. C. L. Merriam of the Men's League of the
Central Congregational Church at Derry Village in Association
Hall before an audience of 130 on Friday evening, February 29
[sic], 1907. An article in the *News* for March 1 says of Frost:

> Thanks were also voted to Mr. Robert Lee Frost, the teacher in English at Pinkerton Academy, for the fine original poem written especially for the occasion and read by the Rev. C. L. Meriam [sic].

A manuscript of the poem as it appeared on pages one and five, along with the bill for typing the poem, accompanied the letter. The poem bore the following signature: Robert Lee Frost.

Newdick was also writing to Frost on the evening of Sunday, August 9, ". . . venturing to amuse you with a chronicle of the week-end and to plague you with some questions." He had spent from Thursday on in "biographical and bibliographical investigation":

> The long day in Derry was both fruitful and disappointing. I combed the *News* from 1905 through 1911 with no discoveries; 1906 and 1911 I went through twice; but "A Tuft of Flowers" was not there, to the best of my belief.

He had begun to wonder if the poem was published before it was read before the Men's League banquet. Frost sent back the letter with his annotations. In regard to the question of prior publication, Frost wrote:

> I didnt write this. I wondered at the time where it had crept in from. Of course it is no high school child's work — you know I just begin to wonder if Margaret Bartlett of Boulder Colorado wasn't capable of writing it. John [her husband-to-be] was the editor and could have published it for her without telling me. My advisorship was purely nominal. You have my permission to ask them. [John Bartlett, on being asked, wrote to disclaim authorship of the poem by his wife or himself.]

On page 681 of the second volume of the Frost biography, *Years of Triumph*, Thompson discusses the fact that, among other things, Frost was not on the advisory board of the *Critic* in March, 1907, the time of the publication of the poem. After reviewing a subsequent request by Newdick that Frost give the matter a thought, he records Frost's reply that he did not recognize the poem as his. He suggested someone on the *Critic* might have wanted to make it seem that he was participating in school affairs or to give the poem the benefit of adult authorship. Thompson was certain, thirty years later, that Frost had written the poem. His speculative theory was either that Frost was amusing himself in his contention or that, more likely, he wanted to expunge from the record poems which did not meet his later standards.

Further in his letter of August 9, Newdick mentions "a two-page anonymous piece called 'A Kitchen in School.'" Quoting fourteen pages from it, noting that it is like "Slipshod Rhymes," which he had found earlier, Newdick wrote: "I *hope* you did it. It's like 'An A No. 1 Sundown,' a capital piece of fooling, and not all fooling either, any more than 'A Record Stride' is all fun." He had preceded the quote with: "Fess up, didn't you write it?" Frost's annotation was: "Probably mine, though I am dim about it." This suggests he did not mind admitting to what he felt he had written.

Newdick's next paragraph noted that "I gleaned small illuminating bits of other information" from the *News* and the *Critic*. "In the *News*, for instance, is an account, before their performance, of the *five* plays you had the *Critic* staff put on in the spring of 1910. Because the account is so very well-written, explains both the immediate and ultimate purposes of the venture, and does not mention your planning and coaching the whole business, I suspect the author to have been we-know-who." Frost supplied another marginal note: "I doubt if I wrote anything like this for the News. There were years when I didnt write a speck of prose."

The next of the results of Newdick's research to be enumerated was: "Again in Lawrence my record of performance was spotty. The library has no file of the *Sentinel* for any of the years in the nineties." Frost's cryptic comment was: "Perhaps its just as well or better."

Further, Newdick informed Frost that, "In the American [in Lawrence] I could get on to no sure track of your column. In 1894, the year you thought most likely, I went through the file for January, July, September, and November, trying to get a foothold. Then I went on into 1895, with similar results." After reviewing some suggestive-only items he had found, Newdick concluded the discussion of that paper with: "So, is there any suggestion you can give me, or any confirmation on my tentative graspings?"

This drew forth Frost's longest marginal comment: "It was paragraphs [rather than epigrams] I wrote. Two I remember the subject of. One was about an eagle that alighted on the flagpole of the Post Office. Another was about women and children gathering coal in the freight yard." In response to Newdick's enclosing copies of the "newspaper sketches of you and Miss White at the time of your graduation from high school," Frost wrote: "We both thought the pictures bad drawings. Some class mate may have kept the original drawings."

In his next paragraph, Newdick told of an unsuccessful hunt in the September, November, and December issues of the Boston *Transcript* for 1891 and 1892 for "the poem about the corn shocks." Frost pointed out his recollection that "The corn shocks poem was in a Lawrence paper of late '91[.]"

As opposed to the failure to find "corn shocks," Newdick triumphantly described his searching through the *Transcript* till he finally found "Greece," a comment on the beginning of the Graeco-Turkish War, published on April 20, 1897. Beside the first eight lines, Frost wrote: "Dreadful, dreadful. I was trying very hard to show sympathy with the people who made me learn Greek."

After quoting the poem he had found, Newdick returned to the poem about the corn shocks: "In 1891 you were still in high school. Had you talked with Hurd before you were through school?" To this and several other questions, he added: "You needn't bother to answer these questions; they are just written thought; and how often I wish I could think of these small but determinative points when I'm *with* you." Frost's rejoined cryptically: "Thou reasonest too hard."

The last of these notes, doubtless sent in an envelope postmarked from South Shaftsbury on August 17, suggests Frost's incapability to believe in meticulous research, though he abetted it and did not forbid it: "Ah what a dusty answer gets the soul that probes too deep into anybody's random beginnings."

Nothing daunted, Newdick continued the factual pursuit, as he was to continue to do as long as he was able. For example, he wrote Miss Clark, on September 24, that Frost was "dim about" the kitchen poem in the Pinkerton *Critic*. Accordingly, he asked her if she had written those lines. Also, on October 11 he wrote to John Bartlett for his opinion of whether Frost had written "A Kitchen in School."

Thompson wrote Newdick a two-page, single-spaced letter on November 24. Evidently, Newdick had sent him various articles, including a review of Thompson's *Chronology*. He complimented him on his style and added: "And also, when, oh when do you find the time for all those articles? Great day! You must have a dynamo inside." Commenting on the Clymer-Green bibliography, he told of his own efforts to conclude a dissertation on Longfellow's early years, a work which became his first publication. His most significant paragraph relating to work on Frost was this:

> News that is more down your alley is this: my work on the "Chronology" got me so excited about Frost's prose that I sold to Frost the idea that he should let me make up a little volume of selected prose. He was surprised when he saw how much there was, and even more surprised when he found out that I wanted to do it for love and not for money. The whole plan is beginning to head up, and he has even made changes in my arrangement, but I don't think anything will happen until next summer, for he feels duty bound to Harvard to get out those lectures for them first. Of course, I'd like to get the lectures for this prose volume, but he thinks that would be discourteous. I expect that Wilbert Snow at Wesleyan will write an appreciation. I'd like to have done it, but when I told Snow about the idea last spring, he said, "Good! And I'll write an Introduction for you." What do you say to enthusiasm like that? I was so pleased to find that he liked the idea that I said "All right," and have regretted it ever since. You know how mistakes live to annoy? Oh well, who am I to think that I was the first to find Frost's prose exceptionally good? Everyone who knows the prose knows the truth. Also, Bill Snow has been able to help me gain Frost's approval, and that is a lot. When I write you again, I'll send you a list of the present "Table of Contents." There are several questions on it which I wish to ask you, but tonight I have too much of a mess here on my desk to clear up before I pack my bag. So my only question is, "*How* can I get Frost to give up the idea about sending those lectures to the Harvard University press?" You know, I guess, that he hasn't touched the stenographer's notes taken at Cambridge.

As the reader will see, this project was not one in which Newdick found pleasure. Nor did it result in publication till three decades later.

Newdick sent Frost by special delivery on November 26 a poem called "A Sachem of the Clouds (A Thanksgiving Legend)" so that it "could reach you by Thanksgiving." Frost's answering letter of November 26 is still being held in the Barrett Collection at the University of Virginia. Perhaps it will be released in time to record comments.

On November 30 Frost sent Newdick a telegram:

MY DAUGHTER LESLIE FROST FRANCIS ON HER LEISURELY WAY
TO MEXICO WITH HER TWO CHILDREN WILL LECTURE
TUESDAY DECEMBER FIRST FOR MRS JOHN ADAMS TWO SIX
FOUR SOUTH ARLINGTON STREET SPRINGFIELD OHIO WISH
SHE COULD SEE SOMETHING OF YOU FOLKS THANKS FOR
SACHEM POEM TAKES YOU TO FIND THINGS.

ROBERT FROST

In addition to expressing Frost's pleasure at the newly-discovered poem, it opened up a new source for Newdick.

In what he called a "chatterish account" of two single-spaced, typed pages of December 6, Newdick gave an account of Lesley's visit with the Newdicks, an account of two lectures Lesley gave in Springfield, Ohio, the highlight of the meeting being an evening when ". . . Lesley showed us scrapbooks, looked over my collection of materials, told of the one-copy magazine [*The Bouquet*] she published in England when you all were living there, and conversed gloriously till one o'clock or so."

After reporting "five or six" recent talks he had given on Frost, he described his own crowded schedule of teaching and other dates, mentioning articles accepted and under consideration. He then gave his rueful first reaction to Thompson's prose project:

The other day, having heard the news from him, I congratulated Thompson on persuading you to publish your prose. As I told him honestly, I am, in so doing, "dancing with tears in my eyes," as the recently popular song put it, because I've been urging such a book with Mr. Thornton for two years, both directly and through Mr. Melcher. But I never made the suggestion or showed my collection of materials to you because Mr. Thornton was sure that the suggestion would annoy you! But the book's the thing; I'm glad it's being put together; and I shall welcome it.

Correspondence with Professor L. W. Payne, Jr., of the University of Texas, brought a welcome note in a letter of January 30: "Just yesterday I saw Mr. Frost himself, and he told me that you were at work on a more exhaustive bibliography. . . ." The echo, through a mutual party, by Frost of Newdick's contempt for the bibliography from which he had disassociated himself would have made his relationship seem more secure.

Because it documented the error in one of Frost's authorship-denials, that of "The Last Minstrel," a letter of February 28, 1937, from Harriette Melvin Tibbetts of Melrose, Massachusetts, recalling her Pinkerton days was of special interest:

> It was our custom at Pinkerton Academy to assemble in chapel for morning devotions, and one morning we found in our hymn books slips of paper on which said poem was printed. We used it as a hymn, singing it to the tune of "O Could I Find From Day to Day." Whether the poem was written especially for us to use in chapel I do not know, but we were quite thrilled to think that our English teacher actually composed the words we were singing.

On April 23, Newdick learned again that patience in waiting for response from his idol was necessary and rewarding. He had sent to Amherst, on December 18, two papers on Frost written by his students, noting: "I've often wished you could know how much the privilege of reading your poems means to young men and women, how almost universally the young people, even as their elders, respond to the poems, from the heart, and how well in their papers they occasionally say things." The papers were "The Heavens in the Poems of Robert Frost" by Helen P. Hunt and "The Twinkling Poet" by William C. Applegate.

Frost's April response was in the form of a package containing two copies of the first edition of *West-running Brook*, both inscribed. For Helen Hunt, Frost wrote: "for her heavenly essay / about the / works of / Robert Frost / Amherst Mass 1937." For Applegate: "for what he called me / Robert Frost / Amherst Mass 1937." Newdick called the two students, inviting them to come to his office "to hear some good news." When he wrote to Frost on April 26, Newdick reported that Miss Hunt "was fairly overcome in almost wordless joy." "I was so pleased," he wrote in a memorandum, "at Frost's generous kindness that when I was on my way out from the Faculty Club, where I bought two cartons of cigarettes, I stopped in Skelley's office and told him about it." The public relations man accordingly did place a story in the newspapers.

Newdick additionally showed his excitement by beginning his letter to Frost on April 26 with this sentence: "This will reach you a day or two after the date above, but none the less I wish you many happy returns of your birthday." The actual date, which is often recorded in Newdick's papers, was March 26. As nearly as can be gathered from Newdick's zealous records, he had not heard from Frost since the previous December. His anxiety is suggested by the fact that he left a memorandum of the fact that he had, on April 13, sent Frost a copy of his article, "Uncollected Poems of Robert Frost," which had appeared in *The Book Collector's Journal* for February. "At the top I wrote, 'For Robert Frost'; in the left margin, I supplied two whole lines the compositor had dropped from my text; all through I made typographical corrections; and at the bottom of p. 1 I called attention to the dropped lines." Perhaps it was this item which drew the response of April 23. Certainly it was a pleasure and a relief to Newdick to hear, whatever the reason.

Just about this time, Newdick had another extreme pleasure; Eva O'Brien Barndollar, of Manchester, New Hampshire, had sent two letters of six and nine pages, respectively, of her reminiscences of Frost as a teacher at the Normal Training School at Plymouth in 1911. Because she was still a student there when *A Boy's Will* was published in England, she had a first edition of the book, evidently obtained through the school. When Newdick replied to her first letter, he averred that he would "give a leg" for the first edition of *A Boy's Will*. With her second letter, of May 31, she sent the book as a gift in recognition of her perception that Newdick's love for Frost was greater than her own regard. (See Item 16, Part III for a review of information supplied by Mrs. Barndollar.)

On May 5, Newdick sent "Dear Mr. Frost" a clipping from the *Columbus Dispatch*, "voicing the community's approval of the Pulitzer awards. And Marie and I wish to join our congratulations to you with the flood of the nation's." At the end of May, John Holmes, poet, columnist, and teacher of Boston, opened, by mail, what was to be a strong friendship with Newdick. Seeing a review of the Clymer-Green bibliography in the *Saturday Review*, Holmes sensed the intense interest of Newdick in Frost and offered correspondence. He also reported that he and another man had recently sat up till half past two talking at the St. Botolph Club. "I couldn't help being struck by Mr. Frost's deprecation of nearly every contemporary poet whose name was mentioned, the first time I have felt anything but admiration for anything and everything he said."

Among other things Newdick told Holmes in a letter of June 2 was that he had had permission to do the biography for two years and that "I now have the first five or six chapters completed in first draft." Referring to Holmes' remark on Frost's attitude toward other writers, he gave a statement of his own biographical policies:

> But as you suggest there are many points that will necessarily have to be glossed over in a biography published during Frost's lifetime. As I have read your articles, quite clearly written con amore, I have wondered just when the shortcomings would dawn on you,— the little flaws that jolt one's hero-worship (or the virtual equivalent). Surely no one who loves the man as well as the poet would give him pain even though he had brought it on himself; so, the unwillingness to give other poets their due, like the long memory for slights and injustices, will have to be ignored.

This same topic came up in a letter to his devoted research assistant, Dr. Burnham. Referring to his confidential note on a forgotten loan from a high school classmate, he said he was amazed at the idea of such an omission but that, "I'm too old not to know that such things happen where one would otherwise hardly even suspect them. There are other cracks in the pedestal, believe me: for instance, a hardly describable hypercriticalness of the work and accomplishments of others in the same field of activity." Though he was certain these characteristics would eventually be recorded, Newdick said he planned to be "like the three famous monkeys."

Newdick's devotion to the best of Frost carried him northward in Ohio to Oberlin College, where RF gave the Commencement address on June 8. When "What Became of New England" was printed in *The Oberlin Alumni Magazine* in May, 1938, it was from "stenographic notes prepared for press by Robert S. Newdick." He had in the meantime checked them with Lesley to make certain the locutions he had recorded were accurate. A note in the June, 1937, Oberlin magazine noted that

Frost had no manuscript. "The speech was taken down in short-hand almost in its entirety, but when this editor tried to patch together the pieces and achieve continuity, she was afraid to tackle it. It was one of those rambling talks, interesting to hear, with very little relation to the occasion. . . ."

An undated letter, presumably the one referred to in the Barrett Collection list as of June 8, can be identified because of the way it fits Newdick's letter of June 11. It was the first Frost had written Newdick in 1937:

Dear Newdick:

My fault entirely about the dates at Pinkerton. I knew I was only there five years. Nevertheless I have always kept the 1905–1911 in Who's Who. I show how I have to be checked upon. Strictly speaking the farming should overlap with the teaching and read 1900 to 1909. It was only for the last two years that I gave up farming and moved into the village to teach full time. I wish these dates could be got right some day.

All full professors at Amherst get an A M degree to make them alumni. It is automatic rather than honorary. It is not conferred publicly with citations on a platform. I dont believe it properly belongs in my list. I wish you had asked me about it.

You would be mistaken in assuming the A M at Michigan meant much to me. I thought little of it in comparison with all the other things they did for me out there. They gave me a great two years in residence. You look the list over in Who's Who and you'll find several degrees I value more than the degrees Michigan gave me however. As you say not all should necessarily be brought in. I wasn't consulted in the matter and was lucky to be handled so tactfully.

I just want to ask you to look sharply into the matter of the Class Hymn. You are probably right, but my recollection would have been that the Bulletin with the poem and all our graduation essays in it wasn't out till after the exercises were over; in which case it would be in behind the order of Exercises by Anon. My wife's mother wrote the music for the Hymn.

I never thanked you for sending the poem about the Sachem I wrote for Thanksgiving exercises. It wasn't so much as I had hoped. The big feeling I spent over it had lingered. It took you to find it.

The Levinson prize wasn't important was it? Small amount and in a small world. Damned if I hadn't forgotten it. It would be well down in the scale. Do you rate election to the P. E. N[.] Club with election to the American Academy and the American Philosophical Society? I can leave a lot to the judgement of others.

Best wishes. Ever yours

"It was a joy," Newdick wrote on June 11, "to receive your letter, and I have been so eager to write you, but hesitant until there should be some word from you." He was, of course, answering immediately.

Mentioning that he had received a copy of the Clymer-Green bibliography, on which he had commented in the *Saturday Review* of the previous November, he reaffirmed "my faith that some day my own bibliography, more inclusive in scope and wider in purpose and method, will be published."

After reviewing various items of Frost research, he noted: "In my reluctance to make a nuisance of myself I try long and hard to work out my own answers growing out of either bibliographical or biographical problems, but on some I have gone as far as I can go alone and am still uncertain. Therefore I venture to enclose two or three with this letter." One of the items was doubtless a single-spaced, typed page headed "The Later Minstrel" and reviewing the very convincing evidence relating to Frost's having written the poem.

The letter concluded: "Most of this summer I shall spend here in Columbus, trying to complete the sketch or first draft of the biography. But I really need to go again to New York and Boston, —and I shall if I may look forward to a day with you at South Shaftsbury or at Franconia at the peak of the year."

Frost's response to that letter is not, uncharacteristically, in the Newdick files, but Newdick's letter of July 7 strongly suggests its content. The opening paragraph indicates another denial of "The Later Minstrel": "Thank you for responding about both the questions and the chronology and the spurious but still curious poem The Later Minstrel—if it's not yours I'll pursue it no further."

Covering such points as the appearance of Newdick's articles on "Robert Frost and the Dramatic" and "Some Notes on

Robert Frost and Shakespeare," the matter of whether or not the Class Hymn which Frost wrote for his high school graduation was published before it was sung, and mention of a "delightful long letter" from Lesley in Mexico, the letter is rather brief. Possibly this was because he had to end it with this plea-reminder: "I'm still hoping you will say I may call on you this summer in the mountains."

His correspondence with Holmes involved discussion of Newdick's thwarted project of doing a book of Frost's prose. This caused Holmes to write on July 8 that "the latest I have heard in New York" was that Thornton planned to do a "book of essays" about Frost: "I'd like to be in it myself but have not been asked." This made Newdick ask on July 12: "Don't you think that *we* might score a bull's eye by collecting and editing a collection of fresh, unpublished essays and poems in tribute to R. F., perhaps for his sixty-third birthday [still thinking in terms of 1875] next spring?" In immediate response, Holmes wrote on July 14 to register interest and to suggest all the problems which would have to be solved.

When Newdick wrote on July 28, he could report:

> I have news about that Holt collection of Frost essays that's on the way: It's to contain the Auden, Engle, and other essays in the recent English edition of the *Selected Poems* plus other pieces to which Frost gives his blessing, such as Van Doren's *Scholastic* essay which you doubtless saw. Let's pray that R. F. may benevolently think some piece of your prose or mine, or both, worthy of inclusion.

In the course of considering the merits of the collaborative tribute book, Newdick gave two good glimpses of himself. Referring to the necessity of extricating himself from the Clymer-Green bibliography, he noted: "Retreats mean bloody feet, and often bruised hearts." And writing of his attitude toward Frost: "As you must surely see, I'm an enthusiast, almost in the eighteenth century sense of the word. But I'm also capable of the work of three ordinary men, when the drive is the drive of devotion."

In the middle of July, Newdick wrote to Dr. Burnham, his devoted helper at Lawrence, about the possibility of hiring an alert high school or college student to find particulars behind this statement Frost had made to him: "It's amusing that I once had a column on the newspaper before columnists were ever known. Of course, it wasn't like the present columns. I wrote about things I'd seen. Sort of prose poems. I remember one thing was about women I'd watched from my window picking up coal along the railroad tracks. Another was about an eagle that flew over Lawrence and alighted on the brass ball at the top of the flagpole on the Postoffice Building. An ardent hunter got out his gun and shot the eagle on his flagpole perch. That was worth writing about, wasn't it? It angered me, of course."

Dr. Burnham wrote on July 22 to indicate he was turning his attention to looking for Frost information in the Lawrence *American* for 1895. However, he was already able to write: "Referring to the 'eagle' escapade, as I recall it, I saw the eagle roosting on the large heroic sized gilded wooden eagle then and now topping the belfry of our City Hall and further recall that said gunner made preparations to use his shell, but Mr. (or Mrs.) Eagle happily flew, before the contemplated deed was accomplished. R. F.'s story may be classed as 'poets license' possibly."

In August, Newdick's friendship with his eventual replacement as Frost's biographer, Lawrance Thompson, had developed sufficiently for him to receive a letter, of August 8, addressed to "Dear patient Newdick." Its seven double-spaced, typed pages are full of discussion of Frost bibliography, much of it quite technical discussion of such matters as how to deal with fly leaves in a bibliography. His general tone is one of friendship and helpfulness. Doubtless his generous remarks on Newdick's "Robert Frost and the Dramatic" were welcome: "Man, you cut circles around any one else writing on Frost. What's more, you know how to integrate your findings so that they make more than the sum of the parts. I don't blame you for being pleased with it. Do some more. For heaven's sake, do some more."

It will be recalled that Thompson had gained approval for a book of Frost's prose, unconsciously thwarting one of Newdick's ideas. His friendship with Frost was flourishing, though his approach, like that of Newdick, was cautious: "I go to see Frost next week. And I have nerve enough to take over with me a couple chapters of my Longfellow book." Evidently, Newdick had told Thompson he was awaiting approval of a visit to Frost, for Thompson offered, "And incidentally I shall ask him if Newdick is coming to see him this summer. The seed may germinate into the letter he just hasn't thought to write you."

That this help was offered in all honesty and sincerity is suggested by a later passage, in which Thompson mentions that his *Chronological Survey* was "published April 26, 1936, which was Sunday, as I remember the day (I know the day is right), when Frost came to Wesleyan to talk." Then he comments: "A bit of biographical information for your notebook. Lord, I'd like to hear you get going on Frost's life some time. You must know more about it than he does! Keep it up. You certainly have the jump on any one else in the field. Had you thought that the one person liable to compete with you on the matter of the biography is Untermeyer?"

During August, Holmes and Newdick continued to consider their possible collaborative book in honor of Frost. They were (as of August 8) both thinking they might not be asked to contribute to the Holt book. After suggesting, in July, a list of 33 possible contributors to their possible book, Holmes reported on August 11 that "A woman in the editorial department of Holt wrote to ask me for a clipping of the account I wrote describing the Frost letters at Harvard. The letter said they were considering it for the book. . . ."

In the course of his letter, relating to their own possible book, he made two interesting remarks about those who did not appreciate the work of Frost:

> The whole matter of literary enemies, and Frost's in this case, is provoking. And you know that although he says he doesn't read reviews, he knows in what quarter the enemies lurk, and he is sensitive to them, as you say. Well, now, who are they? They are people who are behind on reading Frost, who talk their faint echoes of reviews of North of Boston and no new slant since. And they are people who, having the same incomplete trite opinion, have now turned to the left in politics and writing, and regard Frost as arch-conservative, without taking the trouble to find out.

Later he added:

> The number of articulate friends is very great, and of readers enormously greater, and the nature of adverse criticism is that it is topical, faddish, in a cause, and gone tomorrow. We can feel sure that Frost will outlast them all.

When Newdick received word that Holmes could be included

in the Holt book, it was two o'clock on a Sunday morning, on his return from a fishing trip. Seeing nothing from Holt in his mail, he thought, "I'm glad one of us made it." The next day he found, in his mail at the University, a request from a Mrs. Manning at Holt to use his "Robert Frost and the Dramatic." As he wrote on August 22, "I've been treading on air ever since. In his excitement, he had started his letter with "Shake, man, shake! And, moreover, hip, hip, hooray!" The same line was used as a postscript.

The acceptance involved in being included in the book which became *Recognition of Robert Frost* took the sting out of this news from Holmes on August 24:

> . . . I had a letter the other day from RF begging us to abate our zeal for him for the present, in fact suggesting that we can serve him best with such a project if we wait till he is no longer living. So I guess we can't move far in the face of that, though we must not abandon the plan. He says definitely that having friends asked for tributes would make him suffer. He told me all about the pain and coolness between himself and Robinson once when he refused to write for a similar book for EAR.
>
> "You and he," he writes, "can get in better licks for me out of your own affection in the years to come. Promise not to let the world forget me when my address is some graveyard in Lawrence Franconia Amherst South Shaftsbury Florida Texas or California." And then he goes on to suggest that he has been thinking of spending the last of his days in California, ending as he began. I think it would be too bad, and really not appropriate at all; but I suppose he would do it partly for his wife's health and his own.
>
> Of course you see that the "he" quoted above is yourself; and he says elsewhere good things about you, that he likes you, and that he feels you could handle such a book with discretion. But he doesn't want to have to risk it now. In fact he says he doesn't need it now.

When he replied, on August 27, Newdick wrote:

> I confess I am a bit disappointed that RF disapproves for the present, but I thoroughly understand his position, and of course his wish is our law in the matter. Perhaps, as you say, we can keep the project simmering for some

time in the future, and the book that results may be all the better for the longer and inevitably more careful planning. It makes me uncomfortable, however, for RF to be thinking at all of "the last of his days."

The latest message Newdick had had from South Shaftsbury was written on August 1 by Mrs. Frost. Apologizing for long delay in answering, she mentioned unexpected company at the time of the letter she was answering, and then, because of fatigue, it had slipped her mind. Newdick had asked for permission to use two pictures of the Frost children for an article, "Children in the Poems of Robert Frost," which was to appear in *Ohio Schools*. In her second paragraph she wrote that she found herself opposed to the use of the pictures in such a way. She found the associations distressing but held out hope that her attitude might change. Another paragraph of pleasantries included the information that Robert was feeling better than he had during the previous summer. Her close was with her first and last names, styling herself as sincere, and noting that both Frosts sent "kindest regards" to the Newdicks. Then, in a postscript, perhaps influenced impulsively by what she had just written, she recorded that she thought she *was* willing to have the pictures used, appending her initials to the statement.

Pleased as he was to have permission to use the pictures, he would have been somewhat happier to have some word about the visit he was hoping to make. When he wrote to Holmes on August 27, all he could say was, "I have at last decided to travel the early Frost trail again this summer,—Lawrence, Cambridge, Derry, Plymouth. . . ." As will be seen in the notes of the Concord Corners visit of September 1–3, evidently Mrs. Newdick supplied the support which made her husband at least attempt the visit he wanted so much to make. Again, in the notes, "as he rubbed his hair when we had sat down: I was wondering whether I owed you a letter. (Tucky went into hysterics when she heard that.)"

But the trepidation involved in "finding out" Robert Frost in another of his unique ways was certainly worthwhile, as the notes (Item 18, Part III), testify.

What Newdick called a "glorious souvenir" of the visit was one which alluded to the picnic at Lake Willoughby, an inscription in Newdick's English edition of *New Hampshire* which quoted three lines from "A Fountain, a Bottle, a Donkey's Ears and Some Books":

> . . . we faced
> A cliff, and on the cliff a bottle painted,
> Or stained by vegetation from above,
> A likeness to surprise the thrilly tourist.

Below his signature, RF placed a key to identifications to the personnel assigned to the lines. He made a little circle next to "we" and then showed in a note that meant "The Newdicks, EMF and I." Beside the word "cliff" he placed an x and then, in a second note, specified: "Willoughby Cliff, September 3, 1937." (See Frontispiece.) Another souvenir of the picnic was a post card view of Lake Willoughby, eleven inches by three inches, given the Newdicks by Mrs. Frost.

Three other inscriptions were made at that meeting. The Clymer and Green bibliography was autographed under the picture which faces the title page. After the signature is "Visited at Concord Corner / Vermont / September 3, 1937." *From Snow to Snow*, a twenty-page pamphlet published in 1936, was inscribed: "To Robert Newdick my thanks / for the idea of putting some of / my poems in a seasonal order / Robert Frost / Visit of September 3, 1937 / at Concord Corners Vt."

Because of the historical reference in the first line, it may be assumed that the inscription on the page opposite the front cover of *Selected Poems*, 1928, was made during this visit:

> Written in the town [Concord Corners, Vt.] where the first lectures in school keeping were delivered in 1826[.]

Then lines 82–93 of "The Ax-Helve" were quoted. Of interest to students of Frost's memory and language habits will be a notice of the following deviations from the published poem: a comma after *know* is left out in line 82. *Defense* in line 83 is spelled *defence* in the inscription. A comma after *school* is omitted in line 84. The hyphen between *laid* and *on* is omitted in line 86. Line 87 has *ax helve* instead of *ax-helves*. Line 88 has *them* in place of *these*. A period at the end of line 89 is omitted. The comma after *friendship* is left out of line 90. The same occurs after *to* in line 91.

When the Frosts and Newdicks got back from that September 3 picnic, RF took care of the boiling radiator of the Newdick Ford by filling it with water. At the same time, Newdick found

the oil was down a quart or so. Thus, en route from Concord
Corners to Boston, on September 4, "I mailed Mr. Frost a postcard picture of the capitol and in the space for correspondence
wrote as follows:

> En route from Mecca to Gomorrah
>> With frosty water
>>> And a little ile,
>> Not once again
>>> Did Henry bile."

Newdick wrote on September 13 to say that he had arrived
home the previous afternoon, "just a few hours more than two
weeks after our taking off, and with glowing memories more
than sufficient to light us through the autumn and winter. Happiest of all were those of hours with you and Mrs. Frost in Concord Corners and St. Johnsburg and Lake Willoughby. Our
hearts' deep thanks to you both. And we most earnestly hope
that the picnic jaunt did not prove to have been too strenuous
for Mrs. Frost."

After mentioning visits with several biographical sources at
Plymouth, Derry, and Manchester, he recorded a meeting with
John Holmes in Boston. He hoped he had made his "enthusiasm" (tinged with the eighteenth-century sense) more understandable to Holmes, for whom he had great liking.

As mentioned in his notes, RF and Newdick had devoted
much time during the Concord Corners visit to work on *Recognition*. Before Newdick's arrival on August 16, RF had written
to Thornton: "Here are Elinor's plans for the first part of the
book and my list of the essays to follow. We thought 'Recognition of Robert Frost' ought to be a fairly good name for the
book." When he left Concord Corners, Newdick had a mission
to carry to Thornton RF's latest thoughts on the book which
was to honor him. Arriving in New York on Monday evening,
Newdick spent an hour and a half with Thornton on Tuesday
and four hours more on Wednesday: "Our talk was almost exclusively of the book. I gave him the new names and references
that you had chosen (and what copy I had with me), and he had
a secretary make typewritten record of the contents as you
wrote them out (allowing me to retain your original as a treasure) [See Appendix L.]. . . ."

The evidence just presented indicates a distinct interest in
and participation by Frost in a book in his honor. It should be

noted that he was giving cooperation to his publisher, who originated the project. Further, as Newdick wrote of Thornton to Frost in the letter now being discussed, "He has, I found, gone over all of the material very carefully himself, not entrusting that matter to an assistant, and he is making cuts in the several items in that material with an eye on the balance of the book as a whole. Editorially, then, it is his book; and, as you doubtless know, he is taking great joy in the task."

Happily, while he was working with Frost on the *Recognition*, he had no knowledge of remarks made about him by RF in a letter of August 16 to Holmes. In the first place, he wrote, "I seriously doubt if I want any such book of garlands to the living as Newdick proposes." Newdick was really only going along with an idea proposed by Frost's publisher and with which Frost cooperated. "Newdick is all right," Frost reflected to Holmes, "and I like him in most ways—and apparently he likes me in most ways, too. But his zeal for me seems excessive. You can help me there if you will, by abating him a little." Possibly this was why Newdick had to find his way to Frost's house at Concord Corners without the encouragement of the invitation he had so hopefully awaited.

On the other hand, when he wrote to Thornton on September 7, Frost reported having "a good two day talk with Newdick and he goes loaded to the muzzle with my latest ideas . . . Newdick seems willing to help you a lot. And theres a lot to do particularly in the reduction of the things coming under the head of The Idea. . . . It's the part of the book I am most uneasy about. . . . Newdick will discuss with you the possibility of having Ezra Pound in."

The last paragraph of the letter explains in the frankest of ways the ambivalence Frost was to feel toward the endeavors of all such capable, attractive, and enchanted men as Newdick:

> We had a pleasant picnic with the Newdicks on Willoughby Lake. I hope his thoroughness with the surface of me will wear him through into the depths of me (such as they are). I could well afford to have him find me a little deeper than I am. I wish he would keep on getting delayed by new discoveries below the surface till I am dead and out of hearing. I want to be perpetuated: I want the world to know about me. But I dont [sic] want to be told about myself.

FIG. I. *Robert Frost with Dr. and Mrs. Robert S. Newdick during picnic at Willoughby Lake, Vermont.*

With his letter of September 13, Newdick sent a copy of "Design in the Books of Robert Frost," which was appearing in the September *Reading and Collecting*. He requested RF to "Please tell Mrs. Frost, who very kindly read a carbon copy of it, that the essay on 'Robert Frost and the Sound of Sense' has been accepted by *American Literature*, though the editors insist that it be footnoted throughout."

Another note from the letter which suggests the continuing traffic in the search for Frost information is this remark:

> Now that I have looked into my files, let me answer two questions that you asked me and that I could not at the moment reply to exactly: (1) the 1892 graduation program was given to me by Mrs. John T. Lord (Annie Barker). (2) The June, 1892, issue of the *Bulletin* was given me by Miss Edith M. Andrews.

Newdick closed the letter with a reference to the inscriptions Frost had given him, mentioning first he had found in New York a first trade edition of *New Hampshire* and a first edition of the *Selected Poems* (1923). ". . . so already I am accumulating additional items for your inscription sometime!"

> Seriously, again, you must let me thank you again for your great kindness in inscribing my treasures. I hardly glance at them while I'm still with you: I save the first real joy of looking upon them till I'm alone with them. And what a glorious souvenir you made of the English edition of *New Hampshire* by the footnoted lines from the poem ["A Fountain, A Bottle, a Donkey's Ears and Some Books"] we talked of, and that years before had in part grown out of, Lake Willoughby!

In a written note to his typed letter, he reported: "I have put the snapshots into the hands of an expert to be developed and will send you prints soon."

Two days later, Newdick reported on another item discussed at Concord Corners. RF had expressed a wish for a copy of a checklist of holdings of his poems and letters at the Huntington library. The typed list which he sent with the letter consisted of thirty-nine poems on one page, with Newdick's "conjectural annotations." It reiterated a note from "P. Rigney" of the Huntington Staff that "There are also approximately 32 letters cover-

FIG. 2. *Robert Frost carrying water during a picnic with the Newdicks at Willoughby Lake, Vermont.*

ing the years 1894–1929, and one manuscript. This material is uncatalogued, but most of it appears to be in his autograph."

And he thus launched a project which was to take him to California on Frost's behalf:

> As I urged something more than a year and a half ago to Mrs. Frost (for I was fearful then of speaking of the matter to you without counsel): "knowledge of them ought to be in the hands not only of library visitors and neutral-minded librarians, but also of his friends and champions." And if you shall give us permission to have them photostated I shall of course make no use of them whatsoever at any time without your express permission, and meanwhile they would be extremely valuable to me as material giving depth to my background understanding. . . .

The letter concluded with a paragraph about an enclosed copy of "Children in the Poems of Robert Frost," which was appearing in the September *Ohio Schools*. Pointing out that the magazine, the official organ of the Ohio Education Association, went to "many thousands of subscriber-teachers," he noted defensively that he feared the introduction as a bit top heavy with humor that doesn't quite come off. . . ." Yet he hoped "that there will be some touch that you will like as Lesley very generously did." Lesley had written on June 21, from Mexico, that she had "enjoyed the article immensely" and even went so far as to suggest "one or two of my favorite children," making references to "Blueberries" and "Maple."

Uncharacteristically (and thus doubtless significantly) revealing his interest, Frost answered on September 20. The letter was a most welcome commentary on the relationship as a whole and on the Huntington project specifically:

Dear Newdick:

> You showed yourself so amenable on your Concord Corners Willoughby [sic] and your wife is such a fine person, that I feel disposed to make you an offer about those poems and letters in Huntington durance—take it or leave it. I will write you a free pass to visit them if you will go out there and pass critically not only on the handwriting, but on the paper water marks (if any) and general phisique of the poem ["]I had a love once["]. (What a name! What a subject!) Nothing not really important could bother me

FIG. 3. *Robert Frost on the shore of Willoughby Lake, Vermont, 1937. (Photo by Marie Newdick.)*

more than to have that thing accepted of fools as mine. Photostatic copies wont do what I want. The emergency calls for detective work. I have shown you how acutely my mind works in a case of the kind. I dismiss Mrs So and so's [Mrs. Paul Barndollar] claim to have had a copy of my book from me personally. Fortunately it is no great matter. I wouldn't have the poor lady's feelings hurt. The inscription to Ernest Silver is all I needed for confirmation of my notion of how I inscribe books and always have inscribed them when I was actually giving them as presents. I am prepared to swear that I never merely wrote my name and that on an inner page unless the book already belonged to some one else already. Some one was tempted to make a false boast. It shows how important I am to claim friendship with. I ought to feel set up. I was just told that the little I have done to get this hill top into the papers suggests how much a really big person could do. The Innkeeper speaking. He's a fine fellow all the same. You mustnt get angry at him.—We suspect you put the article about the Corners into the Springfield Republican that reached us through the Amherst Record. Mr Thornton tells me what a pleasant and helpful visit he had from you. Mrs. Sylvia Clark has been roused up to ask a favor of us for the Cooperative [word not clear] of N.H.—Did you find the mag. at Plymouth with A Time to Talk in it? The date was after my return from England. Elinor tells me you made a poetical piece of the children. I must read it— mustnt I? I must turn over a new leaf. Thanks for being nice about the children.

The letter was signed "Ever yours / Robert Frost" and dated, characteristically, at the end: "Concord Corners Vt / September 20 12:30 A.M. (We leave / in 9 hours for S. Shafts)." And then he added a final note: "Elinor says I must read the Design article too. You'll spoil me."

On the same day Frost was writing that most heartening of letters, Newdick wrote both a typed letter and a longhand note. The note, to Mrs. Frost, accompanied the snapshots taken in Vermont. "Marie and I cherish the photograph of Willoughby Lake you gave us as a souvenir of our picnic there," he began. And then he noted, "of the snapshots enclosed there's one in particular that we hope you'll like—the profile of Mr. Frost looking up to Mt. Hor." Mrs. Newdick had taken the picture, of Frost in profile, walking along the lake shore (see enclosed picture). Newdick's enthusiasm for it was so great that Mrs. Newdick had it enlarged and colored for him.

The typed letter to Frost, sent, evidently, along with the pictures, which are mentioned as for Mrs. Frost and in an enclosed envelope, mentions an added aspect to the favorite picture: "Marie and I think the best one is that of you looking over toward the hillside where you introduced me to snowberries,—baneberries."

After mentioning the article in *The Shakespeare Association Bulletin* for July and the fact that some items had been cut out of the *Ohio Schools* article, he included two paragraphs which deserve quotation:

> A petition: Won't you please write out for me three or four of the key-lines to passages in Greek and Latin that you cared for enough to memorize? You spoke some for me when I was with you, but I wasn't quick enough to catch them on the fly and I wouldn't ask you to repeat them.
>
> Mr. Thornton tells me he has turned all the copy over to the printer and that he himself may bring up galley proof and go over it with you. . . .

On September 26 he joyfully started a letter with a response to the proposal that he examine in person the manuscripts at the Huntington Library:

> I *take* it! — I mean the offer of a free pass to examine directly the letters and poems in durance now at San Marino. And I'll undertake to smash to smithereens the case for ascribing to you the highly objectionable "I had a love once." — I'll freely admit there are obstacles to overcome for me to get at the papers, but I'll hurdle them in some way. The football team goes out to play Southern California a week from next Saturday, and maybe I can persuade the athletic director to take me along,—for I'll shine shoes or clean spitoons or do anything else to get at those papers. May I have photostats *too*? And is your letter of the twentieth the pass itself? And can't you see me straining at the leash?——

The rest of the letter involves touching base on various research points, mentioning pleasure at Mrs. Frost's taking the article on Frost's poetic children but averring that "you needn't suffer basting by reading what I write . . . ," adding "though I do see you receive copies of all I do that gets into print." Along with several RF-related enclosures, he offered: "I'm sorry Miss Clark has been roused to plague you, and I'm sorry if Mrs. Barndollar's false [!] claim has annoyed you; but I'm glad you've given Mr. Thornton permission to put a few pictures into *Recognition*. I hope he submits the Chronology [which Newdick had prepared] to you and Mrs. Frost for approval."

Another result of the eastern trip was a continuation of the correspondence with John Holmes, who wrote on September 20 a letter chiefly notable because it mentioned that some one had noticed at Bread Loaf the previous year that RF had signed the register: "Robert Frost, San Francisco, Cal." When he answered, early in November, Newdick was able, in addition to various Frost shop talk, to report that fate had dealt kindly with him in regard to classes, one of which had fifty students and the other seven. "It was good to talk with you in the sanctuary of your study," he recalled of the time he had spent with Holmes, "and I'm confident our common interests will be more than sufficient to keep us in touch with each other."

The month of October was featured by negotiations over a possible editing by Newdick of a book of Frost's prose, an enterprise to which previous mention has been made. The flame was fanned anew by a letter of October 7 from Howard F. Lowry, general editor of Oxford University Press. As Mrs. Newdick put it in writing to Mrs. Frost:

> Today, Bob received a letter from the Oxford Press, *asking* him to do a book on the "Prose of Robert Frost." He is in the seventh Heaven at being asked and what it would do for him professionally there is no telling. But—he won't even answer their letter till he hears Mr. Frost would approve. I'm hoping he will, for it means so much to Bob and of course I think he could do a book that would be a credit to both your Robert and mine.

The first thing Newdick did, on having the exciting invitation from Oxford, was to send a telegram to Holt, asking for a wire as to whether Holt had a contract for "any collection of Frost's prose." Thornton replied within a few hours that no such contract existed or was contemplated.

As he wrote to Lowry on November 8, "With Mr. Thornton's telegram in hand, I took counsel with two colleague friends and wrote Mr. Frost as follows [on October 8]:

> Dear Mr. Frost,
>
> I am in a quandary. This morning I received, unsolicited, a virtual invitation from the Oxford University Press to edit "a collection of Robert Frost's critical writing." There is nothing I would rather undertake, for, as you know, the Oxford Press would perform its part admirably on both sides of the Atlantic. And there is nothing I am better prepared to undertake, for, as I remember remarking to you at Concord Corners, I have all of the material collected, tentatively arranged, and ready for selection. However, being interested in all that concerns you, I happen to know that a similar project is at least being contemplated by Messrs. Thompson and Snow. In ordinary circumstances I would immediately inform the Oxford General Editor that I am all set to go ahead, not only because I proposed a collection of your prose to Mr. Thornton as early as May 24, 1935, and because I am loath again to be "scooped" as I was on the bibliography, but also because I am confident that there is room for more than one edition of a good book. But since several friendships are involved, I write first to you, asking whether you deem the way closed or open to me too.

He had, indeed, discussed the letter with two colleagues at Ohio State, Professors William R. Parker and Milton O. Percival. A completely revised first draft of an original letter prepared by Parker remains in Newdick's file.

The extent to which the excitement of his work on Frost, probably intensified by the recognition signified by the Oxford offer, gripped Newdick may be seen in this fragment, "for the Preface to the Frost biography," which Newdick timed at 7:30 A.M., 10–11–37:

> Jane Welsh Carlyle wrote in her *Journal* after Emerson's visit to Craigenputtock, "An angel hath passed this way." Many discerning moderns have written in theirs, after a visit from Robert Frost, "a god hath passed this way."

That I sympathize with the (point of) view of these latter will inevitably be apparent, I suppose, to those who read this book. Yet I have endeavored to write simply and forthrightly, not as if Frost were a god or even a demi-god, but, as he chooses to be, a poetically articulate New England farmer, and with, I trust, a dash of his own characteristic understatement and litotic pungency.

On that same day Frost sent a reply from Amherst about the matter of the book of prose:

Now you make me feel like a green apple you boys are determined to eat. I warned Snow and Thompson I wasn't ripe enough. But I suppose they as the first threat can claim an option on me. You have poor luck. Never mind, remember all the literature Dante got out of the Peach he couldn't have. I hate to be so hard on a friend. Needs must.

Frost's letter was not posted till the afternoon of October 13, perhaps suggesting that he, too, thought it dealt with a matter of unusual significance. Before Newdick received Frost's reply, he had done "a lot of hard thinking" and had written Thompson (on October 15) to say that he was "sorely tempted by this wholly unsolicited invitation" but intended to keep "the promise I virtually made" on November 28, 1936. He suggested Thompson "take the matter up from here."

The first paragraph of the Frost letter of October 11, from Amherst, had made reference to Mrs. Frost's being operated on for cancer:

We are just back from two weeks at the Springfield Hospital where Elinor underwent a serious operation for a "growth." We won't talk about it. We have good hopes. And sufficient to the moment is that she has recovered better than would have been expected with her heart as it is.

Newdick immediately wrote what he called "a man-to-man note in response to the personal news in his letter." His note, significantly, started "Dear Frost": "No, we won't talk about it, but man, you've got to let me clasp your hand across the miles to say our hearts and hopes are with you both."

When Newdick first replied to Lowry, on October 8, he was hopeful that the book he had long visualized might come to be.

By November 1 he considered the chances of the book to be remote and that he was out of the running. Doubtless about that time he received a letter of October 29, setting forth the idea that Frost should bring out the book himself: "Frost allowed as how his wife had brought up the same kind of point but said he doubted if he would ever get to it. He said we'd just let it slide." Thus Thompson thought any one who suggested such a book should be told that Frost was going to do it himself.

On the heels of that statement came one, on November 4, from Lowry to Newdick, stating that he was "determined to carry on." Newdick left Lowry to imagine his joy at this attitude. A good by-product of the jockeying related to this proposed book, which was not published till three decades later, is this paragraph of November 8, indicating to Lowry Newdick's assessment of his relationship to Frost:

My interests I leave confidently in your hands. But will I nill I, I must try to make clear the relations that obtain between Mr. Frost and me. We are warm personal friends: he has been my guest in my home, and a number of times I have been his guest in his home. He hates the words— —and the connotations of the words—"official" and "authorized," but he has given me permission to write his biography, has supplied me with significant notebooks, annotated first editions, manuscripts, etc.; he fills in divers kinds of questionaires for me; and when we are together talks hours on end of intimate personal matters. This in-process biography is the center of most of my research and writing in these my middle years, and nothing must be allowed to imperil it or the friendship which in part it rests upon. Therefore, when you come to the point of making a case for my participating in the editorial work on the book, do make it unmistakably clear that my first interest is the book itself.

In the letter, Newdick discusses Thompson with some distaste. He feels that Thompson has pretended to leave the matter in the hands of Frost while actually maintaining the project. Thompson's letters support Newdick's view that Thompson is persisting, outwardly as assistant to Frost, and casting Newdick as "assistant to the assistant." A letter and a postcard from Thompson in December documented his perseverance in research related to this book. As of November 8, Newdick was telling Lowry he hoped the publisher pursued and obtained the book. "If it works out that there is a place for me, well and good, but in any event get the book, confident that no editor can fail to make a good one out of such rich materials."

Newdick included in his letter of November 9 to Frost the following paragraph:

> Several days before I received your note disapproving of competition, I forwarded the Oxford University Press letter to Mr. Thompson with the suggestion that he take up the matter directly with Mr. Lowry. Mr. Thompson replied after your visit with him, but not quite clearly. If it be true that you are going to assemble your own prose (and that is of course precisely as it should be), I rejoice exceedingly in the prospect of the book! — But shall I not sigh the lack of many, many capital short bits that *you* will disdain to include?

In addition to mentioning correspondence with Lesley in Mexico and reference to the good thoughts being held for the health of Mrs. Frost, the letter also refers to a set of inquiry-enclosures that went with it. One of them was a tentative selection of the Frost items to be enclosed in a textbook being prepared by the head of Newdick's department. On a carbon of this list, Newdick made this note beside "Winter Ownership," an uncollected poem of thirteen lines: "Mr. Frost asked that 'Winter Ownership' be omitted because it needed some more looking over."

A very significant annotation stemmed from an enclosure in one of two letters Newdick dated November 21. The first letter is important for its evidence of his later study of the correspondence he had had with Frost. The letter begins with a request for Frost to look over an enclosed essay. The word essay is asterisked. At the bottom of the page, accompanied by the date, 7–4–38, is a note: "Probably 'RF and the Classics' tho' *possibly* 'The Prose of Robert Frost.'"

A longer letter has an ebullient paragraph of Newdick's plans for going to the Huntington Library in the second half of December as well as to gather impressions of the San Francisco where Frost was born. Subject to Frost's approval, he planned to see an old Frost friend, John Bartlett, in Boulder. "I'm biting off a lot for two weeks, but I'm confident I can chew it because it means so much to me."

Referring to the fact that *Recognition* had been seen by Frost, Newdick averred:

> I'm sure *Recognition* must please you as much as any book of homage has pleased you. I'm thinking not of the physical make up of the book, but of the fact that writer after writer has written of your poems with insight and affection born of gratitude for truth and beauty revealed. Every glance into the book confirms and deepens that impression.

The playfully-confident tone of the following passage suggests how surprised he must have been at the reaction it evoked:

> You'd be amused to know how successfully your allusion in "A Moment of Uncertain Lights" baffled even professional classical scholars (as likewise your allusion to a Greek poet who was a "garbage collector"). I've found the lights in the mythology of Memphis all right, but not in a Roman account as yet—and not in Herodotus to whom I turned on the chance. But don't tell me—
>
> That is, don't tell me *that*. But do please tell me whether the enclosed "Death Song of the Last American Indian" is a bit of your early writing.

The "Death Song . . ." was a poem of sixty-four lines and nine stanzas which Newdick had found in the Lawrence High School *Bulletin*. "Isn't this poem yours?" he wrote on the typescript to "Dear Mr. Frost." In the space at the bottom of the first page, Frost wrote on November 23: "Dear Newdick: No I didnt write this, nor does it seem at all like me. I am unaware of having taken up another person's jingle. You must be very careful in your ascriptions. R.F."

In the bottom right corner of the page, RF wrote "over" and marked it off with an angled line similar to the little box used in division problems. Worked up, apparently, he put considerable force into the P.S. at the end of the poem on the second page:

> And in the other ascriptions too. I feel the great danger of what you are trying to do with me. The word "deeply" for example in your last inquiry ["Can you recall what it

was that was so deeply engaging you then?" Newdick had asked, referring to 1897]. What books of Tacitus was I deeply studying. I never did anything deeply. 'Tis ever thus with the biographer: he will be making the most of everything. You are going to have me a classical scholar. You're one. You must be slow enough with your biography to get the real me through your head. No falsifications good or bad. Sorry I cant be dead and out of your way. Having the real me alive to deal with must make your task so very much harder. What green work all appreciation is. In the Recognition book you will read that I have no sense of humor, that I have a sense of humor, that I have no philosophy, that I have a philosophy. I am praised for having and not having both. Also I am blamed. Cheer up you can go no farther wrong than the best of them. Take your time though. The older you are the better you will understand my foolishness.

The end of the squall was a rather gentle rain. Appended to the annotatem was this evidence of security of employment in Frostian endeavor:

I enclose something for the Curator of MS. at the Huntington Library. Is that the way to address him and do I ask him for the right permission. If not send the letter back and I will write it to your order. My address will soon be General Delivery Gainesville Florida. I should be there by Dec 5 at latest.

The information about Frost's arrival in Gainesville allows the more accurate dating of this recollection of Professor-emeritus Clifford P. Lyons, Frost's long-time friend at the Department of English at the University of North Carolina:

I don't remember Frost saying much about Newdick. We both remember Mrs. Frost saying to Robert about Newdick: "Let's not tell him everything." This was in Gainesville, Fla., probably in the fall of '37. There we first got to know Robert and the family quite well. (Letter of February 2, 1975)

After his initials on the note about arriving in Gainesville, Frost ventured: "Perhaps I should use his name. I've forgotten it."

Newdick's reply of November 30 speaks for itself:

No, no, no, no, no, no, no! Having you alive to deal with
and being counted one among your friends is the central
privilege of these my middle years. Surely you know that:
surely I have not so well concealed the extent of my feelings (from thinking to know and endeavoring to respect
your distrust of anything in excess) as to suggest that I am
deficient in them, or that other than human values were
first. Doubtless you jested, but nevertheless I winced. Has
my zeal somehow annoyed you? I earnestly hope not, and
I try hard to control it.

It's inevitable that some in *Recognition* be out of focus;
a little, plain wrong. Your complexity as an artist will
baffle simplifiers and formula seekers for generations. But
even in wrong-headedness (and the margins of my working
copy of the book are already filling up with cons and queries) there is redeeming right-heartedness.

Yet I shall heed your injunction and be on guard against
wrong ascriptions of my own. Regarding you and the classics, perhaps you were objecting only to the "deeply" in
the set of questions; but if to the paper, I've simply written
clumsily if at the outset I've not suggested implicitly the
distinction between exact classical scholarship on the one
hand and your lifelong fondness for classical literature on
the other—fondness to some extent reflected in your
poems as very few other literary influences are at all reflected there. Regarding the biography, I shall do my utmost to get the real you, through fact and friendship, into
my head and the story. I have no other wish, and need not
have: there are no finger bones in that button box. [See
"The Witch of Coos," lines 151–2.]

Thank you for the letter to the curator at the Huntington: it meets the need exactly. I shall write you at once of
my findings. And perhaps I'll be plaguing you even before
that, for I believe I've spotted your columns of paragraphs
at last!

Marie joins me in wishing that this Florida winter be
entirely to your and Mrs. Frost's liking.

As usual, Newdick signed himself as "Ever yours."
As a further palliative to what he must have reflected was a

waspish reply to a most obedient and adoring servant, Robert Frost wrote Dear Newdick this note, which Newdick marked as of November 26:

> I forgot to say how confident you are of my infallability. Why dont you assume that I may be mistaken about Memphis? I wouldnt intend to be. I hate the definition of poetry that it is just mistakes—learned mistakes. Maybe I was thinking of Mt Ida. But if, as you say you have been able to connect the belief with Memphis, perhaps I shant be proved as wrong in the end as one who sets up to be no scholar and deserves to be.

After his signature, he wrote an appealing line: "Be sure to tell me how I come out."

The next day he wrote to Harold Rugg, the librarian at Dartmouth, who was asking for permission relating to a publication desired by the students. Noting that Newdick was about to examine this manuscript at the Huntington, he refers to the possibility that he will find "something better to preserve than that old thing." In addition to suggesting his confidence in Newdick's capacity to deal with the material, he added the comment that, though he thought there was little in the Huntington file, "there is one about Boston Common on a rainy fall day I might still approve of a little" ["Clear and Colder. Boston Common"].

The hectic correspondence with Frost was accompanied by a group of significant related developments. In July, Newdick had initiated correspondence with Carl Burell, then a resident of Manchester, N.H. who had known Frost as a high school student and had lived at the Derry Farm with the Frosts. All discussion of Burell suggests him to have been a most individualistic person. The seven letters which Newdick received from him contain comments on Frost which intimate how much the informer could tell. He says he is not in the mood to devote himself to giving an account of Frost, because he had sent information to Professor Edna Romig of Boulder, Colorado, and that she was then kept from using it. An example of what he did not say is found in this letter of August 8: "I first met RL FROST in school in 1887 and kept touch with him quite closely till after his return from ENGLAND but IT would be too long a story for me to write now (AS YOU CAN SEE) and would not want to attempt it unless I could know what limitations were placed upon you [.] WITH the begining of his success I began to loose

[sic] touch with him but I have only the most sincere good will toward him [,] but knowing all that I do from first to last and of course knowing his (AND MRS. FROST'S) secretive spots I could not say or do much without his direct request [.]"

When Newdick tried to include a call on Burell in his eastern trip, he found his quarry agreeable enough, but showing trepidation about being away (September 2 to 5) and being unable to entertain guests. Discussing the matter with Frost, Newdick decided to postpone a call on the 73-year-old man. Newdick went along with Frost's idea that he should not go directly from Frost to Burell, the suggestion of undefined emotionalities, possibly relating to the idea that Frost had left Burell behind when he got famous, being presented. The correspondence strongly suggests that Burell had a personality in which Frost could not have been expected to take great satisfaction.

In a letter of September 20, Burell wrote that he would want a subject of a biography to be dead a hundred or a thousand years: "I know only too well what the public wants and will exspect, most of which is not at all practical or expediant to use." Then he continued:

Now for the facts[.] I do not know of a blessed thing in the 15 or more years I knew ROB FROST quite intimately, of which he has any reason to be ashamed in any way or which I suspect he would personally object to being use[d] discretely BUT as I do know his family would object to any use of it whatever [.] ALTHOUGH FROST and I were very good and very real friends we were very different in many ways[.]

In remarks which can only refer to the role played by Elinor Frost in her husband's relationship to the problem, Burell wrote further:

My experience with the woman in Coldado [Prof. Romig of Boulder, Colorado] showed me that FROST (and as of course I know) his family are over sensitive along most lines and I fear your task to give satisfaction will [be] a mighty hard task [.] YOUR greatest accomplishment will be NOT WHAT TO SAY but WHAT NOT TO SAY and under that condition you have a hard job indeed to give a comprehensive history [.] FROST has a fine sense of humor, even if he does at times take himself a little too

seriously [,] but I fear you will find little humor among
the rest of the family.

I am telling you these things in ABSOLUTE CONFI-
DENCE because I wish you well and want to help you.

And help he did, for on November 15 Newdick was writing
him to say that his six volumes of the Lawrence High School
Bulletin, including the period when Frost was a student, had
arrived in his hands. What Newdick was able to learn from them
made an excellent contribution to his knowledge of Frost. The
volumes were not otherwise available.

Newdick was able to suggest, on November 30, that he had
"spotted" Frost's Lawrence newspaper column because of Dr.
Burnham. Burnham had found a column with the appropriate
heading, "The American About and Abroad," published from
December 14, 1894, to October 12, 1897. He sent on November
30 a four-page, long-hand letter about his findings. Listing an
article of April 6, 1895, as the "coal item," the one which
seemed to fit Frost's memory of women picking up coal along
the railroad tracks, mentioning that none of the articles was
signed, he wondered if Newdick thought he had found the right
column. Newdick replied that a first step would be to see if Frost
"confessed" the column.

On December 6, Dr. Burnham copied and sent to Newdick
six pages of sample items from the column. On December 9,
Newdick reviewed for Dr. Burnham the information he had
originally given him about the coal pickers and the eagle. The
work Dr. Burnham was doing was on his mind for, "just east of
Ogden, Utah" on December 26, he sent a note cautioning him
not to let Thompson, who had told Newdick he was going to be
in Lawrence at Christmas, know "where *we've* been looking."
A letter of December 29 reassured Newdick about any breach of
security but also informed him that the article thought to be
about the coal pickers just was not there. Also, no article about
the court house eagle was to be found. "In considering the above
circumstances I hope my efforts have not proved a 'dud'," he
concluded.

As December began, Newdick received a very complimentary
response, by Professor George Whicher, Frost's colleague at
Amherst and a noted scholar, telling him of the "great interest
and value" of his work, as exemplified by "Robert Frost and the

Sound of Sense": "In this paper especially I think you come near
the heart of his 'mysterium'." In his reply of December 7, Newdick mentioned both his mission at the Huntington Library and
the fact that he was trying to find the articles Frost had contributed to farm journals in the Derry years.

Whicher wrote on December 10 to say he could not offer any
clues as to which publications might be involved. "All I recall
is his story about the perching geese, which you have, and his
expressing the pious hope that these contributions would never
be disinterred." (The articles were collected and published in
Lathem and Thompson's *Robert Frost: Poultryman*, Hanover,
1963.)

He also retailed his own recollections of Frostian fulmina-
tions against two manuscript poems in the Huntington wrongly
attributed to him. He facetiously but significantly suggested a
kind of martyrdom for Newdick in tearing up the offending
poems when he got access to them. After that, Whicher dryly
pointed out, Frost would have to grant all Newdick's requests,
after he got out of jail. More seriously, he suggested that Newdick could denounce the wrongly attributed poems.

On December 1, too, Newdick had a letter from Frost's friend
of many years, Ernest L. Silver, president of the State Normal
School of Plymouth, New Hampshire. In thanking Newdick for
his copy of "Robert Frost and the Sound of Sense," he made this
cogent remark: "I remember how Robert Frost would chuckle
as he recalled and repeated expressions he had heard and cherished."

When he had talked with Silver at Plymouth on September
4, he had taken some valuable notes. Silver had Frost books with
inscriptions. One was "To Ernest Silver / Teacher from Robert
Frost / Teacher." Another thanked Silver for teaching Frost
"how to teach." Silver recalled Frost taught ancient history by
means of coins. This reminded Newdick that Frost had mentioned teaching the subject "by illustrations." Silver recalled
that once, when Silver was away, Frost read the students
Twain's "The Celebrated Jumping Frog of Calaveras County"
"as a parable on teaching." Silver quoted Frost as believing that
the way to get a child to read a good book was to leave it lying on
a table. He also mentioned that Frost was "excellent with good
students, by encouraging them by recalling, say at the end of a
walk, a *good* bit and *praising* it."

Having arrived in Gainesville and thinking of Newdick's trip to examine his manuscript at the Huntington Library, Frost wrote on December 14:

I must write you a word of reassurance before you set out on your errand of mercy in far California. I dont want to trouble you too much about your thoughts of me, but I want to trouble you enough to make them long long thoughts. You mustnt let your partisanship hasten you to heroic conclusions. Slow slow. Your use of the word deep scared me. You must be religiously careful not to make me anything but what I am. Of course I know you are resolved on that. But permit me to caution you.

People speak well of the articles you have published about me; I must get my impressions from them since I am so bad about reading my own appraisals. The great test is going to be your handling passim, my literary quality. You can see what a confusion writers make of it in my Recognition. How without seeming to notice it are you going to bring order out of chaos? I am unfortunately without a sense of humor. I am fortunately without one. I fortunately have one. I haven't heard enough to be very sure some one hasnt furnished the fourth corner of the square by saying unfortunately I have one. So, I am told, it is with my having a philosophy. I have one and I havent one fortunately and unfortunately. There are other conflicts less obvious but perhaps more important than these. You must give yourself time to make up your mind about me. Ultimately you ought to be in a position to write a final chapter on me as literature-poetry-that you use beforehand in one of the big popular magazines such as The Atlantic or Harpers. In the end you must stand on your own contribution to the setting of my work right with the world. I dont need to tell you that. You probably know me and my work better than anyone outside my family. You are so much the more under obligation to give me a fresh reading that will show a better understanding than any one else. All right. I wont harp on this. I say it this once and then no more. I look on all or a lot of the flimsy scantling you have got together as useful for the scaffolding of your structure. Some of the details anyway are only valuable as they help you to the main idea. Never

mind if the figure got mixed. I cant rewrite letters of this
length. I used to make it a rule to rewrite absolutely everything with which I saw anything the matter.

Good luck on your errand.

Remember us to the folks. I told you didnt I that Elinor
had been very ill in the hospital? She had a dreadful operation for a growth that makes life seem far along and
sadder. She is down here now with four grandchildren and
enjoying them. Will be sending you a Christmas rhyme-
sheet from the Spiral Press—with the same poem the Saturday Review carries for Christmas.

The remarkable and heartening letter was signed "Sincerely
yours."

When he wrote his first report from Los Angeles on December
21, Newdick had not received the letter just quoted. However,
his account for "Dear Mr. Frost" was just as energized as though
he had the document before him:

> You must have given them a pretty good going over at
> the Huntington when you were here [1932]. They are still
> talking about it. As with a Scottish ballad, there are half a
> dozen various accounts, with certain common denom-
> inators constant.
>
> In your letter of September 20 you spoke of just *one*
> poem ("I had a love once") as erroneously ascribed to you.
> Aren't there *two*, the other one being "Sea Dream"? Surely
> if one must go, both must go, for they are written in the
> same hand on the same kind of paper. Surely both are un-
> like you, even as you were in the early 'nineties,—in both
> substance and style. Librarians, however, are hard nuts to
> crack, and I fear any considerations of substance and style
> are beyond them.

Newdick canvassed such factors as paper and handwriting as
bases for making determination concerning the poems. He
noted that the two poems in question were referred to at the
library as "Frost Apocrypha" and that notations on the blue
folders containing the poems had been changed. He promised
corrected checklists by the end of January.

He closed by telling how he felt about the larger venture of
which the trip was a part:

I can't tell you how grateful I am that you've let me work in these materials. It is as if, like a god, you had antedated our friendship, and had let me, at a distance, glimpse you by "flashes" (charge *that* to Hollywood influence) from time to time through the years. It was not written in my stars that I be an artist; yet I pray, earnestly and humbly, that I may write as a scholar with some measure of an artist's sensitiveness and penetrating truth.

He concluded by wishing both Frosts best wishes "for the holidays and all the other days." (Frost's response on December 28 has not been released by the Barrett Collection at the University of Virginia.)

Newdick's first letter to Frost of 1938, written on January 3, consisted of copies of "I had a love once" and "Sea Dream" of the Huntington Collection, accompanied by a note: "Are not *both* of these poems spurious? I hope you say they are, because it will be much easier for me to make a convincing case against both then against the first one alone."

Frost had already written to Newdick at the Huntington a letter which caught up with him after he returned to Columbus:

It is of course preposterous to ascribe either Sea Dreams or I Had a Love Once to me. They are not in my handwriting, they are not in my wife's handwriting, I didnt sign them, she didnt sign them and I deny having written them. That ought to be enough for gentlemen though scholars. You know how to talk their technical language to these specialists and I miss my guess it you dont get them to throw the two damed [sic] spuriosa out of the Huntington Library or at least separate the two from the poems undeniably and admittedly mine. You may be sure I am grateful to you for what you are doing to clear the nuisance up.

You can't tell what might happen in a house like the Wards' where the editor and his two spinster sisters were all sentimental about poems and poets for the *Independent*: but my guess is the two sisters took turns in taking possession of the manuscript spoils from the office and when there was something so good (in their opinion) they both wanted it, one kept the original and the other made a copy. They may have been careless about the authors names and written some in later even years later from memory when the authors got famous or something and they wanted to find he was as well represented (and as romantically) as possible in their collection. But I spare you my ingenuities. The fact is that I didnt write the poems and you are in a fair way to establish it.

I wonder if either of the poems ever appeared in print in the *Independent*. That might be amusing to look into. I cant help you much with dates. The range of the poems you name is over more than twenty years, I think. The one about the Moth in Winter was written at Plymouth N.H. in 1911 or 1912. Twenty years of a weekly magazine means ten hundred and fifty copies to search through for one or two small poems. I doubt if they indexed such stuff. To find either printed as by some one else would be a fine blow to Huntington pride.

On January 5 Newdick reported his receipt of Frost's "heartening letter" of December 14. He told Frost, as he wrote also to Holmes, that he had "read and reread it until it's nearly frayed!" He was moved to describe to his subject his plan of campaign in writing about him:

> . . . yet one thing I would say, lest anyone deem my papers thus far to be a fair measure of my whole plan and purpose. With the fundamental matters most annoyingly confused in *Recognition* I'm eager to come to grips,—your encompassing sense of humor, your rock-sound philosophy, your unrivalled literary quality,—all of which have meant so much to me from the beginning, all of which grow steadily upon me as I live with them intimately. But from a sense of the responsibility of my loyalty, and not from any other consideration, I have steadily restrained myself so far and built soil; or, to vary the figure, I have been content, while my forces and force increase, to try to take one outpost after another, providing each one seemed to me to constitute an advance and to lie closer to the main objective. Much if not most of my accumulations of matériel I agree to be valuable only incidentally: the true central concerns are scrupulous accuracy, just proportion, and appreciative penetration.

Also, he noted his pleasure in finding the Frost Christmas greeting "delightful as a booklet, splendid as a Christmas poem." As a longhand postscript, he offered, "When I read Er-

nest Haycox' 'A Day in Town' on the train it struck me as un-
commonly good, and I venture to enclose it for Mrs. Frost."

Two days later Newdick was answering the "letter to me at
the Huntington" just quoted:

> I share your indignation in the ascription of these two
> poems to you. I'd like to cuss out the Library officials for
> their not having removed them from the canon on your
> protest in 1932, and to pillory them for their picayunish-
> ness in general. . . . I am prepared to keep hammering at
> them, and shall reinforce every point already made. They
> cannot be trusted, for example, to look into the signifi-
> cance of the paper size, texture, watermarks; but I have
> data in minute detail now and shall present it in a follow-
> up letter.

The same was true of handwriting data. He promised to "prose-
cute thoroughly."

Newdick responded enthusiastically, even conspiratorially,
to Frost's imaginings concerning the possible handling of the
spurious manuscripts by the Ward family:

> And now you strengthen my drive both by the sugges-
> tions concerning the Ward household and by the sugges-
> tion that possibly one or both of the poems appeared in the
> *Independent*. That last is a capital idea! The search will
> take me no more than a couple of weeks, and it will give
> my soul new life to plant *such* a bomb under Bliss and
> Haselden. Under assumed initials, too, and asking with
> guardedness, I can also try the N.Y. Times notes and
> queries' department, and others too.
>
> I must not and will not fail in this opportunity, and you
> know how grateful I am for your encouragement.

During this period, the correspondence between Newdick
and Holmes flourished, several long letters passing in January
alone. In mentioning a noted and controversial review of *Recognition* in the *Saturday Review* for January 1, 1938, Newdick referred to the "same old exaggerating, magnifying, minimizing
[Bernard] DeVoto," thinking of him as "a refreshing influence
in contemporary criticism." He made an even more significant
reference to the book:

> About [Frost] and the book: It should not get out that he
> had any part in it. I was a bit disappointed that he wished

to. The only explanation I can suggest is that he was fearful that no editor could as successfully ignore his enemies as he could. As to the title, I share your feeling that it isn't quite right; but it was his; and that was that.

He also placed his trip to the Huntington in perspective:

You ask whether the California trip wasn't the more important of my Frost-aimed travels to date. Honestly, I don't think so. I think the three summer sallies into New England to be far more important. All I needed at the Huntington I could have obtained by mail, *if* it hadn't been imperative that I examine the paper, etc., of two of the MSS.: the permission granted me by RF on a nearly three-year-old petition was on the condition that the examination would be direct so far as those two MSS. were concerned, — and no MS. may ever leave the Huntington! — But the firsthand impressions of the topography of San Francisco, etc., will be valuable. Now I must figure out a way to get to England again for a few months, to go over the Frost trails there.

As he waited for Newdick's list of the poems at Huntington, Frost had not forgotten he was to see if they included "anything of mine your young pressmen could use for a special edition" (letter to Rugg at Dartmouth, January 14, 1837). A full reaction to the list he received was written on January 18:

The only poems in your list I should care to see are Clear and Colder, Genealogical, Poem incomplete, and To a Moth Seen in Winter. I wonder if the Dartmouth boys under Harold Goddard Rugg could be free to make a booklet of those with nobodys permission but mine. I have a faintly pleasant recollection of at least two, Clear and Colder and To a Moth Seen in Winter. The last is in blank verse isn't it? [Yes] Or is it in rhymed couplets? I made it walking down a foggy icy mountain one thaw in March the year we were at Plymouth. Not everything is as easy to date as that. I wonder which version of a Black Cottage you found out there. I did two versions, in and around 1905–6, one in rhyme which I lost on purpose as a failure and the other that came down with some changes into North of Boston. [The poem in the Huntington consists of eight eight-line stanzas, containing just half as many lines

as the poem in North of Boston. The two poems are different
in every respect but subject.] The date 1914 for it is ridiculous. It was not in book form in May 1914. My head begins
to swim in this confusion of dates. Pretty soon I shan't be
able to remember definitely when I wrote anything. As a
matter of fact, a number of my poems could have three or
four dates apiece on them. Reluctance except for one very
important change (which wouldn't you like to know!) is a
very old poem. Most of your list is recognizable through
the disguise of tentative titles. What's a Summer's Garden? [Several words scribbled out] A Girl's Garden? Then
1897 is a funny date for it[.]

Newdick's response to these comments was written on January 23. He enclosed copies of all the poems Frost mentioned
and included his opinion that Frost could authorize the Dartmouth students as he wished. He made these observations on
the poems:

> The piece listed "Poem—incomplete" is the second
> page of a late draft of In a Vale. A Summer's Garden is
> doubtless very early, and the MS. was written or copied in
> the mid-nineties, when your handwriting was somewhat
> angular and strictly vertical, with very heavy down-
> strokes.
> Both Clear and Colder and The Black Cottage are in
> abandoned versions. I know all such things are beyond me,
> but nevertheless I wish we could have what we have—and
> these poems too. Yet To a Moth Seen in Winter will be the
> Mt. Everest of the booklet.

On January 21, Newdick prepared a "Work Sheet" of all the
projects he was working on. He noted "Robert Frost and New
Hampshire" had been accepted by the New Hampshire State
Federation of Women's Clubs, "Robert Frost Looks at War" by
The South Atlantic Quarterly, and "Robert Frost and the Clas-
sics" by *The Classical Journal*. Typed under "In Prospect and
Preparation" were: *Robert Frost: A Biography*, *Robert Frost:
A Bio. Bibliography*, Robert Frost and Edward Thomas, Robert
Frost as a Newspaperman, Women in the Poems of Robert Frost,
The Heavens in the Poems of RF, The Influence of Robert Frost
on Recent and Contemporary Poetry, Poets' Tributes to Robert
Frost, The Philosophy of Robert Frost, The Humor of Robert

Frost, Robert Frost and the Bible, Robert Frost as a Critic, Illustrations and Illustrators of Robert Frost's Poems, Translations of Robert Frost's Poems, Robert Frost's "Occasional" Verse, The Ars Poetica of Robert Frost. Crossed out were Robert Frost and Free Verse and The Prosody of Robert Frost (in *Complete Poems* and *A Further Range*). He listed twenty-four other articles under Ridgely Torrence, Archibald MacLeish, Ohio, and Miscellaneous.

This period of taking stock, perhaps a time of gathering strength for a new burst of effort on the biography, has been assumed as a time when he probably prepared a longhand list of *Points that Must be Passed Over*:

1. Extreme sensitiveness to criticism, e.g. Hutchinson

2. Remembers old wrong, e.g. Silver.

3. No ear for music, except that he likes ballads, per contra, excellent remark in *The Professor's Wife* [by Bravig Imbs].

4. Not interested in (or capable of) music of the Swinburnian, or even the better Shelleyan sort.

5. Intolerant of the new currents, trends, movements, experiments, etc., in poetry, e.g. Eliot, MacLeish, et.al. and note introduction to *King Jasper*.

6. Negligent of correspondence, e.g. Edw. Garnett, e.g. etc.

7. Unusual closeness of union with wife, Elinor.

8. Children disappointing.

The existence of such a list is, on the one hand, surprising, as it does not fit Newdick's other statements about his ambition to be accurate and truthful. It is surprising in another way, in that it does not list factors covered in this account. Finally, perhaps its main value is that it is attestation of the fact that, consciously or unconsciously, Newdick intended to be a Frost partisan rather than an objective observer.

A letter which Newdick wrote to Mrs. Frost on February 4 but did not send shows his assessment of the importance of her role in the life of her husband. *South Atlantic Quarterly* had just indicated acceptance of "Robert Frost Looks at War." "I'm fairly sure of my ground," Newdick wrote, "for Mr. Frost verified my conclusions in conversation last summer at Concord Corner, but if anything in it could annoy Mr. Frost in the least, won't you please tell me of it?" After a chatty paragraph about John Crowe Ransom and Robert P. Tristram Coffin being at Ohio State, he concluded with, "We often think and speak of you, recalling our happy visit with you last summer, and hoping that the winter in Gainesville is mild and that all goes well with you." He seems not to have had any idea of *his* nearness to death. No reason is given with his notation, "NOT SENT."

During February the correspondence between Newdick and Holmes flourished. Following a suggestion from Frost, Newdick was trying to get a general article on the poet in the *Atlantic Monthly*. Holmes, who knew Weeks, the acting editor, was willing to help. His letter of February 15 contained a page-by-page critique of "Robert Frost's Other Harmony," which was published posthumously in *The Sewanee Review*. The only real Frost note in the letters stems from a bit of ribaldry on the part of Holmes, who quoted a parody of "On First Looking into Chapman's Homer." Approving the Rabelaisian element, Newdick quoted lines on "The sexual desires of the camel." Then he added: "Which reminds me: Have you ever heard Frost cut loose?"

In the middle of February Newdick received a letter from the librarian at Pinkerton Academy. She had been looking for a prose historical sketch of the Academy written by Frost, but she found instead "The Later Minstrel" as published in *The Pinkerton Critic* for March, 1907. The same poem she found to have appeared in *The Derry News* for March 1. The attribution to Frost is definite in each case. When Newdick wrote his thanks about the poem, he added, "though for some reason Mr. Frost cannot remember writing it."

Also during February, in an exchange of letters with Thornton of Holt, Newdick explored the matter of publication of his Frost biography by Holt, noting, "I have not discussed this matter with Mr. Frost in any way whatever." His first letter, on February 12, asks whether Holt thinks it would be better for another house to publish the biography. He mentions a bid from Oxford University Press but says that both he and Oxford want Holt's interest and cooperation. Thornton indicated, in reply, that Holt had assumed Newdick would submit his book there. Additionally, he mentioned knowing that Frost wanted publication of a

THE PINKERTON CRITIC.   13

could not help flying to the big elm tree, for the noise sounded like a gun, and I thought that some one had broken the unwritten treaty between me and the scholars; but I soon found, much to my gratification, that it was only "Ted" and "Stubb;" who had mixed up some kind of mess that they did not know anything about and that had exploded. By the looks of "Stubby's" eye you would think that "Banquo" had been trying to get some revenge for getting killed so many times.

Instead of Mr. Dickey, Mr. Hill of Derry takes possession of the Music rooms now. I guess the scholars hated to lose Mr. Dickey, but they seem to like Mr. Hill, so I guess it is all right. Anyway I continue to hear very musical sounds coming from the old Academy.

On Lincoln's Birthday one hour was given up from the ordinary course of lessons, and Mr. Bingham read a fine story entitled "A True Tribute." It was of recent publication and it was very interesting.

There was also a very interesting observance of the same kind on Longfellow's Birthday. Several of the scholars took part; Mr. Sefton sang a poem of Longfellow's, which began with "I shot an arrow into the air." Mr. Frost wrote a poem for the occasion; it was very good and I am sorry that I cannot remember all of it, but I think you may find it printed in another part of the "CRITIC" if you wish to read it.

Some of the Chester pupils had a good chance to find out who their true friends were the other day, for the track was drifted so badly that the car could not get back at night and they had to find hospitality in Derry.

I had a visit the other day from one of my cousins who lives in Hood's large grove right behind Marion Blood's house. He told me that one Friday night recently a number of young people came to her house and passed a pleasant evening. As he said they were very quiet and orderly and that Miss Clark was there, I knew that they were Seniors.

When good weather comes again and the boys get out practising base ball and training for the track I shall have a lot to tell you, for all I shall have to do will be to go and watch them and listen to their conversation, especially to "Blondy's" bright remarks.

Good-by now, but remember that the next time you hear my voice it will be the welcome Caw! Caw! Caw! of spring.

The Later Minstrel
Robert L. Frost

Remember some departed day,
  When bathed in autumn gold,
You wished for some sweet song, and sighed
  For minstrel days of old.

And that same golden autumn day,
  Perhaps the fates would bring
At eve, one knocking at your heart,
  With perfect songs to sing.

You knew that never bard on earth,
  Did wander wide as he --
Who sang the long, long thoughts of Youth,
  The Secret of the Sea.

You knew not when he might not come,
  But while he made delays,
You wronged the wisdom that you had,
  And sighed for vanished days.

Song's times and seasons are its own,
  Its ways past finding out,
But more and more it fills the earth,
  And triumphs over doubt.

FIG. 4. *March, 1907, Issue of* The Pinkerton Critic.

biography "delayed a while longer": "I should not like to incur his displeasure by bringing it out earlier than he thinks wise."

Newdick welcomed the expression of interest of the part of Holt. He pointed out that he had been "sketching out" chapters for over a year, and had recently been rewriting chapters as well as starting new ones. He felt he was "not far from the home stretch." "I plan now to have the manuscript prepared by the autumn of next year, perhaps in time for the Christmas season, certainly in time for the spring lists of 1940." He acknowledged that Frost had indicated he wanted Newdick to "make haste slowly"; then he suggested "five or six years' concentrated work" did not constitute "haste." "Of course, like you, I shall be guided by his wishes in the matter—even, if he should bid me, to holding the book till he is gone."

Then he pointed out that his professional position would be strengthened by having a definite contract for the book: "Since you do wish it for your list, it shall be yours. . . ." In response, thanking Newdick for his "clearer idea" of anticipated publication, Thornton said he felt "very sure" that Frost did not want any more books done on him for "a couple of years or more." He expressed a desire to sound out Frost when he returned from Florida late in March. He mentioned the possibility that Frost might want another company to "promote his reputation." He understood Newdick's wanting to get the matter settled but counseled him not to worry. "I could find you a half dozen publishers who would take it."

However, a statement on this subject in a letter from Frost to Thornton, postmarked February 23, indicated Thornton must have raised the question:

> I am in a hard place about the Newdick biography. I like Newdick and I am sure he means me the best. I could wish though he were going to be five or ten years later with his biography. I should like to be out of the way or almost out of the way. I have blown hot and cold with him. I think I should feel better if it didn't come from the same source as my own books. And I hope I have still a year or so of grace. Surely he can't be ready quite yet. But if you dont want the book too much please let it go to the Oxford Press. Mind you I don't disapprove of the book. It's probably very well done. The chapters from it that have been published [sic] have been praised by my friends. But I have

had about all the notice I can bear lately—since my Recognition came out. How lucky I should feel if I could be left to self-forgetfulness for a while.

On March 18, the afternoon of a Friday, Mrs. Frost suffered a heart attack. Because the ailment was a chronic one for her, and the experience of such an attack was not new, no sense of crisis was felt immediately. After seven more attacks during the weekend, she stopped breathing on Sunday afternoon, March 20.

Though Frost was physically ill with a cold, threatening pneumonia, and therefore ordered to go to bed and stay there for some time, as well as emotionally distraught, the following telegram, timed at 10:13 p.m., March 22, signed "Robert Frost," was addressed to Newdick at "Ohio State University": YOU HAVE HEARD WHAT HAPPENED MUST SEE YOU SOON IN AMHERST. Only Frost would have worded the message, even if it were sent by one of the family. Also, only he would have thought of being in Amherst soon.

Newdick's response to the news of Mrs. Frost's death was to start for New York, to which Mrs. Newdick forwarded the telegram. Not realizing that Frost was incapacitated, he assumed he would meet him in New York "and to go on with him from there to the services in Amherst and the scattering of the ashes in Derry."

Newdick sent the following telegram to Frost from New York on March 23:

NEWS OF MRS. FROST'S PASSING IN MONDAY'S PAPERS AND
MELCHER'S TELEGRAM PROFOUNDLY SHOCKED AND GRIEVED
US. I CAME TO NEW YORK IMMEDIATELY TO MEET UP WITH
YOU HERE AND GO ON WITH YOU IF YOU WOULD HAVE ME.
THIS MORNING MARIE FORWARDED TO ME YOUR TELEGRAM.
AM WAITING WITH RIDGELY AND OLIVIA TORRENCE . . . IN
READINESS TO RESPOND TO YOUR WILL IN EVERY POSSIBLE
WAY YOURS IN DEEPEST SYMPATHY AND AFFECTION.

The next morning he had a reply from Lesley that her father was sufficiently ill as to make delay of the trip advisable, and that the service in Amherst would be delayed in the interest of keeping him in Florida for a few weeks. She added her assurance that Frost wished to see Newdick, hoping he would be able to make the later trip for the funeral service.

He replied the same day: WILL BE GLAD TO COME TO AMHERST WHENEVER ROBERT WISHES, AND WILL GLADLY COME TO HIM IMMEDIATELY AT GAINESVILLE IF HE WISHES THAT. OUR HEARTS' LOVE TO YOU ALL.

The next day he heard from Lesley that his willingness to make the trip was appreciated but that her father was sufficiently exhausted as to cause need for rest to be preeminent. Alluding to her own sense of confusion, she apologized for a possible delay in sending the telegram and then added a query as to whether she had already sent a previous one. Thus the central purpose of Newdick's dash to New York was in vain, but, as he wrote to Dr. Burnham, "my hope is that Frost will understand from my action more than I was able to find words for in a letter of condolence. . . ."

When he had returned to Columbus, on March 27, Newdick did write this letter of condolence:

Dear Robert Frost,

I've begun this letter twenty times. I want to say everything at once, like a cloudburst, but there seems no power or comfort or use in words when the heart aches so. It was Monday noon before I heard, and knew that ache, and knew what yours must be. Within a few hours I was on what I thought was the quickest and surest way to you— on the way to New York—to stand by you or go with you as you might will for a moment or a week. Then but for Lesley's counsel otherwise I would have come down to you at Gainesville. Now I have come back home, here to wait your word to come to Amherst.

I truly loved Mrs. Frost. I had followed through her life as I have followed yours, and long long ago I perceived the unutterable closeness of the intertwining of those strands. In that closeness I saw with joy a realization of the ideal most dear to me in my own life. Then when it was my privilege to know Mrs. Frost I found her to be all I had been sure she was—quiet, strong, understanding, kind, and gentle. It is a simple fact that her passing is a profound loss to me, but I know with gratitude that she will always live for me as do my own mother and father in mind and heart steadfastly refusing the finality of separation and daily recreating the vital presence.

To you there cannot yet be any words to mitigate the

shock, the grief, the bleak lostness; but man, for what it's
worth, here's the handclasp of friendship and a full heart
of affection.

To Lesley he wrote the next day:

> My heart goes out to you, for I know from my own ex-
> perience something of the double pain you are suffering—
> your own grief in the loss of your mother and at the same
> time the pain of seeing your father suffer in his grief. If
> there were only something I could *do* for you all instead
> of *say*! That was what prompted both my dashing to New
> York, there to join you, and my wish to come down to
> Gainesville. Command me by a nod if there is anything
> you would have me do from here. To you, our deepest
> sympathy and love.

An undated note, probably of March 27, to John Holmes is
valuable for its less emotional reiteration of his assessment of
the impact of Mrs. Frost's death on RF and of her character:

> It is a fearful blow, one I think Frost will not recover
> from, even were all the world to rally to him. There was
> iron, nay, steel in her character, Heaven knows; yet in-
> finite patience and understanding and kindness; and he
> leaned upon her for more than he could possibly have
> realized. My heart aches for him.

And, some time in this period, Marie Newdick wrote to Robert
Frost, expressing her love for Elinor Frost, assuring him of her
sympathy, and reminding him that "our home is always waiting
for you."

Ten days later, on April 6, Newdick wrote Holmes: "No
word from RF. I wish to heaven I knew what one could write
that might succeed in diverting him, for however brief a moment. If you hear anything from him or about him, do let me
know too." In a letter of April 1, he included this line: "The
loss will hasten Frost's own death, I fear, for he was unbeliev-
ably dependent upon his wife." This was, it will be recalled,
one of the factors relating to Frost which must be "passed
over."

His preoccupation with RF's status bid him to write Lesley
two days later:

> The manifold responsibilities you are now called upon
> to meet, I think I have some notion of. Yet I dare beg some
> line from you about your father. Still fearful that any letter
> may be more bothersome than otherwise, I put down im-
> pulse after impulse to write him, though I have in mind
> no questions but simply news of all sorts. Do tell me when
> you think I may write him again.

Too, he sent the manuscript of "Robert Frost's Other Harmony"
to read. "If you approve of it, you need not bother to say so: but
if you would have me say anything differently, or not at all, do
speak of it. I know your father does not care to read such papers,
but your mother used to pass upon them generously for me,
and I have been hoping that you would now."

Lesley's response, postmarked April 15, confirmed Newdick's idea of RF's status, telling him the whole family was
stunned and his father especially. She informed him that the
service for her mother in Amherst would be on April 20, that he
was invited, that he could, however, delay his visit, if considerations prevented his being there, because her father would be
staying on at Amherst and would be "thankful" to see him
when it became practicable. She described her father as not being capable of correspondence but urged Newdick to write as
often as he wished, for she felt seeing and hearing from people
would help with her father's situation. She closed by expressing
her appreciation for his efforts in the past and present.

As might be expected, Newdick replied as follows:

> I shall certainly be with you at the services Friday after-
> noon, and I have made all arrangements here to stay in
> Amherst a few days. My deep gratitude for your letter,
> but the time is so short I shall not try to write to Robert
> before I see him.
> Our hearts are with you to the uttermost.

No doubt, he was intensely gratified to have a telegram from
Frost on April 21:

IF YOU WERE COMING ANYWAY FOR SERVICES TOMORROW
WISH YOU MIGHT ACT AS ONE OF HONORARY BEARERS.

His reply:

YOUR WISH AN HONOR WHICH I ACCEPT GRATEFULLY.

He had, of course, already received the printed invitation: "Funeral services for Elinor Frost will be held at Johnson Chapel, Amherst College, Amherst, Massachusetts, at three o'clock in the afternoon of Friday, April the twenty-second."

While he was in Amherst for Mrs. Frost's funeral, Newdick took copious notes, which are in Item 21, Part III. He also took notes on Frost's revisions in proof of *Collected Poems* (1930). They are on nineteen pages of paper 3⅜ by 5⅝ inches in size.

As he had suggested the pictures of the Frost home in Amherst to Lesley, before he left for home, Newdick wrote to President Stanley King of Amherst College on behalf of the idea of purchase of the Derry Farm to keep it out of the hands of exploiters or ignorant desecrators; "Imagine, if you can, the Derry Farm house of Robert Frost turned into some vulgar tourists' 'home' or antique 'shoppe'." President King responded in a letter of the next day, April 25, calling the idea interesting and saying he hoped to have an opportunity to discuss it with "Robert." Perhaps the two of them would be able to think of a feasible program. (The idea became a reality approximately three decades later.) On May 1 Newdick wrote to "ask only that when you do talk over the matter with Mr. Frost, you make no mention of me. My interest, though entirely unselfish, might possibly be mistaken as meddling."

Before he left for Amherst, Newdick wrote Holmes that he presumed he would see him at the funeral service. After he returned home, he wrote to express his disappointment at not seeing him. Frost, too, noticed Holmes' absence. "When RF asked whether he had in some way offended you, I assured him emphatically that he had not, that your devotion to him was unaltered. However, I'd rather you'd not mention my speaking of the question, when next you see him."

Newdick also told Holmes, "He's putting up a stout front, but he's very hard hit." Ten days later he wrote Miss Clark, "The loss of Mrs. Frost will be a great blow to Robert. . . . Outwardly he is meeting the blow with fortitude, but inwardly he is suffering fearfully."

While at Amherst, Newdick had discussed again the matter of the newspaper column in 1895 at Lawrence. The discovery of the "coal picking" item by Dr. Burnham had excited Newdick greatly. On April 6, he wrote to Holmes: "Have just come upon proof that the Lawrence newspaper column I conjectured to be

Frost's *is* Frost's! And it's loaded not only with 'paragraphs' of prose, but also with early poems. . . ." On April 28, he wrote Dr. Burnham:

> I rush this news to you almost as soon as I have it: Mr. Frost swears that he wrote the column "The American . . .", only from mid-January to mid-March of 1895. That means that someone else started it, and that someone else, or others continued it. It means also that poems occurring after mid-March, 1895, are by others,—unless I can tell from the poems that RF did indeed write them despite his forgetting the fact! Further, the flagpole item, admitted like the coal-stealing item, may set another end date.

The issue of what column Frost wrote for which paper remains in doubt. Thompson, writing his biography a quarter of a century later, expresses as a fact the idea that Frost worked for the American "a little more than two weeks." He got his information about the "coal picking" paragraph from a later search of the files of the newspaper. He quotes a reference to the eagle-on-the-flagpole from a newspaper interview of 1924. He did not have the advantage of the observation of Dr. Burnham. This incident illustrates in miniscule the extreme care which must be taken in regard to all of Frost's statements concerning himself and how they could betray an observer of great acumen and nearly thirty years of experience with the subject.

By the end of April, Newdick was sending papers to Lesley for her comment. The first two were his introduction to the Frost section of the *Anthology of New Hampshire Poetry* and "RF Looks at War," which he had wanted to send to Elinor. Both were scheduled for publication but could be corrected in proof, he pointed out. He indicated his intention of writing again soon "with regard to several other papers."

Newdick proceeded, on May 4, to send Lesley "Robert Frost and Free Verse," "Some of Robert Frost's Inscriptions," and "Robert Frost Looks at War" for her reading and remarks. He gave with each one an explanation of its purpose and intended character. Lesley, who was especially concerned with looking for a teaching job and a place to settle with her daughters, replied that she would read the articles and reply soon, asking for Newdick's judgment on her father's status when he had him alone.

Though he had received permission from RF in Amherst to publish the commencement address given the previous June at Oberlin College, on May 7 Newdick sent the manuscript of it to Lesley: "If there are negative criticisms please let me have them by telegraphic night letter collect." When Lesley returned the articles she had read, she pointed out she had only minor corrections of "What Became of New England," not the kind which could be made by telegraph.

Newdick looked into the possibility of a place for Lesley in a school in Columbus, but he had to report on May 19 there was no opening at that time, adding some suggestions as to other places to look. He mentioned that he had not written to, or heard from, RF since returning from Amherst, "but of course I've been following him with heart and mind." In addition to noting that Frost had promised to visit Ohio State in November, he gave Lesley this account of his time at Amherst with RF:

> We had most of Tuesday together (he allowed me to sit in with him and a group of Amherst undergraduate writers that evening), and Wednesday up to late afternoon and traintime at Northampton. His mind seemed to me to be more active than ever, even too active, Lesley: he was going over and over and over such things as King's accepting his resignation (whereas I have such faith as this, that King may have accepted it thinking to soothe him, thinking not to cross him at this time, etc.), as the College's just recently beginning to collect his first editions (whereas I know the old librarian was a purblind fossil, whose signs of omission can hardly be visited on the College), and so on. He is determined *not* to go abroad, to Greece or anywhere else. And he expressed the hope that he and you and the children might settle down in some small unspoiled New England town in a house large enough for him to have a goodly part to himself, with (say) one meal together a day, and so on.
>
> Of course I felt even more than usually helpless. What was there that I could say that would help at all? I said what I could, fumblingly; and he must have read my heart in my eyes; but all that I wished I could say and do turned in and back upon me mostly unsaid and undone. His quiet, slow uttered courage is magnificent; but can he stand being alone?

We went over some of the letters together, and all of the poems,—those in the Huntington. He called me off the handwriting examination for the time being, puzzled, but thinking that possibly those two poems were in Elinor's hand. As for the poems, he found a number that he had neither published nor drawn from, and those I'm to type and send him for possible inclusion, reworked or as they are, in a book to come.

Newdick's letter of the next day to Frost is self-explanatory and is reproduced in its entirety:

Dear Mr. Frost:

I pray, and believe, that you have not taken me for the ungrateful wretch my silence until now might seem to indicate. The truth is, when I have not been driven by classes, seminars, committee meetings, conferences, and other academic duties, I have been in oppressing personal anxieties which are not yet resolved but which I will refrain from imposing on you at all.

However, I have exchanged several letters with Lesley, since she has generously assumed the function of check-reading my papers on aspects of your work, and since a few dead-lines have recently come and gone. And that reminds me that I was to remind you to send on to me her map of the farm and the accompanying manuscripts.

To complete the list of points I was to remind you of: (a) the curator of the Poetry Room at the Harvard College Library is Arthur T. Hamlin, who requires your authorization, direct or through me, before I may have copies of the letters in his care; (b) Robert Newdick sues for an autographed photograph of his friend Robert Frost; (c) when you have looked into your November engagements you are to set one for us here and let us know the date.

Would you be willing, soon after you come to us, to go up to Ohio Wesleyan University at Delaware, Ohio, for a talk and reading? They most earnestly wish you would, and have asked me to say a good word for them. This last year they responded to two talks about you: one by an advanced student who had listened to your Norton lectures, and one by me. Now they will not rest until yourself come to them. Ohio Wesleyan is of course nominally Methodist, but the religious emphasis is not what it used to be, and the school enjoys a high reputation.

I shall have the copies of your unused poems in your hands within a week. With this letter I enclose an enlargement of a photograph of you and Mrs. Frost at Plymouth in the summer of 1912. Lesley let me have the small original to copy, and of course I am sending an enlargement to her too.

Recently I have received copies of the reports of your talks at Allegheny College and at Andover, and have rejoiced at your carrying on with your customary wit and wisdom and originality.—One fear, however, clouds my thoughts of Allegheny: I spoke of Martin K. Howes as a "dealer," because I have received from him lists of books for sale; but it may be that, like Curtis Hidden Page, he was simply disposing of duplicates for the most part.

The days and evenings of talks with you in Amherst I shall remember always, and you must know how deeply grateful I am for your many other kindnesses to me. I cannot utter the things I would say, but I pray you read them none the less.

Ever yours,

In connection with the appearance at nearby Ohio Wesleyan University, Newdick wrote on the next day to open negotiations about time and fee. Alluding to a fee of $300 which had been mentioned by his Ohio Wesleyan correspondent, he wrote "I believe Mr. Frost might be willing to come to your small school and to jump through fewer hoops for $200. By the way, Frost will not 'dicker' about a fee: he wishes that an offer be made and that he be free rather to accept or reject it without any hard feelings on either side."

In her next letter, on May 25, Lesley wrote of her father that he seemed, in the limited messages she had had, distraught. She noted friends reported him to be exhausted after his first series of lectures. She wondered whether Newdick had reports on those performances, whether there was good continuity of ideas. She thought he was probably becoming too intense, needing to be more relaxed, regretted he had given up the idea of going abroad. Being among people with whom he could not discuss his imagined persecution at Amherst and the death of Mrs.

Frost would have helped him, she thought. She felt the worst thing that could happen would be the emotional intensification which would come from family members being together. She reported that her time at the beach during the previous week had helped her to escape the nervous exhaustion with which she had felt threatened. Gathering her strength for the move northward from Gainesville, she thought disposing of the remnants of three households and taking care of her children would be quite a job.

Two items of special note are to be found in Newdick's reply of May 30:

> At last I have got it through my head that it would be needlessly hard on both you and your father for you to try to arrange to be together for some time to come. There was encouraging word about your father from Professor Zorn the other day: "He has taken a room at the Inn but we see him for a little while each day that he is in town. He has not yet had to face a time of inactivity so that his most difficult time probably lies before him. But he is getting to be much less nervous."
>
> Tell me, please: Does your father have an agent through whom he makes any speaking arrangements? I doubt it, yet I have not been able to give a positive "No" when asked about it. The folks at Ohio Wesleyan asked me to put in a good word for them with him, and I did; but I should be crushed if he thought I was in any slightest way intruding myself into any of his arrangements.

In his letter of May 30 to Frost, Newdick included a query relating a prose article on the Pinkerton Academy by Frost in 1907, the Ohio State Alumni College Program ("on which I have noted several things you may care to glance at"), comment on lectures in Ohio by Ridgely Torrence, and a resume of Lesley's status. "The folks at Wesleyan University are clamoring for me to do more for them in persuading you to come to them," he wrote, as he wondered, "Is there any chance of your coming this way before November?"

Newdick was able to send to Frost, on June 1, copies of the *Oberlin Alumni Magazine* "containing your splendid commencement address at Oberlin last June." He was able to mention its forthcoming appearance in booklet form, on fine antique paper:

I hope you will be pleased with both presentations, and
I thank you again for granting permission for publication;
I am indebted too to Lesley for her fine cooperation. It
would have been a shame to allow this talk to go unre-
corded; and how you yourself could have been disappointed at the time, I don't know,—unless it was at the
apparent (but surely not real) unresponsiveness of the
audience. There are capital things in it, phrased in your
own inimitable style, and it will give joy and stimulation
to all of its readers.

He wrote the alumni secretary of Oberlin of his pleasure "that
you have come to realize the virtue at the heart of Frost's remarks when they are read aloud. Everything of his, whether
prose or verse, reveals itself fully only when read aloud. Catching not only the tone of conversation, but also the very sound
of sense, is the central technical accomplishment to which
Frost has addressed himself for lo, these forty years. And incidentally, the text of a Frost address requires a good deal of punctuation in order to indicate his pauses and changes in thought-
direction."

As May came to an end, Newdick received a letter of appeal
for help from Edith Haskell Tappan, chairman of the committee
which was preparing an *Anthology of New Hampshire Poetry*,
to be issued under the auspices of the New Hampshire Federation of Women's Clubs. Newdick had selected the Frost poems
to be included and had written an introduction to them. To their
horror, the committee had found out that Holt wanted a royalty
of $90 for the six poems included. Frost had written to one of
the committee that he trusted the publisher would not charge
for use of the poetry in the non-profit publication. By writing
to Frost and Thornton at Holt, Newdick was able to get the
charge withdrawn.

Just before he went to Michigan for a week, on June 3, Newdick sent Frost a sheaf of fourteen poems, not published either
as wholes or in part, from the Huntington Library collection.
"I'm praying you publish many of them in your next volume:
I've lived with them pretty intimately for six months now, and
they do not grow dim,—if I may confess to my own fondness
for them."

Only "To a Moth Seen in Winter" was published by RF (in
A Witness Tree, 1942). Four others ("My Giving," "On the Sale

of My Farm," "When the Speed Comes," and "Despair") were used in the first volume of the Lawrance Thompson biography. Thompson's account (pp. 548–9 of *Robert Frost: The Early Years*) throws valuable light on the extreme caution which must be used in considering Frost a source, even in matters related to his own writings. As noted above, Newdick went to California in December, 1937, and "discovered" fourteen unpublished poems, of which he sent Frost a copy on his request. Thompson relates that he first learned of "Despair," one of those of which Newdick sent a copy on June 3, 1938, on March 4, 1962. Frost mentioned the poem to Thompson and asked if a copy of the poem was in the Huntington Library. Evidently, he had a partial memory of the episode of Newdick's getting a copy of the poem nearly a quarter of a century before. To help in identifying the poems, RF quoted it entirely without faltering. Thompson then checked and found a copy of the poem was in the Huntington Library. Thompson asked Frost if he had a copy of the poem; he said he did not. After RF died, Thompson checked Frost's files and found there was no copy. Not being familiar with Newdick's work, though he did know of the 1937 trip, Thompson drew the conclusion that Frost was recalling the poem in full from the time of its composition, 1906, rather than no later than 1937. It is additionally significant, and borne out by such evidence, that Frost was quite unsystematic in regard to knowledge of his own writings.

Newdick had been looking forward to camping "beside a quiet Michigan lake" but hoping he would hear from Frost before he went. Though he had to wait till he returned, he wrote on June 8, "It was a gala Monday, with the arrival of three letters from you in the same mail, after your telegram of Saturday. I think you were having some fun with me, of course, in dividing Gallia into partes tres; but when dux Frost fact; I enjoy a gentle ribbing." Two letters were dated "Amherst Mass / June 2, 1938":

> I shall be glad if Mr. Hamlin would let you have copies of any letters of mine he may have in his keeping. I can't help wondering what they are like myself. I have said all sorts of things in my letters lately. [Presumably this was separate for possible presentation to the librarian mentioned.]

*   *   *

Will have to talk about the [autographed] picture [which Newdick requested in his letter of May 20] when I get to where my things are. [The request was not fulfilled.]

My note book says I am expected at Columbia for a few days ending October 19th. What should you say to my doing Ohio State right on top of that? Could I take a midnight train from Grand Central and be in Columbus in time for a rest in bed before lecturing for you October 20th? October 21st would be better for my health and endurance; but October 21st is Friday and may not be a good night for your public. Another possibility is to wait till late in November when I should be going to Wyoming to help dedicate a room in the library to myself. Do you want to write to me what dates develope out there?

If I come to you or rather when I come to you I wish I might do two or three things of your arranging in Ohio. Theres the one you write about in Wesleyan. Whats all the palaver over price? Cant they pay the two hundred? Or dont you think they should. What are the facts of their life? Please act between them and me. Theres at least one more inquiry from Ohio I may want to ask your help in answering.

Nothing is settled in my mind, but the probability is I shall be scot free next year. So lets sing it in Scotch
"Come open the west port and let me gang free"
with emphasis on the west!

Frost changed his mind about negotiations with Ohio Wesleyan. On June 4, he wired, WESLEYAN OFFERS TWO FIFTY PLENTY. DONT TROUBLE FURTHER I WILL WRITE THEM.

Newdick's comment, as of June 8, on the arrangements for appearances follows:

> I am particularly pleased that you will consent to my arranging some other things for you in Ohio. "All the palaver" about Wesleyan grew out of my fear that you might be annoyed at my taking any part in any such arrangements for you: after the hot water Lankes got me into with you, I move in redoubled fear of the Lord! But if I may act between you and other Ohio groups, I shall be very happy to do so. And unless you tell me otherwise, I'll work around the last ten days of October and mid- and late

Page 182 · On Further Finding Out

November, with a two hundred "floor" for the fee and a three hundred average.

As for your date here, November is better than October because Ohio State does not open until October 4, and October 20th or 21st seems to come pretty closely thereafter. In November, any Tuesday, Wednesday, or Thursday is available, except for the week including the Thanksgiving Thursday and Friday vacation. Let us know as soon as you know. And do plan a cushion of several days with us here at 1294 West First: no one not of your immediate family circle can possibly hold you in deeper affection than we do.

Newdick closed the letter with:

> Be scot free next year? I still don't believe they'll let you! — Still, just in case *you* insist, I'm going to devise plans to intercept you as you gang free through the west port—

The "third letter" seems to have been Frost's notes on the Pinkerton sketch, which Newdick thanked him for "identifying." Newdick had sent a three-page, double-spaced typescript, entitled "Pinkerton Academy." In the upper righthand corner it bore the date of 1906-7. At the bottom of the first page, Newdick addressed a note to Dear Mr. Frost, asking: "Is this the sketch you prepared? For comparison I enclose also the sketch in the 1905-1906 catalogue." In the margin to the left of the first paragraph, parallel to the long edge of the paper, Frost wrote: "This seems to be largely mine. As I remember it, my original was both added to and cut down a little."

On the second page, he ran a line down the left margin beside the following sentences:

> While moving abreast of the times, the Academy has kept unspoiled by transient theory the educational ideals that are not transient. It would be rated as conservative in avoidance of pedagogic experimentation, though less so by comparison with other secondary schools than with many elementary schools. It undertakes to teach with sense and thoroughness the subjects proper to its curriculum. For the rest, its concern is to aim high enough. Work is methodical without subservience to methods. It is held that, for the instructor, "no method nor discipline can

supersede the necessity of being forever on the alert."
Much must be left to the inspiration of the class-room,
reason and native energy.

In the margin he inscribed his endorsement: "This has all my
marks hasnt it?"

Conversely, he disclaimed another passage relating to a statement of the articles of incorporation that the school had among
its purposes "promoting piety and virtue . . .": "I suspect this
is none of mine."

Newdick's view of his communications with Frost at this
time were stated to Holmes in this fashion:

> I hear from RF spasmodically. The other day, after weeks
> of silence, three letters and a telegram came in close suc-
> cession. I've made some copies of poems for him, and some
> speaking arrangements here in Ohio, and he has mean-
> while cooperated by identifying hitherto unknown firsts
> for me, by granting sweeping permissions, etc.

Just as Frost was resigning his post at Amherst, the basis for
his "scot free" reference, one of his students, Benjamin P. Atkinson, was writing, on June 6, a letter to a friend, Elizabeth
Cady Stanton, a graduate student at Ohio State and a friend of
Newdick, giving a picture of student reaction to him. He mentioned a dinner with Frost attended by six students who had
attended an informal class with Frost during the year and who
had ushered at Mrs. Frost's funeral services. Atkinson gave as
an example of Frost's genius his stating, in a discussion of styles,
that he thought it a matter of one's self-image.

After the dinner, Frost sent away the two other professors
who attended and sat in the moonlight, talking about capital-
ism, Communism, Walter Lippmann, the stock market, and
miscellaneous other subjects. The student felt the experience
was the ultimate in conversation. When the students were leaving, their teacher gave each of them an inscribed copy of his
collected poems, expressing to them his thanks, presumably
for assisting at the funeral service.

The student felt that Frost embodied, in his own unique way
the virtues of kindness, wit, wisdom, beauty.

The student recalled that the eleven who attended the first
class session with Frost were speechless as they walked away;
they had had a draining emotional experience. After the dinner

184 · *On Further Finding Out*

meeting at the end of the year, one student cried and experienced depression, presumably on hearing Frost's announcement that he was to leave Amherst. The student thought Frost would not have time for looking back to sad memories, that he would live wisely in the present.

The students had been planning to start a magazine, but the departure of Frost had made them lose their confidence. Atkinson's epitaph for the project was that what had been learned from Frost was too indefinable to be put in words.

Having had a telegram from Frost on June 10 that he preferred to be at Ohio State just after being at Columbia and that he wished "YOU COULD FIX DATE," Newdick both telegraphed and wrote on June 14 to say that he was to appear at Ohio State on Thursday evening, October 20. He asked if he should arrange engagements during the following week. He also included a review of five of his publications to appear in the rest of the year: "Relatively, all such papers are by-products: the core of all my thinking, you know."

When Newdick wrote to Frost at the beginning of July in connection with arrangements for RF appearances, he asked: "Do you know where you will be in mid-September?" The heavy duty of the summer quarter would seem less difficult, he explained, "if I may hope to see you at the close of it." There was no known response to this query. The next letter to Frost, on July 10, concerned itself entirely with setting the date for an RF appearance in Warren, Ohio, and at Ohio Wesleyan University: "I need to know . . . what dates are still available for other Ohio organizations during that week." Newdick had become well-established as RF's midwestern agent, without fee, of course.

A letter of July 14 mentions dates tentatively arranged for October 20, 25, and 31: "Please forgive my importunity, but won't you authorize me to confirm these dates? Program chairmen are anxious until their arrangements are concluded." In addition to asking what date had been set, if it had, for Ohio Wesleyan, he expressed himself as "proud and happy to be entrusted with the opportunity to arrange the schedule for your Ohio swing in October. And I surely need not add that I am anxious that I make every move and play exactly as you would have it." He needed to know whether three talks a week were "sufficiently strenuous," whether he could schedule talks before October 24 and after October 31, whether dates in November were already engaged. "Just let me know what room I have to turn in, then you may forget all about details and schedule and all, for there are more Ohioans clamoring for you than there will be time for."

RF replied on July 15 by telegram: OCTOBER 31ST ACCEPTABLE WILL YOU ARRANGE OTHER DATES THAT WEEK HAVE REFERRED WESLEYAN AND ATHENS TO YOU HAVE YOU HEARD FROM THEM. After Newdick replied with a wire and letter of more scheduling details, Frost sent a telegram which said simply: LEAVE EVERY-THING TO YOU.

Frost wrote a letter on July 20. It opened with a reference to a visit being paid Newdick by his friend Paul Weidner, one of whose letters Newdick had sent to Frost: "I remember your letter from Weidner very well and the pleasure it gave me. You are lucky to have friends of your youth still with you." Of the scheduling, he remarked:

> Anything you say goes with me in Ohio between the dates of October 20th and 31st. Thats eleven days—twelve inclusive. It seems as if I ought to be equal to at least five in that time. I mustnt go much over the 31st, not more than a day at most, for various reasons.
>
> Its a great relief to have the engagements taken off my wretched hands. I say I have nothing left but work and ambition. But I sometimes doubt I have even those. I show no disposition to work and I have only ambition when it is summoned by an audience present to get me talking.

At that point the letter stopped once, being signed. Presumably as an afterthought, he placed the word "over" after his signature and began writing of something that troubled him greatly, his sense of being wronged at Amherst College, from which he had just resigned:

> Did I fail to speak to you of my resignation from Amherst? I had been on the verge of getting out for two or three years. I got rather a jolt when I discovered that the president was only too anxious for the chance to get me out the minute I should give him an opening. There has been a bad misunderstanding about my relationship to the college this last twelve year term. I thought I was a regular professor with all the rights and privileges of a professor, among them the pensional. But it turns out I wasn't. My salary was never budgeted by the trustees as I was prom-

ised by Pres. Olds it would be when I came back to Amherst from Michigan. I was simply kept in a fancy way [sic] out of the pocket of some rich alumnus. I should have suspected as much from the talk that has been going round about my lack of gratitude. To whom? For what? I had assumed from the pressure put on to bring me back that I was wanted for value I could confer. The relationship had become something disgustingly personal and patronageous without my realizing it in time. Pres. King has been so mysterious both in his determination to get me out and in refusing to give his reasons that I have arrived at him as my guess as to what rich alumnus was my keeper. I have been through a lot of hard thinking for this result. He has been having a grand pose of magnanimity before the trustees in not having let me know of my obligations to him. He is done with me partly because I havent shown my appreciation [sic] by coming to hear him talk in Chapel and faculty meeting and perhaps just a little because he is spending much of his own personal wealth on doubling the Amherst plant in his administration. No bitterness about the plant be it understood. I am a good deal displeased with myself in having been such a fool as to have been so cheated about my standing

(Lawrance Thompson says in Volume II of his biography of Frost that such accounts as the foregoing are part of a protective myth to assuage guilt over Frost's failure to perform as Amherst College expected. Outstandingly, Thompson found no evidence of Frost's being forced to leave the school; contrarily, Frost mentioned leaving for several years.)

Newdick, as might be expected, having no information other than that supplied by Frost, responded sympathetically on July 22:

To have the pleasant visit of a letter from you, always makes me deeply happy. This news of Amherst, however, is distressing, primarily because the whole business has given you so much displeasure, but also because King has shown himself to be so monstrously stupid, crude, and unimaginative. When you told me in April that you intended to resign, effective July 1939, and gave me some of your reasons, I felt sure that there had been simply an accumulation of misunderstandings: it was unthinkable

to me that King or anybody else in authority at Amherst
could entertain any thought of countenancing your sever-
ing relations with the College. I was certain that the apparent willingness of King to discuss your leaving was no
more than what he deemed to be a subtle way to avoid
even the semblance of crossing you at a time that was painful and difficult for you. Now to realize that you were
wholly right, even more right than you then suspected, is
shocking. And even if King has been posing in false magnanimity for some time in the background, it is well nigh
incredible that on the very basest ground of policy he
should now relax the pose! Or can he see no farther than
his nose and his cheque-book? It is *you* who have conferred
honor on Amherst all these years, not Amherst on you.
The veriest innocent must realize that. The country over,
to men of letters, scholars, educators, even wise administrators, the relationship apparently obtaining between you
and Amherst, has loomed as an ideal which they have
tried one after another to reach as best they could for their
own schools within the limits of their institutional capacities. Now when they learn, as inevitably they will, of
King's real attitude, the condemnation heaped upon him
will be crushing. And when six or seven academic generations of Amherst graduates learn the truth, the College
may well be shaken to its foundations. This is not rhetoric:
it is plain, Carlylean fact. Read the long excerpt I enclose,
with only names omitted, from a letter from one of your
men [Atkinson] in the class of 1938 to a friend of mine.
By the heart of Amherst, which is to say by the men of
Amherst, including those whom you have touched only by
your presence among them, you are, and always have been,
respected, admired, and loved—even to the point of many
tears. King and his ilk be damned!

At the same time Frost was writing him, on July 20, Newdick
was writing two letters. A short one, dealing with engagements,
mentions the telegram in which Frost left everything to Newdick. This had ended his anxieties: "I have no fear of taking
responsibility when I am *bidden* to, though I confess it is foreign
to me to *assume* any. Now I shall proceed with assurance, ever
taking the utmost care regarding your well being and satisfaction." Frost was seldom in more devoted hands.

The other letter dealt with the efforts Newdick was making to get copies of letters Frost had written Thomas. Newdick had already made copies of Frost's half of the correspondence between the two men. At that moment, failing to reach Mrs. Thomas by letter, Newdick had a friend of his in England making personal investigations, which were hopefully to result in acquiring copies of the letters: ". . . I shall be profoundly grateful if you will write a line to Mrs. Thomas, assuring her that I do have your permission to obtain copies of the letters . . . ." The upshot of the matter was that Mrs. Thomas did not have the letters, at least some of which could have been in Thomas' possession when he was killed in battle.

Doubtless thinking how different the reaction of Amherst students was from that of the college's administration, Newdick wrote, on July 23, to Atkinson to suggest that he spend his summer in writing an account of his association with Frost during the past academic year. His interest was great enough that he prepared a long paragraph, suggesting the content of the proposed account, concluding: "You would close, of course, with the story of the last evening at the Inn . . . and the aftermath of the young man . . . who broke down and wept. . . ." Even though Newdick thought it would be "making literary capital of sacred friendship" to publish an account during Frost's lifetime, he thought it should be published eventually and that there would never be a better time than the present for recalling the events. Aside from helping a biographer, the account would "contribute to the just fame of a major poet with a genius for friendship."

The response on July 29, from Atkinson, was quite positive. He was quite ready to record memorable things Frost had said about education, people, writing. He had already written a close friend for memories and was regretting not keeping a journal. He thought the account should be kept private, for the group was a vivid friendship, rather than a class. He thought the ideas which had come from the relationship were sacred and that all in the group could object to a public record of them. Perhaps this attitude is the reason the account has not been written.

Late in July, Newdick received a letter from Lawrance Thompson, then the curator of rare books at the Princeton University Library. It gives a useful insight into the man who replaced Newdick to become Frost's principal biographer. Thompson expressed his thanks for a copy of "What Became of New England," commenting:

. . . There is something sad about it to me, because I feel
Frost on the defensive in a way that I don't like . . . .
   I'm not talking so much about what Frost says in this
talk or what he implies. Things bother him too much. He
rises to defend ideas now—ideas which he would have
thought strong enough to take care of themselves, years
back. He wasn't the kind to write answers to the criticizers
of his reviews, was he? And yet he now comes out in defense against those voices which might just as well be
ignored.

He added, "Whenever Frost speaks, he says something worth
listening to." He thought the address worth preserving. "And
I'm proud to have a copy of it from you. But I think you know
what I mean about Frost on the defensive." He amused himself
by saying his strongest bond with Frost was his inability to get
letters written. Practically, he suggested Newdick's sending
copies of a magazine to Lesley: "It will be of more value to you
to stand in with her. I have never met her, I'm sorry to say."

"Do you know anything about Mr. Frost's summer plans?" he
asked, adding, "I want to see him, but haven't any idea where he
is now." Mentioning his desire to do more work on the prose
project, a thorn in the side to Newdick, he concluded by offering: "Remember that when you want a critic on any of your
Frost chapters, I'd be delighted to offer any friendly suggestions
that I could."

John Holmes wrote on August 6 with much news about RF,
the result of a visit with Thornton at Holt's:

   . . . Of course Thornton talked a good deal about RF and
we speculated about the future. T. thinks RF will take
Carol and Lillian and go to Calif. to live. RF told me when
I was up there over the Fourth that he thought of living in
Boston this winter and writing the Norton lectures.
   I got a ride with Dale Warren again and spent Friday to
Sunday afternoon there [South Shaftsbury], sleeping at
Carol's house, spending the afternoons at the Gulley, and
mornings walking in the orchard, and evenings (nights)
sitting up in the living room, at the red house, talking. He
wrote out in various books I had taken some five unpub-
lished poems, including the two that will appear in the
September Atlantic. . . . Wish I could give you a full account of all that was said.

But one thing was that RF asked us to come up and spend some time with him at the Gulley. The way it has turned out is that we're here [Easton, Pa.] till about next Wednesday, and driving to South Shaftsbury. RF will be there two or three days, then leaves for a month. Perhaps to Concord Corners, but I don't know that . . . . we are urged to stay as long as we like, and if that's the way it still seems to be when we get there and see him, will probably stay into September sometime.

A letter of August 17, from John Holmes, whose invitation to stay at the Frost home had held up, contributed very helpful information:

We've had a memorable week-end here at the farm. RF has had meals with us, and slept at Carol's. . . . RF and I have walked in his fields, and talked, and Saturday night he read to Sally and me. He is pretty nervous and restless, wants to be on the go. He trusts you wholly, and speaks of you with pleasure in your devotion. . . . . He left here yesterday for Bread Loaf, and then Concord Corners, to stay until the 25th of Sept. We're here until the first. . . .

I have been exploring the books, and have a couple of things to report to you though I fear they're none of your business, and he might not like it if he knew I found these things. . . .

In the first place, you'll recall that I said that at Carol's house there are three or four composition books, in which Carol had written stories and descriptions during the years in England, apparently to give RF for Christmas. In this house I found one of the same things written by Irma. They're priceless for spelling and the child's mind (dated 1913) and they also contain certain lights on the family life and movements, unaware. . . .

Then I found here a carbon copy of a typed journal kept by Sidney Cox, called Walks and Talks with RF. He met RF in 1911, when RF was teaching at Plymouth Normal School. He has kept a very good account from notes of conversations, so that you get an approximation of some of the lavishly used talk. Letters are interspersed, a good many of them, from England and then afterwards, and Cox fills in between so there is continuity. I think he drew on this journal for his monograph a little, but not much. There are

excellent descriptions of RF and Elinor and the various
houses where they lived. You really ought to get your
hands on it. . . .

      *   *   *

Cox's journal contains many passages from RF's letters
arguing his theories of speech, sounds, and the fight he
must make to establish this new idea.

      *   *   *

RF gave me a free hand in quoting him in my book. . . .
RF read one of my essays in it and said it is the real thing.
But he wants me very much to give up all writing except
poems, and wrote as much in a book he inscribed for
me. . . . what he is after is keeping one's self to one's
self—. . . .

In Newdick's immediate response (August 20), he first mentioned his memory of his own "glorious day with him and
Elinor" at South Shaftsbury in 1936:

Right off, too, I must thank you for giving me renewed
assurance of Frost's trust in me and fondness for me. Such
news is always welcome, and I am glad that you are so built
that you take pleasure in passing on good news. During
the days that I spent with Frost in April at Amherst I felt
as I did on leaving him and Elinor at Concord Corners in
September, that only a disaster could make even the
slightest rift in our eye-to-eye and heart-to-heart understanding.

Of course, Newdick was intensely interested in Holmes' discoveries and commented on them at length in his five-page letter. He also commented on the Frost children, referring to "two
capital days—capital save for her [Lesley's] near exhaustion
from prolonged grief—in Amherst" as well as her helpfulness to
him in regard to reading manuscripts.

He noted that RF's telling Holmes to drop everything but
poetry "is as ultimate a blessing on you as an artist, John, as
RF can give. . . . But I must agree with you that no two life-pat-
terns can be the same. . . . And whether he realises it or not,
RF himself has popped into and out of the world of men much
oftener than he thinks he has."

Two of his paragraphs in the five-page letter bear so directly
on Newdick's work with the biography that they must be
quoted:

In the quest for facts I have written literally thousands of letters: the correspondence file makes a five-foot shelf in itself. Ultimately of least importance, they are yet the first foundation of interpretation, are the substructure on which ultimately rests the spire of criticism. All three are or should be woven through a proper biography, though finally, as Frost says, I must stand by my success in putting his work right to the world. But I fear I grow too talky in my enthusiasm. . . .

Have I told you I have returned to writing on the biography? I've done three chapters so far this summer, despite the terrific heat, despite more than usual household anxieties, and despite the heaviest academic load I've ever carried: a whole chapter (instead of the usual phrase or clause of the sketches) on Frost's few months at Dartmouth; another chapter, the next, on the following nine months, stressing his six months in the mill and his published and unpublished "proletarian" poetry ("Clearly Frost was a practicing American worker's poet before most of today's noisy academic 'proletarians' were out of rompers."); and a chapter on his first acceptance by the *Independent*, the Lanier business, and his first realizations concerning "the sound of sense" and his determine [sic] to follow the less travelled road. Only the last is more than a good first draft. The virtue of any first draft is its disclosing points on which I need further data.

In his immediate response, Holmes (August 23) gave further important glimpses of the Frost family:

> . . . It is part of being here that I understand him little by little more for seeing the house, the books, and so on. For instance, it came to me the other day, looking at a little white shed that stands across the brook, that some people would have planted ten-foot fir trees as a screen for it, trees bought from a nursery ready-grown, because they couldn't wait. But not RF. For one thing it probably never occurred to him to surround it with anything, and for another, nothing inside or outside the house is unnatural that way. It is the house of a farmer who is also a man of letters, in good taste, but done without straining or forcing anything out of its rightness. That pretty well covers him.

One also sees his generosity and willingness to spend on his family what he makes. He said he had "turned the checkbook inside out for the children."

. . . Carol is very shy, talks little, and I feel a gulf between us, imagined mostly from my side, perhaps, but maybe there. His father said he had, like all the children, tried writing, but had given it up, and had felt bitter about it. "We don't talk about it any more," said RF. Carol's wife is deaf, you know, and that tends to shut him up still more. He said to me he is self-conscious about shouting to her, though nearly always she has her machine with her. She is a wonder herself, and I know has trouble with his moods, which are dark and rebellious. He has a rare smile and twinkle, though. He deprecates himself, humbles himself somewhat, and seems acutely conscious that maybe he appears to me like an ignorant farmer. I embarrass him, and I feel that perhaps I make him jealous, since his father has given me so much time and thought, given me this house, and shared talk of books and writers. Carol never sits in on any of that, though RF and Lillian wish he would.

RF said that when Carol first took over the farm down below, he tried hard to shut his mother and father out of his life, and make an independent go of it, but was finally unable to, and now gets some regular help. But I think it still rankles. He is proud. He must be his father's son. RF says it discourages and embitters Carol to know that his father makes as much in a night or two lecturing as he can make in a year of hard work. Carol works terribly hard.

Prescott would stand out anywhere, and although he now has interest only in mechanical things, there is the same inventiveness and thoughtfulness there. We like him very much indeed.

Frost in his response to what was, in effect, another biographer is seen in these notes on the one-hundred page journal of Sidney Cox:

. . . My impression is that RF has had this journal for a long time. He has only partly read it, if a slip of paper with notes of certain pages and passages are any indication. He seems to have been inspecting it for deletions and has deleted a few sentences here and there. It looks like a checking-up at Cox's request, but when he was sent it is hard to tell. I guess at some years ago, because the entries end about ten years ago.

Holmes also referred to one of several explorations by Frost of a change in publishers:

> Thornton's break with Holt's is still some months off, in the spring, I believe; and Tom Wilson is said to be going with him. RF has said to me at first off the record, and then with specific directions to do some sounding, that he would like to transfer all his books to Houghton Mifflin. He admires several people there. I've taken him at his word and written back and forth to them about it, knowing some men there well, and they are much interested, and mean to proceed tactfully toward getting him. This is still very much to be kept quiet, and we'll see what we'll see. But I think you ought to know of the possibility. I wonder how you feel about it. Would it distress or please you if the change should come about?

Holmes closed the letter with unique and incisive comments on the place of Elinor in RF's life:

> I hope (this a last thought) that you're going to try to give Elinor some careful attention and a good deal of space in your book. You know what an influence she was, a real one, in the poems. She had a darker mind than his, he has told me. Her own letters to people would be interesting. RF has a good many of them—or had—unless he has recently destroyed them. It would be a delicate business to get what you need from him about her, but she's absolutely a vital part of his picture and always was. She was inscrutable in many ways, shy and untamed, and fiercely watchful. She never went to his readings more than once or twice, but suffered at home. And by the way, in his own suffering over them, he told me that just once he was driven by a friend to some college to talk and when he got there told the man to turn around and take him home, which he did. Sometimes at the station he would phone home and say he wasn't going, and then hearing her voice, decide he would. Not that she told him to, but that he wanted to test himself that way.

On August 14, RF had written to Newdick as follows:

> Do you suppose you could tend to the enclosed for me? You are probably better acquainted with the facts of the case than I am. That is to say you are probably less deceived than I am self deceived. I loathe going over this ground more than once in so often.
> Trust you are all flourishing in summer heat somewhere pleasant.

The "enclosed" was a request from publishers of the *Standard American Encyclopedia* for corrections and additions to their entry for Robert Frost. Newdick submitted on August 22 to the encyclopedia a listing about three times as long as the one it replaced, reflecting all the devoted research he had done. It covered two typed pages. He wrote RF on August 18 that he would send him a carbon copy of the article, "—but of course you needn't bother to read it." He added that it was a "real joy for me to be permitted to do anything and everything I can for you, and I'm hoping you will let me serve you just as often as you think me capable of handling the business in hand." He also enclosed the completed schedule of six appearances, between Thursday, October 20, and Tuesday, November 1, in the Ohio cities of Columbus, Athens, Delaware, Cleveland, Warren, and Cincinnati. The fees averaged $250 and thus totaled $1500. "Marie and I are making all plans for you to make your headquarters for the entire time with us with both a bedroom and the study for your exclusive use." (This represented considerable reorganization and crowding in a small house.) If RF approved, Newdick was planning to drive him to the various points in his car. "You may be sure I shall protect you from all impositions to the utmost of my power." He reported having told a Cleveland woman: ". . . I can assure you that Mr. Frost will graciously autograph copies of his books that may be brought up to him after the talk and reading. He is very kindly to all friendly persons, and I have never known him to refuse an autograph save to persons who thrust mere blank slips of paper at him."

Also included in that letter was a

> . . . prayer for a copy of your *Collected Poems* annotated as to places and dates of composition and so on. As I work

through the years with equal eyes on facts and poems I come to a good many conclusions of my own, but I'd rather be more sure than I am of myself. For example, you may not have *written* "Into My Own" while you were teaching at Messer's Crossing, but you had the experience and the thought then, though it may have welled up in words only long afterwards. And I know you know I'd not exploit such a book but keep it close almost as thought.

Something Newdick did not do was to correct the date of RF's birth in the encyclopedia reference. He had written to Holmes on August 20, for "your *very* private ear," that "there is much evidence that RF was born not in 1875 but 1874." Even though this was one of those facts known better to Newdick than RF and though he wrote in ink "Thursday, March 26, 1874" as the date of birth in the unpublished manuscript he left, Newdick was not ready to publish the new date. Perhaps it was because he had just received an equivocal letter from Dartmouth College. The record there showed his birthdate as March 26, 1874, but the date had been transcribed into school records from the record blank Frost, as a student, had made out. Thus it was in the writing of another and subject to possible error. Newdick was on the point of realizing how fundamental a point of information might not be clear in his subject's mind.

At the beginning of September, Newdick had so many "eager requests . . . from college groups all over Ohio" that he wired to ask whether RF wanted to add several dates in November. Another possibility was to make another tour later in November or "in the winter or spring." Frost telegraphed on September 3: DONT YOU THINK I SHOULD MAKE A LATER TOUR. To a succeeding telegram, asking RF to set dates, to allow assigning them to colleges, or to indicate postponement of consideration of the matter, there was no reply.

A letter from Holmes, who had returned to his home in Somerville, Mass., on September 4, revealed two glimpses of Frost. One of these has to be considered in deciding the status of Carol: ". . . RF phoned from Bread Loaf to tell Carol to drive over and take him to Concord Corners. But when we stopped next morning to say good-bye, Carol said his father had told him to wait a day." Holmes had read Newdick's paper on RF's inscriptions in books. "Couldn't you speak of his way of writing in a book a student wants to give his girl, so as to protect himself from having his volume come on the market inscribed to some unknown female? He gets the boy to sign, too, then writes, From us Both."

In his responding letter, September 7, Newdick spent most of a page writing of work he and others had done on the project of making such poems as "The Death of the Hired Man," "The Generations of Men," and "A Hundred Collars" into radio plays. Newdick had long been aware of RF's thinking and writing of the dramatic element. He and those who worked with him prepared several scripts before finding that RF was deeply opposed to such treatment of his work.

He included in this letter a comment on Holmes' statement in his letter of August 25 about the importance of Elinor:

> . . . your note on the importance of Elinor in the life story. You are right: that last is of prime significance. In the life story I have a number of such threads to weave in: early, there's the father, almost brutal in many respects; then and until 1900 or 1901 there's the mother, one of the few who understood him and encouraged him; from 1885 on for fifteen years or so there's the grandfather, who dimly understood but whose values were nonFrostian values; then from 1890 on (I believe they became engaged in 1892) there's Elinor, the greatest of them all, and after that there are but friendships and acquaintanceships of affection and interest, though not of influence.

These two paragraphs seem both revealing and self-explanatory:

> Do you think, as from this distance I have been inclined to, that RF spent so much time at Bread Loaf this year in an effort to throw himself into activity that would in a measure be distracting? The end of an early summer letter to me ran as follows: "I say I have nothing left but work and ambition. But I sometimes doubt I have even those. I show no disposition to work and I have ambition only when it is summoned by an audience present to get me talking." Then followed two extraordinarily closely written pages of bitterness about the Amherst mess, these added as a kind of postscript.
> Earlier he had said, concerning the business of his coming out to Ohio, "It's a great relief to have these arrangements taken off my wretched hands." Of course I wrote

him at once that I was very happy to be of any assistance to him, and added a thought capable of extension into the kind of secretaryship of which he spoke to you. All I could do the next six months from here, I should be happy to. Then I could give him the six off months, or a chunk of them, next year, wherever he might be. But perhaps what he would want done for him cannot be done at any distance, and maybe I'm not the one in any event to try to do it. Yet you know I should be happy to serve him as I can. Possibly he may bring up the subject when he's here next month.

Another paragraph relates to RF's mention of his "boyhood and youth friendship with John Thom," a black porter in the Boston South Station. "He will not, however, respond to letters." In asking Holmes to call on Thom to get his reminiscences, Newdick explained his finances. "I can't possibly get over East this summer: two spring trips exhausted my vacation means, and then some! I hate to break the pattern of seeing Frost every summer since the first, but I'm hoping to make up for lost time when he's here."

A letter of Holmes (September 11) provided news of what RF had been doing "up there":

RF didn't stay at Bread Loaf because he found activity distracting, I think, so much as that he wanted to take John Cone north with him and John's vacation was delayed, so RF waited. He was to be taken by Carol the day we left, Sept. 1st, but the weather looked rainy up there and RF phoned a second time for them to wait a day. I assume that he is at Concord Corners now, has been there a week, and found no such accumulation of mail that he would miss yours in it, because he had everything sent to Bread Loaf till he left. He spoke of his appreciation of your making Ohio arrangements.

This letter also included the text of Robert Frost inscriptions in Holmes' books.

When Newdick responded to Holmes, who had mentioned the possibility of his speaking, arranged through Holt, in Columbus, Newdick expressed the hope Holmes would come while Frost was there: "It would be just like the old fellow to propose to present you." In the course of discussing plans, he revealed, specifically, the trouble the Newdicks would go to in accommodating Frost:

> And of course you must plan, whatever the time of your coming, to stay with us. We have three upstairs rooms plus a bathroom. This time we've planned to give RF our bedroom and my study, the three of us sleeping dormitory fashion in Jim's room (if we don't, as we may, send Jim to stay with his grandmother while RF is here, inasmuch as he likes relative quiet and is not too keen on small children, though he has always been most gracious to Jimmy). If you come while RF is here, as I think you should, you will be made welcome on the studio couch-bed in the study.

Another revealing observation comes from Newdick's letter of September 15:

> I wonder if John Cone took Irma and the youngster up to Concord Corners. I talked with Cone that day in Amherst, dined with him in the party, and then talked some with him afterwards. He struck me as a steady, dependable fellow. And I was glad for that impression, for I had gathered that it had been up to RF to finance him through *two* educations, one in landscape architecture, then another in architecture.

On September 17, RF wrote his reaction to the idea of the radio plays:

> I'm afraid I couldn't let you do what you propose to do with my poems on the radio. It would drive me crazy to have parts of them turned into prose. It can't be you quite realize what a poem is. Any translation hurts it. And there is absolutely no excuse for translating a poem into other and worn words in its own language. What's more I am not ambitious to use the radio in the present state of its programs for the spread of my work. I have a very low opinion of the people running it, which is only confirmed by the necessity you are no doubt under of mangling my work to make an educational hour after their own hearts. It would never occur to them to have you read the poems as they are. It might be tolerable to have three for instance read the Generations of Men, one the girl's part[,] one the boy's

part and one the descriptive part. But even then that has no attraction for me.

The rest of the letter dealt with a pleasanter matter:

> I can't tell you how much I appreciated your work for my lecture tour in Ohio. I may have seemed indifferent about extending it to more colleges. My health and endurance had to be thought of. I didn't know what to say. There was the uncertainty too about when I was expected at the University of Wyoming and and [sic] Iowa. I have bitten off a great deal for this year—too much perhaps. I have managed to get Wyoming postponed from November to May and Iowa too I think. All to the good. I mustn't go into winter weather all shucked out with the social part of the lecturing. There's where the danger of exhaustion lies.

Writing from Elizabethtown, N.Y., and giving his next mailing address as "St Botolph Club 4 Newberry St Boston Mass," he closed with, "It wont be long before I see you all."

Newdick shared his disappointment over the radio plays in a letter of September 20 to Holmes:

> Here's an honest-to-gosh SOS. Yesterday I had a letter from RF. Three-fourths of it was all one could ask, and it wound up with a note of pleasure that it would not be long until he was with us all. But he turned thumbs down on the proposal to adapt any of the poems as plays for radio: poems are poems, the radio holds no attraction for him, etc. Two years ago, before I knew him so well, and before I knew myself so well, I should have been crushed. And of course it's possible that *this* may be as bad as fear can make it, though I pray not. He wrote from Elizabethtown: maybe L.U. [Louis Untermeyer] had got him down. He's coming to Boston soon—gave St. Botolf's [sic] as his next address. If the matter comes up, do rally for me—if it's possible under heaven. Where I feel pretty confident of understanding, I'm a creature of sudden impulses and enthusiasm,—though I can and do play a mean hand of poker when that's the game. But Maxwell Anderson is *writing* for the radio; so is Auden (*F6*), and MacLeish (*Fall of the City*); and even snooty T.S. Eliot is giving approval to radio arrangements of his plays (*Murder*, et al.). And I

was eager to show the cock-eyed world, still too little conscious of RF, that his poems are *plays too*. That is,—I mean this, as I don't have to emphasize to you—the drive was to take *him* to a larger audience:—I confess the involved sin of "adapting" a *poem*. But should damnation lie therein? Reassure me "when, as, and if" you can.

At the same time he was smarting under RF's rejection of the radio plays, he got a letter (of September 17) from Lawrance Thompson, giving much revelation of the posture Thompson was to take as RF's biographer. His subject was his book on Longfellow, to be published in November, 1938. He detailed his disgust with the Longfellow family, which had required him to submit his manuscript to the family for approval of the publication of the material he had been allowed to see. The family had refused permission to use more than twenty passages Thompson had built into his book.

The work Thompson had done had been made possible and necessary by the garbling of sources by the "official biographer," Samuel Longfellow, the poet's brother. His summation of his method has great relevance to the work on Frost for which he was awarded the Pulitzer Prize. Out of deference to the extremely valuable work of Professor Thompson and to the belief of his widow, Mrs. Janet Thompson, who generously has authorized other quotations used in this book but who believed Professor Thompson would not have wanted his letter quoted, the writer will not paraphrase the material for which quotation was not allowed. However, it may be stated that the letter seems, in this writer's opinion, to embody a commendable determination to hew to the line of truth with a courageous attitude toward objections raised by people with subjective attitudes, a perennial problem of the biographer.

Because of the difficulties with his Longfellow manuscript, the publication of which had to be postponed for several months, Thompson had not seen RF that summer. Nor had he heard from him, and he was greatly interested in getting to work on his book on RF's prose. He was particularly interested in seeing RF's Charles Eliot Norton lectures, delivered at Harvard in the spring of 1936, get into print. He had talked with people in Cambridge and found "everyone is eager to see the lectures in print because they thought so highly of the lectures—But the University Press has no desire to press the matter, and will

never bother him about it, although his failure to come through
with the promised lectures would make the only exception in a
long series of annual lectures." Thompson thought Newdick
should help Frost by influencing him to prepare the lectures for
publication. Thompson saw the unopened package of stenographic notes of the lectures when he visited RF at Amherst in
June, 1936. RF said then he had no wish to make the needed
revision for publication. Thompson speculates that RF burned
the notes and states that the strongest reason for not doing this
chore, which was stipulated in the contract for the lectures,
was his admitted indolence (*The Years of Triumph*, pp. 674–5).

The conscientiousness with which Newdick prepared for the
visit of Frost is suggested by the fact that he started to ask correspondents, more than a month in advance, about the poet's likes
and dislikes, particularly with regard to food. Two responses
seem particularly valuable:

> I think the following is a good rule to follow. Mr. Frost
> likes very much to be left entirely alone before he is going
> to speak. In other words, if you are going to have him talk
> in the evening he likes to go somewhere and rest and not
> have to say a word to anybody. Also, he eats a very light
> supper before talking. This usually consists of a cup of
> warm milk and one or two raw eggs, then after the lecture
> is over he enjoys sitting around and talking with congenial
> people. At that time he likes a fairly hearty lunch. This,
> I believe, is the principal thing you need to know. He just
> hates to have someone give a dinner for him prior to his
> talking, which makes it necessary for him to carry on a
> conversation with people. It upsets him dreadfully. In fact,
> the more you can leave him on his own and not confine
> him to any set rules the happier I believe he is going to be.
> (H. B. Collamore, Hartford, Conn., September 19, 1938)
>
> Frost has changed his habits somewhat since Elinor's
> death, and you will need to feel your way, but these hints
> may be helpful. He was not sleeping well when he was
> last with us and was sitting up late. He likes to have com-
> pany—a few congenial people. Also he prefers a bed with
> box springs, if possible. He takes a very simple breakfast,
> no coffee, but a glass of milk and toast or muffins. For
> lunch and dinner he has generally a good appetite and likes
> hearty simple things. Steak always went well, or roast

beef, and he likes ice-cream. He used to be fond of ginger ale in the evening and refused alcohol, but lately he has been taking a high-ball or cocktail.

You know, of course, that he does not like to talk much before a platform appearance, but welcomes a chance to keep on talking afterward. He also likes to go out and stroll around almost any time, but particularly before going to bed. (Prof. George F. Whicher, Amherst College, October 13, 1938)

As he had done at least several times before, Newdick drew up, on September 26, a formal memorandum concerning an issue in his Frost research.

I believe, for two reasons, that a poem by Robert Frost was published either late in 1911 or early in 1912:

(1) Mrs. Barndollar—Eve O'Brien—had a memory of seeing it (when it was pointed out to her by her English teacher at Plymouth Normal School) and then of asking Frost about it, to his embarrassment. (I talked her out of her memory, on the basis of my record! But now I think otherwise.)

(2) Extract from a letter from Robert Frost to Susan Hayes Ward, dated Plymouth, N.H., February 10, 1912: "Enclosed is another in print. The Marion C. Smith you were talking about when I was with you I was very certain I had heard of somewhere, but I didn't know where. Heard of her? Yes it is almost as if I had met her in the pages of the Companion."

(3) The "record" shows nothing in print for 1911, and in 1912 nothing until October.

The statement serves as a reminder of Newdick's meticulous dedication to accurate research and to the multiple bibliographical problems caused by Frost's heedlessness and wilfulness in matters of memory.

The next day he wrote to Frost to report:

We're all looking forward eagerly to your coming to us three weeks from Thursday. And you can be sure of protection from all but the very minimum of the "social part of the lecturing." I'm responding to all bookstores that you are *not* available for set autographing sessions, to all radio

newscasters that you do not give radio interviews, and to
all our lecture sponsors that you are averse to being dined
before an appearance though you may consent to an informal meeting with a small group afterwards. As for writing directly to you, I have countenanced only the letter
of the Harvard Club of Central Ohio, which would like
you to dine on Friday evening, October 21. And here at
1294 with us, everything possible will be arranged for your
convenience and comfort.

As an addendum, he managed to say some of the rebuttal he
had in mind in regard to the radio plays:

I've come, somewhat the worse for the wear, from the
stratosphere where your counter radio blast took me,—
have come down right side up and stand at attention, nay,
at salute. I should not have obeyed that impulse, even
though I had been brooding resentfully on the radio plays
and adaptations of Eliot, Auden, MacLeish, Anderson, and
others, and then heartily thought you might say, mutatis
mutandis, yes, young man, you may try my verses,—
knowing I knew how much JM [John Milton] resented the
tinkering. I must learn to shove impulses to one side and
to control the will to extend your empire even among bar-
barians.

Another kind of problem was presented in a letter of September 28 from Professor Whicher. Newdick had asked for copies of
inscriptions RF had done for him and of verses written by Frost
for Whicher at Franconia. In the case of the inscriptions, Whicher felt the fact that both parties were alive made it undesirable
to quote the words written. In the case of the verses, Whicher
found Frost had retained a copy and thought Frost should be the
one to give out the lines.

The beginning of October brought a long and interesting letter from Lesley, answer to one Newdick had written two weeks
before. She wrote of spending time at South Shaftsbury, getting
her father "from the Adirondacks," going to Pittsfield to look
over The Open Book, a bookstore she had owned since 1923,
and preparing to move to Washington, where she had found a
place in the King-Smith Studio School, after spending several
more days with RF in Amherst. She and her children started for
Washington in the afternoon of Wednesday, September 21, at

the time of the historic hurricane, which they encountered near Hartford. The travelers encountered falling trees, poles, and wires, were marooned for seven hours in a farm house with about a dozen others, and finally reached the home in Hartford of Mrs. Vachel Lindsay, who was expecting them for the night. Instead of one night, they stayed three, finally reaching Washington on the Sunday, having had to give up New York plans. In Washington, she had been busy getting her children settled and getting acquainted with her new school. She was both pleased and concerned over the anticipated lecture series for the fall. She felt there was significant danger of his overworking himself, that he needed to slow his pace. She was pleased to know he would be in Newdick's hands in Ohio; she depended on him to shield him from social demands and to help him to get sufficient rest. She thought he was getting less sleep than he should and noted a rapid loss of weight. Her view was that he was compulsively (though consciously) involving himself in endless, exciting talk which would induce a breakdown. She understood him to believe he really should do less and that he hoped someone would restrain him. She thought the routine of the Newdick home would be just what her father needed to prepare him for the effort involved in the readings. As far as any material needs were concerned, she felt he was among the easiest of people to satisfy.

In his reply to this letter on October 3, after expressing his satisfaction in Lesley's surviving the ordeal of the hurricane, Newdick expressed his appreciation of her guidance with regard to entertainment of her father: "And you may rest assured that I'll protect him from all I can, including me! I'll hate to, but I'll even push him into his room, as you say, and make him try to sleep." Then he brought forward an idea he had been considering for some weeks:

> You say you'll write again soon, and you must, if only to counsel me on the following idea. I know your father has felt of late the need for some one to relieve him of handling minor business details and letters. I have, next year, from April to October free of academic duties, and I *can* arrange temporarily to be free of them at any time: What would you say to my offering my full-time services for that six months' period, or longer? Of course for no pay: my compensation would lie in the privilege of being with him

when he wished either to talk ad lib. or to give me instruc-
tions. There would be no problem as to the times when he
wished simply to be alone: I could continue, in those intervals, my own reading and study. That would be no different from my program now, for, save that I perform my
academic duties, I devote almost all of my time to the
countless ramifications of study and preparation for the
biography. And there would be no problem regarding my
family, for Marie understands that my RF studies are
central in my life as a scholar and so has given the idea
her approval. What say you? Dare I suggest it to your
father? If so, should I speak it or write it?

The result of Lesley's broaching the idea to her father was
mentioned in a letter Newdick wrote her on December 8:

> For the big question as to whether I dared propose sec-
> retaryship to your father, he answered emphatically in the
> negative at the outset of his visit. Of course I had no way
> of knowing that he had already made arrangements for all
> the secretarial work he might have; and I think he gathered
> from what you told him that my gesture was more gran-
> diose than I thought it to be. I think also, certainly I pray,
> that he deems me less an Old Man of the Sea on his shoul-
> ders near to than at a distance!

On October 6, Newdick received a telegram from Kathleen
Morrison, who had begun her duties as secretary to RF, that he
was in a hospital in Boston with a "cold." He wrote to Frost that
he was "dreadfully anxious" but was—"emphasizing" in his
thinking that he was also reported as recovering. He presumed
that he had been exposed to the hurricane. He acknowledged
word that RF had accepted an invitation to a dinner being given
in his honor by the Harvard Club of Central Ohio on the evening
of October 21.

The idea of some of Frost's Amherst friends that he was trying
to leave his recent life behind him seems to fit the mood of a remark written to Louis Untermeyer on October 12. He was back
in his apartment, at 88 Mt. Vernon St., and ready to sing the
"Take the Road Song" from *The Beggar's Opera*. He was to set
off the next day for "Columbia and Columbus."

Frost informed Bernard DeVoto from Columbus that he was

"out here with my faithful biographer." Having spent 18 and
19 October at Columbia University, he arrived on the Thursday,
when he was to give his Ohio State lecture in the evening. He
was in Newdick's hands until after his appearance in Cincinnati
on Tuesday, November 1. Under his care and guidance he met
all his responsibilities and came through the series of occasions,
social and literary, with great success. Looking back on it a
month later, Newdick wrote Thornton:

> His twelve days here with us were glorious. There
> wasn't a single thing that went the least bit wrong, to my
> knowledge at least; and there was good reason to think
> that RF enjoyed himself as thoroughly as his tempestuous
> mind will allow him. Of course he'd withdraw into him-
> self some few hours before a public appearance, and of
> course there was, as regular as clock motion, the aftermath
> of depression each time; but the intervals were capital,
> and there was talk nearly unceasing then. I believe we are
> closer than ever before. The very thought of a biographer
> at work is something to dismay him at a distance, but he
> finds me less fearful close-up! — I tell you all this because
> I think you'll be pleased to learn of it.

Doubtless, everything was not glorious. When the writer first
met Mrs. Newdick in 1972, she remarked that she really did not
like Frost but pretended to for her husband's sake. When asked
for reason for the dislike, she related the following incident,
which could only have taken place on October 20, the evening
of his appearance at Ohio State. Knowing that Frost ate little or
nothing before a reading, she asked him what, if anything, he
would like at the regular time of the evening meal. He said a
boiled egg would suffice. Mrs. Newdick prepared that at the
same time she prepared a platter of steak-and-potatoes. When
he sat down at the table with the Newdicks, he ignored the egg,
declared of the food on the platter, "That looks good!" He then
proceeded to eat all of it.

All that has been recounted has demonstrated repeatedly that
Newdick put Frost before himself in any way which could be
identified. The episode just mentioned would be minor as compared to the continuing and repeated efforts expended on Frost's
behalf. Mrs. Newdick evidently did not argue with her husband
about his devotion, but she did not share it. In a note to Mrs.

Newdick, the writer mentioned that some of the public thought of Frost as a white-haired gaffer. She wrote beside the remark, "He was a despot!"

Thompson, who was glad to get the written version of the Oberlin commencement address, had asked Newdick to be certain to have transcriptions made of his remarks in Ohio. He had been following this procedure himself, in building up the prose collection on which he was working. There is no sign that any full record of any of RF's talks was made, probably out of deference to his known aversion to having notes or recordings made when he spoke.

Newdick, of course, made many pages of notes as the result of the time he spent with Frost. (These will be found in Item 30, Part III.) Selections from clipped newspaper accounts may suggest the character of some of his remarks to various audiences and the responses to them:

> From the time Professor Robert S. Newdick began his glowing introduction to the moment Frost had recited the final line of his concluding poem, the audience, which taxed the capacity of the ancient auditorium, alternately responded with hushed silence and shouts of merriment. His subtle, sly wit made the evening a memorable one.
>
> More than 1000 heard him; so many, in fact, that seating the audience delayed the address half an hour. Many stood and still felt themselves rewarded.
>
> Wearing high-top shoes, a soft white shirt with black bow tie slightly askew, the coat of his tuxedo suit open, Frost started the fun with silent grimacing when Newdick, his host, who is also writing his biography, introduced him as one of "Plutarch's men" and likened his speech to Marcus Cato's.
>
> The poet didn't alter the mood. He spoke of poetry, and "said" much of his own. To the delight of his admiring audience he interpolated his recitations with anecdotes concerning the origin of many of them.
>
> To the joy of those nearby, he dropped his voice now and then to poke dry fun at many an outworn notion and an occasional stuffed shirt.
>
> A serious artist, he demonstrated that he doesn't take himself too seriously. Spoofing the dogmatists from Aristotle to the contemporary young English poet, Stephen

Spender, and not sparing his own slips, Frost made just two arbitrary statements. He said:

"I have not much use for political programs, nor have I much use for literary programs."

(Ohio State University, October 20, as in the *Ohio State Journal*)

Undaunted by Professor Ransom's reference to his listeners as "a group of earnest collegians," Mr. Frost proceeded to draw a little wintry earnestness from them, much to their own delight, and substitute some of his own warmth. Leaning easily against the lectern, one hand gesturing the air, the other riffling a book's pages, he dissolved the awkward barriers between lecturer and audience, as few men could have done.

Mr. Frost described his own poetry as a remembrance of things past, the recollection of impressions long over, which passed unnoticed at the time. Thus, the feelings quickened as he stood by a dark lake's edge in winter might become the subject of a successful poem years later. These feelings are the "delight end" in poetry, and the source of its strength. The poet can "take a little run towards wisdom" but never so far as to die into a systematizer. Philosophy only exists when it is imaginative, and poet should not perish in closed systems of knowledge, which think to explain all that it is necessary to know or observe in life. Mr. Frost read selections from his own poetry at the close of the lecture, and received more encores than an opera singer.

Following the reading members of the faculty and a few students had the privilege of hearing Mr. Frost speak more informally on poetry and ideas at President Chalmers' house. He spoke and read until a late hour, and none were tempted to leave.

"Every one lives in wait for the enjoyment he will derive from the pinnacles of delight which punctuate our lives," said Mr. Frost. "During the interim," Mr. Frost continued, "I putter to avoid the otherwise inevitable period of melancholy and boredom."

(Kenyon College, October 23, as in the *Kenyon Collegian*)

"Poems," said Mr. Frost, "are fireflies. They represent our lucid intervals and glow only for a moment."

Explaining his reluctance when requested to reveal any

"meanings" in the verses, he said, "That's what I wrote; that's what I meant."

"My most naive praise," Mr. Frost continued, "comes from people who say that they like my poetry because they have a farm in Vermont or because their mother was born in New Hampshire."

He explained that his poetry is not regional in a geographic sense. It concerns realms, not places. "People who really understand the poems have lived in these realms," he added.

Following these introductory remarks, Mr. Frost read several recently published lyrics and selections from his "Collected Poems."

Included in the poems read were "The Road Not Taken," "The Tuft of Flowers," "Snow Dust" and "Departmental."
(Ohio Wesleyan University, October 26, as in the *Ohio Wesleyan Transcript*)

"Don't miss any of the tricks." Robert Frost, with a friendly twinkle in his eye, gave this advice to college poets when he was interviewed shortly after his lecture here Wednesday evening.

And how to become a poet?—"Read poems, lots of them—good ones, not cheap things—and read them enviously. See how it's done. I think they put it this way, 'don't miss any of the tricks.'"

What to write about?—"I would say, begin at pleasure and arrive at wisdom. Too many young poets want to write about philosophy at first, to worry about the world when they start out. But really, you need not have wisdom when you set out, because you'll end up with enough of that by the time you are forty!"

What sparks inside you, Mr. Frost, to make you write a poem? How are you inspired?—"With a fascination of pain or delight. Young poets should begin to write of delight and then gradually work into the other."

And when you began writing poetry, did you do it for your own pleasure or for an audience?—"I do not like that 'for your own pleasure' idea. A poet is never without the sense of an audience; he has something to say to somebody and that is why he writes it."

Now for something more general, Mr. Frost: What views

do you hold as to the quality of contemporary poetry as compared to the verse of 20 years ago?—"About 20 years ago," he said as he opened a book to autograph it, "editors of magazines and newspapers began to use quite a large amount of poetry, and since then the demand has varied. In the past ten years it rather faded, and now I wonder if it isn't coming back." He closed the book after signing it, and then interjected, "Oh, somebody is always howling about poetry."

Quizzed as to his opinion of present day regional poets, Mr. Frost confided, "You know, I have been called a New England poet, and that is only natural because much inspiration comes from things closest to you. However, I've been told that one of my pieces about the Himalayas was the best I've written. Really, I'd rather be called an American poet."

(Ohio Wesleyan University, Gene Tartt in the *Transcript*)

"It's fun in the beginning and ends up in knowledge."

He read several of his own poems, including two old favorites, "Reluctance," and "The Death of the Hired Man," and spoke of the ruthlessness of poets.

"Many otherwise splendid poems that could last forever are ruined by the very force of their own strength," he said.

He urged embryonic poets in the audience to start with simple things, and not, he said, "to start from Aristotle and work backward."

(Ohio Poetry Society, October 28, as in the *Cleveland Plain Dealer*)

In the opening part of his address Frost paid a tribute to his friend Ben Atkinson, son of G. F. Atkinson, formerly of Warren. Ben Atkinson, a Harding graduate, attended Amherst College where Frost was an instructor, and is now teaching at Syracuse University.

Frost's talk was delightfully informal, the talk being more in conversational form than in the usual lecture type. From time to time he pushed back his snowy white hair from his brow and seemed to be making a keen study of the audience.

Frost declared he had no training in English when a boy, but his studies did include Latin, Greek and mathematics. He said his first poetic expression was at the age of 15 years.

The things that great men are required to do were spoken of by the poet, who concluded this thought with the statement that "such men are considered authorities on things they know nothing about, and must serve as judges in all kinds of contests until they really have no time of their own."

The reason a lot of folks do not like poetry, Frost said, is because they are "sore heads."

He stated that he would like to make an anthology of British and American verse and said that the English have treated American writers rather poorly except Poe, and he (Poe) has been treated too well for the work which he did.

The speaker said he is not strictly a moralist but draws his thoughts rather from the spiritual.

Among the poems read were "Birches," "Stopping by the Woods on a Snowy Evening," "The Road Not Taken," "Cliff House Beach," "Peck of Gold," "The Runaway," "Death of the Hired Man," "Departmental," "To a Woodchuck," "Precaution," "Not All There," and "Mending Wall."

No interview was obtainable, but Frost after the lecture did answer some written questions.

Asked if boys and girls of this generation who are reared with all of the freedom of expression of the age are better or worse citizens when they grow up, he said: "I believe they are better for the freedom gives them self-reliance."

He also believes that the repeal of prohibition has "done something to youth," for everywhere he sees much drinking of highballs and cocktails.

Asked if the high school student of today is a better English student and uses better English than in 1920, Frost stated: "By all means, no." He also said that in spite of the swing craze of the present time there is some real poetry in the modern dances.

(Warren, Ohio, October 31, source unidentified)
Robert Frost expressed belief that poets had a better chance for survival of their work than prose writers.

"Of course this is true," the poet hedged, "if the future can be judged with any security at all by what has gone before. But this world is changing so rapidly in so many ways it's hard to be any kind of prophet."

The New England poet pointed out the preponderance

of poetry handed down from the earliest times as compared with the amount of prose.

"So," he said, "there is compensation for the poet in the hope of permanence, when he falls short as he so often does in remuneration for his work. Great poetry survived when empires fell."

Frost disputed emphatically the contention that poetry was "dying out."

"It is as 'alive' as it ever was," he asserted. "Poetry is not at a low ebb at present nor is it at a particularly high peak. It is going along about as usual. There are a lot of people who enjoy the simpler, homespun verse at all times and there is a smaller audience that deeply appreciates the finest poetry. It was so in Shakespeare's time. It is true today, as well."

The mission of the poet, Frost said, "is to entertain and to sustain men's souls on the finest planes. The poets are not lax on the job today but are fulfilling their mission. A great deal of fine poetry is being written."

There is a dearth of strictly religious poetry, he observed. There are no Francis Thompsons and no poets writing verse that stands up with "The Hound of Heaven."

As a matter of fact young poets with the inclination to write religious poetry might specialize in that field to their advantage, Frost thinks.

His own greatest exhilaration in writing is "to see if I can make each poem sound different from all others I have written."

(Cincinnati, November 1, George Elliston, newspaper unidentified.)

Most of the items RF inscribed for Newdick were done on October 30. On the reverse of the fly leaf of a first edition of *New Hampshire* he wrote "For Robert Newdick / October 30 1938." On the opposite page he wrote out the entire twenty-four lines of "Happiness Makes Up in Height What It Lacks in Length." Eight minor changes from the published version are these: Line one has comma after *oh* and *world* omitted. Commas at ends of lines two, three, thirteen, and fourteen are omitted. Comma is substituted for dash at end of line six. "Robert Frost" is signed at the end of the poem.

Newdick's copy of *Recognition of Robert Frost* has inscribed on the fly leaf: "Hoping Robert Newdick / will find some of these / critics were somewhere / near right in their / opinion of me / Robert Frost / October 30 1938." The lack of punctuation is typical of all Frost notations. Frost signed the book again under his picture on the title page. A second copy of *Recognition* has a signature under the picture which serves as the frontispiece.

An Exhibition on the work of Robert Frost, Allegheny College, May, 1938, was signed by Frost on the front cover and dated at Ohio State, October 30, 1938. A booklet, *The Chapbook (A Monthly Miscellany)*, No. 36, April, 1923, edited by Harold Monro and published by The Westminster Press, London, has on page three of this issue, containing *New American Poems*, the poem, "On Stopping by Woods on a Snowy Evening." On the blank portion of that page, beneath the poem, Frost wrote: "For Robert Newdick / October 30, 1938 / Columbus, Ohio." On the same day Frost signed a printed paper doily from the Granville (Ohio) Inn and Golf Course.

Two manuscript poems were probably autographed for Newdick during this visit. One is the original working manuscript of the poem later published in *Time Out* as "A Loose Mountain." Here it is entitled "Telescopic." The twelfth line of the published version reads "Nor find in dew the slightest cloudy trace," whereas, in this version, Frost wrote, "Nor find in morning dew the slightest trace." Also, the last two lines of this manuscript do not appear in the published version: "The way we did the Great War and the curse / That followed after of defeatist verse." The last line has "after of defeatist" substituted for words crossed out. After his signature he placed the notation: "For Robert Newdick / A very first." The other is the poem, "It Is Almost the Year Two Thousand." The most significant deviation from the published version is the substitution of the word "their" for "this" in the last line.

One miscellaneous souvenir of the Frost visit to Columbus is a telephone bill listing calls to Washington, D.C., on October 22, Cambridge, Mass., on October 27, New York on October 27, Cambridge, Mass., October 28, all doubtless made by Frost. Another is a list of twenty-six people instrumental in the various appearances, made by Newdick at Frost's request, so that he could send each person an autographed book as a token of his thanks.

It seems likely that the following meditation, unfortunately undated, may have come out of the intense experience of the twelve full days with Frost:

Can it be written,—this which I have risen from the half-sleep of dawn to write? We shall see. It has come so often—and I have so often been aware of it at that time— that at last I've won the struggle to rouse myself and write it, or try to.

"It" is the half-mystical, almost God-like (if I may say so) living *with* Frost in the creation, recreation, and understanding of his poems. (Even I had not guessed they were so much with me.)

It's as if I am a super movie producer-director-cameraman. Nothing, practically nothing, stands long in my way: there are means for overcoming almost every obstacle in my quest.

I see Frost then as a great brooder—with an infinite sense of humor. He looks long and he looks hard; and when he's through looking there's little that has escaped him— "something must be left to God."

He chooses to look, and to brood, with the equipment nature gave him. (Only interpreters, like me, need the movie magic of portion and power to command all means.) When he looks up, to the stars and the heavens and to Heaven, he looks with the naked eye only, but with how sharp an eye! There's a character in one of the poems who burned his house and used the insurance money to buy a telescope. His impatience, I should say, much amused Frost,—amused him in itself, and amused him also in its futility: what more could such an one see?

And when he looks down he looks by himself, long, patiently, hard. He has no impulse to reach for a microscope: what more could it reveal that counts in the world man really (as opposed to speculatively) lives in? He looks at an ant on the tablecloth running into a dormant moth, and lo, there's the beginning of "Departmental." Or, out of doors, he looks at a growing plant so intently that he sees it shouldering each crumb as it comes.

I think the poems are of these origins with one common denominator, namely, himself: (1) his self-communion;

(2) his communion with self and wife (sweetheart, in some of the earliest pieces); (3) his observations of what would amuse both of them in the telling.

The self-communion is significant. There is, yes, the need for "Revelation,"—but before there is need for that there is something to reveal, something observed and wrought out largely alone and in silence.

Equally significant is the communion with Elinor, and the having of her almost constantly in mind. (How good it was, for such a lone wolf as he, to have found his life-companion of head and heart and body so early in life!) Sometimes it seems to me the poems are half hers. Certainly no one will ever rightly or fully understand who does not take full account of the lover-sweetheart, husband-wife relationship. Why, one knows *her* from the poems almost as well as one knows *him*!—

What of love in called "larger" senses: love of fellow-men, love of God? Well, in a word, [I must hasten; the clarity of the vision at halfwaking grows dim.] it must be obvious, I think, that one who himself so deeply knows love will be, more than another, inclined to believe, albeit wordlessly, in a somewhat similar love among men and women generally,—and even, though here one will move even more cautiously, between God and man. It's bound that is, (to say it differently) to predispose Frost to a fundamental hopefulness quite the opposite of Hardy's fundamental despair.

A word as to my object [this, happily, I am going to say, and it remains clear]: It is to explore the poems in all their meaningfulness as to surprise Frost, if he ever learns of my understandings; to catch every glint of every phrase as if I had been present at all the jogs and pains of birth; to miss only the bits that *never were* said in words but only by glances and half smiles,—and even some of those! And I think I can do it.

This four-and-a-quarter-page, longhand statement-of-faith was preceded by a sheet, on which the only writing was: "(Confidential: To be destroyed.)" It may be surmised that the extreme emotionality of it left him abashed. It would not in any way be detrimental to anyone.

Newdick put Frost on the train for his next date in Pennsylvania at midnight on Tuesday, November 1. On November 4 he wrote Holmes that "I'm still pretty well burned out, especially with internal haemorrhoids (Sp?) from carrying a heavy suitcase too far." Having "dropped *everything* for RF," he was groggily catching up.

On November 6, he was in correspondence with the faithful Dr. Burnham of Lawrence. He was evidently reflecting what Frost had told him when he remarked, "One trouble with Lawrence correspondents is that now, after the lapse of years, and after Frost has won fame, they refuse to remember what an outcast or pariah he was for years in his own community! If they'd discuss *that*—Maybe they would tell us about such things but not write them."

He was still writing about Frost's visit going off "without a single hitch," but, as he told Whicher of his eight triumphal appearances, he added, "But I had to get used to his next day depression." Whicher replied that he was pleased to hear about Frost, that he had not had news since a few hours before the hurricane struck; he had heard recently, from Bernard De Voto, of a forty-five-dollar taxi ride Frost had taken from Hartford to Boston.

An Ohio State student had tried to arrange through Newdick for Frost to look at his poems. He was advised that "Mr. Frost was too close to exhaustion while he was here from his cold and his arduous schedule to go through your thick packet of verses." The suggestion was made that he select no more than four and send them with a letter to 80 Mt. Vernon St., Boston. "In that event, omit the pieces in free verse, for free verse doesn't rate very high in Mr. Frost's scale of values."

Newdick's first letter to Frost after his departure was written on November 11. It announced, "The ties came the other day, and we immediately sent yours on to Boston. I'm enthusiastic about my set, and thank you." (The gift from Frost to Newdick is not mentioned otherwise.):

> We've missed you, more than I will say. And from everywhere you were, the letters keep coming in and chorusing. We must have him again! Will he come this way next year?

The rest of the letter and a separate one on the same day, discussing an appearance at Iowa State College in October, 1939, show that he had already begun to be the agent for a trip the next fall.

He wrote, on November 28, a letter to which he had been giving thought for a long time, to Professor Sidney Cox of Dartmouth College, of whose long friendship he had known and of whose journal Holmes had written him: "I know that you have a Frost book in mind, and for my part I shall welcome it." The letters he had from Frost would make a welcome second book. He was writing to ask for the use of the Frost-Cox letters of the 1912–1915 period.

Frost wrote to Newdick on December 2, addressing him for the first time as "Dear Robert":

> Who are some of the people I am under obligations to for my late pleasantness in Ohio? Give full names and addresses. For example: Mrs. _____ Redhead _____ at Cleveland Ohio. I thought I would square it with them by sending autographed books. Leave out no one however unimportant. There were two ladies running the thing in Cincinnati weren't there?
>
> It isnt thought best for me to try Ohio any further this school year. I have three or four near New York[,] four or five in the west and five or six in Lawrence Mass for the spring. That should take as much out of me and put as much back as is good for the bad in one season. I am just off for Washt and Balt. I shall do a couple in Florid[a] probably and one at Norfolk on the way south later. Youd think I was a flee fleaing. Mrs. Morrison will discuss things with you.
>
> I'll never forget my visit with you—what I read to you and what you said to me. The point I tried to make was that I was a very hard person to make out if I am any judge of human nature. [This sentence is quoted by Thompson in the Introduction to his *The Early Years*.] I might easily be most deceiving when most bent on telling the truth.
>
> We'll talk about collecting my stray papers and lectures later. It may be you will have to publish them with the Holts if I make a new agreement to stay with them. My relations with them are in a parlous flux.
>
> Remember me to the family and the Scioto River.

Before he could receive that letter, Newdick had written Frost, on December 4. Mentioning that Frost said he liked to receive letters but did not care much about writing them, Newdick said this was a letter without the usual purposes, "just a

letter, a lame substitute for the privilege of talking with you."
This letter was addressed to "Dear Mr. Frost." It was misad-
dressed and returned. By the time that had happened, Newdick
had the "Dear Robert" letter of December 2. Thus Newdick
wrote, when he mailed the letter again, this note: "Dear Robert—This was written and posted as dated, but being misad-
dressed was returned. I venture to send it again for what still
remains alive in it, and because my more recent letter assumed
this one. R.N."

As one might guess, the first-name basis was quite pleasantly
significant to Newdick, who had hastened to reciprocate in the
note. His letter of December 12 uses that address and remarks
on the point:

> I have been very happy, as you knew I would be, in your
> letter, particularly in your promoting me to first-name
> friendship; and in this reply, through sureness now of your
> personal regard for me, I overcome all my old hesitancies
> and respond as I have long wished to address you.

The business of the letter was to list eight people, of the
twenty-six on his working list, to whom RF could send autographed books.

Newdick wrote Frost that he had had a "very friendly response" from Sidney Cox and permission to use the letters for
which he had asked. When he thanked Cox upon receipt of the
letters, he sent along a "preliminary sketch" of the coverage of
Frost's months in England. He included in his letter this very
suggestive paragraph:

> You put your finger on the central problem when you
> say it's going to be hard to write of him with the inevitable
> admiration and affection and yet to show him as always
> something of a rogue. There's almost no limit to the admi-
> ration and affection, as I think you know. And I am bound
> to show him exactly as he was and is without seeming to
> be (as I will not be) playing up the mischievousness and
> roguery for any writer's or reader's reason whatsoever! — I
> think I told you Robert was with me for twelve days last
> month. Over and over he told me, with illustrative exam-
> ples, with what he regarded as illustrative examples, what
> a "bad" fellow he'd been, how "unmoral" if not indeed
> "immoral." So I know he wants that streak made patent.

Yet I do think (and I'd like to know whether you agree)
that right now, and since Elinor's death and L's [Lesley's]
lambasting him, he's *overly* insistent on the shadows.

Cox had written on December 2, echoing Frost's lines, that
Frost did not seem to change but that he was always surprising,
baffling any effort to find a formula to represent his qualities.

When Newdick returned the borrowed letters to Cox, an
accompanying letter of December 9 made reference to what
has long been a problem for those who have had the benefit of
RF's intimate comment:

> While of course I shall not quote the disparaging com-
> ments on other writers, I am very glad to have read those
> first appraisals. Frost has been very lucky, and knows he
> has been very lucky, in having had so little of his devas-
> tating criticism of fellow writers passed on by reporters
> and interviewers. There's something about him that
> begets a kind of protective attitude on the part of those
> who are privileged to hear him talk.

In his letter of December 12, Cox first of all commented on
Newdick's picture of Frost in England. He felt Newdick's chapter caught a lot of the way Frost worked, his low-pressure dedication, his acceptance of assistance, his confidence amid questioning, his resistance to being ignored. Cox and his wife
approved the account which showed Frost could maintain his
humor amid struggle, that he had a shrewdness and intelligence
not tainted by bookishness. He was pleased to see Frost admired
by thousands for his "broad human commonness" while the
more esoteric writers were dependent on a coterie of solemn
specialists.

As valuable as those remarks were, after making a few suggestions relating to style, Cox outdid them in giving Newdick
the benefit of the essence of twenty-five years of observation
of their subject:

> . . . I know he hates to be described as mellow, in the
> sense of too gentle and sweet to be dangerous. He thought,
> years ago, that the world might fall into the hands of the
> roughs because the fine were too soft. And three years ago
> he remarked sharply, "I'm no Jesus Christ." He's always
> differentiated himself, though not so much by assertion

as by behavior, from the prim and the ladylike and the
hyperaesthetic. I can remember a talk in Littleton in 1922
or about in which he used the phrase, "Wait until I see,"
making the point that the time for evaluating a man's
action was not until his objective had a chance to be accomplished, and implying that if some injury or some
deviation was involved the quality of the performance
might silence objection, without entirely exempting the
intervening act from disapprobation by an unimaginative
moralist. But don't say he was ever a pragmatist, either.
The thing is an actor has to do some wrong. He has always
reserved the right to be ruthless in pursuance of poetry,
sometimes almost savagely holding within himself that
he'd make the poetry so good that it would make up. All
through my acquaintance he has shocked me. It has been
a slow realization for me that good acts and good character
that rise from well balanced instincts, good feelings and
the effective remembering of past feelings is sounder and
finer than good acting that rises from thinking about being
good. The former kind may include much of the devil, but
though it is not pious and proper nor saintly, as a rule, it
is productive and involves good performance such as no
sensitiveness to taboos provides. For instance, he has
always spoken his real feeling about people in confidence,
often in flagrant violation of the taboo about talking behind folk's backs. He has no scruples such as are involved
in what some professors call professional ethics. In fact I
don't think he ever had rationalistic scruples. He doesn't
need rules and principles against meanness because his
feelings are not mean. If his feeling is harsh, severe, scorn-
ful, he often shows it, though not without a feeling for
the person involved and the person spoken to. You saw
how he "teased" Louis the night of the funeral. He is always a tease, a fighter, a snapper of bonds he didn't forge.
He even likes at times to be misunderstood—in preference
to being understood wrong. He professes his unmorality,
I think, truthfully and from of old, too, scorning to resem-
ble those of us who profess being gentlemen, never re-
vengeful, never hating, never ferocious, out of pusillanim-
ity, or out of complaisance, and who fall into ugly, indirect
meanness because we dared not be boldly bad. And then

professing roguishness, and bragging a little, playfully, of outwitting a horse-dealer or a pettifogging set of examiners who were passing on his pupils, he is free to be generous and honest and full of virtue, in the Roman sense, without solemnity or smugness. You will hear of disapprovals of his that will be offered as proofs of a puritanical attitude toward sex, or toward snobbishness. But those acts arise out of his own taste and his own feeling for unmixed emotions and for being real, and his own feeling for other people's feelings rather than from taboos. I think he's always been good and always held an opening for a wholesome devilishness. And once in a while he does something absurdly overbearing, through pride.

Newdick had found that RF had, in Kathleen Morrison, the secretary and agent he needed. Newdick mentioned having a "pleasant letter" from her in connection with RF's desire for Newdick to serve as Ohio agent as before. Mrs. Morrison had indicated in her letter (December 8) that RF had had eight appearances in the East in November after leaving Ohio. Four more were scheduled for December and six for March. This had involved some principles which seemed to fit his needs and capacities. She thought he should not tour for more than two weeks at a time: "The let-down that follows one of these trips is terrific and the nervous exhaustion makes it impossible to get any work done." She thought he should have three profitable, intense periods and then no other appearances. She thought he ought always to have a day's rest between towns. Performing, moving on, and planning the next speech was too much to expect him to do in comfort. The impression one has is that he had placed himself in competent and considerate hands.

When Newdick wrote to Thornton on November 26, he mentioned that Frost had informed him that Thornton was going to leave Holt. He wrote two paragraphs about Frost materials he hoped Thornton could help him get from the publishing house before he left. Thornton did not reply, but, on December 28, his successor, William Sloane, did. He spoke of discussing Newdick's letter with Frost in Boston. He expressed interest in the collection of Frost prose pieces, asking that it be sent along if it was presentable. He also wanted to know the progress of the biography, including when Newdick expected to have it finished.

The correspondence between Newdick and Sloane in January was quite productive. In a letter of January 3, Newdick wished Sloane well in his new post, asked whether Frost was staying with Holt, reviewed the career of the prose book (going back to his original suggestion of May 24, 1935), and asked two questions: "(1) whether Mr. Frost is agreeable to your having the volume instead of OUP; (2) whether you are really interested in the volume." The first question would decide whether he would send anything for examination, "because I must in all respects be loyal to RF." If the second were true, he would have to reassemble all the materials which he had recently merged into the biographical materials.

Two weeks later, Sloane was able to write that Frost would publish all his future writings with Holt. RF wanted Holt to do the "volume of stray papers and lectures" rather than Oxford University Press. Yes, they would be interested in the volume of prose for the end of the year. In regard to the biography, he mentioned RF's "embarrassment" in regard to it, his desire for its delay, the fact that RF wanted Holt to do it, and that all material in Holt files relevant to the biography would be available to the biographer.

Naturally, this information was very helpful and encouraging to Newdick. It left out one important point: "I take it that he [RF] gave you the impression, at least, that he approved *my* doing [the prose book] rather than . . . [anyone else]; and I'll hope that he makes the point unmistakably clear when he writes me next." And he gave insight into the relationship between biographer and subject as most recently experienced:

> You are quite right in your impression that Mr. Frost is somewhat embarrassed by the thought of his biography, though you know he cooperated with Munson on a sketch some ten years ago. While he was here in Ohio I tipped off those who introduced me to introduce him, not to speak of me as his biographer, much less as his "official" biographer; nevertheless, he sometimes would turn to me while he was speaking and ask, "Is that right, Boss-z?" And while we talked long hours together of matters I as biographer could never possibly have uncovered by myself, he would sometimes interrupt himself to exclaim, "But we're both of us absurd in this!" and then resume. He finds me more embarrassing as biographer at a dis-

tance, that is, than when we are tête-á-tête as friends. But neither he nor you need fear that I shall rush the biography to market: I have given it my days and nights for five years now, and there still remains much to be explored as well as written. (Letter of January 19)

In a letter of January 26, he asked for publicity to be sent to Iowa State College for RF's appearance there the next October. He enclosed "an essay on Mr. Frost's prose" which he thought might be a basis for the foreword to the book of Frost's prose, with regard to which he also wrote:

I think I shall have the tentative materials for the book of Frost's prose in your hands not later than the tenth of next month. And here's an important point I have so far forgotten to mention about that book: it is understood, between Mr. Frost and me, and now among us three, that whatever royalties may accrue from it are to be payable to Mr. Frost. Perhaps I might be paid a very small flat sum to defray the costs of photostats, typing MS., etc., but even that is not essential.

Sloane had mentioned a forthcoming edition of Frost's *Collected Poems*. This made Newdick think of a "small service" he might render if the book had not gone to press: "In the past, the special and general editorial supervision of the text of Mr. Frost's poems has, in my opinion, been lax, permitting the intrusion of inaccuracies, inconsistencies, and confusion . . . my sole concern is RF and his poems. . . ." His cooperation in textual matters was Holt's for the asking. In addition, he asked for assistance in getting a copy of a clipping from the Holt file on RF. On January 30, he wrote, thanking Sloane for sending a copy of RF's response to the National Institute gold medal award. In his great enthusiasm for that document, he wrote:

I think it ought to go into the book, and I hope he will agree to its appearance there. At all events, I'm pleased inside me to realize that I've shaped the materials for the book, just today handed to a colleague and friend for criticism before I sent it on to you, precisely to the end-point of Frost's response.

In addition to arranging engagements for RF, he was preparing for the appearance in Columbus of John Holmes on February

25 and 26. In a letter of January 22 he discussed various details of that appearance and noted: "Top news is that apparently I'm to go ahead with the collection of RF's prose for Holt."

Two paragraphs of this period, related to arrangements for RF, give valuable glimpses of RF:

> You are very wise to be planning to make use of the microphone and the public address system. Frost *can* make himself heard through a large auditorium; but he makes many "asides" that except for a few in the very front rows are lost unless they are picked up by sensitive microphones. That last plural was deliberate: I suggest that three microphones be placed around the lectern, so that no matter what direction he faces there will be one mike that will pick up his voice directly.

* * *

> Fifteen minutes on his feet before the whole student body would drain Mr. Frost almost as much as an hour before an evening audience. He knows only one way to do a thing, and that's with his whole strength. It wouldn't be fair to impose on him the necessity for two high voltage discharges in one day. So *the* thing must be just the one or the other, the morning or the evening, though, as I wrote you earlier, a lesser thing, such as a luncheon or an after-lecture supper, may be arranged, and at that he will be glad to talk and read again.

On January 26, Newdick wrote to RF reviewing the elements covered in the Sloane correspondence, mentioned concluding the Iowa State arrangements, touched on the coming appearance of Holmes in Columbus, referred to a lot of work connected with preparing for a new course in American literature, noting that he was slated "to be given an increase in salary, promotion, and direction of the departmental offerings in American literature." He unwittingly added, "We'll see." He restricted himself to:

> One petition, selected from many I'd like to make: If you are willing for me to see your letters to Thomas Bird Mosher, of which there are seven or eight preserved, won't you write me a letter to send on to his widow in Portland? Miss Elizabeth Lamb, Mosher's secretary for many years,

insists. I'd like mightily to see the letters, because from them I know I can prove to myself that you had not offered a book of poems to an American publisher before you went to England, and also that an American publisher asked you for a book of your poems before any book appeared but after you were pretty well committed to the firm of David Nutt. [The letter was returned from Key West on February 14.]

On February 1, Sloane wrote to say that the *Collected Poems* was already on the press when Newdick's offer to eliminate errors was received. In spite of a tart statement that what causes most errors is the author's making last-minute changes by letter and telegram, he did identify the offer of help as generous and stated his regret at not being able to benefit by it.

A paragraph about the prose book referred to the royalty arrangement as very generous on Newdick's part, indicating Sloane had no knowledge of it. Then he mentioned that, two weeks previously, RF had said he was in the embarrassing position of having "about eight" people who wanted to write the preface to *his* book, one which would contain many prefaces. He added that he could not comment further on the essay Newdick had sent him until "Robert Frost's own mind is more crystallized on the whole book."

Naturally, the mention of so many other possible participators in the prose book struck a nerve: "Eight! I knew of three, but eight sends me reeling!" Newdick quickly got his balance, though, and continued:

> But it oughtn't to: I've known for years now what a curious pack we extreme Frostians make up; how each one likes to think of himself as the closest to the throne, though in part that is owing to Frost's apparent intimacy with everyone with whom he opens up. And trust Frost, with the shrewdness of Mark Twain, to spot the absurdity in anybody else's writing the preface to his book! Absurd, that is, except for the fact that it is a book he may safely "permit" but could "do" himself only with grave peril. On that last point I talked with him frankly, and I retain the impression that he agreed with me. However, whatever he decides about a preface or foreword will be agreeable to me. I'd like best for him to write his own. I'd like least his admitting a third person, and I honestly think it might

look bad for all three. Or maybe the book could go without any formal preface or foreword at all, relying on the *design built into the arrangement of its parts*.

He added his opinion that "*all* of the text" should "pass under Mr. Frost's scrutiny" before going to press. He also gave some examples of "textual confusion."

In his reply, on February 8, Sloane admitted that eight might have been hyperbolic. He gave his opinion that any preface should deal with the circumstances of the book rather than the material in it. He also mentioned that Frost had several times spoken of examining all that went into the book. Sloane was looking forward to more discussion of the book on his return from Florida. On that same day, Sloane sent Newdick an autographed copy of the new volume of *Collected Poems*, at "Robert Frost's request." The book was mailed on February 16. Newdick wrote, in anticipation of it, "Can I really believe RF put me on the list? You see, I suspect your own thoughtfulness to be manifest here." On February 17, Sloane reported that RF had thought of it on his own, without prompting.

On February 11, Newdick sent a letter of two and a half pages, to precede the manuscript for the book of Frost prose, which he was about to send. In addition to discussion of kinds of material included and possible titles for the book and their merits, these two paragraphs seem of continuing interest.:

> As for the by-line, it is important, I think, that the part of the editor be minimised [sic] throughout. The substance that makes the book the book is all Frost's. The editor is chiefly a device (a) to protect Frost from hostile critics who might resent any implicit avowal on *his* part of his significance as a judge in literary matters generally, and (b) to make possible the collection of small, scattered, yet significant bits from out-of-the-way interviews, partial reports of talks, etc.,—bits that an enthusiast will be pardoned for setting some considerable store by. Minimising the editor's part would, I think, mean keeping headnotes or footnotes terse and factual. It would involve also, in the by-line, a somewhat new phrasing of his part in the work. The most that could be said would be Collected and Arranged with Notes and a Chronology by . . . . Better would be simply Selected and Arranged by . . . .
>
> Finally, like the matter of the proper title, the organisa-

tion of the book is a fundamental consideration. Frost's own care in the organisation of books is marked and effective,—so much so that I was able to make the "design" of his books the subject of an entire article a few years ago. It follows that any book presenting his writing should be wrought as carefully as possible into a significant pattern of patterns. The dominant pattern, the pattern of the whole, ought to be indicated by the title of the book. The lesser patterns ought to be suggested by the lesser titles set over the natural groupings of the prefaces and parleyings.

He pointed out that he was to be clear of teaching duties from April 1 to October 1: "Most of those six months plus I plan to devote to the biography, but I shall be fortified, professionally, in not rushing the biography if meanwhile there will be a substantial related piece of work accomplished."

In the midst of sending off the manuscript of the prose book, Newdick received RF's letter of February 12:

> At it again are you [referring to arranging appearance dates]? The certainty begins to be established that I shall be seeing you in the fall. I'll have things to tell you by then.
>
> I have just been to Cuba with Paul and Mary Engle. The land is motonously [sic] rich and full of beggars. Any souvenirs were made in Chekoslovakia[,] Paris or the United States. There is no native art or craft. The Engles made good company and so did our grimy little Cuban interpreter who was educated at the normal school at Mansfield Penn and for three years in the American navy.
>
> I am still at a loss what harmless to do with myself.
>
> Perhaps I had better seek money. I dont have to keep telling you my gratitude.

As a postscript to the letter Frost gave his address as: "c/o Hervey Allen / Coconut Grove Florida / till about the twenty second / then, I expect, Boston again."

Newdick replied on February 19:

> I was very happy to have your note from Hervey Allen's, and I am hoping that by air mail this response will reach you there before you start for Boston. . . . It's good to have the news of you direct and to learn that you've been enjoying Florida and Cuba with congenial company.

Mr. Sloane wrote about a week ago that he was sending
me a copy of the new edition of your Collected Poems, and
yesterday the book arrived. Thank you sincerely. What
your poems themselves mean to me, I won't try to say.
But surely I may say I warm to the wisdom and power of
your prefatory essay, some of whose elements I dare to
think I was privileged to hear taking verbal shape when
you were here in Ohio last fall. And I delight in the new
and attractive binding of the volume.

We are already looking forward to your coming out to us
again next fall. My only regret is that the near-week at
Iowa State must necessarily cut down on the time available for the state of Ohio. You know how gladly I make
these arrangements. I won't bother you with or about
details, nor with contracts, except when as at Iowa State
some official red tape requires them.

Early last week I sent to Mr. Sloane, for preliminary
examination and consideration for the proposed book of
your prose, a large collection of materials, a plan for or-
ganizing the materials with consistent and significant
design from the title-page through the last of the obiter
dicta, and a long letter of one-sided discussion—in lieu of a
conference. But I'll be much more comfortable when *you*
have spoken some further word about the book. As it is,
I'm trusting that Mr. Sloane rightly understood you. I hope
he did, for in less than a month now I enter on a half-year of
earned vacation from all University duties, and then will
be free to give my full time to the work.

I asked Mrs. Morrison to send on to you, if she thought
you would care to see it, the offprint of "Robert Frost
Looks at War" from the South Atlantic Quarterly. With
this letter I venture to enclose a half-page newspaper
article from today's [Columbus] Dispatch, on John
Holmes, who will be our guest next weekend. John is
another of the five friendships that have come to me in
some way through you.

To Sloane he wrote, the next day, "Let me be honest in my
dishonesty." Then he quoted the paragraph in his letter beginning with "Early last week" and ending with "whole time to the
work." And then came the following explanation, relating to
matters beyond its particular instance:

The *dis*honesty lies in the suggestion that you may have misunderstood. I'm sure you didn't. But I do want RF to speak out and not let the matter go by a kind of default. Many things between us have gone by default, and — so far — happily. Nevertheless I prefer assurance. I'm pretty sure you'll understand my concern and smile at the disingenuous device.

Without question, the major event of March was the passage of three letters between Holmes and Newdick. The first was from Holmes, started on March 6, stating his very great enjoyment of being with the Newdicks: "You made me feel that the whole of Ohio is very friendly and stimulating." Only the first page was written on March 6; it stated RF had invited him to lunch the next day, after which Holmes could finish the letter. It was not until March 12 that he did so, conceivably at trepidation over what he was going to write. He does not give any explanation for the delay but plunges in:

SUNDAY MARCH 12. The lunch with RF was very good. We stayed in the apartment, and he cooked things himself, including the best fried chicken I ever ate. I can't remember much we talked about, but felt a sinking at the heart when I spoke of you and the fine impression I brought back from Ohio. His old stubbornness boiled up again, and he said he would have to have a showdown with you—though I couldn't see just what he meant. But metaphorically he said he had spent his life heaping up piles of building material—friends, experiences, memories—and leaving them behind him unused to be used sometime when, as and how he wished. He said that this material he feels is his possibly for poems, and that once shaped by another hand isn't quite his any more. I am simply reporting. You can judge what he feels.

Of Frost's appearance at Tufts, about which there were early difficulties, Holmes gave this report:

. . . However, the occasion was a great success. The chapel was packed, and he was in rare form. Of course, to my obvious anxieties I had the added and more secret one that he might be feeling contrary, or half-sick, or something. But not so. There was just enough pleasure to his sense of biography and importance in the occasion to give extra effort, and make a talk I heard several people say was better than the talks at Harvard at the Norton lectures. His theme was play in the realm of wisdom. He read the three poems he had read 24 years ago at Tufts, The Sound of Trees, Birches, and Road Not Taken. He said, by the way, that the latter described Edward Thomas, and not any incident of his own life.

The length and concentration of Newdick's reply of March 15 attest what an emotional matter the writing of a biography of Frost by Newdick was:

Well, here I am, back from the depths. In reading, at noon, that part of your letter written on Monday the sixth, I glowed. Then I passed on to that part written Sunday the twelfth, and willy nilly I hit bottom. I ate lunch, but the food lay in an undigested ball in my stomach. Then I went to bed, thinking a nap might bring me back, but it was no go. For dinner I simply went through enough motions to deceive Tucky, for I had no desire for more lead in my mid-section. Next I tried writing short semi-business letters, but when I'd rewritten one of them four times I knew I couldn't hide there. Finally I went off to a movie, Idiot's Delight. That, believe it or not, did the trick . . . .

You can guess what set me down, and you must forgive me for writing first, and possibly in this letter only, of that—RF's tirade. I tried, you remember, to prepare you for that,—and perhaps at the same time was trying to prepare myself. I can think of no one, literally no one, of whom he has spoken to me, from Elinor on down, against whom he has not spoken at one time or another or repeatedly, with blasting and devastating force. I was therefore quite sure that in speaking with others he would take me to town too, that I could not reasonably think I would be a solitary exception.

But this is the first time that I've had an honest report of it. And you mustn't, seeing what it's done to me, be sorry you made the report, for I am not. I am glad, and grateful to you. As an intellectual person, I was prepared for it; as an emotional person, I find I am not. Finally, of course, intellect will dominate, and when it does I shall be able to profit by what I have learned. For surely in his outburst *the* tender spot was exposed, namely, that the past is and must remain his marble quarry as an artist.

As a reasoning creature, I can have no misgivings. I have never exploited personal contact with him. I have never divulged the contents of any of his letters that I have or know of. I have never made public any hidden knowledge that I have come by through him. I have written strictly by the record, i.e., his poems primarily, then the criticism, then the bibliography, then the facts of other public record. Further, though much for me depends upon the biography and though this present reluctance of his is relatively new, that is, of the last two years of the five I have been working, I have assured him I would go slowly, indeed that I would hold everything for his nod of assent. These are fundamental considerations, and not mere rationalizations, that my reason recalls.

And as a creature of emotions, I am utterly and completely certain of how I stand with him. I give friendship openhandedly; I am slow with affection. I try to take every man at his best, yet I am slow to believe; in fact, the more I wish to believe, the slower I am to believe, and I am slower still to act upon the belief. And despite all the evidence, small bits and large chunks, despite even that fine letter I showed you which he wrote me on the eve of my departure for California at Christmas 1937, I would not admit to myself until after he left here last October that all was clear and certain between us fundamentally. I *have* feared the "knifing" of jealous ones, for I know from seeing him in company how he will lead a critical one on to be more and more critical of one absent, and I have sometimes felt that he fed upon such criticism as a sort of inverted praise of himself, though I have steadfastly refused to be so tricked myself; and some of that fear, as I disclosed to you in speaking of Mrs. Morrison, DeVoto, and McCord, I must admit still to exist. Yet the conviction truly remains, emotionally and intellectually, that knifers always end by slipping and cutting themselves more harmfully than they have injured their victims, and that I have been too completely honest in every aspect of our friendship and of our relationships beyond or rather outside of friendship to be caught.

I am writing at night by the clock, but in the morning of the friendship and may I say affection between us. And what I ask now is that you will do more than report, that you will put your mind to this with mine for enough of a stretch and give me your impressions and counsel, for I wish to live in no fool's paradise. You said: [Here Newdick quoted Holmes, beginning with "His old stubbornness" and ending with "judge what he feels."]

It's in judging what he feels that I feel your impressions and analysis will be helpful to me. I can't see how any of the material is "shaped by another hand," and so less "his," how it can be so thought of, before publication of the biography, none of which he has seen, and all of which waits upon his nod, — and some of which he has offered to read in order to assist me with the chiaroscuro! And I think I told you that I told him I had made it a point not to follow on his trail with continuing friendships unless his friends first made overtures to *me*. "Showdown" implies opposition? In what? Not surely as in poker, from which he draws a figure in *A Further Range*, where one player tries to outfigure, outmaneuver, outwit, outbluff, another! No matter what analysis I attempt, I can't make the pieces fit a pattern, either in themselves or in relation to patterns of the past between us. And I can't think of an analysis that defensively. I'm self-deceptively avoiding. I do therefore need talk-over and counsel, and I hope you'll have time and the heart for it.

Puzzled, and possibly confused, but solidly yours.

When he replied on March 18, Holmes said he had been afraid he was "throwing back a small bomb" but did not expect it would hit quite so hard. He thought Newdick had answered all his own questions: "In other words, you had prepared for it. As you say, the mind expected and was ready for some wild-animal move on Robert Frost's part, but the beast hurt."

I appreciate that you appreciate my not holding back on what I heard Robert Frost say. Let me review it, and comment on it. He actually said nothing more than that what is his is his. I think that knowing him for an untamed, wary, stubborn, easily alarmed man, you can well be prepared for such flights any number of times. It is a variation of his non-conforming. He wants you to write about him;

then he ducks; then his egotism and hope for future reputation works again and he wants the biography; then some
deep self-accusation will come up and he'll think what the
hell, leave me alone, why force myself on posterity; and
then more profanity. In other words, he's a touchy animal,
and you have to expect this sort of thing. As a good trainer,
you ought not to jump so nervously.

The rest of the letter made these significant remarks about
Frost and Newdick:

You are working with a wiser foresight than anyone
who has made his acquaintance, because you do not borrow his light, do not try to crowd into the camera picture
of Frost. The others, whose names we know and suspect,
will certainly crowd themselves right out in the end. Your
sincerity and reasonableness and thoroughness will take
you through to the goal you have in sight. Lean on those
things you have already built, and they will support you.

You quote back at me what sounds very ungrammatical
and cramped as a report of what he said. Let me trim that
and make it right. We were eating in the apartment; he had
cooked the meal. He was in calm mood and good humor;
twinkling, even, I had meant to tell him at some length
about you and your work and resources, and thought I was
but introducing the subject when I said I had just been to
Columbus. But he damped it and me. He said then that he
would have to have a showdown. He said that he felt (I
didn't say this before and I think he is wrong in thinking
it and should be corrected) that you needed the biographical rights for your own advancement, and that while he
was perfectly glad to see you get ahead, he didn't want to
have the biography written on those terms only. I felt very
badly. I felt that he was being cruel, probably careless in
putting it that way, and unhappy himself. All that I wanted
to tell him about you, which was strong in me from the
Columbus visit, was choked off. He then made the comparison I told you of, his past and the heaps here and there
of building material; the metaphor his own. Looking at the
way I said it to you, I really think you need not feel as badly
as you do. You might, as you say, expect that he'd dodge
and parry in this way.

Others will destroy their own value to him, but you will strengthen yours. This is one of the trials of it. I wish you could see him more often. If you did, this sort of thing would not bother you, because it would be a matter of daily and weekly occurrence, as you already know is likely. You wouldn't mind such a remark at close quarters, in other words; but as reported by me, which I assume as a faithful report, it takes on sinister color. This is true of any man's letters to anyone anywhere; it is one of the risks of distance. My feeling is that you are very firm with Frost, but must be ready for his sudden turnings and twistings; it is harder for you when you hear of them from a distance.

As a matter of fact, I want to make it clear that what he said he perhaps forgot the next day. You will know how to take a remark he makes: he talks all day and every day; you can't pin any one thing down as final, so for heaven's sake take what I have told you as relative. Take it as merely a flash, a signal, a hint that your way is not smooth ahead—but no more than that.

I am afraid I hurt you. But not because I said something that is not so; I reported out of friendship what happened. I wish it hadn't exploded in your face so loudly. You have all the qualities in you that will win RF if you could only be near him. Letters, however eloquent, are not very effective. If casually and naturally and constantly you could be with him or in his reach, or he in yours, such a jam as I seem to have pushed you in need never happen. You would take it in the day's talk. My point is that you really know that is so. It is only seeing a casual remark in a letter reported, and then worrying about it, that makes you feel so bad. Now, have I made clear my sense of your soundness about the approach to him you have adopted? I think your instinct is extraordinary; that word in its simple sense. You know the right road; trust it.

Surely what I have reminded you of fits a pattern you really know, a pattern of personality (RF's) and behavior you already have seen and recorded. I think, finally, that what you have gone through as a result of my abrupt reporting of a remark is evidence of your worthiness of the job undertaken; you only need to be in close touch with

him to make him feel at ease with you. You are as sensitive
as he is, I now feel; as open to breath and look and hint;
and as deeply honest. Don't worry. Don't feel badly. Take
it, if you can, as the price of being the one you are, and the
sign of being the biographer you shall be.

Earlier in the month, Newdick had written this view of Frost
to a man in Melrose, Massachusetts, who wanted to include
him in a series:

I would suggest that in writing him you make him a
concrete and definite offer. Name the sum you can afford
to pay him, and I may say I never schedule him for less
than $250. As for dates, name a definite list, however long,
so that he or Mrs. Morrison can make a choice. And be
sure to say something about the esteem in which you hold
him and the esteem in which the audience will hold him.
And, finally, it might be well for you to write to him in
your character as a private individual rather than in your
capacity as an agent, that is, on your personal letterhead.

At the same time, March 7, writing to a magazine editor,
Newdick gave a review of his writing program in reference to
Frost:

You didn't specify just what kind of an article you would
like from me or what kinds the *Review* looks upon favorably. My program in writing of Mr. Frost, while the mag-
num opus of the biography is coming along gradually, is
not to repeat myself, but in each paper to handle—with
some finality, I hope—a different aspect of his life or writing. At the present time I have two essays in my work-
book that might now go out, a shortish one on "Robert
Frost and Free Verse," a longer one on "Some of Robert
Frost's Book Inscriptions." You might not think the latter
a likely subject, but you would be surprised at his variety,
tact, humor, whimsicality, and so on, in that sometimes
burdensome business; and if you wished it I could furnish
also a photograph made of him autographing a book at the
Boston Book Fair last November.

Of course I have many "subjects" listed ahead, and notes
already prepared on some of the subjects; but in general
I prefer to write an article first and to think of placing it
only after it's done. One I might now write up for you,

because I am on the point of doing so anyway, is one dealing with the verse-tributes that have been paid to Frost, and it would be timely now because the current issue of *College Poetry* focuses on Frost. Otherwise my writing time for this coming spring is pledged to a portrait of Frost for the *Atlantic*.

On March 15 Sloane wrote to report that he had had a brief telephone conversation with RF about the prose collection. Frost was eager to enlarge the section of "deliberately written" pieces and to decrease the number of stenographic reports and excerpts. Sloane said he would prefer a book which was Robert Frost's best prose rather than all of his prose.

In that letter and as of March 30 he discussed the material in the Holt files referent to RF. He reported himself to be under explicit orders of the board of directors not to allow the materials out of company possession for any reason. The main point seems to have been that some of the documents dealt with "flaws in certain of Mr. Frost's copyrights." He said there was nothing "secret, disgraceful, or sensational" in the papers.

On March 26, 1939, RF received at Apartment 30, 88 Mt. Vernon St. in Boston this telegram: GREETINGS AND GOOD WISHES ON YOUR BIRTHDAY from THE NEWDICKS. By this time Newdick was reasonably certain it was RF's 65th birthday.

It was in April that Newdick was able to turn his attention fully to his work on Frost, as he thought for the next six months. Thus it seems reasonable to guess that several sheets headed "Why write a biography?" may have been written as he started that period of unobstructed work; the document may also have been a result of the heart-searching caused by Holmes' report of RF's remark. Just after the heading Newdick wrote this syllogism: "Man: light on work:: work: light on man."

Three elements are enumerated under the topic of "How write a biography?":

Fact, surely, not fancy or even half-fancy. F. and h.f. make for pleasant reading, but reader never knows where one leaves off and other begins,—or writes either!

Thesis—if any—emerging *from* facts. The thesis biog. like a lawyer's argument: may be brilliant, but only one side. Thesis may change; facts won't.

Facts have their levels, tho even taken above. E.g., facts

of dates, facts of private peculiarities,—one desirable, other not—certainly not for a living person: too snoopy. Authors expose themselves as artists, not as individuals: no invasion of rights of privacy. Boswell or Johnson?

Newdick's second sheet was headed "Poetry of *ideas* primarily." Under that he had four paragraphs:

You can go through the *year* with Frost: *you can go through life with him. His* life, yes, primarily; but, because of thinking that elevates the particular into the general, *all* life too.

But not in barren intellectual terms: in *dramatic* terms, whatever the form. Drama at the core: man in action—with self, with others, with ideas embodied, with abstractions (so the circle back to self is completed).

Drive of ideas is at fundamentals. So conversation; so poem. Poems of course were condensed, concentrated economical: more artistic.

Functioning first, yes; but, then, afterwards, expressive —bold words, grouped to express one idea, chosen to express mood—often a mood that is apprehended more than comprehended. Double meanings—triple—quadruple!

The third page of the document concerns itself with:

Related ideas. A central unvarying philosophy. Matured young—or born old! Development, no doubt; but hardly change. Evolution accepted, with *corollary of* STRUGGLE! No use for wishy-washiness. Toughness of fiber: physical, mental, spiritual: (a) work, (b) hard thinking, (c) blinder-free conjectures, intuitions, groping, readings. Reliance on (a) and (b); (c) a metaphysical playground. No victimization, even by evolution-struggle concept. Keep doing, keep thinking, keep feeling. Carlyle, not Pater, Arnold, not Wilde; Wordsworth, not Swinburne, Dobson et al.

No lyrics *just* songs, melodies, and so on.
No narratives just story.
No dramatic bits just conflict qua conflict.
Each what it is, yes; but more, too.

And he concluded this attempt to capture his own attitude

toward the work which so absorbed him with this statement on the fourth page:

> The only right justification that one can have for looking narrowly into the life of an artist lies in the conviction that thereby one can throw more light on the artist's work and so promote greater understanding and appreciation of it. Conversely, however, the work throws light on the man. Where both are worthy and admirable, both may properly be regarded for themselves.

A letter to Sloane of April 3, the period to which the foregoing ruminations have been (arbitrarily) assigned, speaks for itself in showing Newdick in another mood:

> Let me first thank you for your letter of March 30 and then respond to it. I think I must have given you a wrong impression of the kind of factual matter I am looking for. I should not think of including petty legal points in the biography. What I am after here is the "story," and a story I know there is, though every fact must be checked. Suppose I tell you what I know or think I know, and ask my questions as they come up? I shall make no effort at style here, but simply at substance. Here goes:
>
> (1) While in London in the summer of 1914 with her daughter, Mrs. Henry Holt heard of the furor Robert Frost's *North of Boston* was creating in literary circles, bought a copy, and brought it back with her to her farm home in Vermont, from which she wrote Mr. Frost, then living at Little Iddens in Gloucestershire, a note of appreciation.
>
> (2) Mrs. Holt called her husband's attention to the book, and he forthwith entered into negotiations with the firm of David Nutt, imported sheets, bound them with his own title-page inserted, and published the book late in December, 1914, or very early in January, 1915.
>
> (3) When Frost returned to America in the spring of 1915, he had difficulty in getting Thomas' son through Ellis Island; but, with the assistance of friends, among them his new friends at Henry Holt and Company, he succeeded.
>
> (4) Pleased with the success of *North of Boston* and with the author thereof, Holt then undertook to bring out his works in America from then on. In England, Frost had

agreed to let Nutt (i. e., Mrs. Nutt) have the next two books after *A Boy's Will*, not (as in the case of *North of Boston*) from imported sheets, but from its own plates.

(5) All of this was while Alfred Harcourt was manager of Holt's trade department, and it was Harcourt who got from Frost the MS of *Mountain Interval*, published in 1916.

(6) There was a contract entered into between Frost and Henry Holt and Company that provided for a minimum regular income for him for some years in the future. That minimum was subsequently increased to $3000 a year. Later (last year) it was reduced to $1500,—though Frost's actual income remained constant because royalties and permissions exceeded, indeed doubled, the base figure.

There you have, in brief, the whole "story" as I know it now. And all of those points are ones to be used, except, of course, the figures and facts of point 6. You see how that story, from the very beginning, sheds a factually golden light on Holt's—points 1, 2, 3, and the first sentence of point 6. You see also—point 4—of what solid service to Frost his publisher proved to be in helping him out of an intolerable position, namely, that of being bound to Nutt on an entirely one-sided contract. (Point 5 is relatively unimportant.)

All I wish is to have these points approved as accurate from the records. And I should like, for my own guidance in seeing the panorama of Frost's life unfold, to have the dates attached to the facts, as nearly as dates can be attached to them. And if there are any further facts that heighten the understanding I now have, I should like them,—just as I should like facts, if there are any, that change the picture in any essential point. Certainly neither RF nor HH&Co. nor RSN wishes to be a party to any but a strictly factual representation. And there need be no mention of the fact, which I and every publisher knows, that neither *A Boy's Will* nor *North of Boston* is protected by copyright,—though I take it to be a tribute to American publishers that no one of them has ever, to my knowledge, pirated either book.

It may be that you understood what I was driving at from the outset, but I have written thus lengthily because it seemed to me that you and the directors were thinking of me as trying to pry into minutiae that are not now any of my business and never will be. I shall be entirely content with what *you* may give me, in a letter, from the records, as really pertinent. I suggested that I do the looking only because I thought it would be an imposition to ask you to examine them. And you already have my word that I shall use nothing in print anywhere that is not approved both by you and Robert as to both substance, context, and implication.

Now let me speak to your letter of March 15.

It's capital news that Mr. Frost will add to the deliberately written material for the book of his prose! And you are quite right that the book should be, as nearly exclusively as possible, made up of his best prose rather than of all of his prose. There's time enough in the future, maybe a generation or two hence, for a meticulous gathering and publication of everything. The book of a living author must be one that justifies itself through itself,—even when the device of a "collector" is employed,—if it prove that one be employed.

But you know, as I do, that there's no rushing RF, on anything. I'll mention the book from time to time, and so will you, so that he will know there's no loss of interest; but he must be the one to move. You know, however, how eager I am to move, and I know you'll let me know when I may. Meanwhile, suppose you let me have the typescript back for me to put into a shape that RF might see without disappointment.

After the end of the letter, Newdick wrote in the lower left-hand corner: "What were *your own* impressions of the suggested organization?"

On the same day he wrote a query concerning RF's Swedenborgian background. It is notable for the following considerations: "I know that Robert and Elinor were married by a Swedenborgian clergyman. But was that only out of deference to the convictions of Robert's mother? Or is it a fact that Robert himself was for a while a Swedenborgian? I have never been able to get him to say positively. . . ."

On April 9 he wrote to "Dear Robert," mainly about the scheduling he had been trying to do. Pointing out that it had been "nearly two months now since my last letter to Mrs. Morrison, to which I have not had an answer," he pointed out that "I can rest easily only after you give your final approval to the schedule for your Ohio lectures next October." His discussion of the proposed schedule is of interest for what it displays of his conclusions about and consideration for RF:

> To make the schedule as clear as possible I have made a kind of annotated calendar and map. You will be through at Ames on Friday night. Nearly three full days are allowed for the trip from Ames to Columbus. We are hoping and planning that you will make your headquarters in Columbus with us. I have respected your wish and made no Columbus engagement for you, but Granville, Delaware, and Springfield are within an hour's drive from Columbus; Oxford is a three hours' drive—driving at 35 or so—about a hundred miles. Every speaking date is cushioned by a day for rest—two at the week-end. And on your Saturday here, Cornell will play Ohio State in the stadium.
>
> However, in order that I may meet your wishes, I have set only one of these dates finally for you, that at Springfield; and I can close up the schedule, as it were, if you prefer: Oct. 23, Granville; Oct. 24, Oxford; Oct. 25, Cleveland; Oct. 26, Delaware; Oct. 27, Springfield. But that would be a killing pace, and I hope you will not choose to undertake it. The present schedule, with cushion days, is in line both with last year's and with Mrs. Morrison's counsel. But do please let me know your pleasure in the question of the schedule so that the various program chairmen can be reassured.

Patience was needed. On April 21 he sent a telegram to a group in Louisville: WROTE FROST TEN DAYS AGO. WIRED YESTERDAY. NO RESPONSE YET. But patience (and effort) were rewarded. He was able to write on April 29 that "Robert Frost has now given his final approval to the schedule I have arranged for him next autumn. . . ."

In a letter of April 27 to Holmes, Newdick gave this picture of his work on the biography:

> I'm concentrating day after day after day on the biography. That means many hours at a stretch in note-finding, note-jotting, note-arranging and-rearranging, until the data fall into patterns and patterns of patterns. It means

constant consciousness that the man matters because of
the poems, that all included fact and interpretation point
either to the shaping of the man positively or negatively,
to roads taken or not taken or not taken for long. It means
writing, rewriting, typing, revising, retyping, until at
length there emerges what may legitimately be called a
tentative first draft. I suppose fiction must be just as difficult in its way. . . .

Probably the Harvard chapter was at that moment a particular
focus, for he wrote Holmes on May 3 a note that, "I hope you've
put off any careful reading of the chapter on RF at Harvard—it
has gone through drastic revision, and probably will be recast
again!"—The chapter as he left it uses the Sheffield quote in its
entirety.

In response, Holmes having read both of the "Harvard Days"
chapters, made this comment:

> It seems to be true of RF, as you say in the second ver-
> sion, that he is always absorbing more than he realizes.
> That has deep implications. I was startled to see Sheffield
> so accurately and mercilessly pictured. He still teaches,
> now at Wellesley, and belongs to the English Lunch Club,
> and I see him now and then. I see you have removed some
> of the description of Sheffield.

As busy as Newdick was on the manuscript, he was not too
busy to be concerned with maintaining a good relationship with
Lesley. He wrote her on May 10: "Though I've been troubled
for some time now at no word from you I'm trusting that all is
really well, that if in any way I gave a shadow of offence you'd let
me speak to clear it up." He enclosed a "short new paper" (title
undisclosed) which he hoped she would "read and pass upon."
It seems unquestionable that he hoped to have her contribute
her observations to the RF biography, something which had not
happened so far. "It's been many moons since I turned away
from the central work to write an article, but reading in the
poems the other day with an eye to the out-of-doors, the impulse to do this one overcame me. . . . [allowing the idea the
article might have been "Robert Frost's Way with Flowers," one
of the last he wrote.]" ". . . on new writing I want your approval
or disapproval, according to our understanding." The identity of
the essay sent to Lesley is made practically certain by the fact

that he sent, on the same day "a short, slight, but I hope personal essay on one aspect of Robert Frost's knowledge of nature" to Sloane. He asked Sloane if he had any objection to as long a quotation as he had made from "Blueberries." The essay on "Flowers" quotes fourteen lines from that work.

A letter of which Newdick was never to know, postmarked May 18, from RF to Sidney Cox, who had doubtless written of his relationship to Newdick, made some very pertinent remarks. Because Cox wrote two major documents related to Frost, one before and one after this letter, the comments on Cox-Frost compliment the ones on Newdick-Frost. The letter was written on the specific occasion of Cox's being granted his full professorship at Dartmouth. Frost says he makes Cox out to be forty-five. What is he going to do with the remaining half of his life?

> One thing more to day and then I will have done with indoctrination forever, the agreement to date from the day of your promotion to fullness. I should think we could afford to be a little easier in the spirit without any risk of losing your invaluable affrontery. Positively that's my last. Lets lay off being personal with each other. Let our object be to be objective. Lets tell each other ideas we have. I have always hoped you might sometime publicly remember me in writing, but I got discouraged by the way you started off on my having sought you at least as much as you sought me. What the hell has that kind of inferiority superiority got to do with two people like us? Unless I have got him stopped the poetry editor of Time is presently going to deal with me in some such deplorable scandalousness. Newdick will be too personal. There is only you left to be uniquely mental with me mind to mind. Maybe I ask too much too vaguely. Damn it I dont want to dictate the book. What Henry Holt printed was all right [*Robert Frost / Original "Ordinary Man,"* Holt, 1929]. But you could go still higher into the thought realm for my taste. . . . I lead a life estranged from myself. I had a wretched time in Florida. One friend, my secretary has taken me in hand to keep me lecturing and talking as of old. But I am very wild at heart sometimes. Not at all confused. Just wild-wild. Couldnt you read it between the lines in my Preface nay and in the lines? All the more

reason for your being objective with me. Nothing can save
me for any more verse but unscrupulous reality.

On May 28, Newdick wrote to "Dear Robert" that "since our
last word from you the snow *on* the ground has gone and come
back in great balls of white set in foliage *off* the ground, but you
are ever in our thoughts and we have taken pleasure with you in
the Ralph Waldo Emerson fellowship at Harvard." Noting a few
activities, he pointed out that he had "been writing otherwise
as energetically as the highwaymen come riding." He concluded, "It's a long time until next October, and unless you
flag me down I'll be looking you up for a call when I come to
New England in July. Don't flag!"

A month later, Newdick received notice from the secretary
of the Graduate School at Ohio State that he was being granted
"$75 to be used as travelling expenses in obtaining further
material in connection with your biography of Frost." For that
day, this was very eminent evidence of the strong interest,
maintained over several years by departmental and administrative officials in the work on Frost, which produced a steady
stream of articles, to total thirty-one items, in four years of the
most intense, dedicated, and thoughtful work. By that time, as
he wrote Dr. Burnham on June 23, he had "sketched through
the biography from Frost's birth to 1905 . . . ."

On July 5, Newdick's secretary, Jean H. Hammond, acknowledged "receipt of your elongated package" from Miss Sylvia
Clark of Derry. "I am sorry to have to tell you that Dr. Newdick
is in the hospital suffering from an appendectomy. At the present time his condition is serious, but it is believed that as soon
as he can digest food there will be improvement."

Lettered in at the bottom of the sheet which has the carbon
of the Clark letter is the following copy for an undated telegram:

Robert Frost
Apartment 30, 88 Mt. Vernon Avenue
Boston, Mass.

   Bob Newdick died rather suddenly last night. Letter
follows.

                                        Paul R. Weidner

The date given in other such letters to Frost informants is July 7.
Naturally, the wheels of research, which Newdick had

worked so ardently to place in motion, continued in motion.
The day after his death, a librarian in the California State Library at Sacramento wrote:

> I have read your chapter on Robert Frost's boyhood days
> in San Francisco with much interest. It make me eager to
> read the book when it is published.
> You seem to have captured the spirit of San Francisco in
> the 70's and brought it to life. Of course you know that
> San Franciscans were very annoyed over Kipling's remarks, but the description does work in beautifully with
> your subject. . . .
> I do not detect any serious errors in the manuscript.
> I checked the newspapers to see if I could verify the date
> of birth of the sister but I was unable to locate a notice for
> either date.

To this correspondent, Miss Hammond wrote, on July 10, a
few more details of Newdick's death: "He had undergone an
appendectomy and was doing very nicely, but an infection
(septicemia) set in and proved fatal. Everything happened so
rapidly that it completely stunned us and we are still somewhat
upset."

Newdick had been attempting for a number of months first to
get an address for Edgar Gilbert, RF's friend of Lawrence days.
Gilbert, very busy head of Gilbert Research Institute in Morristown, New Jersey, had begun to consider how he could record
what he knew of Frost, for whom he had both affection and
admiration. One result was that he introduced Frost when he
appeared at the Morristown YMCA on May 4, 1939. On April
26, he appeared before the Rotary Club of Morristown to speak
about Frost in preparation for his friend's anticipated appearance. The following paragraphs from an article in the *Morristown Record* of April 27, sent to Newdick by Gilbert, as related
to statements by an eye-witness of Frost's life in Lawrence,
seem worthy of quoting:

> Mr. Gilbert reviewed the ancestral antecedents of
> Robert Frost whom he referred to as "a New England
> Yankee."
> In "The Death of the Hired Man," Mr. Gilbert said that
> Frost reveals the influence of his early days. The inspira-

tion for the poem came from the experience Mrs. Frost and her children had when Mr. Frost, Sr., died and the bereaved family was taken in by his parents who gave the newly arrived dependents a grudging reception.

Robert Frost was deeply influenced by his mother and many of her sterling qualities live in him.

The article concluded with the notation that "The speaker said he would be particularly interested in watching Frost read his poems because he seems to be creating as he goes along." Gilbert had heard Frost read Shakespeare in the mill where they worked together in Lawrence.

Gilbert sent, on July 30, to Newdick, a copy of the introductory remarks he was invited to make when RF appeared on May 4. Reminding his listeners that he had on several occasions in the past month "told you of the life and work of Robert Frost in order that you might more fully enjoy the literary treat that is before you this evening," Gilbert told the audience, ". . . he saw through a world that most of us never see until it is pointed out to us." He felt he could say of Frost: "When we first became friends, nearly half a century ago, a poem was his life. In the years that have followed he has made his life a poem." Thus Gilbert was substantiating Frost's recollection of his intense and consuming interest in poetry when he was in high school at the age of fifteen.

In opening the letter, which came too late for Newdick, Gilbert apologized that his personal work had kept him too busy to reply earlier. He devoted his first paragraph to criticism of the garbled account of Frost's lecture which appeared in the *Morristown Record*. He refers to similar distortion of his own remarks in the several times "I talked . . . before organizations of the better type of mind, to get them interested in this very interesting man and imbued with the desire to hear him." He enclosed the clipping of his talk before Rotary, "which you will read as illustrating and justifying my complaint." Thus it is not possible to tell whether he was actually responsible for the interesting observation that the core of "The Death of the Hired Man" is parallel to the reception Belle Frost and her children received in Lawrence. He apologized for not getting an account of the Frost lecture: "Sitting as I did on the platform with Bob and Nuttle, I could not gracefully make even notes. . . ." Of response to the lecture, he noted:

At any rate, the lecture was fine. The audience was certainly delighted, both with his penetrating and humorous remarks on literary matters in general and with his rendition of his poems. Many had brought with them copies of his books, and after the lecture pressed him to autograph them, which he did very graciously with little pointed comments and advices. I have talked with many who attended, and have been gratified with the consensus of approval expressed. What more can I say to you, who knew they would like him? Incidentally there was a substantial sale of the several volumes of his poems at the local bookstore, particularly the March edition by Halcyon House, selling at the popular price of $1.59 and including the collected six books.

He sent these notes of Frost on the lecture circuit:

I met Bob in New York upon arrival of his train from Boston, and brought him home for a brief rest and supper before time for the lecture. He was very tired from his hard trip through the West, and still was scheduled to lecture in Lawrence, Mass. the next evening. So I had to get him back to a returning train at Newark after midnight, in order that he could pass the night on the sleeper and be ready in Boston the next morning for a conference with president Conant of Harvard. Too heavy a program for a man in his tired condition. But he recuperated very effectively in the few hours that we had before the lecture, and showed a well trained self denial in refusing dinner and satisfying his needs with the raw yolks of a few eggs, a roll and a little fruit juice. Mrs. G. was quite concerned as to his ability to sustain the long effort of a lecture. But he surprised us by stepping out upon the platform appearing years younger and with much composure. However toward the end he was plainly getting tired, perhaps to his audience not noticably so.

One incident in regard to the preparations for his visit here was interesting. As is customary when persons of importance are to visit this section in any capacity, the society people are accustomed to seek to entertain them. A wealthy supporter of the "Y" had asked the pleasure of entertaining Bob, and planned to get up a dinner party of socialites. But through his secretary, in messages from Boston, it had been learned that he could not think of undertaking any such functions prior to his lecture, and that he must arrange for prompt departure in order to meet his Boston and Lawrence engagements. In view of conditions, we made his stay here as carefree and comfortable as possible.

Having tantalizingly recalled in an earlier letter that he remembered Frost reading Shakespeare aloud against the noise of the machinery in the mill in Lawrence where they both worked, he ended this letter with the admission that "we are as far as ever from the write up of my early acquaintance with Bob in the days at Arlington Mills." He was delaying his account in the interest of being able to "scrupulously do justice to Bob both then and now." He assured Newdick that "I will compose something for you that will represent an effort on my part to cooperate with you." If he ever did write such an account, it did not reach any student of Frost.

In expressing for Newdick his appreciation of Gilbert's cooperation and helpfulness on August 3, Miss Hammond wrote that "at this time Mrs. Newdick is in the East making arrangements about the completion of the biography of Robert Frost."

What RF responded when he learned of Newdick's death is not precisely known. Mrs. Newdick has said she does not know what she did with his letter. She thought it contained a reference to Frost's poem, "Happiness Makes up in Height What It Lacks in Depth."

A letter to Lawrance Thompson, on July 17, indicates some of his reaction:

> . . . But there's all the sad problem of Newdick's literary remains to consider. I need your advice. You knew him pretty well and how completely he had thrown his life into writing mine. I am told [evidently by Mrs. Newdick, who mentioned this to the writer on June 15, 1972] his mind ran on me in his last delirium. [Newdick also kept inquiring, Mrs. Newdick recalled, if there had been any word from Robert.] What is a miserable hero to say to worship like this? I naturally want to deal tenderly with his memory. You be thinking my predicament over and come only when you can. . . . But there is the reason for an early visit

that Mrs. Newdick is coming for a visit some time in the summer and I should like to have seen you before I see her.

Thompson has reported that he had written, some weeks before Newdick died, for permission to do the book that became *Fire and Ice*, an interpretive volume of 1942. In his letter of July 17, Frost had replied that book could give him "nothing but pleasure." When Thompson visited Frost, he was offered the status of official biographer. This arrangement, RF is reported to have said, would give him a stock protection against people who wanted to do his biography. Thompson agreed on July 29, 1939, accepting the proviso that the official biography was not to be published till after Frost's death, which Thompson probably did not imagine, if he allowed his thoughts to linger on the matter, would be as late as January 26, 1963.

Because it has not been possible to ascertain the exact date of Mrs. Newdick's visit to Frost after her husband's death in the summer of 1939, it is not known what role her visit may have played in the appointment of Thompson. The friend who accompanied Mrs. Newdick on the trip recalled that Mrs. Newdick visited Frost on two different mornings and the two women and their two sons visited Frost during one evening. Mrs. Newdick recalled only the evening: "We sat all one evening in his cottage and listened to him talk about his living alone and joy at Bread Loaf." She added her concentration on what was done and said was weakened by "my thoughts about Bob, who had died earlier that month." Presumably, Frost did not offer any effective help in the matter of getting Newdick's work completed. Very possibly, he did not know how. Too, he probably lacked volition to bring to completion the appearance of any biography of himself.

One piece of evidence of Frost's attitude toward Newdick, in retrospect, is seen in a conversation of 1941, recorded on p. 238 of Louis Mertins' *Robert Frost Talks Walking* (1965). Mertins, whose degree of devotion surpassed that of Newdick, was castigated for doing research on RF in Lawrence and Derry. It was all right, Frost said, to "look up things here in California," where Mertins lived. He did not want them to "come back here where I am living and start nosing about in the years that are over." He said what was remote did not bother him. "When it's near is different." He did not mention he already had a formally-appointed official biographer. But he did say:

I went through all this with Newdick. I suppose I killed
him. You see, he was going everywhere, always carrying
a big brief case packed and jammed with notes about me—
notes gathered here, there and every place. He had amassed
no end of stuff—and it *was* stuff, nothing else much. There
must have been over a million words of it. Much of it was
made up of newspaper interviews, and a newspaper story
makes the worst kind of biographical material. Reporters
rarely get a thing down right, the editor, who always
knows so much more about anything on earth than the
man who wrote the story, changes it to some inane thing,
giving a wrong sense to what you are supposed to have
said. A man's biography made up out of one's repeated
speeches, or interviews, would be a horrifying mess.

Yes, I suppose I killed Newdick. I remember seeing him
at Ohio State, and riding on a train with him. I scolded him
for digging up my past, as have you too. I told him I
wouldn't stand for it, and he'd have to stop it. It broke
his heart and he died.

Of course, I didn't exactly kill him. He died during an
appendectomy, but I didn't help him any. He died very
young. Now his wife is sitting on his manuscript. Holts
wanted to buy it from her, but she demanded an outra-
geous price for it. She wants somebody to collaborate and
finish the book, giving her husband due credit—giving her
due cash.

The last document directly relating to Newdick's work is a
typed letter of December 30, 1953, from RF to Mrs. Newdick:

Dear Marie:

Of course all that material should be in some one's
hands who knows how to take care of it. I have spoken of
it offhand to several but now I will go to work seriously
to help you sell it. We must see if you can't get a car for Jim.
It was good to hear from you. You bring it all back—my
stay with you and the last midnight ride with Robert on
the train coming East. You speak of my letters to him.
I wrote letters in those days, didn't I? I hardly write any
now. You'll hear from me soon or from someone else possibly Mrs. Louis Cohn of the House of Books in New York.

Always your friend
R.F.

After January 1 and permanent address:
35 Brewster Street
Cambridge, Massachusetts.

That was the last Mrs. Newdick heard of the matter. In sales conducted by the Hamilton Gallery in 1966 and 1967, she realized about $10,000 from various letters and documents. The only use made of Newdick's material so far consists of peripheral mention of Newdick in Thompson's biography and the use of one of the letters sold in the *Selected Letters*, edited by Thompson.

III. Newdick's Research Findings

Introduction

When Part II, the narrative of the relationship between Frost and Newdick was first written, the view was taken that the discovery of various information about his subject and his excited response was part of the story.

However, it was true that the units of undigested information were an impediment to the flow of the account. Thus the information is presented in this separate section, ready for the use and edification of those interested in Frost, and not acting as an intrusion in the main element, the excitement Newdick found in his association with Robert Frost.

The reader is informed that the material here presented is an abbreviation and a selection of what may be found in two full file drawers of material. Examples of what may not even be suggested, even in this way, are the bibliography which Newdick prepared, practically complete to his time, and a manuscript of Frost prose selections.

Newdick's Research Findings.

ITEM 1:   Notes for August 29, 1935.

ITEM 2:   Notes for August 30, 1935.

ITEM 3:   Notes for August 31, 1935.

ITEM 4:   Notes for September 1, 1935.

ITEM 5:   Professor Sidney Cox's Summary of Frost as a Teacher.

ITEM 6:   Miss Sylvia Clark and "An A No. 1 Sundown."

ITEM 7:   Professor Henry C. Morrison Meets Robert Frost.

ITEM 8:   Nuggets of Early 1936.

ITEM 9:   Recollections of Newdick's Visit to Frost on July 26, 1936.

ITEM 10:   The Letter of Louis W. Morse.

ITEM 11:   Findings of Dr. J. Forrest Burnham.

ITEM 12:   Observations of Frost's Classmates, Lawrence High School.

ITEM 13:   The Robert von Moschzisker Letter.

ITEM 14:   Conversation with Wilbert Snow.

ITEM 15:   The "Hair" Episode at Dartmouth.

ITEM 16:   Observations of Mrs. Barndollar.

ITEM 17:   Letter of Professor William Ernest Hocking.

ITEM 18:   Newdick's Notes of the Visit with the Frosts, September 1–3, 1937, Concord Corners, Vt.

ITEM 19:   Letter from Edgar Gilbert.

ITEM 20:   Letter of Charles L. Hanson.

ITEM 21:   Newdick's Amherst Observations, April, 1938.

ITEM 22:   Letter of Miss Elizabeth Nelligan.

ITEM 23:   Reminiscence of Justice Louis S. Cox.

ITEM 24:   Relating to Preston Shirley.

ITEM 25:   Robert Frost Inscriptions for John Holmes.

ITEM 26:   Letter of Miss Nettie McQuestin.

ITEM 27:   Letter of Robert Lincoln O'Brien.

ITEM 28:   Manthey-Zorn Observation.

ITEM 29:   Recollections of a Sculptor.

ITEM 30:   Newdick's Notes of Frost in Columbus, Ohio, October, 1938.

ITEM 31:   Professor Sheffield's Recollection.

ITEM 32:   The Selheimer Material.

ITEM 33: Frost Addresses in San Francisco.

ITEM 34: Mrs. Hall's Map of the Derry Farm.

ITEM 35: Burell Documents.

ITEM 36: Membership in the Society of the New Jerusalem (Swedenborgian).

Item 1:

Notes for August 29, 1935.

The following are the notes taken by Newdick after spending August 29, 1935, with RF:

Mother taught at Sullivant Ave. School in Columbus, Ohio. [He once went out to see the school when he was in Columbus.]*

His grandfather and uncle disapproved of her gave her no help in getting a job in Lawrence, as they could easily have done. She got job at Salem, a poor one. The incident of liking the bread because it was good, of making a regular order for it, and then of the necessity of cancelling the order because the family couldn't eat the bread and she couldn't afford to throw the money away. [Let it not be forgotten that half of Frost is Scottish; there's been a bit too much of New England talked.] Schism in the community: Election and vindication on reemployment issue. Next year, two schools! Resignation at end of year. Job in Salem through a friend. [Silver's father (longhand note by Newdick. W.A.S.)] (Not through the family.) Tough customers. F home from Dartmouth for this reason, among others. Asked for mother's assignment and given it, she taking a lower class. F had to beat up the roughies — the only time in his teaching experience. John Hare drew a knife on him, but F disarmed him. F refused to bring charges but asked that the knife be kept as evidence, a memento. John had, it seemed to F, a bad eye, a bad look. On enquiry years later, however, he learned that John was a selectman [technical New England term].

Grandfather disgusted with F. Elinor (Mrs. F.) begged for a farm: the one near Derry for $1,200.

*Newdick's notes employ both brackets and parentheses. The sources of interpolative material, where they could be confused, are keyed by the initials R.S.N. or W.A.S.

Uncle also disgusted. Left his money to a school, for a fence. Here read the poem In Neglect, the one Pound spotted and asked about.

At Derry the F's had no callers for eight years. [i.e. until E.B.F. born and died. (longhand note by Newdick. W.A.S.)]

Hay fever hit F annually about Aug. 15. F not a medicine taker; tried medicine once, with bad results. Tried sealed room: fainted. In good shape until Aug. 15, then miserable.

Swapped farm help with John Barry.

Out twice after eight o'clock in eight years.

In Lawrence one day met Wolcott who knew of F's refusal to be taken under Ward's wing on Ward's terms. . . "What are you doing now?" "Farming a little." "Getting along all right?" "Well, I'm thinking of trying teaching again for a little cash." W knew of opening in Pinkerton Academy, right in Derry, and knew some of the trustees. "Allow time for a letter, then go call." Called and was received by Merriam after being kept waiting. M had received the letter but was suspicious and hedged. To put it up to the other trustees he read F's poem The Tuft of Flowers at the Men's League banquet in the Congregational Church. Those who heard it liked it and crowded around F afterwards. (He had been too bashful to read the poem himself.) Chase came to the farm several days later with the news of the appointment, a part-time one, at fearfully low pay. Had pneumonia the first year.

Principal was old Dr. [Bingham, Geo. W., teacher of Latin. (Newdick longhand note. W.A.S.)]

F disgusted by fuss made about putting on a play a year; so he put on four: *Faustus, Comus,* one of Sheridan's, and a modern one. Dr. Bingham encountered F on the street and buttonholed him. F was fearful at first. But the Dr. was offering the communion service of the church for use in the Circe scene in Comus! Thus F tacitly shamed the complainers at one play.

[Much that F condemns is condemned tacitly. Note the silences in the tribute to Robinson. He won't say what he doesn't really believe. His silences therefore are as eloquent as his sayings, if one can interpret them aright!]

Soon a full time job.

Thereafter began his pilgrimages north for relief from hay fever.

An enemy in Reynolds.

Silver, coming to look over the job as principal, marked F for dismissal. So Chase. Then came Morrison, inspecting, — and spending two of his five hours in F's classes! This Morrison now at Chicago, where he has the reputation of a slave driver. M's approval was more than the equivalent of a degree, the point, or one of them, that both Reynolds and Silver resented.

Now the F's were invited places; now Silver was enthusiastic. But F never quite trusted Silver thereafter.

[F has always been, and still remains, keenly sensitive, and he has a capacity for remembering unkindnesses, though at the same time he is now forgiving.]

Mrs. Pettee's husband a forger, for $10,000. He and F friends after his release from jail. But he never really caught on. Long walks together for a while. (Here F confirmed Mrs. P's story of the origin of Rose Pogonias on one such walk. Here too I told him of Miss Clark's keeping an A-No. 1 Sundown.) [See information developed later in narrative. W.A.S.] Difference between the sisters, Miss C. being unhappy, caustic.

F once attended an informal dinner party at the house. The guests had no part in the conversation: The sisters told anecdotes to each other for the benefit of the guests.

[Miss C. resented Bartlett's (presumably John. W.A.S.) account of hostility toward F, but I felt that F rather agreed with B.]

At Pinkerton, F. gradually took over all the English classes: 35 periods weekly; seven classes daily; no rest periods. F would make the windows rattle one period, would stall the next.

Was in line for principalship; indeed, was offered it. This was after questioning Reynolds' calibre to Chase, so killing R's chances.

F has an enemy in Jack Harris at Amherst. H a friend of E. A. Robinson's; translated some with him. A warhorse, a worker. F once left Amherst because of Harris. Had conference with president, then with him and Dwight Morrow, trustee. Praised the hewers of wood and the drawers of water—and went off to Michigan. Immediately the authorities at Amherst woke up and began to request his return. H is still venomous and rude. F: "I didn't get along by warfare; I just slipped in."

[F is extremely sensitive, and knows it. Suspicious. Needs reassurances. Is determined not to be any sort of "case."]

On the Frost scholarship: Some of F's talks are successful, some not. After a good one (The second at Amherst this last spring) the president took him by the arm on the way out. F: "I told you I was going to ask you for something; everybody else is." "Ask ahead, to the half of my kingdom." F: A scholarship; a scholarship of a new kind: testing a man's ability to live with himself; no travel abroad or in country; no courses; might work at a simple job; accountable twenty or forty years hence; could drop at half year or hold for second year; not necessarily an artist— might be a philosopher; no appointment committee—president and F to be sole judges. President: "How much." F: "Not too much; perhaps $1,000." P: "Do you have a man in mind." F: "Yes; there's a likely young man, the ivy orator. Come out and hear him." P: "I don't care about that. If I can raise the money overnight I'll make the announcement tomorrow. A good many of the alumni are in town." Both went out then to hear the ivy orator read his poem, a good one. The announcement came at a ceremony the next day. F doesn't know where the money came from; perhaps the president dipped into his own pocket. The president is normally a rather cold business man; but, F thinks now, he must really be friendly. The boy the son of an insurance man.

The story of W. K. Brown and "Goodbye and Keep Cold": Mass. State College's Sears: pomology O.K., versification should be mended. S wouldn't believe that B[rown] didn't write it until he saw it in a book of F's. Sheepish ever since. [I told of quoting poem to Miss Hall and of her pointing out what forty below had in fact done to their apple trees.] [See later correspondence. W.A.S.]

Friends with Robinson. Admired him more than any other fellow artist. Later stuff, a falling off. Incurably romantic. Fun in Miniver Cheevy.

Asked for preface for R's last long poem. F: "I don't write prefaces.'' F's first piece, a short one, dealt with the thesis that one can be as serious in philosophy only as far as one can go in play. King Lear. Happiness in words and phrases. This later lost. Break at time of Merlin: "Don't!" Gravely: "I've already done it.'' What everybody was doing in 80's and 90's; Guinevere; deadly. Macmillan called long distance.

Came back from answering at outside phone and wrote again (afraid to wait for letter; it might annoy him, and then he'd write nothing), this time bringing in more Robinson, particularly a conversation re the difference of men: What constitutes a difference? Real differences and false. Poems like algebra and geometry — false. What do you do with your difference? Are you afraid of it or proud of it? And so on. No mention of *King Jasper*. Macmillan's letter requested 2,500 to 5,000 words. All off. Philosophy of life totally different; can't tell just why. F like Matthew Arnold with think [sic] of the Iseult with the children. R off on the slant of the love story. F would think of King Mark's impossible position. The mockery of Miniver Cheevy a mockery of R himself.

W. H. Ward, Maurice Thompson. Visit at office. [Frost later said *No Visit* (longhand note by Newdick. W.A.S.)] W curious about the "Lee": "Southern?" Asked re Lanier too. Ode form for elegy (a la Lanier). W influential, would have pushed for F and made a difference. But F read Lanier, didn't care for him, and said so. A crucial decision, this to follow his own difference. W disgusted. "Then why," I asked, "did the Independent buy later poems?" It was W's sister who insisted on that. —Stacks of MSS. in the office. Casualness of it all. A valuable glimpse of an editorial office. Had had another in Boston. [Hurd (longhand note by Newdick. W.A.S.)]

The Boston venture: Charles Hurd, who had gone to Boston with poems and short stories, met discouragement, and settled down to newspaper. So H discouraged F, but he (F) stuck around for a while. Finally driven to walk back to Lawrence by hunger: ate berries on way, and was sick. Poem or two in Transcript.

The New York venture: Took some pieces of furniture down from Derry to New York; rented a flat; visited editorial offices, e.g. The Sun.

Secretary Wallace a friend. Collier the Indian Commissioner a

Communist. E. S. Sergeant sentimental re Indians. Indian boy at Santa Fe: story of Buck and Doe. Later sentimentalized the version to please Miss S. Wallace on English cooperatives. Collier on Indians as Communists: no property; no money; etc. Indians increasing. Take over country? Back where we were years ago.

F unwilling to republish Bulletin pieces. Of course. But surely the list for the record? Perhaps that.

Favorable to large, cooperative bibliography. Asked re price.

Played football in h. s. Ill after games. No medical attendance then.

[F once wrote the whole issue of the Bulletin, then resigned.] [R.S.N.]

Often gets so far behind in his mail that he throws away a batch and begins again!

In London: Had never heard of Pound. F. S. Flint, after promise, introduced him. Given card. Over by church walk, dropped in. "Hear you have a book." Over to Nutt's to get it; no word on way home. "Find something to read." Chuckle at poem; F knew by chuckle it was In Neglect; told P of uncle leaving money for a school fence. "You don't mind if we like this, do you?" Later: "Go along home now." First review; entirely independent. The story of Skipworth Cannel, the fortune, the pen and ink drawings, and poetry written while you wait. The three bundles: *Smart Set, Egoist, Poetry*. This disillusioned F who took himself seriously. P on Amy Lowell: "I'll have the old gal think she was born writing free verse!" Liked to play Maestro. Jealous of others. Abercrombie and Gibson—"Well, if you will frequent the purlieus of Literature!" — "You are doing the short story, aren't you?" "Well, for the sake of argument, say I am; what about it?" P took thirteen-page short story from shelf. F pointed out ten pages of background. P annoyed. — P now nearly friendless: eager response recently to enquiring college student.

Harold Monro: horse-faced, wall-eyed, two-faced: arm around shoulder, then a nasty crack. Book shop and magazine, bad business. F called on last visit to England. M rude, then gave a party, then remarked re an anthology, "Only the best in this; you won't be in it." Then luncheon with Eliot: not a success; the two don't talk the same idiom.

Item 2:

Notes for August 30, 1935.

The association between Newdick and Frost on the second day, Friday, August 30, yielded the following meticulous notes:

Drive up old road by the 1915 house of the Lynch's. New front porch. View of mountains! New overhead wires. Clump of trees behind house, brought down from the mountains and planted, —Assyrian planting, i.e. a woodchuck in every hole. The Torch, the maple up the hill behind the house. Had chickens. The garden was on the slope to the left of the house. Sold some land to Raymond Holden. Ernest Poole and his ilk: big car, dinners, etc. Holden's wife a bitch; ugly, too. H's money ($150,000?) with Louise Bogan, then married. Another on string now. His new novel re first wife. The Liberty Range: Lafayette, Lincoln, Liberty itself. Walking; skiing. No money down on farm ($1,000); so might as well have chosen a better! *Did* take the farm from under the owner (see New Hampshire).

Stop at camp, inviting Marie and Jimmy to tea at four-thirty.

Drive up to hills of Derry-Franconia days. F's first venture up this way was by himself, to Bethlehem, in search of relief from the hay fever that had plagued him for years. Hotels full. One Irishman introduced him to another by the name of Lynch who took him in, and subsequently his family, and, in 1915, again. Mrs. L., Mr. Thayer, and the cider. The story behind The Fear: "The Quane iv th' Road." Subsequent history of the woman: the house-burnings, etc. Marriage, but no go. Callahan and the burned hotel and Mr. L's remark, "Let him that set the fire put it out," while papering and without turning his head. The story of The Self-Seeker: botanist friend. F used to do a deal of botanizing, not realising the connection with his hay fever . . . thought the result of a cold. Jews, singly and as a race. Indians?

At camp, Jimmy twirled his baton for F; F tried it, with little success. The talk re "charms" of early days.

Mrs. Frost at door to greet us: sweet-faced, white-haired, reserved.

Monument for the man who first struck on the idea of blaming it on the world! F says he never did. [I would not be taken as ever having rebelled.] [See line 12 of "Not Quite Social".]

Electrician's helper in 1893. Was bobbin boy earlier. Tramp through south, ostensibly in search of a job. Column on another Lawrence paper (not the Sentinel). NRA: "More heart than brain and more money than either." Talk of the poor, mean well, *but*—. Mrs. F even more antipathetic. Masefield's not a false difference, — the new old. Bridges, in *talk* untrue to himself. Lunch with him first in London, arranged by   . A flop. B says one can't talk about poetry, that is, versification, unless one knows and uses the terminology of music! Book on Milton's metrics is better. B's violence at Ann Arbor: Mrs. B had to take him upstairs. Sat on his feet and rocked back and forth in the heat of argument. The scholar in him overcame the poet.

Mrs. F. did high school in two and a half years. College likewise; entered in 1892, out six months attending ill mother, graduated '95.

F remembers another Gk. teacher at H., one who didn't care whether his attendance was regular or not, so long as his (F's) work help up to his (F's) A standard!

F taught night school in North Cambridge. 1895. [R.S.N. long-hand: 1897] Failure: young.

Taught evening class in Lawrence in 1896 [R.S.N. longhand: 1898]: new books.

In Camb., Mr. and Mrs. F. lived with her parents. But they gave up Cmb house about 1897: one reason for F's leaving Harvard.

Reynolds' nasty remark re football tickets at a teachers' convention: "Let's see, Frost: *you* didn't stay at Harvard long enough to get football tickets, did you?"

President of Parent-Teachers' Assoc. at Dow Academy in Franconia. One or two years, maybe three. Used to read once a year to them. Some of the children educated there.

". . . let them in all over you": a phrase F. used Thursday regarding too inquisitive people.

The man of Mending Wall: Gay (on the farm toward Boston), not Barry (on the farm toward Derry).

F did put up the seat I photographed back in the woods. The brook is the original of Hyla Brook. [And *there* it is a west-running brook, too!]

At the farm, [at Derry] F. knew the flowers all right: devil's paint brush, black-eyed Susan, etc. And the trees, even to the taste of the bark: pulled off a twig and had me taste it: like checkerberry.

Mountain Interval: see Thoreau and Emerson. RR used form Inter*vale*. So also Brown (of B and Nichols School). B never forgave F for the end F upheld in the controversy. Philologist upheld F. Article?

F an expressionist in writing.

One-third heritage, one-third environment: these alone enough to make a difference—in the Frostian sense of that word, e.g. wherein lies a man's difference?

F and the reading at Columbus [in 1922]: the new book, uncut; so the necessity for a knife, and hence the request of Andrews. Andrews afterwards a bit nasty in a pleasant way, insinuating that on F's part it was a stage-play. F not under the necessity of such a stage play. An unkind in book too (The Reading and Writing of Verse). F didn't meet Taylor at all. Liked Denney [Ohio State University English Department members].

Composition and literature should be taught together in a college department of English. There shouldn't be two departments, as there used to be at the U. of Michigan.

F no believer in transplanting animals or birds artificially. Or anything else, for that matter. [This ties in with the poem about The Danger Zone, the one F wrote into the fifth printing of his Collected Poems for me and then took back, because he mistakenly thought I didn't like it, whereas the truth was simply that it didn't immediately yield to full understanding and I couldn't honestly pretend an understanding I was without or an enthusiasm that had not yet been born.]

While in neglect [catch the poem-title] F said his poems were not the fashion of the moment. Mrs. F said they were *too good!*

"Design," not collected, in part because F was fearful the experience was too special. A question that: what is, and what is not, too special experience.

Parlor Joke, doesn't like. Argued with him that it is an angry poem, that none of the others are, that it extends the range (not of his interests, for see e.g. The Lone Striker and also The Self-Seeker, but) of his visible emotions, etc., etc.

F has not kept either clippings or first editions. Is a bit amused and somewhat annoyed by bibliographical pother. Neither did Mrs. F keep clippings. As they said almost in chorus, they lived in the present and the future, not the past! [Contrast the voluminous scrap-books of Percy Mackaye!]

Nothing to the story of the Huntington Library MSS. *They* out there continue to ascribe them to Frost although he denies their authenticity. His offer to give them something really his, if they would destroy what they have, refused!

Direction was to take one poem or the other, but not both: the man's a thief.

At Harvard, F disliked the talk of "credits." Cut classes often. Lived on Ellery St. opposite the library. Read German with Mrs. F. Second year she went to Lawrence when her folks did. He was distracted, and gave it up the next year.

Sheffield, the "bearded lady" at Wellesley now. Miss Nancy-ish. Invited F to home: nothing in common. S used to be laughed at while he waited for precisely the right word with which to express himself.

G. R. Elliott and "The Ladder of Love" nonsense. Dualism, too. F must speak to him, a close friend who knows much of his (F's) mind.

In 1912 Silver tried to dissuade F from going to England; no job on return! Perhaps a small school, but not at the normal school.

Did no real farming in Eng. Garden started in October! Artichokes for two families. No go, of course.

F. was living in Abercrombie's house at the time of the incident of the gamekeeper. Gibson no help. G a snob. [Frost threatened as trespasser for walking through an estate.]

On F's last visit to England, A's wife carried on embarrassingly: A had had too much wife, too much family responsibility, etc., etc. Lugubrious occasion (F's word).

Grandfather: he and F used to talk, and agree, re [Grover] Cleveland. Occasionally though rarely, they played cribbage. He saw what F was up to, though most folks didn't. F, in response to the proposition about the year, "Give me twenty, give me twenty, give me twenty," over and over, like "an auctioneer." Grandfather bitter over son's death, disapproved Mrs. F's "westernisms," etc.

Regarding the biography of Frost: the two Davidsons working at cross purposes, then F suggested Munson, who had just written something F rather liked. Munson, however, of "the other crowd." See, for instance, the dedication to Hart Crane. M's biography not well done. [R.S.N. longhand note: NB-Nothing of Romig.] [Note later Romig correspondence. W.A.S.]

[A neighbor told me that each of F's children had a special talent: Marjorie for flowers, Lesley for animals, etc.]

The incident of opening the letter from Macmillan's for him, then reading it, and his exclamation: "It *is* done!"

F likes Robinson's Mister Flood.

Fancy G[amaliel] Bradford keeping all those letters, and having everything in shipshape! F has destroyed many, perhaps even most. Perhaps L. Untermeyer has saved F's. [Published in 1963.]

The pictures I took of the old farm at Derry: The house the same except for the absence of a hedge of rose quince. The birches *are* the climbing kind.

Porcupines stupid. Have to be touched before they sting. The dog with quills in his mouth; chloroform: death. Ps bite twigs to make the apples fall.

Tennis racquet in corner. F was hoping for a game this summer. Got to playing again last winter in Florida.

Read no book through until he was fourteen; was playing baseball, raising hell, etc. Sister read six or seven a week.

Seemed a scholar in high school; walked off with things.

On quantity in English verse: How long is oh? In pain the oh may be drawn out all night. Step on a person's foot and the oh may be second-short. Similarly, how long is through? The accent is what counts, not the visible or the technical length.

Bridges cock-eyed on quantity. [Also Saintsbury?]

F would like to look into the development of metre of accent from the meter of quantity, —from the late Latin into the old French.

Bridges kept one foot in the "other crowd." So-called "new" stuff, "like blowing a baloon up from the outside."

Holden "off" in his sketch, particularly with regard to Mrs. F. [Possibly refers to Raymond Holden's profile of Frost on pp. 25–7 of the June 6, 1931, *New Yorker*, though Holden has no reference to either mother or wife of R.F.] In his car F goes up a hill in first if he's by himself, in second if he's talking. Has Chevrolet now. Had Oakland before. He lurches off toward the side of the road when he turns to talk.

Hands in pockets, mildly rattling money and keys. [So also Lowes.] Twinkle, now and then in eyes, eyes capable of many expressions. Brows, heavy, rise and fall. No tie. Shirt open at throat, gray suit. [See Blackington pictures of 1937.]

Re girl's school at Bennington: disgusted at ruling that "no girl should go nude who is not beautiful."

Disgusted with much of the so-called "new" in education.

Not trustful, quite, of either Gray or Lee of The New School.

"Only an idealist would do that!" That is, hire a girl teacher on part-time, give her twenty hours a week, and pay her only a thousand dollars.

No late nights now, because Mrs. F sleepless.

As electrician's helper, trimmed carbons.

My Butterfly written earlier than 1894. [R.S.N. longhand: 1892]

Poem in Transcript, about 1897, the time of the Greek War. No pay for this.

Also Corn Stalks about 1900, in a place he forgets. [R.S.N. long-hand: 1891!]

F spoke of the clouds as "combing the summit" — a sign of "weather," meaning bad weather. Also, a "dragon" [of mist] coming up the Notch means weather.

Ran down hill from Lynch's — on the other side of town.

At thirty to thirty-two, deciding he must do something decisive. [This he was saying Thursday, not Friday.]

Frost told Green the name of the man to whom to write concerning the Lawrence High School Bulletin, "the fellow who was squirrel enough to have kept the file." [R.S.N. longhand: Carl Burrell]

Mrs. Howard Mumford Jones has one squib of Frost's,—the one Melcher has a copy of. [The one shoe smelling of Pacific, the other of Atlantic salt!]

Abercrombie in America at Johns Hopkins University lecturing last winter. Didn't let F know he was here. F happened to read of it in the paper.

Apparently on the outs now with Cestre [French critic and translator].

Knew of Feuillerat in Figaro recently.

Had scholarship at Dartmouth, worth $90.00. Room then was $30 a year, board $2.50 a week. Was monitor, took attendance, etc. Left without seeing the dean. No fault of Dartmouth's. [F never blames anything on others, so far as he is concerned.] Fault, if any, was F's.

F doesn't want to be anybody's "case" — doctor's, psycho-analyst's, or father confessor's.

Made good grades: see record at Harvard.

Told F re Torrence at Miami, of T's possibly becoming Ohio's laureate, of T's recent book for the Japan Society, etc.

Told him also, when asked, re Talfourd [R.S.N. scholarly interest]. Also about Lowes.

Wife took over his mail for two years. F finds a stack of mail discouraging to the writing of anything else.

Plans to go South again this winter; so will be at Amherst earlier than usual this autumn.

Refuge from grief (Margery) [Marjorie Frost Fraser, who died in childbirth in 1934] in work. Callous? [No!]

Stark Young a disrupter. Obtained R. Utter's virtual dismissal. Utter not a bad man. Y misrepresented U's attitude toward his teaching work: said he hated it. F sorry for anything he said to give the dismissal an opportunity to be. U on West Coast now. [R.S.N. longhand: Utter died recently.]

Andrews out at Amherst to make way for Stark Young. Then F came along, at a good salary. Hence, possibly, Andrews' meanness and caustic attitude.

F doesn't like to quibble re lecture fee, as with the folk at Bennington. Likes an offer that permits him to take it or leave it. Or likes to name price and get it without talk.

Has dim pencilled letters of Edward Thomas. Wishes them transcribed.

Three years in England cost $3,600, — $1,200 a year. Came home broke.

Young people are never interested, or rarely are, in their ancestors. Older ones are. Bartlett and the Winthrops, from the Plantagenet line. F [as I suspected] didn't cooperate with N. S. Frost in the F genealogy; hence the errors therein re F. F too slow in answering. NSF an old man.

Ray Stannard Baker killing himself on Wilson's biography. A mine for others? But a biography ought to be readable. A biographer needs a selector. Accuracy in bibliography, I suggested, and interpretation and criticism in biography, along with the facts.

Was rushed into Mountain Interval by Alfred Harcourt on porch at 1915 Franconia house. H then with Holt. Book didn't sell well. Compare A Boy's Will. Not sufficient time to impose on its design any satisfying sort of unity. F likes design, I suggested, with instances. Yes, he responded. Poems in M I wouldn't have been different, but there's something to the way they are put out.

Recollected from Thursday: H. Monroe refused stuff for *Poetry* before F left for England, then took Pound's reviews of ABW [*A Boy's Will*] and NoB [*North of Boston*] and published The Code. She said later she had been out of town when the first F stuff came. I don't believe F quite believes her.

Three of Margery's [Marjorie's] poems in a recent issue of Poetry, of which F gave me a copy. Slender volume of M's work to be published soon by the Spiral Press (Blumenthal). This latest "nice" of H.M.

Farms still to be bought cheap: 100 to 200 acres for $1,000. After paint and repairs, worth $10,000.00.

F slowed up when he first fully realized what he wanted to do: write. Never talked much of it. Not even up to and through 1912. But note grandfather—

Doesn't like Florida. Where he was last winter, 8,000 of 10,000 on relief.

Abercrombie wrote the *Nation* review of NoB. Note also the *Nation* at the end of the year! [R.S.N. longhand: Included *NoB* among best.]

Poem in The Egoist? Early in 1914.

Recollected from Thursday: Lore of oxen in The Mountain perhaps not exactly right; F never drove oxen himself; but he's often worked beside them.

Agreed that ski jumps were bosh. Learn young, as his children did. Long runs in the mountains. One near there [Taft?] of 21 miles.

Recollected from Thursday: One buries one's self in one's later years, and usually doesn't know it.

F's fingers on his face, then in his hair, pushing it forward and so mussing it.

Re my list of Uncollected Poems, said he was always looking for good poems he might have omitted.

"Design." Mrs. F liked. General interest? Where does general interest leave off?

Recollected from Thursday: The Amy Lowell piece was written

out for a reporter who couldn't get it straight otherwise. [Note a no-pay piece; yet observe place in Cox's Prose Preferences.]

Carol has four children, oldest six. [R.S.N. longhand: RF has four grandchildren!]

Item 3:

Notes for August 31, 1935.

These are the notes taken by Newdick after spending August 31, 1935, with Frost:

At lunch with Mr. and Mrs. F. at mountain inn. Mr. and Mrs. Hibbert guests also. H talking with F records for phonograph. H from OSU; knew Andrews, writes Graves, etc. Records made new way with new equipment in Bell laboratories. This one for Natl. Council of Teachers of English,—not to be confused with other Columbia records. Mrs. H is daughter of Ashley Thorndike.

Frost's story of Wallace and [left blank] and the Indians again, well told.

E.[dgar] L.[ee] Masters and record. M no success after Spoon R. Anthol. Told group of hearing of M's trying to sell MSS. to dealer in Washington, D.C. M's prose bad. Most of poems too, — metrically and otherwise. Was mean, cruel, to Carl Sandburg and also to F. Angry at divided chapter in Amy L's book.

Meal served at table, home style. Caramat Inn.

At home after three-forty:

Father drinking whiskey, drinking blood for consumption — taking F with him! No talk, or almost none. Would tease F sometimes in evenings and on Sundays, in bed, in tub, etc. Once didn't speak to wife for six weeks. Ambitious, Worked himself to death: Cleveland's first campaign. Disappointed.

Mother sometimes a reviewer. F remembers a lovely copy of Herrick's poems with engravings. Died 1901.

Sad story of sister. Precocious. F no good through the grades — played ball, raised hell, etc. Took entrance exam at Lawrence: at the rate the officials proposed he would enter high school at

17. Instead, he graduated from L.H.S. at 17. [See later discussion of confusion over birth date. W.A.S.] Answer: attended small school in the country — at Salem where his mother was teaching: went through arithmetic in a year; algebra easy for him; was good at Latin. Took exam again, and entered h.s. with sister. This perhaps a blow to her. Soon at top of class, though he did no talking about it. She jealous. F's quarrel with her, e.g. re her reading Latin aloud, his putting her out, her coming to window along roof ledge, etc. Also, she neurotic in love; and F was called in when he shouldn't have been. His mistake, too, was to be severe. She became a model in New York; thought her work important. After his scorching letter, she gave up the job, but she never forgave him the letter. . Then she taught in several places, but was hounded by illusions of pursuit. Often came to him for money. Once lived awhile with them, but was fearful of being imposed upon. At end, screaming, screaming for F to protect her from F!! Died about 1917 [R.S.N. longhand: 1929].

F had flu during the War.

To be biographer, but to avoid term "official biographer": F doesn't like it, for it smacks of pretentiousness. Moreover, he doesn't want the thing to be burdensome to him. Will send me stuff as he finds it or thinks of it. Will write to people who are loath to open up. Will straighten out chronology of what he did from 1892 until marriage.

At the hotel from nine-thirty until twelve-thirty:

Lounge occupied, took dining room — small table in corner, partially cleared of its setting.

Talk re the Natl. Acad. of Arts and Letters. F. Beacon vs. R. U. Johnson, the secretary, who had used official position unfairly. This only time F appeared there, simply to take his chair once. Disgusted. So also Bliss Perry.

Talk re T. S. Eliot at dinner at New York. Would read poem if F did. F said he'd *write* one while E spoke one. E's effort was the one with recurring "Mother." F said this apparently from the ballad *Edward* with a bit of a difference. Remarked to Lowes that poetry was the least quoting—or should be — of all the forms of literature. On the contrary, said Lowes, it is the most quoting; it's the business of you fellows to quote, in one way or another; and it's our business (i.e. that of the professors) to tell you where you got it! F not warm to this. F's poem was faked, that is, it was the one Mrs. Jones and Melcher have, the one about the reproaching shoes [Who's too old for walking]. E said F didn't take the occasion seriously enough. Most of the older poets were disposed of off hand. Burns was, Eliot sniffed, perhaps a song-writer, but surely not a poet. [This was what, according to the newspapers, F disagreed with.] E was baited all evening, but didn't seem to become aware of the fact, wearing his pretentiousness haughtily to the end. A joke. [See what F said of E at The New School one day.]

F's pile of notebooks, fixed-leaf ones, not loose-leaf; heavy reddish paper covers. Much frayed, some of them, from much handling. [Evidently the poems are seasoned quite a while before they are published; indeed, I can prove this to be the case, and perhaps should in a short paper.]

F's reading in a conversational tone of voice. And by conversational I mean conversational. No raising of the voice. The tunes are the tunes of speech, the rhythms the rhythms of speech. He read each of the shorter poems twice. [This, from other reports I have, seems to be his regular practice.]

I remarked that he *did* observe the line-ends, by pauses, albeit often short ones. He agreed: Of course. Then I told him of Melcher's saying he did not. [And Melcher has been his friend for twenty years, and has heard him read many, many times.]

We had only a very brief talk re versification and metrics, both of us, I think, intending to return to the matter for a longer discussion, but time not offering thereafter. But in a rapid running-over of ABC's we agreed perfectly: there must be communication; there must be a pattern to play to and fit on; accent dominates over quantity, in fact quantity is what you make it; etc., etc.

More from the afternoon session:

At mill in 1892: Billy Golden (still working in the mill). [R.S.N. longhand: No, dead.] Ed Gilbert: attended Dartmouth; became h.s. master; is now head of a chemical company. [Write to these for reminiscences.] Pocket Shakespeare. Boxing, wrestling. Oily floor. Long hours, something like 6:30 to 6:00, a sixty-hour week. Job that of a trimmer of carbons, hard on a cloudy day, easy on a bright one.

(Billie Poole, from Princeton, interrupted at lunch: wished F to consider changing publishers.)

Job for a few days in Boston in an architect's office as a blue print boy.

This while on the week's venture to Boston to try to get a foothold.

After return from Dartmouth, took over Mother's school. In fact his Mother's difficulties were the prime reason, I venture, for his leaving Dartmouth.

At Canobee Lake for the following summer.

Story of the Shakespearean reader who wished an advance agent. F's letter got him (F) the job. F insisted the man read in Boston before competent critics, in order to obtain some material for advertisements. F arranged for Clapp of the Transcript to come, for Rolfe, and for a few others. Got a hall, too. They couldn't give the fellow a boost. The reader from Portland, Maine.

Back to Lawrence, walking all the way: had gone three days without food.

Worked in mill all winter at Lawrence.

Job teaching in district school at Salem. Walked out and got it. This 1894–1895?

Will lecture at State this fall. Will name date later. Will also conduct conference for aspiring writers. $150.00 to $200.00. Will be guest at 1294. [Newdick's home.] So will Mrs. F. Have questions written out. Hold conference after reading and talk.

Haines the botanist? [R.S.N. longhand, evidently written in later: John—see *Recognition*] Ralph Haodson [?] introduced Edward Thomas to Frost. T had heard of F and wished to meet him. F had read nothing of T's but had heard of his stuff,—had read one regarding Spring. T came down to Little Iddens. T leaned on F. T at college had had money, but had got into a forced marriage (see his wife's As It Was). T wrote at least one book a year about the roads of Eng. Biography of Marlborough; publisher called for 2,000 [R.S.N. longhand: 20,000?] words; at which end; asked T. F brought T's son to America. Trouble at Ellis Island. Charley Burlingame's note to Fred Howe, Commissioner at E. Is. One pink, the other red. F indignant at hearings: "Tell them 'No!'"

Re Garnett's change in tone in reviewing NoB [North of Boston] and MI [Mountain Interval]: G had written F asking F to get him a job; F, busy, was tardy in answering; second letter from G: "Who do you think you are? I helped make you; I'll help tear you down!"

More from the conversation at the Inn: [Caramat Terrace]:

Lyric set to music by Louise Homer's husband; she asked him to come to hear it; he didn't.

F doesn't like to hear his lyrics set to music. Says each has its own tune. The tune of the music kills the tune of the lyric proper. His word was "steals."

Cecil Yapp has a record of Mending Wall, so Hibbert said.

Electrical Research Products, Inc., 250 W. 57th St., New York.

F had to use loudspeaker at Mayflower Hotel in Washington, D.C. Doesn't like them.

Likes hall at the New School in New York: the best he's ever read in.

Columbia University has a series of records of Frost's readings. [There should be a page of this in the Bibliography.]

Item 4:

Notes for September 1, 1935.

These are the notes taken by Newdick after spending September 1, 1935, with Frost:

Mr. and Mrs. F drove down to our camp in their car to bid us goodbye. I already had the tent down and away, for it was ten-thirty. They were to stay only a few moments, but it was after noon before Mrs. F. finally got us apart!

We wished to photograph Mr. an Mrs. F together, but she is camera shy; says she never permits her picture to be taken as she doesn't photograph well. [There should be a good picture of them together.]

I read to F to have him tell me whether I read rightly — most of Birches. He said I did read rightly, making allowances for inevitable differences, and apart from the accent in one line, wherein the accent should be "to take the stiffness *out* of them."

A recollection from Saturday: F assured me, an important point, that I do follow him closely. And of course he agreed that this matter is fundamental for either a critic or a biographer.

Another recollection from Saturday: He had read the first draft of Some Uncollected Later Poems of Robert Frost and approved it. He was prompted to speak of passion, and to ask me what I understood by the word and the concept. I answered as best I could, saying that of course I took it to be essentially powerful emotion, and, was a rule of thumb, more powerful as it was less declamatory and spectacular in its manifestation. I did not mean at all anything sensuous, much less sensual. And according to my basic understanding, his poems are full to the brim with passion, passion restrained, passion disciplined, passion under control, but unquestional [sic] powerful passion. I think this pleased him. He went on to tell me, then, about [name deleted out of deference to Mr. Untermeyer's statement in a letter of October, 1973, that the description is not appropriate]—one of Louis Untermeyer's numerous wives, and a particularly nasty one: one capable, F said, of emptying a piss-pot from an upstairs window without looking to see, or caring, whether anyone was below; a congenitally dirty, filthy creature, albeit beautiful.

He told me also that he had been cultivated by The Masses and other such papers. They'd like to claim him as a "proletarian" poet. "You're really one of us," they assured him. "Yes?" he responded. But he didn't go down to the office and hobnob with them. The consequence was, a change of front. That's frequently the case when he refuses to be lionized or to be drawn into camps.

Saturday night I told him something about my mother and father and we were led naturally into talk of death. He told of his talk of death with grandson. As often, F simply questioned. [If one isn't alert he'll find Frost making him do the talking!] He told also of the exaltation of his grandson after his teacher learned he was Robert Frost's grandson.

F likes to talk and speaks of the fact. But he knows, he says, that if he talks too much he empties himself. He won't talk unless he has something to say; he won't lecture merely to be lecturing. His lectures aren't written out; each one is different, for between any two of them his thinking has gone on from where it was to some other point. When the line of thought ceases to develop, F drops it. He needs to be much alone, he ways; he's never so social, paradoxical as it may seem, as when he's alone, for then the thoughts develop that later emerge in talk or conversation.

As he had laid down some principles on which the biography was to proceed, I responded that there were some that I wished to state as guiding my working practice. One was that I would rather cut off my right hand than give him pain. He broke in at this and said he could see that; that Mrs. F had remarked the night before that she could see that he and I were going to become really good friends. Another was that I placed first the virtue of accuracy of fact and statement and interpretation, that I should speak the truth as I saw it or not speak it at all. A third was that, for my part as a student of American poetry, I classed him, like Weygandt, in company with Emerson, Dickinson, Whitman, and Poe, and rather above Emerson and Poe as having more on the ball. These points, I remarked, need never, it seemed to me, be spoken of again; but I did think they called for expression, albeit briefly, once.

F is as considerate of Mrs. F as a lover in his teens. And her eyes shine from their depths when they rest on him. Here are two other rare souls who have held and kept their love fresh through the years.

Again from Saturday: F read me the first piece on Robinson, and also the second. In response to Macmillan's frantic request for a longer "introduction" for King Jasper, he'll put the two together, inasmuch as they easily go together, but he vows he'll do no more. He doesn't mention King Jasper. He doesn't care for Robinson's later work. When he heard that R was at work on the King Arthur stuff he pleaded with him, "Don't! Please don't! That will be too much like the stuff poured out in the generation before ours, and in our younger days." But R drew himself up frigidly and said, "But I've already done it." This, I believe, was the Merlin. One allusion in the introduction, which we agreed would better be entitled A Tribute than An Introduction, will be missed by many, — the allusion to R's wishing F to drink whiskey with him: the "bitters." 'F, you're hoarse.' 'No more than usual.' 'Yes; you are; you've got a cold.' 'Nonsense.' 'Yes, you have; don't you think we ought to take something for it.' Then F caught on and they drank.

In later years, Randall told me, R did not drink at all himself; but he always had the stuff on hand, and enjoyed his guests' enjoyment of it.

F recalled how he and Pound talked of R in London, delighting in R's "and thought and thought and thought and thought about it." The fourth "thought," they agreed, was R having fun. And one of F's theses is that a man can go no farther seriously than he can go in fun. R forgot that. In Miniver Cheevy, R poked fun at the romantics. Then he proceeded to go the whole ticket himself. F couldn't see either the subject or the interpretation of the subject. For his part, F said, he would have seen King Mark's position quite differently. Matthew Arnold did too. But most of the romantics went in, and go in, for the story on the traditional love basis.

Saturday evening I suggested that F play a game with me for a while: to check my understanding of his mind I'd name authors old and new that he approved and disapproved. He agreed to play the game, and we started off. First of all, I ventured, he approved heartily of M. Arnold as a poet. Yes. Most of Swinburne, except for acrobatics and felicitous insincerities, was washed up. Yes. Browning he'd approve of, in almost all of the pieces, but especially the Ring and the Book. Yes. (And here he broke in and quoted a deal of Browning, some things only phrases that stick forever in the mind.) At a distance, too, he'd approve Dryden. Yes. And so it went for a while longer. This whole thing I thought of as a desirable checking-up on my basic understanding of F. Could I, in short, with more than chance or average accuracy, project his mind as he would project it.

It often appeared in conversation that there are two crowds—his word—in the literary world: the new new and the old new. F of course stands with the later. He discounts the performances of the former, nailing the speciousness at the root of their enterprises, that is, the desperate desire to be new at all costs. Recall here the story of Ezra Pound inventing new newness for this man and that woman and so on, and then convincing them that always there had been that new newness in their work. See, e.g., what Pound did to Amy Lowell: "I was amputating her sonnet appendix this morning. I'll have that old gal thinking she was *born* writing free verse!" The "gal," says F, is accurately remembered, for P could be colloquial when he was not posing, e.g. as when he raised his head and remarked, while reading the first copy of ABW, "You don't mind if we approve, do you?" with the royal or editorial "we" rather pompously and pontifically brought out.

Item 5:

Professor Sidney Cox's Summary of Frost as a Teacher.

Just as he was receiving the remarkable document Frost had sent him, on October 16, 1935, Newdick heard from Professor Sidney Cox, a member of the English faculty at Dartmouth College, who promised, and was to give, every cooperation, at the same time mentioning the book he was later to write and publish. His summary of Frost as a teacher is worth reading:

. . . In doing well with that subject you will put into writing the most original and creative, but also distrusted, ideas and ways of teaching put into action in this country in my lifetime. [Cox wrote in the margin of the typed letter this additional note: Not that he was, is, or would be a reformer. Always humorous. W.A.S.] He is so importantly different from Dewey, so much more inclusive, profound, playful, beyond the powers of mechanized minds, even the most capable and successful. What readers will do with him as a teacher of the art of the gradually vanishing teacher is say, smiling, "Well, of course, he is a genius." And I suppose those he has taught have some of them been geniuses. . . . He is not assimilable to any concept; he relies on imagination and imaginatively unified knowledge, starting with the concrete of the student's felt experience and gaining extension by metaphor. There is no college or university in the country that trusts the adventurous, passionate, inwardly-disciplined, self-formed intelligence sufficiently not to discount any such teaching as Robert practices and would like to see.

Item 6:

Miss Sylvia Clark and "An A No. 1 Sundown."

One of the people Newdick had visited in August 1935 was Miss Sylvia Clark of Derry Village, N. H. Knowing of her intimate knowledge of a rare occasional poem by Frost, who "recalled the piece joyously, and was pleased that you had kept it . . . ," he asked her for a copy. She sent a copy of "An A No. 1 Sundown" and gave the following account of its composition and survival:

One afternoon while Mr. Frost was teaching at Pinkerton Academy, I called him and Miss S. D. Bartley, our Librarian, to admire with me a very brilliant sunset.

Their choice of adjectives did not seem to me to be worthy of the wonderful display of color and I upbraided them severely for their lack of enthusiasm over what I termed "my show." The next morning Mr. Frost gave me this little poem, and I have kept it among my choicest treasures. (Letter, 12/3/35)

On December 11, Miss Clark decided to send Newdick the original manuscript of the Sundown poem "to place in your collection of papers regarding our friend Robert Frost." The excitement he felt in the research on Frost was suggested in lines Newdick wrote on December 14:

I have been walking on air since the arrival of yesterday morning's mail, for in that mail came your kind letter and the priceless gift of an original and I believe unique manuscript of Robert Frost's!—Ordinarily I fight shy of exclamation points, but I found it impossible to refrain from that one, and indeed I feel like writing a whole row of them to give visible embodiment of my joy, thus:!!!!!!

He mentioned the new manuscript with that of "Not Quite

Social" and the notebook and averred that he already had gifts enough for both Christmas and the New Year.

Item 7:

Professor Henry C. Morrison Meets Robert Frost.

Newdick had written to Professor Henry C. Morrison of the University of Chicago in November 1935, to tell him that Frost thought "it was you more than any one else who discovered him," adding that Frost believed Silver, the principal at Pinkerton, had him "listed for dismissal." After an exchange of correspondence, Professor Morrison gave, on December 10, the following account of their meeting, without waiting "to hear from Mr. Frost."

I was at that time head of the State Education Office in New Hampshire and as such was responsible for the certification of those secondary schools in the state which were, under the law, entitled to charge school districts not maintaining high schools of their own with a tuition for pupils coming from such districts. This function entailed inspection and I suppose the inspection was further affected by my own personal interest in teaching.

On the occasion of this particular visit of inspection I dropped into a classroom in English literature and was at once struck by a rare phenomenon: a class of boys and girls of high school age were listening open-mouthed to the teacher who was talking to them about an English classic. As I looked at the teacher I saw slumped down behind the desk a young man who was commenting on the work he had in his hand and perhaps other work by the same author on the desk. He was neither raising his voice nor cutting up any pedagogical monkey shines but rather talking to them as he might talk to a group of friends around his own fireside. But he "had them" as few other teachers ever do "get them." I do not know that I stayed about a great while and spent most of my time in his classroom. I do not remember that. I do know that I stayed long enough to size up the situation and saw: First, that he knew what he was talking about; and second, that he had some genuine love of his own apparently for the pieces of literature about which he was talking. I thought then and I think now that we have therein the largest part of the teaching of literature or music or the fine arts or noble living of any sort to young people.

I did not know Mr. Frost at that time but I invited and urged him to come over to Exeter soon where I was holding a teachers institute and just talk to high school teachers about how he taught literature. As I recall it he rather demurred at the proposal, professing that he knew nothing about the subject of teaching. Anyhow I finally prevailed and he did, on the day appointed, appear. I recall, with some amusement, that I have seldom seen anybody so thoroughly overcome by stage fright as he was, but he did what I wanted and made his point and afterward I came to rely upon him a good deal in his general field to simplify the whole problem of the high school teacher of English literature. Something was accomplished, but after all you can't accomplish much with people who do not know the field, whose love for literature has consisted chiefly in passing college courses in the subject and who oftentimes have been dumped into that field because they could not teach Latin, Science or Mathematics.

Well that was a long time ago. On the surface things have changed a good deal; at the bottom they have not changed at all. What was good teaching in literature as Frost did it then would be good teaching today.

In the sense of the incident as thus described I "discovered" Frost after his principal had already discovered him, for as I recall the circumstance it was his principal who called my attention to him. But to say that I discovered Frost in the larger sense, is, of course, ridiculous. I had not the faintest idea of his capacity as a poet. Nobody was more surprised than I when he burst upon us on his return from his visit in England with a great reputation already formed.

In another sense I did discover him as one of the valued friends and companions of a whole lifetime and although it is many years since I have seen him, those days before the war and our talks together constitute a greatly prized memory.

Item 8:

Nuggets of Early 1936.

As 1936 began, Newdick had an energetic biographical research program under way. The following are three nuggets, never before published, which he panned in one month:

I always think of Robert Frost, the neighbor. Ever kindly—intensely human—delightfully social but having no patience with show or pretense. He takes as much interest in the humblest of his country neighbors as in his acquaintances in the higher walks of life. It seems to me the most outstanding characteristic of his personality is a profound love of humanity and nature. He seems ever to be reaching out for the soul of things, and whatever he finds be it beautiful or ugly, is met sympathetically and understandingly. All seems grist to his mill but the final product is free from grit or bitterness, soothing to the heart and spreading kindliness as a ray of sunlight sweeps a mountain valley.

Robert Frost is a delightful converstionalist. A chat with him is always to be remembered. His keen sense of humor is at once apparent. It bubbles forth like a mountain spring and is just as refreshing.

Always evident is his love of nature. He delights in long walks through the woods. Nothing gave him more pleasure than to start out with his son, blankets and fish rods in hand and climb perhaps over the rugged top of Mt. Lafayette and down into the wilderness beyond for a night or two under the stars. His poetry to those who know him, seems tinctured with the peace and understanding of one who communes intimately with nature.

H. L. Johnson, M.D., Franconia, N.H.
February 5, 1936

The joy of calling on the Frosts is never to be forgotten by their friends. The home had an air of cordial hospitality rare indeed.

I like to think of the lovely low rambling white cottage. It nestled into a hill of evergreens to the west and nearby was a stately old grove of sugar maples with fine paths through which I have traveled with Mrs. Frost and the children. There was always something unusual about the birds or the flowers or the sunset that you must just not miss.

The wide piazza on the front always invited one to sit and gaze down the winding bush grown road into the valley to the right. Or down the mountain side on the left. Mr. Frost would often call attention to the distant flicker of headlights as motor cars wound their way in the evening slowly down the "three mile hill," or as they approached from the Easton valley. You feel his thoughts, unspoken then, but later you somehow felt when he read a new poem that you had heard it from him before when he called your attention to some subtle beauty that only he could put into words.

Sarah C. Johnson, M.D., Franconia, N.H.
February 7, 1936

I knew Mr. Frost before he became famous about twenty three years ago. I remember how well he liked to walk and would walk to Bethlehem Village every day when the weather permitted[;] his young son Carroll was always with him [being] then only a small boy[.]

Mary MacPherson, Bethlehem, N.Y.,
February 14, 1936.

Item 9:

Recollection of Newdick's Visit to
Frost on July 26, 1936.

Valentine of Syracuse just leaving. Has been in N. Y. senate.
From Syracuse. Annoyed at reference to Democrats in S. as of
"another class." Wondering about ideals. F. likes him.

Mr. and Mrs. F. looking rested. Lovely white old farmhouse.
Glorious view; clear sweep to "West Mountain" (really the
Taconic Range), with Mt. Equinox (5,000 ft.) in distance. Clear
day; so appeared close. No other habitation near. Yet farms,
hedgerows, etc., visible on distant hillsides. Mrs. F. likes this.
F. prefers wilder, that is, more natural view at Franconia place.

Late in aft. talked of stones in wall about the house, making the
terrace: quartz, limestone. Limestone de luxe equals marble;
market for which is now largely gone. I said my geology was
too, but he went on to explain the process of the formation of
quartzite, and later talked of Shailer at Harvard.

Evidently Shailer was one of his H. professors who interested
him. S. delivered neatly worked, out, hour-long lectures,—little
stump speeches, F. called them, or essays. The sort of thing
Hamilton Holt believes he has emancipated the academic world
from, said F., with a trace of kindly malice. F. repeated a large
part of one of S's lectures on earth strains. I recall part of it, about
slate being broken in Kansas: 'farm exploding, leaping into the
air.' Bend slowly, all right, e.g. glass. Sudden strains, something
must give, and does.

F. would now enlarge Bread Loaf concept. One can start from
form and work on to substance, or from substance and on to
form. B. L. started from the form end, largely. Now how about
a professor of unsystematic philosophy? F. wouldn't ban the
regular profs. of phil. in the Us.; they have their place keeping
the whole business alive. Yet unsystematic phil. has its place
too: the materials of thought worked out in essays, so to speak,
from twenty minutes to an hour long. Prof. to be capable of it,

students to be taken in and helped to realize their capacities for it. E.g., when F. talks he "commits" an essay.

Ex.: "Where Is the Place of Ideals and Who Are the Custodians of Them?" the theme of his first talk at B. L. this summer. (Nowadays there are usually two such talks, one at each session, i.e., the summer school and the writers' conference.)

F. to do the Harvard tricentennial ode. First time he's engaged to write a poem to order. Doesn't think poems come that way. Certainly not often. Recalled, however, "By the rude bridge that arched the flood," etc., containing two great lines, "two lines that certainly are poetry: Here the embattled farmers stood and fired the shot heard round the world." "*Might* write, he said, without mentioning H.[arvard] Might write of *his* tricentenary, i.e., of the Frosts to Amer. in 1636. "They'd hate me if they heard me joking about it, I suppose." Sec of all the alumni said, "We haven't in mind anything like the Commemoration Ode, but like one that we have been singing ever since," namely, "Fair Harvard."

Asked also to do ode for Phi Beta Kappa celebration, Alpha Chapter, I believe at William and Mary. Would like to, and would like to go down, but doesn't know. Hasn't answered man yet.

C. E. Norton lectures also to be written. So, a busy summer ahead! And no ideas as yet—

How he got the job at Pinkerton: In Lawrence, met Wolcott (name I missed last summer). Asked re money; replied he was looking for a place to teach. Said W.: I know a trustee at P.; go round to see him in about a week, after he's had a letter from me. F. did: Merriam. The Tuft of Flowers at the Men's League banquet.

W. had come to know F. because Ward had asked him (Wolcott) to look him (F.) up, after stuff sent to Independent. Had come to know each other. He used to look at F's poems. He was the man who complained that the poems were too much like talk. (Not a college professor, then, as has been said.) F. took hold of the idea at once: "If that's the tone of talk, watch me now," or words to that effect. W. a preacher in Lawrence.

I observed that J.L.L. would have a hard time tracking F's poetic

antecedents and influences. This was after we had got to talking about F's pref. to *Dartmouth Verse, 1925.* F. had recently
seen that pref. again. "Didn't you like it?" I said, impulsively;
"It has some fine things in it," and I quoted 'a poet must begin
as a cloud of all the other poets he has ever known.' F. smiled
and said he did. I said, I shouldn't have said that, at least that
way; but that I did think it had had time to get cold and for him
to read it dispassionately. He said perhaps he had grooved his
brain by the writing, and liked to have the groove caressed. The
whole thing ended in gay joking and banter. This, I think, was
at the noon meal.

Shortly after I came we all sat down to a meal, though I tried to
excuse myself, saying, the truth, that I had had a late breakfast
and a bit of lunch (a soda) in Bennington. Pork chops; potatoes;
beets, buttered; bread and butter; etc. Pineapple was to be dessert. F. said ice cream would go well with it. So we drove down
to S. S. and he bought ice cream and a pie. Meanwhile I bought
orange marmalade and raspberry jam for Mrs. F. Dessert ignored
pineapple: apple pie a la mode.

After lunch we walked over the farm. Up to the clearing toward
the top of the drumlin (I think that's the word: something like
a medial moraine). A long sweep of birch trees across the uncut
field of hay, now pretty well burned up and gone beyond seed.
Saw a gateway he cleared in the trees opposite. Also the place
"where two stones almost meet," the abode—the crevice and
burrow—of his Drumlin Woodchuck. Saw part of open well:
water in spring but not for long; not deep enough, perhaps.
Picked a low-growing pine, used in making Christmas wreaths.
Also spireflowers in the field, or at the edge.

Re trees, more now, says F., than a century ago. Small, not six
feet in diameter as then; but numerous. They take the fields
again if left to their own. F. brings some in and plants them
occasionally, e.g. about the house, or, rather, mostly on the hillside to the right (east) of the house.

Farm about a mile east of S.S.: take small road, then take lane on
farm. Telephone, I believe, though I didn't see it. No electricity.

Rough plan of house: [not reproduced]

Cool day. Fire in aft. and at night. Large fireplace, with old crane, hook, and original "shovel." Comfortable natural wicker chairs. Blue floors. Old Orientals. Pictures.

Chapin's full face portrait of F. in dining room. Chapin has the other port.[rait] of F. C. sold it to John Erskine, then got angry at E. and took it back. E. had been buying on payment basis.

Business of C's arranging for F. to talk for $75 guarantee, plus, if any plus. Old checque. F., annoyed by lack of frankness, complained. Fifty more, later. Didn't care about money; hated old cheque and raw deal. This made breach with C. for some time, now apparently healed. F. doesn't know of any port.[rait] owned by the Morrows.

Letter from Pound at Rapallo as soon as first lect. at H. could have been reported by a toady. "Cheap witticisms." F. once crushed P. and earlier cheap witticisms; "Never mind those; I'll do the witticisms; you do the shitticisms." P. said, "If you don't know better, shut up; if you do, stop lying." F. paid no attention.

J.L.L. started F. off at H.F. didn't want anybody after that. [Refers to introduction to audience at first Norton lecture in March, 1936.] (Evidently, and from his letter to me, too, L. not there thereafter.)

F. saw G.L.K.[ittredge] several times, but didn't call on him, as he wished to. Saw Lowes at dinners too, and Bliss Perry also, I believe.

F. asked about work here at N.Y. State Coll. for Ts. I told him. He asked, Dissatisfied with Cox? I said, No; they think very highly of him, and said to me, He's the man whose place you are taking this summer. We talked of C's novels. I spoke of fault of professors in writing of college life. F. agreed, tho' Mrs. F. was inclined to disagree.

I spoke of Imbs, suggesting it was a pen name. No, said F., the real one. He (F.) came out well in *The Professor's Wife* because editor of publishing house was a friend, i.e., Lincoln MacVeagh.

McV. deleted Imbs's record of F's indiscretions in talk at the professor's house, i.e., Lambuth's. "Came off well there."

How F. went to N.H. Normal at Plymouth in 1911: Played along outgoing head (Crock?) and incoming (Silver; still there) on deal re putting money into a camp; publishing invitation to state supt. (Morrison); then refusing to put money into deal! F. watched politics, e.g. Crock helping Silver in return for S's placing C's son-in-law (Now Washington newspaper man) at Pinkerton.

F. going to see Silver at Plymouth on Wed., July 29. Has S. forgotten? F. never does. Often forgets offence, remembers there was an offence; sometimes memory brings it back, usually does, but not always.

S's wife then an invalid living in Maine. Later she recovered and lived in P. for four or five years. Died. S. gay with ladies? Discreet, anyway.

S. and the F's lived together in P. S. brought in friends too. But angry at F's not putting money into camp,—a little F. still had coming from his grandfather's estate. S. threatened F. if F. went abroad, but F. had insisted only for one year.

F. knew he couldn't die at P. He knew also that he'd have to face the world. A year at P. would give him a send-off of a kind, build him up.

F. never played ball with radicals. Dial. Little Review. Then how in the Seven Arts? They came after me! F. likes to have things hauled out of him; doesn't submit anything anymore; hasn't for a long, long time; no part of his income, to amount to anything. Did little for Seven Arts: a poem, perhaps, and the play. Liked Waldo Frank, but W.F. hated and hates L. Untermeyer. F. writes, so does F. occasionally.

Stop war? Why not begin with traffic accidents?

Much talk of accidents seen, at time and afterwards; talk of cars, braking, etc; talk of Consumers' Research Bulletins and syrup story of Berle's; our experience on ret. fr. Charleston, S.C.

Talk of grandson, Irma's boy. Tough. Teacher difficulty. Result: investigator. Investigator's chagrin learning who Irma was. —What's coming if things go on, because for protection one always demands the right to regulate. Talk of old age pensions: ought to be put off as long as possible; ought to be given on oath—and not on pauper's oath either. Leave self-respect.

Nature for us or against us, a man asked F. Ans.: We're here, aren't we? So, by however narrow a margin, N. must be for us. However, the balance may be upset in any individual case. e.g. the New Orleans gambler who lost steadily year after year at cards, and e.g., the person who has more than his share of luck.

Frost killed apple-crop this year; so Carol hit.

Recognizing the old R. F. farm, I stopped there first on the main road. Carol's wife told me how to reach R. F.'s farm, after talking with Carol a moment. Top of old place newly painted red.

F. told of ins and outs of Middlebury's Bread Loaf: The Battelle who left an inn to the school; part inn thereafter, part school; all changed now for school purposes: better board at less money.

Talked of Gay, retiring head, Owen, incoming head, Eaton, who makes F. a bit uneasy, and others. John Farrar conferred on it, i.e. the conference end, an unwelcome Bohemian atmosphere for a while.

David Morton there at B. L. this year. Full prof. at Amherst. Influence did it, perhaps the Morrows'. King somewhat reluctant to take him, but did, and promoted him rapidly. He poses: poetry can't be taught; so holds class ten minutes; etc. Relieves F. of the crazy fringe of sentimentalists. Another theory: life of art, art itself, superior to life, truer than life, etc. Pretends to be a bear with the ladies. Came from Vanderbilt. Doesn't like to pay bills, and is otherwise Southern. Students take to him; faculty disapprove, inevitably.

I asked whether B. L. faculty by invitation or application. F. said he didn't know; was I interested? Yes, I said, if by application: I wished to avoid a faux pas.

He gave me Ed. by Poetry reprint, proof of new bookplate by Lankes, auto'd first ptg. of *A F. R.*, [Number 581 of 803] auto'd first edn. of *N. o B.* (one of the 51 bound in blue then stripped and rebound) and three auto'd Sev. Sht, P's for distribution where I deemed fit: friends, special students, etc. He'd have given me a first edn. of *A B. W.* [*A Boy's Will*], too, but the one copy on hand, first handed to me, was found to be partly auto'd to L. G. Armstrong (I believe that was the name).—He remembered making a memo at 1294, but said he had lost it.—I refused a first trade edn. of *C. Ps.*, Elliots' *Cycle*, and others. I feel at such times desperately in a spot: I'd like to have them, but I feel more that I've no right to two of anything by gift.

[Newdick's copy of the limited edition had arrived in time for R.F. to read from it at Ohio State but had evidently not been autographed. The inscription reads: For Robert Newdick / particularly / from his faithfully / Robert Frost. The Nutt, 1914, edition of North of Boston has written on the fly leaf: For Robert Newdick / to bibliograph / from Robert Frost / gratefully / 1936. Possibly this was when he inscribed the Jonathan Cape, 1936, *Selected Poems*: To my friend Robert Newdick / success in reading the four / prefaces in this book / Robert Frost. The authors of the prefaces were W. H. Auden, Paul Engle, C. Day Lewis, Edwin Muir.]

I gave him a reprint of R. F., Teacher and Educator, explaining I hoped the articles and bibliog. would stir up the animals in the big tent of education. He smiled. I asked whether he found me to be accurate in my representations. He said yes, and added that it amazed him where I found all the stuff.

He had said as we started out on the walk over the farm that he was grateful for what I was doing and had done. I depreciated the importance of anything I had done, but made clear that I intended the things as acts of homage. He wouldn't allow the deprecation, saying such things were solid, were far more than reviews and impressionistic studies and such, and that he appreciated them.

I asked whether I might write to Silver. He said yes, and asked whether he should mention me Wednesday. I said I'd be grateful if he would; such would make the getting easier.

While we three were in the room where he keeps the small stock of private things at this place, we talked much of C. L. G.[reen] and S. C.[lymer] I learned that C. has gone back to work in the bank in Boston, that he will be glad when the Bibliog. is finished (G. having got on his nerves), and that he last winter said there was room for all of us. I made clear the whole business of the Green smashup, quoting an example of G's take-it-back-iveness, speaking of consulting Melcher, etc., etc. At this time he (F.) spoke to Mrs. F. of a certain Holmes's writing him recently about a biography. I said nothing at this, and nothing was said to me.

F. was grateful for the transcribed Thomas letters, and let me cut off an autograph of one. He asked whether I had spent any money on the project, whether he owed me anything. I emphatically said no. I offered to do any other such work he might wish done. He said he thought of none at the moment.

He thinks he left a big box of stuff back in an attic room at the old 1915 farm in Franconia, full of letters, etc. If so, what treasure for someone!

He told me the gamekeeper business: the g. snooping in the hedge, glowering at F. and E. T., etc.; following the G. home, challenging him to fight, the G's refusing; T's coming up, the g's going for him, T's cowardice (or so it always seemed to T: "That's why he went to war," said F.); the g's having the police after F.; W. W. Gibson's doing nothing for F., though he moved in high "county" society, and could easily have put in a word with Lord Beecham [R.S.N.: Beauchamp?]; Abercrombie's taking it up at once when he heard of the matter; Lord B's unbelief of the g's lies and his letting, i.e. insisting the g. go off to the war. F. at this time at The Gallows, Abercrombie's cottage,—named per. fr. Callow(s), a name Masefield uses in a poem, incidentally,—Farmer Callow(s).

F. said he was not disillusioned by seeing English literati at close range; that he never expected anything of anybody until he had seen them.

He and Mrs. F. recalled how regularly one of these would say of any other, "A nice chap, but he can't write," or "Nice chap, but it's too bad about his writing."

F. knows Babette Deutsche has lately attacked him, e.g. *A B. W.* [*A Boy's Will*] so imitative that she can't imagine how anyone took it in the first place. On this score F. said "The Blessed Damozel is written all over Trial by Existence." I said I thought I saw traces of Shelley; he thought little likely, for S. had never loomed large to him.

We talked of Tennyson again, of Morris's forgettable facility, of W. V. Moody. F. quoted false lines; I countered with an idea I thought sincere, i.e. "You are not of us," they said, from the poem in which the ship of the world's state is carried through to a question, later resolved somewhat in The Brute and others. . . F. didn't remember anything so good.

F. knows the other crowd won't soon forgive his barbs, e.g. in the pref. to *King J*. He's willing for there to be experiment; he's experimented on his own, destroying the results; on the whole he prefers to let the others do the experimenting, sticking meanwhile to what he knows he can do.

A rich talk for a while on sound images vs. eye images. Images lie at the heart of poetry, certainly; communicating them, recalling them so they live again, something seen to something seen again, is poetry. But too much on eye images. Any Lowell. He's sought particularly sound images. How one says Says you! or Oh yeah? or the like and countless others. (Here goes the aggrieved tone of voice.)

Spoke of Thompson's *Survey*. He too knows there are errors. I read a bit from the tentative review for the *A. G. Q.* [*Amherst Graduate Quarterly*.], letting T. out on the score of accuracy because of the pressure for final copy and proof. T. got dope from Snow, "who never could get anything straight," said F. E.g., the *Atlantic* story is hardly at the expense of E. Sedgwick, but at exp. of someone if the office: "We regret we have no place for your vigorous verse."

F. told of calling on Briggs, dean, to say goodbye. (He hadn't bothered to say goodbye to the dean at Dartmouth.) B. was kind. Later B. sent a letter, a "to whom it may concern" affair, telling of F's standing, his leaving of his own choice, etc. I think F. remembers B. gratefully. F. long kept the letter, but no longer has it.

Mrs. F. says F. has no copy of that graduation picture of his mother. I must see if I can get that Duncan one for him, though he has the gloss print I sent him. Mrs. F. says F. has another picture of his m.

The woodblock of F. in the *Survey*, Mrs. F. says, originally on G. Munson's book, the dustjacket. I must get that dustjacket. —F. auto'd that in my copy of the *Survey*.

Story of San Francisco days: On barn, baiting Chinamen; they climbed up after the boys; F. jumping, banged lower teeth through lower lip; long a lump there, pretty well absorbed now after 50 years.

Story of curing wart with balm of gilead bud rubbed on. This after talking of my grandmother's "balsam" preparation, virtuous through its alcohol probably. And this after story of grandson's mangled hand after disobedience, a hand still bandaged.

F. remembers only 4 full years at Pinkerton. Says first year he took pneumonia and had to drop out. Remembers going in with a class and out with it.

Item 10:

The Letter of Louis W. Morse.

On October 1, 1936, one of Frost's former students, Louis W. Morse, at Pinkerton wrote Newdick. His recollections give a rare glimpse:

My recollections of Mr. Frost are that he was a genial and friend-ly teacher and easily won his way into the hearts of his pupils. I do not recall that he was ever cross with anyone: perhaps he had no need to be, for his friendly attitude toward the students commanded their respect.

In teaching literature, he sometimes read biographies of writers to the class and we took down notes from which we were to write papers to hand in. He taught the study of Shake-speare's works in an interesting way. After we had read a play, he would assign various parts of the speeches to different stu-dents to learn, so that they could recite them in dialogue in the class room, in the manner that it would be done on the stage. I might remark parenthetically that during my years at Pinker-ton several Shakesperian plays were creditably produced, in costume, by the students in the academy auditorium. Among these were, "Julius Caesar," "Macbeth" and "As You Like It." These productions, however, were under the direction of the teachers of elocution.

In his teaching of composition, Mr. Frost liked to bring out originality in the students' work, and the unusual in their writ-ing won his praise. For instance, in a little poem I once wrote for the *Pinkerton Critic*, the school magazine, about childhood memories, I made reference to a place which we, as children called "Over-the-wall, Over-the-wall." This pleased him great-ly, and he said it was the unusual in writing that captured the attention of the readers.

I am sorry, I have not been able to find any papers with annotations by Mr. Frost, but am enclosing a slip with brief notes which I took down in one of his classes; though probably it will not be of much interest to you.

The notes are, as a matter of fact, quite revealing. Notes Morse indicated were "taken about 1908" were from Frost's remarks about "kit Marlowe":

Great blank verse writer. Great blank verse given [written above: created] strength by him[.] Not so great as Shakespeare. Enough to give new kind of poetry. M's life lends itself to playwriting for it was tragic. Murdered in tavern when young. Know more about him than Shakpre. Marlowe irreligious man. / *Read Dr. Faustus* / short play—16 scenes[.] In writing about it, quote some passage.

Story Faustus sells his soul to the devil. Had learned all he thought he needed. Makes up mind to be magician.

As an afterthought, dated October 4, Morse wrote on the reverse of what seems to have been a half-sheet of paper: "It probably is not generally known that Robert Frost started to grow a full beard while at Pinkerton Academy. I believe it was toward the last of the school year, and my recollection is of a rather stubbly growth."

Item 11:

Findings of Dr. J. Forrest Burnham.

In response to a Newdick letter of September 1936, Dr. J. Forrest Burnham, of Lawrence, began on October 19 a most helpful correspondence which was to last for nearly three years. In his first letter he gave the names of the 32 members of Frost's graduating class at Lawrence High School, complete with addresses, "gathered from various sources" for all but the six who were deceased. He also included in his letter a series of clippings and notations relating to Frost's career at Lawrence High School.

On January 31, 1937, Newdick wrote Burnham to thank him for the list of Frost's Lawrence High School classmates, which he had been attempting to get since December 1935. He expressed himself as "unutterably grateful for your kind and generous assistance." The correspondence and accompanying legwork over the next two years made the language appropriate. By April 7 Newdick could report that he had heard from more than half of the survivors of the class. "Some, of course, could remember nothing that they deemed of interest, but others recalled all sorts of illuminating bits, such, for instance, as that when he was reading Caesar's Commentaries *Frost followed the directions in the text and constructed a wooden model of that famous bridge . . . all in all. I am far richer in biographical material. . . ."*

In addition to arranging for Ernest C. Jewell (a member of the high school class after Frost's and a friend of some years) to read Newdick's manuscript on Frost at Lawrence High School, Burnham collected such unique items as "a letter which is a copy of one received by a friend of ours from another friend":

I remember well the family of White the carpenter, but did not remember that he entered the ministry. I am not surprised for as I remember him, he was quite a religious man and although not exactly a fanatic, he had very decided views of his own. While not living in poverty, the family had very few luxuries and my memory of their home pictures a rather barren spot. . . . [When one of the White girls was sick] they asked a younger sister what she thought the invalid would enjoy—expecting her to name fruit, eggs, or chicken, but the sister insisted that red carnations would give her more pleasure than anything—. . . I met Leona (or Elinor) and she had been painting the portrait of a big shaggy dog and boarding him at her house in the country while painting him, and she complained that between the food he ate and the cost of her paints, she would get little profit of her labor. The last time I saw her she was in a very unhappy state of mind. She had given birth to a baby that had lived only a short time, and she was miserable because they would not let her have the child in bed with her and cuddle it and love it for the short time it lived. [Suggests "Home Burial."] She complained bitterly of her husband and said he was very heartless to her. If this is the White girl that married Robert Frost (I have forgotten the name of the man she married) she must have been older than he, for she was about my age and in a biography of Frost . . . the date of his birth was given as 1875. Perhaps it was one of the younger sisters he married, but the atmosphere of her married life as I sensed it from my interviews with her, seems to correspond with the idiosyncrasies of the poet Frost. A young woman living here knows him and says he is a bit queer. But he has, at least, made such a good name for himself that he had a part in the Harvard Tercentenary and the winter before that he gave readings at Harvard.

The foregoing note, bearing his rubber physician's stamp and date of May 23, 1937, was with a regular letter of informational notes and a "Confidential" aside:

I have noticed a certain atmosphere of coolness in partial relation to our investigation here, and perhaps without reason, altho I doubt the reservation it may be associated with, not by the Jewels, that the male member of the firm under investigation has been charged with accepting a financial loan from Mr. J. in past years, which has never been liquidated.

It is greatly to be regretted that one should ever uncover any skeleton in a closet in geneological studies, yet it does often occur.

In placing an individual on a deserved pedestal I wonder if it is not proper that there be no cracks in the base.

On March 2–5, 1938, Dr. Burnham, following a suggestion Newdick had given him, consulted, in the Salem, N.H., Public Library, records of The Board of Education of that term appropriate to Robert L. Frost. He found that Frost had taught the spring term of 1894 for 11 weeks at a wage of $24 per month in No. 9 School. He had twelve pupils who took instruction in reading, spelling, penmanship, arithmetic, geography, grammar, composition, and history. In the fall and winter of 1895–6, he taught at the same school for nineteen weeks for a total compensation of $114. He also received a dollar for wood and $2.50 for a "janitor."

Later in March, not being satisfied that he had thought he had found the "coal picking" item in the Lawrence Daily American, *Dr. Burnham rechecked the files. On March 29, he wrote "Hurrah!" He had found the item in the third column of page 5 of the issue of February 2, 1895:*

I am going to betray a confidence and worse than that, a poor man's confidence, but only in the hope of compelling for him your natural if unrighteous sympathy.

There are a lot of women and children that have let me see them looting coal in a yard near here. They come with buckets and gather it piece by piece under the coal cars. It is feverish work keeping warm, for such people. And the curious part of it is, they will not take the coal otherwise than from off the ground, which necessitates their twice handling it, once from the car to the ground, and again from the ground to the bucket. The moral strain attendant on such work must be excessive and one suffers to watch them skulking and stooping all day.

The column in which this item appeared, "The American About and Abroad," appeared from December 14, 1894, till October 12, 1897. Though he did not find the eagle-on-the-flagpole item, Dr. Burnham did report poems in columns of July 1897 and thereafter.

On June 23, Newdick sent, among other queries, a request to Dr. Burnham, in Lawrence, that he look in Lawrence news-

papers for possible mention of RF's birth: "But it occurs to me that Robert's father would have wired or written word to his father when the first child was born, and that grandfather Frost would have seen to it that a notice was inserted in a Lawrence paper."

Item 12:

Observations of Frost's Classmates, Lawrence High School.

1. My memory of Robert in those days is most pleasing but not especially definite. I was a bit older but not enough so to fully appreciate the eager rosy cheeked boy who stuttered a bit in his enthusiasm over his ready translations of Cicero, Virgil and Homer.

   I do not believe he ever failed or said, "unprepared." . . .

   Several years ago I made a brief call on Bob and Elinor in their temporary Amherst home. They were delightful, so truly the poet and his charming wife. Elinor was a girl of rare spirit and refinement. She belonged in the literary atmosphere of a poet's study, but Josephine Spaulding would tell you that there were years of taxing interlude between high school courtship and poet's study.

   Harriet W. Carter, February 21, 1937

2. As a senior I occupied the seat directly opposite Robert Frost and was always deeply impressed by his wonderful intellectual ability, high ideals, and great literary genius.

   He always seemed to live in an atmosphere of lofty thoughts and high aspirations.

   Anna H. Desmond, June 22, 1937

3. I remember that during his high school career, he constructed a small wooden Roman bridge, following the descriptions in his Latin book, which the Latin teacher displayed in all the Latin classes and considered it quite an accomplishment for a school student.

   Ellen G. Dunn, before February 17, 1937

4. When the news of the marriage of Elinor White and Robert

Frost reached me I was happy for them. She, the studious woman whose modesty was worthy of imitation. He, the earnest and honored young man who had no time for pranks or play. . . .

The children owed much to their cultured mother whose sweet face was framed in graying hair and who always wore a smart bonnet.

Grandfather Frost had an aristocratic air and was very severe. Were he living today he would be proud of his famous grandson.

Helen A. Ford, February 20, 1937

5. I am returning herewith the manuscript you recently sent me ["preliminary drafts of Chapters IV and V of the biography of Robert Frost"]. So far as my wife and I can recall, the facts are substantially correct. The poem, "La Noche Triste," was published in the April, 1890, number of the Lawrence High School Bulletin, of which I happened to be editor. At the time, no special significance was attached to the publication: I was just anxious for "copy."

Ernest C. Jewell, May 10, 1937

6. . . . Robert was tall, slender, square shouldered, a young man with blonde hair. He always acted the gentleman towards his teachers and classmates.

Intellectually he was the outstanding scholar of his class. Perhaps his greatest literary achievement is the poem he so kindly composed for our graduation. Incidentally, we of the class, believe it his greatest work.

While Robert was always a perfect gentleman with the soul of a poet, he was also physically rugged. One day a fellow student made a statement concerning Robert which he knew was untrue. With a display of physical force Robert compelled the fellow student to retract his statement.

Josephine L. Kane, February 5, 1938

7. Yes, I heard him when he spoke before our College Club in Lawrence in 1925 and an interesting feature of that evening

was the singing of the 1892 Class Hymn, which he wrote, by members of the class who were present.

It was my privilege to play the piano for the singing as I did in 1892 when we graduated—and, as Robert sang with us, that feature of the program made a great "hit" with the large audience.

Annie Barker Lord, March 20, 1937

8. Frost was not by any means a good mixer in high school days. He flocked very much by himself, as was perhaps natural in view of the rather plebeian character of our class. He dwelt like a star, apart. It was evident by senior year that there was affinity between himself and Elinor White—sort of a Browning and Elizabeth Barrett affair. Both of them, of course, people of the highest grades but not seemingly anxious or even perhaps able to click in the most of the rest of us [sic].

Frank B. McAllister, November 14, 1937

9. There is not much I can tell you about Robert Frost, or Rob, as we always called him. He was rather grave for a high school boy, though always pleasant to meet. His sister Jean was also in our class and we always went to her for help in our Latin.

Ruby S. Ralton, February 11, 1937

10. If Bob had only told us he would some day become famous, we could and would have paid more detailed attention when he was with us. However, as he was shy and retiring when in school, he left only a hazy memory. By this I do not mean that he did not have a personality of his own for he thoroughly did, but it was scholastic, and that was something the high school students in our class gave him credit for.

As I remember him, he was a rather large framed lad with a tawny mane of blonde hair, rather dreamy-eyed, with almost a pink and white complexion, although he was by no means effeminate. He was always so far ahead of us in his studies that we accepted the fact long before we graduated that he would be the valedictorian. The same applied to

Eleanor White, who was quiet, retiring and not one of the sky-larking crowd. However, she was very pleasant and a favorite in the class. That Bob and Eleanor should gravitate toward each other seemed only natural and caused no comment among us. While both were fine, wholesome students, liked by everyone, still they seemed to work and belong on a plane of their own.

The only incident I can recall was the football career of Bob Frost. In those days the football team was without benefit of coach, or an expense account. The captain was boss in theory, if not in fact. Discipline was something hard to enforce. During our senior year I was captain of the football team. Before the season was under way the players were lax in reporting for practice, and as we had so few boys capable of playing they got away with it. At last I concluded I would discipline the team and promptly laid off some of the players. To fill a place, as a last resort, I asked Bob to play with no idea he would do so. It seems he was anxious to play, but would not ask and no one ever thought of inviting him. I will never forget how dumbfounded we were when Bob played his first game. He was like some wild animal let loose. He charged, tackled and played like a fighting bull, he had no fear. Right then and there he became one of us.

Before this we had given him recognition for his brains. Now he had demonstrated he was a regular fellow behind his quiet manners, and that it would be just bad judgment to start a quarrel with him.

Thomas L. Sullivan, October 11, 1937

Item 13:

The Robert von Moschzisker Letter.

Newdick received a letter from a good Frost friend, Robert von Moschzisker, of Philadelphia, dated October 5, 1936. He had found Frost lived near his summer home in 1916. "We were so impressed by his writings that we called, and found them living in a very primitive little white house, perched on the side of a hill, overlooking a beautiful mountain view [Mt. Lafayette]. The children were all quite young, but all seemed to be helping in the house and on the place." His observations, gained through a friendship of twenty years, are worth recording:

When Robert Frost comes to Philadelphia he frequently stays at our home and his very presence always stimulates. We have had some delightful times together when he has read and talked, in his own chatty way, far into the night. Our talks always cover a wide range—religion, politics, art, economics, and of course, poetry.

His most impressive qualities are, to my mind, his absolute honesty of thought and clearness of vision, his utter dislike of sham and false principles.

Mrs. Von Moschzisker and I might tell some stories of the early poverty that he endured to make the poet which he became; but we would not care to do so.

Robert told us once that he could write only after he had had some change in his life or had in some way suffered. This may explain his many changes of habitat.

Frost has a great charm as a public speaker. Early last summer he was given a degree by the University of Pennsylvania. After the ceremonies, the graduating class of the Law School had a luncheon at the University Club. Frost attended this luncheon and was called upon to speak. Now, as you probably know, fourth-year law students are rather a "hard-boiled" set; but Robert conquered them so completely that, after a ten minute talk, when he attempted to say good-bye, the audience arose and demanded more.

Item 14:

Conversation with Wilbert Snow.

On January 29, 1937, Newdick participated for several hours in conversation at the Faculty Club at Ohio State University with Wilbert Snow, long a friend of Frost, from Connecticut. He recorded several pages of "added knowledge," of which the following might be considered to be of general interest:

S says F hard on contemporaries. Quoted Mark van Doren: "If he'd just say something good about any one of us!"—S had Lambuth's attitude toward Imbs for the latter's book, in which MacV. saved F by deletions. [Imbs' book, *The Professor's Wife,* is about a very snobbish English professor and his wife.] S takes "Build Soil" to be largely fun—*or* F hasn't thought his politics through. I said I refused to get into politics with F. S said he sometimes got F so mad he (F) wouldn't speak to him.

S says you can depend upon it it's good if F says so. F wrote S a fine letter when S's third book of poems came out. Sandburg made a copy of the letter, so that it would surely be preserved; so did a chap in the English Department.

Re F and the Harvard Tercentenary: F really upset by the asking of Masefield too. But Conant had no choice: The Lamonts, who gave $500,000 for the roving professorship, great friends of Masefield, made the request that Masefield be asked! (Compare with Lesley's emphasis on the no-degree business.)

Item 15:

The "Hair" Episode at Dartmouth.

Even as Newdick was receiving testimony as to the gravity of Frost's behavior in high school (in Item 12, Part III), he received the following balancing evidence from Carl H. Richardson, a Dartmouth classmate and namesake of "the victim" of the following episode:

The Junior Yearbook issued by Class of 1894, our Freshman year, contains an act set forth under the caption "Hair."

Three persons take part, the victim, the first conspirator and the second conspirator. The Victim, announces that he needs a haircut. The First Conspirator (Robert Lee Frost) remarks "It is a good resolution." Then the Second Conspirator says he and his pal can do a good job and save the Victim 25 cents. The Victim agrees and the Conspirators proceed to cut a strip of the hair from the forehead to the nape of the neck and then crosswise from ear to ear. The First Conspirator (Frost) holds up a mirror to the Victim and immediately a roughhouse ensues, not alone with pillows, but with furniture, and as a result, the Victim left college, never to return. Now Frost must have had some real humor in his make-up to have done this. (April 27, 1937.)

The yearbook section cited by Richardson (not the Richardson mentioned in the scene) appears on p. 151 of Aegis, *published, 1892–3 by the Junior Class of Dartmouth College, is as follows:*

HAIR

A Farce in One Act

Dramatis Personal [sic]:

The Victim . . . "Parson" Richardson

First Conspirator . . . Frost
Second Conspirator . . . Hazen

The Victim: I swow, boys, I guess I'll have to get my hair cut; I haven't had a hair cut for a year and a half.

First Con.: Good resolution.

Second Con.: Say, Parson, we can cut hair to beat four of a kind; better let me do it and save a quarter.

The Victim: I swow, boys, you're awful kind; get out your shears and peel 'er off.

(The conspirators do "peel 'er off," by entirely cutting the hair from a strip running from the victim's forehead to the nape of his neck, and also from one ear to the other.)

First Con.: (Holding a mirror in front of the victim) Now, Parson, don't that look nice?

(The victim gazes upon his reflection in silent terror for a moment, then bolts from the room, leaves college, and when last heard from was waiting for his hair to grow.)

Copied from p. 151 of *Aegis*, published 1892–3 by the Junior class, Dartmouth College, by Carl H. Richardson, Boston, Massachusetts, April 27, 1937.

On March 18, 1938, Carl H. Richardson of Boston, a Dartmouth student in 1892, wrote his answers to nineteen questions Newdick had sent the month before. Most of the answers do not concern Frost directly, but two additional notes may be recorded. In mentioning the "Hair" incident, Richardson dated it as happening on October 5. The editor of the Aegis, *published in March 1893, referred, under the heading, "Our Departed" to "the scholarly Frost and [Guy Waldo] Richardson, the emblem of piety and righteousness." Confirming other accounts of volatile activity, Newdick's respondent noted: "There were some pretty lively boys rooming in Wentworth Hall, where Frost lived; I find a reference to some of these boys as 'Wentworth hellers'. I remember a football rush very well and can see Frost in my mind's eye now, working toward the center to get the ball; he had a heavy head of hair and was a nice looking boy."*

Just at the end of August 1938, Newdick received a curious note, typed at the bottom of a query he had sent out, from Guy W. Richardson, the butt of the "Hair" episode. His recollection of the matter:

I have very pleasant memories of the student days at Dartmouth, in the fall of '92, when Robert Frost was one of my classmates. I had frequent talks with him, but the incident I recall most distinctly was when he proposed giving me a phrenological reading. He examined my head very carefully, and made some comments that seem to have been justified by future developments. I regret that I have not been able to renew my acquaintance with this distinguished man, except for a brief interview at the close of one of his lectures at Harvard a year or two ago, so I cannot say whether he has ever been seriously interested in phrenology.

As well as constituting a warning concerning the unreliability of informants other than RF, this account, containing the substitution of phrenology for haircut, suggests this informant's subtle way of suggesting to RF (should he see the note) that he remembered very well what was done.

Item 16:

Observations of Mrs. Eva Barndollar.

Mrs. Eva Barndollar, who had been a student at the Normal Training School at Plymouth, New Hampshire, in 1911, when Frost was teaching there, sent Newdick two letters of reminiscence in May 1937. Unfortunately, when the writer found her still living in Manchester, New Hampshire, in 1974, she declined to give permission to quote her letters. Thus the following summation of her valuable comments is given.

She recalled Frost as conducting in his classes an open forum, covering a wide range of subjects, speaking in a low voice. He gave examinations occasionally, she thought, to meet school requirements but thought he never graded them. Being convinced he probably put the papers into his stove, she wrote, on one occasion, instead of the answers to his questions a flippant and irrelevant discourse. After several days, receiving no grade, she stopped after class to ask how she had done on that paper. After a moment's puzzlement, he assured her that she had done quite acceptably.

The students found his mannerisms both intriguing and endearing. He usually entered the classroom breathless and late, giving any of various excuses. The students thought he had simply become engrossed in reading. His hair was usually awry; his coat buttons might not be aligned, and he might not have on collar or tie. The fact that his trousers bagged at the knees did not bother the students, for they found the movement of his mind fascinating. His patience, tolerance, and friendliness were impressive. As he sat in his chair leading the class into the intricacies of human behavior, he poised himself on his spine, his hands in his pockets. He was recalled as having a spare figure, bent posture, plentiful hair splotched with grey, spare and active hands, and eyes which were incisive though compassionate. His pallid complexion made Miss O'Brien think his health was not of the best.

The same intense response to current events which inspired Lesley, at five, to start down the road outside the Derry farm house with a kettle of water to pour on the Russians (1905) evidently was displayed in the classroom. When the Titanic sank, the class spent the next class hour discussing imagined reactions of those who went down with the ship.

Frost enjoyed a good classroom argument. He baited a student who recommended to him a best-seller, repulsing good-humoredly the aroused assault of the class.

Just as he found it hard to keep to the exact time of class meeting, so, in the weeks before his family arrived, he found it hard to arrive during the designated serving hours in the dining room. He was noted for appearing unapologetically just as dessert was being served.

His physical activities centered on tennis, which he played with pleasure and knowledge but without endurance, and hiking. He tramped about the countryside with his children on occasion. When he took the class to Mt. Prospect, a matter of thirteen miles, he enlivened the trek with observations and stories about nature, for which he had an obvious love.

When the students learned their teacher had published a poem, they were surprised and then expressed their pride in this exploit on the part of one of their teachers. He had evidently given no hint of previous publication. He seemed embarrassed, like a boy caught with his hand in the jam jar.

When he went to England in the summer of 1912, the students who had expected to see him on returning to school were disappointed. However, Mrs. Barndollar and probably others got a first edition of A Boy's Will, autographed. Costing seventy-five cents, the book's modest brown binding, having flecks of gold woven into the fabric, seemed appropriate to its author. His former student liked to recall he had taught her to value common things.

When Newdick responded to Mrs. Barndollar's first letter, he asked if she had had any papers Frost had marked. She replied she had kept for a long time one on which he had marked that it was lively and that she should keep up what she was doing. Though she wrote she did not understand his comment, she recalled being delighted that he had read one of her papers. She added he always gave her good grades.

Mrs. Barndollar had lost a notebook she had kept of Frost's remarks, but she still recalled his insistence against hypocrisy *and for following one's own bent. She thought he felt people could choose their own status in life, whether good or bad.*

She remembered the consideration Frost had for her on an occasion when she had a cough. Thinking she needed more rest, he told her she was excused from class so that she could be outside in the sun. Because she found this endearing, she insisted on going to class, though he tried to dissuade her.

Frost's sense of humor was strong in Mrs. Barndollar's memory. She thought her Irish wit helped her catch on when others did not. Quoting one of his puns, she could still see his broad grin when he said it.

Frost, she recalled, had made an arrangement with a bookseller to get reduced rates for quantity purchases. He gave her advice which led to her purchase of Palgrave's Golden Treasury, Marcus Aurelius' Meditations, Emerson's Representative Men, and Wordsworth's Complete Poems.

Though she no longer had pictures she had taken of Frost, having sent them to him at Michigan (where he supposedly received them without comment), she still had an image of Mr. and Mrs. Frost before their small house in the school campus. She had on a high-collared white waist with wool skirt, the hem of which touched the grass. Frost stood smiling, his head characteristically tilted to one side, holding perhaps a twig, his sweater unbuttoned. Another picture showed him with several of the girls at the school, and possibly another showed him with his son or a daughter.

When the writer asked Mrs. Barndollar for permission to quote her letters, the sense of her reply was that she was afraid what she had written might be considered controversial, that she would not want anything derogatory to be printed but would want her admiration for her memorable former teacher to be on record. In that spirit, the gist of some twenty pages Mrs. Barndollar wrote to Professor Newdick and to this writer has been recorded here.

Item 17:

Letter of Professor William Ernest Hocking.

On May 1, 1937, Newdick received a letter from Professor William Ernest Hocking, a professor of philosophy at Harvard University. It provides an excellent insight of Frost's attitude toward Harvard or any other school:

In 1916, I received a letter from our class secretary containing a list of lost men, i.e., men unknown to the secretary, because they never answered any of his letters. Our fifteenth reunion was approaching, and he wanted to round up the lost sheep. The name of Robert Frost was near the top of the list. I didn't know, at that time, that Frost had ever been in Harvard,—he hadn't mentioned it. And I took it for granted that our secretary had ordinary discretion, and that this must be some other Robert Frost. However I enquired from the college office where Robert Frost lived, when he was an undergraduate; the answer was Franconia, New Hampshire. This looked suspicious. I wrote to him to ask whether he was ever a member of the class of '01. He did not answer . . . he seldom does. But the next time he came in for several days conversation I asked him about it, and he admitted the truth. He had taken courses with Barrett Wendell and a Professor Parker in Greek. He abominated Wendell's affectations and as for Parker—Frost knew quite a little Greek on his own—he found him a pedant unwilling to receive any enlightenment from his class. So he dropped out, and tried to be spurlos versenkt. But owing to my detective work, he was caught; and at our twenty-fifth, he actually appeared and read us a poem. But nobody would call him an enthusiastic Harvard man.

Item 18:

Newdick's Notes of the Visit with the Frosts,
September 1–3, 1937, at Concord Corners, Vt.

The Irish came into northern New Hampshire chiefly, at first, as cooks. Consider their names: Lynch, Callahan, Ash, Fitzgerald,—cousins, many of them. Lynch was the original of O'Toole in "The Cow's in the Corn."

Bethlehem: H.W. Beecher's writing of it brought it to F's attention. Cowpox. [What that word precipitates, I now know not.]

Let them that set the fire put it out! [Reference to "The Cow's in the Corn!"]

Thayer, the Yank neighbor of the Lynches, who would come in for cider. As he was leaving, Mrs. L. would say: Ah, God love you, Mr. Thayer; come often! When he was gone, she would exclaim: God damn your black soul to hell! (And this before the F children.)

Reading Tacitus led to impulse to return to Harvard for more of the same.

Much novel reading at one time. Lew Wallace: The Far God. Also Prescott. Much interest in Yucatan.

Carl Burell: Pembroke, behind the hill; so Orion, in "Canis Major."

Friend in buckling-down days at school in Salem under his mother: Charles Peabody, who became a mason. Wouldn't study grammar, but got it out of the corner of his eye from the work of the others. Arithmetic and geography, yes. Once stuck another boy with a pin; so, mother whipped him then and there.

His mother considered apprenticing him to a cabinet maker. But the cabinet maker not enthusiastic. So he went on to L.H.S.

Worked for an architect whose hobby was conchology (shells), wrapping shells for transportation. The architect was dissatisfied with the way the work was done, and complained about it,—the only time anyone really complained about work he did.

At Willoughby Lake, botanizing, F. pointed out to me: snowberries, that hide under their leaves; bane berries; Clinton, with three purplish berries in early autumn; etc., etc. He knew everything I asked about. [He once told Thornton he had never failed to place a specimen anywhere in its class and family, though sometimes he found a species unknown to him.]

Friend in German Department at Amherst: Otto Manthey Zorn.

Prose contributions to a farm journal about 1905–6–7. [Whicher put me up to asking about these.] Got in bad about geese. Had to follow up in a reply, and did! [But no mag. title from F!]

"The Lost Follower": Religion. Army and Church.

Hay fever came on cir. Aug. 15–20. Cough, closed nose, etc., etc., until Jan. Ragweed!

Poem in Plymouth N.S. mag. 1915 or 1916: "A Time to Talk." [R.S.N. longhand note: In Pinkerton Critic Earlier!]

Miss Newell for first-year Latin. A taskmaster. Caesar with Miss Lear. Then Virgil with Miss N, and finally Cicero with Miss L.

F fed up finally by the grind: "mark-sick," he called it. He *sold* the Hood medal to a jeweller!

John Thom, now at South Station, Boston, a friend of H.S. days.

Carl Burell, an excellent botanist, in "The Self-Seeker."

At Fobes' cottage about 12 years. They mostly away. Would take no rent: rich; said rent would go for income tax.

Frank McAllister finished up last year as ed. of H.S. Bulletin after Frost quit.

Re *Dearborn Independent*: Ed., Cameron. Asst. ed., Pierce Cummings. Re N.W. Ayer & Son. (Forget meaning of this last notation.)

At Mich., rented from Bernice Stewart; place now at Ford's Dearborn Village. F himself not pleasant: put off anti-Semitic drive on his editors! Fired 'em in a batch.

Four echoes in *A Boy's Will*:
(1) verge of doom: Shakespeare;
(2) "Trial by Existence": Rossetti's "Blessed Damozel" with reverse English and then some;
(3) when wintry winds do blow: ballad (I ventured: Shakespeare);
(4) with a silver pin: ballad.
On this point, contrast B. Deutsch in her recent book!

Other echoes in F: deliberate: but few. Note argument with Lowes. [We talked of this before. R.S.N.]

In San Francisco in 1932. [Out there for Olympics, etc. R.S.N.] Abbotsford [Hotel. W.A.S.], once called "Brogan's Folly." Blanchette. (What *does* that name mean? A friend of those days?)

Wild youth, esp. on coast. In with Seth Balser, who ended up a confirmed criminal. Broke and entered, more than once, too.

Did not feel responsibility toward family until about 1905. But, I objected, for those first 30 years you had some philosophy! Yes, perhaps. It was wisdom and art. Never cared for art alone. Or put it this way: philosophy and form.

F says he has never been "Bohemian," has always regarded civic virtue and domesticity, e.g., as worthwhile. (This point marks the end of my few written notes. Now for a page or two of recollections and memoranda.)

We drove up to Concord on Tucky's reassurance, not mine, and engaged a room in an o. f. house, owned by Mrs.   , on the main drag, the road from St. Johnsbury to (I believe) Lancaster. We had had a tip from the man who used to own the creamery, who also told us of the first normal school at Concord (the part now called C. Corners) in 1823, which was celebrated with a pageant in 1923.

Shortly after noon I went out, getting lost thrice on the way, and approached the temporary house (the one that Irma and John are to have) with some doubt. Someone had seen me coming. F met me cordially in the doorway, hand outstretched. As he rubbed his hair when we had sat down: I was wondering whether I owed you a letter. (Tucky went into hysterics when she heard that.) I remained until 6:30 or 7:00, and F invited us both up, and then to dinner at St. Johnsbury, the next day at 10:30. That was Wednesday.

Thursday we drove up for them, then on to St. Johnsbury for dinner, an excellent one. F and I shopped for groceries and a pillow. Then back to C.C. There F and I talked, and E.M.F. and Tucky. When we left, about dinner-time, we had plans made for the morrow: we to prepare the picnic, they to select the place.

Friday, then, we all went to Willoughby Lake, north of St. J., where the Fs hadn't been for 20 years or so. There we had our banquet-lunch. Afterwards F and I went botanizing along the side of the hill. We drove back to C.C., and there had our "postscript" meal from lunch surplus. F and I went for water and got into a long talk that took us into the dark, so that EMF and Tucky came for us. I took Tucky to town and then returned. I left F at 2:30 A.M.,—the end of three glorious days.

Much of the talk was of the book *Recognition*. I urged the inclusion of something about Michigan in the Places section. I urged also the inclusion of a number of omitted friendly names: P. Colum, A Kreymborg, etc., etc. F agreed on all these points. Then we worked on the plan of the book, its "design," working out Portraiture, The Idea, etc., etc. At last I took with me to N.Y. the nearly final plan for Thornton.

The talk on the walk for water was in re Carl Burrell. He a queer duck,—maybe sexually perverse. Has married two shut-in women. Grandfather F. fixed it up that C.B. went to the farm at Derry with the Fs. CB had the cow, etc. After a year or so, he left. The deal was a hard one for CB, but that was not RF's doings, and he resented B's intrusion, for that's what it amounted to. Grandfather F was afraid RF couldn't get along, didn't know enough.—As boys, they used to botanize, B being excellent.

I offered *not* to stop, as planned, to see CB, and F preferred this, saying my going from him to B would at least seem to be ambassadorial, and that if relations were to be reopened he should make the first move, maybe by giving CB $25 annually for his shut-ins.

When we stepped out of doors on that last night, or rather early in the morning, there was a strange light in the north. Could it be Northern Lights? We waited for our eyes to get used to the night. No; just a strange light on the underside of a cloud. Then F swept the heavens with his eyes and began to talk in intimate fashion of the stars, which were extraordinarily bright: the Northern Cross, Orion, the Pleiades, — one constellation after another. He knows the stars as he knows flowers, botany.

When we talked of the Eng. edn. of SPs [*Selected Poems*], he voiced his annoyance at the tone. I tried to explain that, saying it was the *least* condescending I had ever read from two of those four pens (Day's and Auden's). Mrs. F agreed with me when I read the last paragraph of the AGQ [*Amherst Graduate Quarterly*] review in carbon copy.

She, by the way, read "RF and the Sound of Sense" and voiced her liking for it, gently, as is her wont. She read other things, too, and expressed similar liking. She said to Tucky, "I hope Mr. Newdick isn't left someday by Rob's poetry going into eclipse," or words exactly to that effect. She and Tucky got on easily and pleasantly together.

RF would hear none of the preliminary sketch-chapters for the biography, but the assumptions all the way were that of course I was going ahead.

Re the Huntington Lib. holdings: He examined the list, correcting one or two of my guesses, denying the authenticity of "I had a love once," etc., but not yet granting me permission to go over the material. He expressed a wish for a copy of the checklist, which I subsequently sent on to him. (I'm making this memory record on Sept. 25, 26, 1937.)

We walked over the several properties he got in this latest real estate deal: the house up towards the "inn," the several "lots" up the way where the postroad used to be, examining the upper spring, looking into cellar-holes, etc. He and EMF were a bit annoyed at Hall's Pond becoming Shadow Lake when there are already several SLs in Vermont. [R.S.N. longhand note: Suggested I buy a lot there!]

Tucky took pictures both at the house and on the picnic. One can look from the front yard across the river (which is not visible) to Franconia.

David McCord had been there for three days before I came along, for once getting away from his mother! — Irma and John were to come up the day after we left. There's no place F can really get away.

F raised the question, to quit trying to get away, that is, to talk the rest of life away, or to seek real seclusion where (as he wrote to Holmes) he could lay a few lays. He talked again of never being so much with people as when he's by himself, meaning that then he composes the poems that delight so many readers.

He made treasures of an armload of books for me, Friday night, by inscriptions. I liked particularly that in the Eng. edn. of NH, though that in From S to S thanks me for an idea — which Thornton says he had independently! Well, no wonder: it was so obvious to a reflective reader. [See Appendix G.]

At my request, too, he inscribed a first of MI [*Mountain Interval*] for Billy Graves, who so much admires him and who has let me use MI for months.

Much, much talk of the problem of the rich and the poor, and the difficulty, if not indeed the impossibility of getting them together. That place, e.g., where Frost is listed as a trustee (or something of the sort), which aims to be a real community center, — but for him the place was packed with dress goods, how people looked down on them, etc. There was no lessening of the looking down because of his and Elinor's book-learning, either.

He told of getting the money when he was at Derry. The farm was tied up, but it was to come to him, and he knew it could be made into security. Derry lawyer no help. Manchester lawyer was. Then the fuss over the insurance, with finally the home office stepping in and examining F. He got the ins., $600, all he ever had; and carried it until the farm was sold. It was a revelation to F that he was as shrewd, nay shrewder, than many with whom he dealt. That business played a part in his becoming less unsocial, in his coming out, so to speak, about 1905, 1906. — He said he wanted the money chiefly for more capital investment; but the investment didn't pan out well. The Derry lawyer recently tried a sort of blackmail upon him! (He named these names but they're gone at the moment. Maybe I can add them later.) [R.S.N. longhand: Blanchette.]

There's no point in recording the details of the talk re *Recognitions*, but it was jolly good that I took along my whole Frost library of materials, for almost everything was made use of in some way or another.

Much talk on war, too, particularly after I said that Mrs. Whicher didn't seem to understand, had thought him *over* emphasizing. He sees war as inevitable among nations, as contest between individuals. Compare traffic accidents: part of the price we pay for rapid transportation, for speeding the tempo of life, for broadening the country we've seen, etc. It's simply inevitable, — nature. This brotherhood business is wishful thinking. He has a poem, not yet published, re the two hands, the one we hold on with, the other we hit with: we can't hit quite hard enough to break entirely the hold of the holding hand, and, conversely, we can't hold quite tightly enough to prevent hits. Who, he said, can walk if holding of hands.—I told him of my essay, written *before* this talk and making, from other materials, the same point. (I didn't add that it has a sort of postscript on the holding to a faith, though I'm as certain as ever, nay, more certain, of that faith of his: God can count on me never to be disappointed in him.

On a last sheet which had nothing else typed on it appeared: "On this sheet I'll add bits that come back to me from time to time. (Oh, to be Boswell!)"

Item 19:

Letter from Edgar Gilbert.

On December 31, 1937, Frost's longtime friend, Edgar Gilbert, after negotiations going back to the preceding July, sent Newdick this illuminating paragraph:

Yes, as Dr. Burnham has told you, Bob and I were work mates and had been brought up in the same neck of the woods. He lived in Salem while I was in Methuen, then he in Methuen while I in Salem, then both in Lawrence, and working together, later I teaching in Methuen and he in Pinkerton Academy just beyond Salem. He entered Dartmouth several years earlier than I. We had much in common and would be good pals. We read Shakespeare's thunders to the hammer of the heavy machinery of the electric power plant, and sang his sonnets to the purr of the brushes on the big dynamos.

Item 20:

Letter of Charles L. Hanson.

On February 25, 1938, Charles L. Hanson, a Frost friend of twenty-five years' standing, responded to Newdick's request of the previous September for Frost insights. Hanson had sent a six-page typescript, recalling how, in their early friendship, "His shyness retired behind his trust and he enjoyed my unabashed appreciation of his work."

Of his Harvard lectures in 1936 Hanson recalled that his welcome on the occasion of the first lecture was memorable:

He had never heard any such demonstration on his behalf in any part of the country, and to have it occur in Boston—with its reputation for reserve if not coldness—was upsetting. It was all he could do to keep his poise and begin to address the enthusiastic crowd. Haltingly, tremblingly, he did the best he could under the trying circumstances, his pleasure almost overwhelmed by his sense of helplessness and defeat.

Three other Hanson glimpses add importantly to a view of a rather vulnerable and approachable Frost, one whose reality is at times forgotten:

A few evenings later as I was walking by his Cambridge house he came out to post a letter and insisted on my going in. Against my inclination, for my intention was to give him time to get settled before calling, I yielded. When I left, he said he would walk part way home with me. Soon we reached my home, more than a mile distant, and I asked him in. No, it was too late. But it was not eleven o'clock, I urged. "Well, you have crossed my threshold; I'll cross yours," and in he came. The next hour, in which he chatted with my wife, one of my daughters, and me was a memorable one for us all. He was at home. We were all friends. He could say what he pleased. He could trust us with his doubts, his fears, his hopes. He and I had gone on from where we left off years before, and he seemed to enjoy renewing the friendship as much as I did. In discussing some criticisms of his verse he expressed doubt as to whether one particularly distinguished and notable critical man considered his verse poetry, and I took keen satisfaction in assuring him that this critic had told me years ago that he was favorably impressed. It was obviously a genuine relief to Frost to have the matter settled.

When he rose to go he said in his timid way "You'll steer me out of your front yard a bit, won't you?" I gladly agreed to do so, although unwilling to tell him I had been counting on doing that very thing in order that we might be by ourselves. The talk was perhaps more intimate. Suddenly he turned to me: "You are the Hanson whose *English Composition* I used in teaching at Pinkerton Academy, aren't you?" It was clear that I was, and the talk went on. As we approached his gate, he stopped. "Why, you have come all the way back with me. It doesn't seem fair to leave you here." But the hour was late and I suggested he had better turn in rather than walk halfway toward my home.

Yet it was not "unalloyed." One evening he confided in me that he had been invited to be the poet at the meeting of the Harvard Chapter of Phi Beta Kappa. That he could manage with material on hand, but he had also been asked to write an ode to read at the Tercentenary celebration. That was almost too much. He had never written anything to order. Once a woman who had admired his "Birches" had importuned him to write a similar poem that would appeal to girls, one that would describe her feelings when as a very small child, tempted by an older sister to swing on a birch, she was left by the mischievous sister hanging in midair.

He could turn that request off with a smile, but with Harvard it was different. Sadly he remarked, in his slow, tired voice that is almost a drawl, "Well, I suppose a man might do that sort of thing once in a lifetime." But it did not accord with his habit of writing only what he was impelled to write.

A few days later he faced in my school an eager group of several hundred boys who at once put him at ease and drew from him his very best. I do not see how he could have said a thing better or read a line better. There was no hesitation, no doubt. He and his audience were one, and the spontaneous outbursts of appreciation and applause must have thrilled him.

Next day a boy who had never before been able to finish a poem brought me one that had been inspired by Frost. It was printed in the school paper and a copy of it went to the poet. The generous man replied by sending the boy a volume of his "Selected Poems," with a greeting that left the lad speechless.

The Frost whom Hanson knew had written him in "a typical sentence from a recent letter": "What a funny predicament a small success in poetry can land you in."

Item 21:

Newdick's Amherst Observations, April, 1938.

Selected excerpts of Newdick's letters from Amherst to his wife supply important observations:

The college chapel was of course lovely, banked with flowers over the altar and pulpit—and around the bronze urn that holds Elinor's ashes. (The Derry plan still holds.) The regular funeral service—from the book—was held, but with no sermon—just a prayer. Very short, and very well done. The family sat to the right (facing the altar), the honorary bearers to the left, and others behind. . . .

Afterwards, to about 6, RF and Lesley received the bearers and their wives at the Zorns, and there was tea and much talk. The familiar post-funeral atmosphere was almost entirely absent, thank God. I had especially good talks with Thornton, Melcher, Thompson, Cox, and Lesley. She will read MSS. for me as her mother did. She said she liked The Other Harmony but would read it again. RF said (tho' I saw little of him at this time) to give the *Ox. Un. Pr.* the contract.

Later, RF brought four of us to dinner here at the Lord Jeffery: his son-in-law John, Louis Untermeyer, Sidney Cox, and I. Marvelous shore dinner. Then to the lounge for talk until about 10:30.

Today RF is going to Dartmouth to see Irma, who couldn't stand to come down for the services. He'll be back tomorrow.

No shadow or faintest suggestion of anything amiss. [Evidently in regard to his doing the authorized biography. W.A.S.] On the contrary, all the talk, of *every one* else as well as of RF, is that all is set. Not that I was anxious, but I do like reassurance—and I daresay you do too!

RF looks better, far better, than I expected he would—and yesterday, that despite the fact that he hadn't gone to bed the "night" before till 8 a.m. Melcher said F said he hadn't been away from Elinor for more than a month in more than 40 years. And that most of his thinking had been wound around Elinor's silence. . . .

The F's are not in their own home, but staying with the Zorns. (Letter of April 23, 1938, 10:45 A.M.)

. . . I found a call from Lesley; so I went over to Elliott's to meet her and talk—about her mother's last days, the threat of pneumonia to Robert thereafter; about the poems and letters in Huntington, particularly the two denied "poems"; about family pictures, of which she gave me three—Mr. and Mrs. Frost at Plymouth (1911 or 1912), the Sunset Ave. home here (which RF sold at once to the college when he got back, because he'd never enter it again), and Marjorie; and much else.

RF, I hear, had another almost sleepless night, getting off at noon for Dartmouth and Irma. There, Lesley thought, he might really get a good sleep, because, she says, Irma *won't* sit up till all hours with him! I hope so: if he doesn't get some soon, he'll crack; anybody would. I expect him back tomorrow. . . . He really apologized for going at all,—but Irma *is* his daughter! And if I know RF I'll get back in intensity what I may lose in *spread*.

Whicher was telling me the urn was engraved with the date R met E. And he planned it all this way; if he should go first, years ago, it occurred to me today, while I was reading again the last lines of "On the Sale of My Farm":

> Only be it understood,
> It shall be no trespassing
> If I came again some spring
> In the grey disguise of years,
> Seeking ache of memory here.

(Letter of April 23, 1938, 11:15 P.M.)

. . . Lesley took me across town to the Sunset Avenue home, and I explored the downstairs, particularly RF's study. . . . Later I had the idea the inside of the house ought to be photographically recorded. . . . [This was done.]

So I came back here and composed the enclosed letter to President King in regard to the Derry farm. Lesley says the ashes will not be scattered until all the family can come together, but that her father wishes to make preliminary arrangements very soon. Tonight he's at South Shaftsbury with Carol, then I think tomorrow he'll come on back here.

. . . Lesley's saying that I was her father's guest didn't make me *blue*. That is, that he'd pay my inn bill. I'm not so sure as she is—
(Letter of April 24, 1938, night.)

This is the first time I've felt really stalled, for still there's no word from RF. God knows what he ran into at Irma's and Carol's, for none of the children have too much self-capacity; so I'm not annoyed at all.

. . . There's no difficulty with Thornton. He's out, or on the way out, at Holt's,—and I think he advised RF to approve OUP!

. . . Mrs. E. said today that Mrs. Z. is really ill, and that RF will *not* be able to stay there when he comes back, but will probably have to stay at the inn: routine going on around him upsets him! . . .

Well, upon very short rations of fingernails. . . . I *blocked out* the Dartmouth chapter from beginning to end, writing it sketchily . . . out of writing, too, grew another list of questions for RF!
(Letter of April 24, 1938, 7:50, 10:45, and 11:35 P.M.)

The following are Newdick's notes of conversations with Robert Frost at Amherst in the period April 21–25:

Is against Pepper's bill. Applauded Booth Tarkington's comments, and added plenty of his own!
RF *seemed* to crack at the assumptions of "progressive" education.
Agreed to make a specially annotated copy of *Collected Poems*—when written, where, origin or special circumstances, etc. Thinks he has done one or two like this; thinks he remembers one in England. This came after I told of hearing of one he made, then withdrew and destroyed.
Agreed to write to Harvard for me in re letters, to send Lesley's new Introduction (as she requested), and to come to Ohio in the autumn for talk, etc.

RF with a class: Large, 80–100. Half sheets of paper. Write when you have something to say, i.e. if out of what I say—tangential to it, or if from somewhere else entirely. And write not every day, but once or twice a week. Pay no attention to me if an idea comes to you in class: write it down! But no telegraphic jottings: make sentences.—RF would read them walking home, and often was pleased. Of course there were loafers, e.g. the boy who picked him up at Middletown and brought him home, to whom Frost said, from the boy's lack of work, 'I ought to fail you, oughtn't I?' The motto of the class: Those who will, may; those who won't, must. RF never carried out the threat of the last—either at Pinkerton or at Amherst. This annoyed the "regular" pedagogues.

Later, RF said he wasn't fitted for regular classes, Six, eight, or ten meetings a year best for him and them: gave them *concentrates* of his thinking.

RF said he may do a book on educational experiences, largely anecdotal.

On Lesley: Says she has no sense, likes to gad around, to flock with people, especially those with "names." Tom McCann would announce a novel tomorrow if she'd give him the title proposed. But she frets about tuition-free education for children. Why not a small N.E. town, ordinary schools? In the end he'll probably have to set up a place for her, with a wing for himself; take maybe one meal together a day. RF says he doesn't get on well with people, even his own.

In re Henry Holt & Co.: RF would like to buy his list from Holt and place it elsewhere. Maybe he can. 'Do they think you're too good to me?' he asked Thornton, in my hearing. 'Only one,' replied Thornton. That one, of course, was Bristol.

RF was shocked when he found he had repeated himself, e.g. the harp-like figure in A Lone Striker and in The Death of the Hired Man. He tries always for different tones, and of course to avoid any repetition.

Lesley all right as check-reader, as Mrs. Frost was.

RF on Amherst: King seemed eager to accept resignation. Budget $40,000 short. ($9,000 for house: about what he paid for it and put into it.) Harvard lectures began it? RF's refusal to come up to NY last winter for alumni doings. He did one such talk for alumni in Boston. Frost surprised by King's eagerness. Again, Amherst just now buying RF books for Converse library.

Memo: Get dope on RF's likes and dislikes from Mrs. Zorn, Mrs. Elliott, and Collamore, for his coming to Ohio.

The trip to the South: Sailed from NY to Norfolk / on day McClelland elected mayor of NY /. Then tramp steamer to Elizabeth City. Invited on party, which turned out to be a drinking party, at Nag's Head: drinking that night; duck-hunting the next day; then more drinking. The friendly saloon-keeper, who in a measure protected him, and who later introduced him to Mr. Lamb of the newspaper and to Mr. Sheep of the seminary. By the latter he was taken out to meet the girls, whom he might be engaged to teach. The time in the lumber-camp, and the smells. Slept with a worker. The freightcar, the stove, and the negroes and their songs. Bumming on the railroad: his kit taken by officers on one, razor, etc. The Negro who drew a gun, but was overcome. In Baltimore, called on Vrudam (?), well known as a philanthropist, interested and writing for the Boston *Arena*, a professional uplifter, whom he had heard of, and, I believe, in whom his mother was interested. He took a long look at Frost, then reached in his pocket and got a handful of small change and held it out. As Frost, embarrassed, reached for it, some fell on the floor and rolled, and Frost had to scramble for it. Sick from such an experience. Stopped at little grocery, kept by a man named Williams and his family. Starved, drank 6 cups of coffee right off. F engaged to look up new customers, but not especially good at it. The Williams family, however, took him in as one of themselves. Contrast the professional uplifter! At last F's mother sent him money to come home. All the time he was ostensibly looking for a job.

RF doesn't know whereabouts of "brown box" of old photographs Lesley spoke of.

RF sold Hood medal right away.

Wore glasses in H.S. Has had to use them again recently too.

[Many questions on Dartmouth asked and answered and written up at Amherst in rough draft of Dartmouth chapter.]

Poem of RF's not written down, but heard orally:

They say the truth shall make you free.
My truth will bind you slave to me.

RF never liked Utopias, never liked welfare workers.

Ask Laura Simmons in re his No. Cambridge teaching. She hostile.

Grandfather ceased work cir. 1885, and retired, taking over

responsibility for the house, save for occasional work as a sheriff's deputy. RF never heard him or grandmother laugh: a heavy-hearted household.

Shoe-making, Salem, bet. 1886–1890: Nailed shank; 3 nails on each side. Piece work; make $1.50 a day—the best pay he made for a long time! Not always busy; at those times off swimming. Held nails in mouth, but mother didn't know that.

Signature on 1896 letter is Elinor's.

The New York sally was around Christmas-time, 1904. For a month or two. Took some furniture down, rented a flat. Looked up editor of the Sunday *Sun*. After a long wait, got to talk with him: "Have some MS. to leave." The editor made no answer, simply pointed to an office boy and walked away. Frost says he never was a very good applicant.

This fits into the pattern of what was true but has not before been noted, i.e. that Frost made regularly (he put it this way) one or two efforts a year to get on his feet, to get money for doctor bills, etc.

In 1903 the effort had been to write for a farm journal, tho' he couldn't or wouldn't recall its name. One article was on an agricultural show or a fair that he wrote up. Another was on geese. On the latter, he felt that the editor had let him down.

In 1905 there was the effort too: Manchester reporter. Query: Did RF say he acted as the Derry correspondent, or just what?

In 1906, he made an effort to get another district school, as in the 'nineties,' but unsuccessfully. Query: at or out of Salem again?

At Harvard, for first year's scholarship given a detur: Shelden's Table Talk, and scholarship worth $300–400. Father's detur, once, had been Bartlett's quotations.

At H., took entrance exams in Gk., Lat., Eng., Fr., Physics, etc. *Had* taken, 1891, Hist., Gk., and Lat.

Friend at Harvard was Waddell Catchings, who broke Saks Fifth Avenue in later years (1929 about).

Prize readings of RF: For Pulitzer prizes about 10 years ago, i.e., cir. 1928. For *Opportunity* about 9 or 10 years ago. Recently, read for the Campfire Girls. Telegraphed the dope, i.e. his judgment. Got a rhymed letter of thanks from the youngster. [Read also for *Gypsy*, as I know.]

I saw a reporter of the *Amherst Student* interview RF on April 27. What did he write up?

See the Amherst Record for the list of honorary pallbearers.

Why wasn't John Holmes there? "Butinsky" (alias "Lion-Hunter") Bailey was, afterwards. Of course John Cone from Dartmouth, N.H.

Preacher did well. His glances to RF and family. Bronze urn: "1891–1938". Flowers in profusion, well arranged.

Frost gestures:

Rubbing nose with the 2 and 3 of rt. hand, folded back.
Open hand over face and down.
Wrinkling nose.
Spreading hands, palms down.
Opening and closing both hands with a kind of tossing-away
    motion.
One hand, half closed, short movement to the right.
[See the Disraeli photograph.]

See Mary Austen's Memorirs [sic] in re RF and Madam Bianchi!

RF never away from Elinor before for more than a month.

". . . how much of my thinking was wound around Elinor's silences."

Geode in Yale Review.

Whicher repeated to me RF's poem in re the temperature at Franconia, and promised to send me a copy.

RF and stealing pig in San Francisco?

Scrawny Harry Smith, EAR's friend, RF's enemy.

RF and Mrs. Goodwilly of Baltimore: dinner, aut. 1937, despite RF's explanations; flowers for Elinor's services, but no call.

Pictures of . .Mayan sculpture and Yucatan views in Sunset Ave. home: lifelong fascination for RF.

RF disliked being cultivated and patronised by the rich, esp. if Mrs. F overlooked. Therefore glad to get away from Franconia.

Mrs. F did everything for the children; therefore, they relatively helpless.

She realized their health none too good was result in part of under and mal-nutrition in early days, and told Mrs. Elliott so.

Otto Zorn really a disciple. Never argued with RF. Never objected, unless for F's protection and well-being. Fine man, fine mind,—one refusing to become embroiled in college politics.

RF suggested Pease for Pres. of Amherst. P. later to Harvard as Prof. of Greek. Then Smith turned P. against RF, mildly. P would not invite RF to sit down when RF called on him.

RF's voice a bit shrill when he is disturbed or annoyed. Children have this characteristic too. You can tell from another room when he is annoyed, disturbed, upset.

Lesley said: Her mother overdid when she heard that after all her heart was in pretty good shape. But would put down book, remarking, "My, I'm getting lazy!" then pitch in. Pains like angina: morphine; sleep. But next day, still pain: therefore *not* angina, but occlusion. Talked: told RF to take walk. More morphine and sleep: shocks *visible* to the bedside watcher: never woke again before death came.

Item 22:

Letter of Miss Elizabeth G. Nelligan.

In August 1938, Newdick succeeded in getting the recollections of Miss Elizabeth G. Nelligan (letter August 15, 1938, Cambridge, Mass.) of Frost as she knew him as the principal of Shepard Evening School in North Cambridge during his first year at Harvard, 1897–98.

I remember him very distinctly for his kindly and courteous manner. I was very inexperienced as I had not finished school at the time. There were a great many young men who registered very early in the course, some of whom just came for fun, and to upset the order of the school. I do remember that in a short time he weeded out the young men who were not serious in their work. He always had a large green felt bag filled with books.

He visited the rooms often during the course of the evening; and would often ask the pupils questions about their work. While I knew that Evening School was just a stepping stone to something better, he was really interested in the teachers' work and in the progress of the pupils.

I have had a strong suspicion for many years that the young school principal at the Shepard Evening School was the renowned poet Robert L. Frost, but until I received your letter I was not positive. [Miss Nelligan's brother, Prof. Richard Nelligan, retired, of Amherst College, was Frost's next-door neighbor in Amherst, but Frost was always away when Miss Nelligan visited there. R.S.N.] I often thought I would like to have asked him if he were the young man under whom I worked in '97–'98.

Miss Laura Simmons formerly lived in Cambridge. As I remember, she found the discipline rather hard, and no doubt Mr. Frost had spoken to her about it. [When Newdick finally found Miss Simmons, she had no memory of Frost.]

I am enclosing the recommendation which Mr. Frost gave me

at the end of the term. I would like to have you return it to me if possible. I have kept it all these years as I could really feel that he would be heard from later.

Miss Nelligan, a school principal, concluded by saying that she felt his encouragement and kindness had helped her: "As my very first teaching was done under his supervision, I really feel that had it not been for his kindness and helpfulness, I could not have reached my present position. . . . I certainly deem it an honor to have been associated with him." She added a postscript: "The school term was from Oct. 1 to Apr. 1, and school was held on Monday, Wednesday, and Friday evenings from 7:30–9:30. I could not conceive of Miss Simmons or any other teacher disliking [as RF was evidently correct in saying she did] Mr. Frost as he was always most considerate and helpful. I do remember that he always seemed rather tired, no doubt due to the many courses which he was carrying."

The recommendation which RF wrote, dated "Cambridge Mass Feb 21 98," reads as follows:

To whom it may concern:—

Miss Elizabeth S. Nelligan has just completed a term's work as assistant teacher in the Shepard Evening School of this city. She has been entirely successful both as an instructor and as a disciplinarian. I take pleasure in giving this testimonial of her ability.

R. L. Frost, Principal.

Recent examination of school records in Cambridge has revealed that, when Frost was appointed, at the school committee meeting of September 23, 1897, his salary was set at $2.50 per evening.

Item 23:

Reminiscence of Justice Louis S. Cox.

By coincidence, [See Item 15.] Newdick received, in a letter of September 6, 1938, a Dartmouth reminiscence from Louis S. Cox, a justice of the Massachusetts Supreme Court:

One [matter] is an incident which occurred after we had been in Hanover but a matter of a week or so as freshmen. When the freshmen and sophomores were playing the customary fall games of baseball, some one in our class brought out a '96 banner. This was instantly resented by the sophomores who charged the freshmen. Clothes were torn as well as the banner, and the opposing forces surged back and forth upon the campus for some time until the sophomores had gained possession of the greater part of the banner and had retired to one side of the diamond. It was then that Frost rallied the freshmen, most of whom were unknown to one another, and with a remnant of the banner in his hand led the freshmen in a charge across the diamond and against the sophomores. I can see him now out in front of the huddled mob as he led them to the charge.

The other matter is indicative of his love of fun. Frost roomed in one of the old dormitories with a man named Hazen, now dead, and another named Richardson. Money was very scarce in that room, and, although we entered college on the fifth of September, it was not until some time in November that Richardson thought he needed a hair cut, which in those days cost twenty-five cents. He made this known to his roommates, whereupon Frost suggested that there was no reason for him to pay for the hair cut because he, Frost, and Hazen could give him one. Richardson assented to this and Frost sat him in a chair and proceeded to give him a hair cut, but instead of following the conventional method, he cut a strip about two inches wide down to the scalp from Richardson's forehead over the top of his head and down the back to the nape of the neck. He then cut a corresponding strip from one ear up over the head and down to the other ear. About this time Richardson realized that something was wrong and interrupted the barbering to look in the mirror. I can not repeat the conversation which followed, but the upshot of the matter was that Richardson packed his belongings into an old bag and walked down the hill to the Railroad Station at Norwich, and we have never seen anything more of him. There is some irony in the fact that Richardson is now the secretary to the Society For The Prevention Of Cruelty To Animals.

Some years ago, when Frost was here in Lawrence, I asked him if he remembered the incident and his eyes twinkled and his engaging smile spread entirely over his face.

Phrenology indeed!

Item 24:

Relating to Preston Shirley.

Early in September 1938, Newdick received an intriguing note from the nephew of Preston Shirley, who lived across from RF in Wentworth Hall at Dartmouth:

. . . They were both Sophomores [Frost was at Dartmouth from September to December, 1892, only as a freshman. W.A.S.] and became close friends as they had a common interest in literature.

After Preston's death on July 10th, 1905, Robert Frost wrote an article in some magazine—I do not recall the name of it—and sent me a copy.

I sent it to Preston's sister . . . asking her to return it, but I have never been able to get it back from her. . . .

. . . I think this would give you first hand information of Frost's life at Dartmouth.

When Newdick wrote to Mrs. Carolyn Shirley Leonard, of 157 Bowles St., Springfield, Mass., she said she would be glad to continue to search for the "article of which you wrote." Then she added, tantalizingly,

As I recall, during his brief stay at Dartmouth College, Robert Frost maintained quite a casual attitude on attendance at classes, and he and my brother Preston amused themselves by playing practical (!) and sometimes crude jokes on those living on a lower floor of "old Dartmouth Hall."[sic] Would you desire an account of these performances, and of the various other "capers" these two particular students offered students and faculty?

As I remember, my brother Preston died on August 8, 1905, just two days before his thirtieth birthday.

In reply, Newdick supplicated to be told at least what peri-
odical the article was in. He emphatically did want the anec-
dotes suggested: "Frost has said that what he most enjoyed at
Dartmouth was acting like an Indian in a college founded for
Indians, and from what Judge Louis Cox and others have told
me, Frost and Shirley outdid the Indians."
Mrs. Leonard evidently never wrote again. However, on Sep-
tember 20, Mrs. Barron Shirley, widow of the brother of Preston
Shirley, sent pictures of her husband's room at Wentworth Hall
and the following reminiscences:

I will describe the rooms as I remember them. Evidently one
large room had been changed to a suite of three by partitioning
off the west side, and then dividing that room into two. It gave
a window to the study where the desk is, the bedroom which I
have not found, and the living room where the coal stove is.
This room was entered from the long corridor on the second
floor, and the doors were made of boards going horizontally
across them and without panelling. You cannot imagine anything more barracks like. The doors had to be very strong to
withstand the onslaught of the Sophomores. My husband
knocked a man out with a ball bat and didn't care if he killed
him, he said; who had persistently annoyed him. Robert Frost
and Preston were gentle souls and had no such personal en-
counters, at least, I never heard of them.

The rooms looked toward the Observatory on the hill, and the
living room overlooked the college pump, and also the ash-pile
where the students emptied their trash, gathered up at infre-
quent intervals. The bedroom—if I could find it—contained a
washbowl and pitcher as there was no bathroom, so far as I
know, in Wentworth Hall at that time.

Preston had a brilliant imagination and Robert a memory of
nature scenes that were pictorial in their minuteness. I take
keen pleasure in his poetry for I have seen so many of the scenes
he describes. "The Rose Pogonia" for instance, recalls pogonia
meadows that I know, and his poetry comes to mind when I see
them. There is a Psalm-like quality about his descriptions that
gives the keenest pleasure.

I suppose in your study of Robert Frost you have come across
the painful schism in the class. Preston had a great deal in keep-

ing this alive. He was editor of the Dartmouth and his word had great weight. I do not know what it was about, but I think if you write to Rev. Charles E. Merrill of Boston. . . . . I believe he graduated in the class with Preston and was one of the "outs." It was a painful procession of graduates, about 19 in cap and gown, and the rest in their ordinary dress coming in and sitting in the back seats at their own graduation. I believe the wound is healed now. . . .

I suppose you have a photograph of Robert Frost in his college days. I had one but I cannot find it, and I cannot find one of the books he gave me. I fear I must have loaned them to a member of the Woman's Club here in Durham who was writing a paper on the poet and borrowed them. If you have none of him, I will make a further effort to find it.

These are the exact words in the copy of "A boy's will" that he gave me
"Mrs. Barron Shirley
From Robert Frost
with thanks for a glimpse of the old room in Wentworth."
He sent me two books when I wrote to him after he had sent my daughter Elizabeth a book saying as nearly as I can remember it
"Elizabeth Shirley, a sophomore in Smith
From Robert Frost
who was a Sophomore with
Preston Shirley at Dartmouth."

Item 25:

Robert Frost Inscriptions for John Holmes.

A letter written by John Holmes on September 11, 1938, included this revealing response to Newdick's request for copies of inscriptions by RF in Holmes' books:

1) in a paper-covered Boy's Will, inscribed after Elinor's death, he wrote 8 lines, the last 8 in Trial By Existence, especially significant — "leaving us crushed and mystified."

2) in the 1934 Boy's Will he wrote the four lines beginning "We make ourselves a place apart" ["Revelation"] because he wanted me to feel at that time that I would be "really found out" and published. This was when he was lecturing at Harvard.

3) the least rare of the English North of Boston he gave me, writing To John Holmes from Robert Frost. I think he differentiates a gift and an inscription, because the two above, which I owned, say For John Holmes from Robert Frost.

4) in the Chapin North of Boston he wrote this summer "To John Holmes with strongest wishes for more and more poetry from him to the exclusion of all other forms of writing, from Robert Frost. South Shaftsbury Vermont. The Gulley Gulch. August 15, 1938."

5) In the limited edition of West Running Brook, which I owned, he wrote out a new poem, which he titled "Lines Written Last Autumn," [published as "November"] with a footnote to say he meant 1937. It begins "We saw leaves go to glory-" and is, I think, one of his best. This signed For John Holmes.

6) In the trade edition of Further Range he wrote out Desert Places, because I suggested that poem when he asked me

what I liked best. He dated it, May 27, 1936—I was at his house in Amherst, but he didn't put the place in. This poem he signed To John Holmes, so maybe he isn't consistent.

7) He gave me the limited edition of Further Range, No. 282, and inscribed it "To John Holmes from his always faithfully and affectionately Robert Frost South Shaftsbury Vt July 10 1936"

8) In the English edition of the same he wrote out another new poem about a speck on a piece of paper, long and funny and running over to the next page. ["A Considerable Speck"] This he signed For, and dated.

9) He gave me a paper-covered Snow to Snow, writing "To the poet who reviewed me R.F." I had just reviewed Further Range.

10) In the 1923 Selected Poems, which I took to Vt. this summer, he wrote "To John Holmes from his friend in these matters Robert Frost as of 1923."

11) In the 1928 Selected Poems he wrote again the leaves all go to glory poem ["November"], with, by the way, some different wording from No. 5 above.—whether a revision or faulty memory I don't know.

12) In the present Am. ed. of Selected Poems he wrote "Proclaimed the time was neither wrong nor right—" ["Acquainted with the Night"] Robert Frost To John Holmes. He was speaking at the NE Poetry Club and was sore because he wasn't in evening clothes and had to share the program. He boiled all evening and was pretty tart when he spoke.

13) In the British Selected Poems, the one with the 4 essays, he wrote three lines ["A Hundred Collars"] I can't find anywhere in the books,
What I like best's the lay of different farms
Coming out on them from a stretch of woods
Or over a hill or round a sudden corner
Robert Frost

For John Holmes
South Shaftsbury Vermont
July 2 1938

14) And in the Collected Poems, which he gave me, he wrote
To my friend John Holmes the Poet.

Item 26:

Letter of Miss Nettie McQuestin.

Another letter of September 15, from Miss Nettie McQuestin, of Boston, recalled visits to the house she shared with her mother and sister, an elocution teacher: "I remember his calling it 'the little house in the steep street' as he poetically termed our home and my invalid mother was especially fond of Mrs. Frost." She remembered:

In the summer of 1914 when Mr. Frost and his family were living in England and my sister and I were traveling in Europe[,] we were invited to the Frost home. It was Mr. Frost's intention to have my sister read to his poet friends that they might get an idea of the "American style" of reading poetry. He also hoped to arrange a similar program to be given at the Poetry Book Shop in Holborn, London. Unfortunately the war upset these plans so that what might have been red letter days did not occur.

Item 27:

Letter of Robert Lincoln O'Brien.

On October 3, 1938, a letter was received from Robert Lincoln O'Brien, of Washington, D.C. Newdick had written him for verification of a story that a Derry minister had recommended the poetry of Frost, a member of the Pinkerton Academy staff, to the editor of the Boston Transcript. *The event, probably of 1907, was verified in the following:*

I went to Derry Village one evening to speak when I was on the Boston Transcript and the Rev. Charles L. Merriam was the Pastor of the Congregational Church in that place. The world called me the editor of the Transcript. I had that title, but I really had nothing to do with anything except the editorial page. All the other departments were highly organized and systematized and under the control of persons who were very insistent upon maintaining their own authority. One of these was the man who passed on the poetry. Quantities of it were sent in. People were usually offended because it was not used. My chief relations with it was to take the poetry sent to me to this man, getting his rejection and then writing a letter trying to let down as easily as possible the disappointed author. In this state of mind on my part, I was approached by Mr. Merriam with the information that a young man in the school named Robert Frost, of whom I had never heard, was writing excellent verse. There is usually some such person in every village and Congregational Church in the United States. I think I was rather short in telling him that I did not want to look into it, without giving the explanation which I have given you in the earlier part of this letter. I always have felt very much ashamed of myself, although I am not sure that the Transcript organization would have received, realized and accepted the greatness of Robert Frost. I have several times taken pleasure in casting my vote as a member of the Pulitzer Board for him, and have hoped in that way to make belated amends for my shortsightedness.

Item 28:

Manthey-Zorn Observations.

On October 7, 1938, Professor Otto Manthey-Zorn, one of his preferred associates at Amherst, gave some observations both of his habits and his troubled relationship with the college:

Lesley is probably right and Robert will no doubt enjoy your hospitality most if you run your household just as you are accustomed to have it. Since he knows and likes you so well he will not hesitate in the least to ask for the things he wants or make suggestions about small comforts which you could not anticipate. He has liked a quite warm room at night with plenty of covers on his bed, he has been used to taking only a little milk and hot water when he gets up late in the morning, a hearty meal at noon and a light supper have been his preference. But I have reason to believe that Robert has changed quite radically within the last months. I have seen him take a very complete breakfast and sit for hours at a late dinner and omit neither bread nor wine. However, you cannot depend upon me for accurate information about that. Robert has been very much put out about Amherst since last Spring and is apparently also disgruntled about us. We have seen very little of him, and what we have seen of him leads me to think that he is still a very confused man who acts as though he must get away from everything connected with Amherst, even his friends, in order to regain himself. You will, however, have a splendid two weeks with him, and once he has arrived at your home you will find that all the little details will take care of themselves.

When Newdick thanked Professor Zorn for his observations, he reassured him that RF, however disgruntled he was about Amherst, could not be "in any slightest degree" be put out about him. "I believe his loyalty in friendship is close to his tenaciousness in family ties, and he has always spoken of you as his closest friend in Amherst."

Item 29:

Recollections of a Sculptor.

Part of Newdick's inclusive and exhaustive research related to pictures and sculptures of RF. He had realized that one who makes an image has to observe carefully, and wrote many letters eliciting the recollections of the artists. At the end of January, 1939, he received this glimpse from Florence Reeve Fiori:

You asked me to tell you something of the circumstances of Mr. Frost's sitting. They were not altogether happy at the outset —Mr. Frost was not very well at the time. He had been exercising too strenuously on his farm, and Mrs. Frost was afraid he had strained his heart. It was therefore easy to understand her reluctance to have him pose. When she said "I know these artists—they take years to finish their work," I realised what I was up against. I asked for three sittings, was promised two by Mrs. Frost, and ended up by getting four—thanks to Mr. Frost's kindheartedness! Since sitting meant just that[,] he really did not exert himself, and I rather think he enjoyed those few hours —I know *I* did. It was a delightful experience listening to him talk about anything at all. His interest in Nature seemed inexhaustible—I remember he spent several hours talking about "bees," and I had the feeling he could have continued for days without tiring me or himself.

The sittings took place right on the college campus at Amherst. We used a room on the ground-floor so that Mr. Frost would not have to climb any stairs. Mr. Morton was very helpful in digging up some good photographs of Mr. Frost, and in this way I was able to finish the head in short order.

Item 30:

Newdick's Notes of Frost in Columbus, Ohio, October, 1938.

April 13 and 14, 1939, Newdick devoted himself to the task of typing the notes he had taken in October, 1938. They are preceded in his file with this note, written as though intended for another reader:

The forty-odd pages of notes that follow are recorded from talks with RF, and the lectures and readings I heard him give, during his visit with us late in October, 1938.

Of course there's much in mind that I could write up if the object were the accumulation of notes for themselves. What I've not written I'm sure will stay without record. So, for that matter, would much that is here written. But there's much detail that might slip away, I fear; or that I should like to "document" with sureness from a more or less closely dated talk.

I have not expanded the notes I took down at nights after we gave up talking or at intervals during the day when I had the opportunity and time.

The reader might need to know that the notes to follow were typed on thirty-eight sheets of regular-sized paper, practically all entries being single-spaced. Generally speaking, as will be seen, Newdick had organized the material he had recorded by topics, using a separate sheet (or more) for each heading, some of the headings being topical and others chronological. Several pages had only three lines on them. The notes are arranged as well as seemed possible in order of personal-to-less-personal:

CHARACTER

Says he's a gambler. Likes to win, o. c., and plays hard and ruthlessly to win. But can take a loss.

He thinks he's pretty skillful in handling people, in manipulating them to serve his own ends when he wants them to.

Says he's immoral, and has always been so. Adds that maybe all life is, if one gets something done. Would have lived with E without marriage, but there was E and his mother to think of.

Is aware of only one change in himself — his attitude toward perfection. As a youth he wanted it perfect; couldn't use a copybook he had spoiled by a blot.

Later, though just when might be hard to say, he came to like the imperfect, the raw, the painful, grief, etc. I instanced the closing lines of "To Earthward" and there, he agreed, this is said.

Thinks he has more in common with business men than with most (so-called) poets. Executives are ruthless: they can't be bothered with details; they sweep small matters aside. Executive to the point of being an executioner: ruthless. (Ruthless is a favorite word with him lately, I observe. So also is the word fishy.)

See in this connection "Provide Provide" which some think he shouldn't have written — or published!

PERSONAL

Wears a coat like a cape.

Walks aisle in train. Also, like countryman, gets up to door when nearing his station.

Smokes cigarettes occasionally. Never smoked pipe or cigars.

With medicine, cuts doctor's doses when driven to use it; but refuses most medicine, even cough drops, throat lozenges for speakers, etc.

Drinking loosens his tongue at once, at length upsets him.
   At Bread Loaf, 1938, *appeared* to drink heavily, in order to out-noise Lee Simonson. Had a stomach-ache 2 wks thereafter.

Shirt 17 or 17½, except dress: 16½. 33 sleeves, 34 for dress.

Night shirts, not pyjamas.

Shoes hightop, half-laced, half over hooks.

Cheap socks: no mending—walks too much. Cotton.

Blue favorite color for ties, etc.

Yet Stetson hat, made-in-England-of-British-wool topcoat.

Clothes no consideration, though,—nor their press!

Preferred Granville Inn to Maramor,—per. bec. heard much of M.

Not often absent-minded, but forgot shirts going to Cleveland. Once at Dartmouth forgot vest, and Mrs. Lambuth much distressed.

GESTURES

Rubbing right eye with back of right fist, then drawing his opened hand down across his face.

Flinging outward with his fingers, with hands about lower-chest high and about as close as if to catch a softball.

Beating with his right hand—for emphasis; sometimes too to the "time" of a poem.

A tossing of the right hand outward from the wrist, as if throwing something away,—about lower-shoulder high,—something like the familiar "So Long" gesture.

ELINOR WHITE FROST

Her f. a minister, late in life—theological school without college. Unitarian?

Then went back to his business, wood-turning. Worked for Safford's father.

Descendant of Peregrine White of Mayflower and of Whites who fought at Concord.

Her m., like f., also of good stock, and of a good family.

M. kept a nice house, but had to take in boarders.

356 · *Newdick's Research Findings*

Elinor had ( ) sisters:
>One, who became an invalid, recovered thru Xn Science.
>>She hated RF, and thought Elinor unhappy. Looked in on them scornfully and pityingly.
>One went to Boston and became an artist. Leona?
>>RF now good to Boston Book Fair because of Fuller, who gave Leona's dau. a job in his bookstore.

RF did not go to funeral of E's mother, but she did,—and she went also to see her sister.

Elinor's a fine mind. R never encountered a better: clear, hard, no compromise. She didn't *believe* in starting anything you couldn't see the end of—yet she lived "unsoundly" that way with F for years.

No compromise. But surrender. She gave in to his way in the 90's: he broke her to it.—Then she resented going back to the world!

Among her classmates at College, Mrs. Owen D. Young.

Enemies broke their engagement for a while, damn' near ruining RF. She became engaged to another man, too! But RF won ... [1894?]

She came home from college in 1893 to calm him down during the spring and summer. At Canobie Lake with her m. and s. Leona, artist, who found insanity in husband's family and left him,—but later went back to him.

RF says she was never interested in his prose or talks.
>She never read the lecture I put into shape, or those Thompson did.
>After the Poetry Society dinner, she remarked that R was amusing. but said nothing, he noted, as to his sharpness or depth.

Nor did she take much interest in his later poems, tho' she liked the one about the perfect day. She disapproved of the publication of "Departmental." And "The Hardship of Accounting" she disapproved in *principle*!

She hated doctors, except in child-bearing.

She hated child-bearing, esp. for her children.

Blamed it on God, a la Hardy,—but RF feels it comes back on him.

She hated FDR. A passion with her. Said she would kill him, if she had the strength. "Charlotte Corday?" asked RF, laughing, turning it off. But she didn't join in the laugh.

When Hoover was elected she clipped the Times editorial. That's the earliest F has found, that's when it all began—long before FDR elected.

During her last five years she turned away from him, turned her face (1) to mourning the death of the Republican party, (2) her own dead, Margery, and (3) the failure of the other children —though, RF says, he was no good for that long!

She turned *to* pro-Republicanism and hatred of the New Deal.

Even outsiders, Amherstites, could see the rift between them in politics — and his dancing to cover it up! But she went on clipping, clipping, relentlessly clipping, day after day after day, — clipping all that damned FDR, nothing that was in his favor. And the facts and figures she knew were amazing even to experts. . .

During those last five years she took politics seriously reverted. He never excited for himself, but did his best for her. Read papers daily then, with her. Almost never now.

She complained of the nation's living beyond its income. He said to her he was sheepish in thinking he's (i. e., they'd) always lived that way. But she didn't get the "sheepish."

In later years she quarrelled with all bills, thought them too high. (He says he read this somewhere recently.) But he's always been careless with money, witness "The Hardship of Accounting," which she didn't like because it wasn't nice.

SINCE ELINOR'S DEATH

Would hate any other woman claiming a part in his earlier life and poems. There was none. There might have been,—just as his energy might have gone into drinking instead of into poetry.

Women are now writing him letters, telling him their ages and charms, inviting. . . (I told him, from Dad's experience, this inevitable.)

Needs, wants feminine companionship and friendship, and will have it. Is fearful of arrangement with K. Morrison—for her and Ted, rather than for himself. If he were Ted, he wouldn't permit it! A bit fearful too of Mrs. DeVoto, though the D's are used to freedoms of this kind.

Kay was in his "class" at Bryn Mawr—Reeling and Writhing Club.

In 1938 about a week in Mass. General Hospital.
Got up once to go out to get food, but they brought it finally. Still sweats and has pain in his chest (Oct., 1938).

Would like to get away. But where? And what do? Must stay and get around, or the book sales will fall off.

Receives about $3000 a year in royalties and permissions. Is guaranteed $150 a month. Used to be $250. Changed under Thornton.

Frankly acknowledges part played in popularity by anthologies.

May do a book about his educational experiences and devices. May use K. Morrison's help in preparing it.

A backlook at Amherst: Whicher firm, but cold. Eliot's religiosity. Zorn turned King's spokesman. F knows he should have gone to hear King.

RF tried to break with Holt's, but Bristol refused. (This since April.)

THE CHILDREN

RF says he played with them a good deal, up through the Franconia days, 1915 et seq.

E. g., he found out with them all that could be done with hoops.

But they stopped when he stopped; didn't go on by themselves.

On Elinor's feeling their failure in later years, see other sheets.

IRMA FROST

Hysterical, like Jeannie.

John, her son, has the look of fear in his eyes.

But her husband, John Cone, is wonderfully patient.

MARGERY FROST

RF says he knew, when telegram called them back West, that M was lost and that life, in a sense, was over.

Out there, RF carried them all,—so they thought him without feeling.

ELLIOTT FROST

It was his death that led RF to write "Home Burial."

Not that Elinor went off so, but many he knew did, e. g. a woman who lost her son beneath a street car.

And Elinor came near it.

CAROL FROST

He really suffers an impediment, says F.

Dark, smouldering, silent, resentful, feels beaten.

Resents his father's making as much in a day or so as he makes all year.

Tried poetry for quite a while. RF couldn't see anything in it,— but he never discouraged: it might be good anyway! But family resented fact he didn't *en* courage.

Must leave Carol an annuity. All the other children understand.

Carol could make a living, the farm costing him nothing; but he always manages to find a way to lose on some "improvement."

Lilian, his wife, village-ish, jealous of others.

The son, Prescott, was Elinor's favorite. RF told Lilian so: a mistake, because now L will watch narrowly what RF does with his worldly goods.

But, so far at least, Irma's John is a smarter boy, and more promising.

LESLEY FROST

M. [Dwight] Francis, formerly husband of Kay Francis, and now husband of her friend.

Two Daus: Lesley Lee and Elinor.

Lesley gave RF "the works" in Florida—on the miserable life he, a genius, had given his wife and children, and their resentments—no settled home or friends or associations, etc.

Then he shot back at Lesley a devastating blast. No more, now, on either side: he will not jab; he says he's no Jabberwocky. But his mood is bleak.

And Irma disagreed with Lesley, thought Elinor had had what she wanted out of life.

BELLE MOODIE FROST

Deeply religious. Presbyterian—Unitarian—Swedenborgian, taking the last two steps in SF.

Told son of Wallace and Bruce. (Father told of RELee)

Read Edward Bellamy's *Looking Backward* aloud.

In New Zealand the son of his mother's bro. still lives,—who, like her father, was lost at sea? *Orkney*. Fifeshire?

See much on sheet headed Lawrence, 1885–1900.

W. P. FROST, JR.

At death, manager of the *Post*, a Republican paper. Hated *that*.

F remembers hearing boy say, "There [is] crepe on your door."

Anecdote of dime lost in board walk. . .

Irreligious, even blasphemous. Could swear half an hour without repeating himself.

Brilliant, but unscrupulous. Once taken into custody in L. by U. S. govt. officers for blackmailing L. whorehouse-keeper. Mother's brother, his uncle, Colcord, a politician, had influence, and got him out of it.—This was the grand-uncle of F's who left his money for a school fence and so begot "In Neglect."

WPFJr. the kind of politician Lincoln Steffens exposed.

Shook boy out of open window 4 or 5 stories up.

RF his office boy last year or two.

Exacting.

Loyal to his friends.

Friends with Henry George. (Mother also fond of George.)

Associated with HG in a newspaper venture.

Told son of Robert E. Lee.

[I think F was molded by his father, i. e. turned in upon himself. Then this tendency was not checked by his mother,—and so he had to find himself,—as he did cir. 1906.]

JEANNIE FROST

Had typhoid, probably owing to the way they lived.

Thereafter she had curvature, and thereafter was never "right."

She died in an institution, a mental case, 1929.

TOWARD THE ARS POETICA OF R. F.

Takes no stock in "inspiration." Just fitness, and "something extra."

If, he says, a poet doesn't make words do things, he's no "maker."

RF can quote good things endlessly,—or by the apt bit or phrase.

Just loose and strict iambic.

F distressed that so many boys who are struck by poetry are "nuts" e.g. young Lowell at Kenyon, a psychological case. There are other similar ones there too.

As for MacLeish's "We don't know, we wonder," RF says we *do* know. E. g., we know the U.S. is better than any place else. *If* the question is in re life, or the world, another matter.

When he's not writing poetry, he's "puttering"—his name for everything else.

Alvin Johnson of New School said something good of RF, "You are a democrat at least in your belief in the equality of tools."

RF quoted Elinor applauding Wilbert Snow to Mrs. S. for S's standing for poetry instead of for money.

Chas. Cobb (sp?) at Amherst insisted only 4 beats in Keats' "A thing of beauty is a joy forever." 5 to RF

RF debunked Irish, Yeatsian, poetry of *no* accent. It's in the *words*! E. g., not BE-GIN or its opposite, or BEgin, but beGIN.

I suggested great poets had no time or inclination to pose. F said Yeats came closest to being a great one posing. Said Yeats said every man has to choose among seven poses. [Where?!]

Object: to make each poem sound different.

On tone-images:
Runs in STOPPING BY WOODS
Pauses in THE DEATH OF THE HIRED MAN

Frost's figure for poems that only two or three understand: like after-dinner anecdotes, ostensibly told for point, yet blunted, so that no one gets the point, and so the essential purpose is defeated.

Nonsense to say "A poem should not mean but be." It should be, of course; that's first. But it should *mean too*.

The so-called "new" program (he said at Ohio State): a) literal, truthful; b) symbolic, meaningful—all this as *old as poetry*!

Not a descriptive poet. A des've poet is thru when his desc'n is done. F describes, true enough. But he also has the meaning there—if only the "meaning" of the self-righteous tone (of a woman) at the end of THE RUNAWAY.

Iambic, strict and loose. His, he says, usually strict. Stresses, with one or two, or, sometimes, three (this rare, but see The Listeners of de la Mare) light,—and sometimes none, e.g. . . . . *don't watch out!* But *never* four or more.

Hendecasyllables in one poem. Not noticed. (Yes, Colum.) Carefully done, an extra light syllable thrown in regularly.

"A poem ought *at least* be as good as the prose it might have been."

If no surprise for the reader, none for the writer, and vice versa.

RF can *feel* what the length of a poem is going to be, once he starts to write; but he doesn't know.

And there's no saving of a good thing for the last: *pile it in!* The end will come of itself—or it wasn't really a poem after all.

No practice work: every try "for keep." Often wrong, o. c. But no sketching for him, no trials.

Never wrote on assignment, not even on self-assignment.

Tried, for Harvard Tercentenary, and Phi Beta Kappa poem, to show he did have the courage to do bad work,—but shingles, on one side of face, saved him.

A poem begins in delight, and makes a little run to a bit of wisdom.

Admits the philosophical interest. Loves philosophy next to poetry. But knows danger of *taught* wisdom. Wisdom, true wisdom, must be *learned* wisdom. F wants knowledge dumped all around him, and *on* him. Then—two and two together?

The form should be there, but the poet should hit it so hard as to shake it, to make it tremble, to make the reader feel it may be broken—as sometimes indeed in Emerson it is broken.

Force, power, can come only from such ruthlessness. Tennyson does it occasionally. Browning usually does it, at least so far as the metric form is concerned.

Pig-headed stupidity, trying to get variety out of metres. Young sometimes say, We have hair on our heads, let's do it, let's buck the wall of metre.

If ever any variation in Milton's meter, M unaware of it.

Shakespeare's
  Let me not to the marriage of true minds, etc.
is perfectly regular iambic.

Unstresses: usually one or two; on the margin, none—or three, —but not an unlimited, uncounted number.

Boynton's statement in re RF is satisfactory.

Metre-beats and voice-beats are not the same, but *both must* be there for *poetry*.

RF thinks Virgil in
  *A*rma vir*um*que cano
where Virgil apparently wrenches the accent, normal, of CAno to caNO really said it hoveringly, nearly as in prose Latin, not giving too much to the metre.

In Sh's line above, not phyrric and spondee, but 2 iambs.

Finds self speaking in rhythms when teaching, unconsciously following a pattern.

See Technique

Delight is source of all art, must be in all, art, even tragedy.
  No art *is* life; there's always an element of play. *Lear?*
  See the name of it—a play.

Thing (a special Frostian word) results from delight written down, composed, according to form—even tho one's own variant of that.

Wisdom, much or little, at the end, or scattered through. Not just words, pretty words, phrases, tunes.

Add re poems in "classical" themes in youth, e.g., Caesar's Lost Transport Ships, Hannibal, A Dream of Julius Caesar, etc.

TECHNIQUE

A whole poem in one sentence without punctuation: DUST OF SNOW.

Poem of same length and structure, every verse a sentence: WHAT 50 SAID

Linked stanzas and what he called "repetend": STOPPING BY WOODS . . .

Elaborate rhyme schemes: THE GRINDSTONE, THE LONE STRIKER

Sonnet in one sentence, one figure: THE SILKEN TENT

DIALECT

Scotch—in no poem
French-Canadian: THE AXE-HELVE

Yankee: BROWN'S DESCENT
  Yankee old crone: WITCH OF COOS

Irish: THE COW'S IN THE CORN

Drunk: A HUNDRED COLLARS

POLITICS

Says he is not naturally partisan, is naturally above partisanship, as an artist should be: big enough to embrace both sides, all sides.

(Here really goes much noted under Elinor . . .)

Is not sure FDR wouldn't agree with all he (F) says, and with what many others say, in *principle*. But the *necessities*. . . .

And RF isn't sure but what the poor *should* have their turn. Perkins and Hopkins, however, indicate a permanently socialistic pattern.

Called the Sudentenland settlement in Czechoslovakia, right. Won wagers.

Likes to think ahead so, philosophically.

Sees alliance of England and Germany as natural and in time inevitable. Italy hasn't physical stick [stock?] to be truly great. Or the resources. Stock thinned by admixture with African, etc.

In another mood, or questioning: "The world can't have been made for the weak and the poor."

RELIGION, GOD, AND THE BIBLE

"Where is this God I hear so much about? Where *is* he?"

So F suddenly asked me in the railway station at Cincinnati, Nov. 1.

At another time, he quoted the Bible, "Make friends with the unrighteous." A problem passage, a crux,—like X's blasting the fig tree that had no figs,—and, in the Apocrypha, His blasting the children. And compare Provide, Provide—which some tell him he shouldn't have written.

SEX

See also SINCE ELINOR'S DEATH in re fem. companionship, etc.

A strongly sexed man. Attractive to women, tho' not bristling. But faithful to one, who was satisfying.

Yet not condemnatory of those of wild and promiscuous youth.

Much in the poems on this score:

PUTTING IN THE SEED
Emphatically so

DEVOTION
With the note of holding the curve to an endless repetition

With the line, Love at the lips was once. . . .

Others

PEOPLE

M. Boie of Atl. Mo. a "bitch"—likes to play with husbands of other women.

D. Canfield likes men about her and crazy about her. Domestic and faithful; but likes air of being *almost* swept away, and F feels this in the novels. Mr. C usually in a kind of hiding. The F's see that the children meet the right people, etc.,—as the F's hardly ever did. (RF int'd in acct of DC and WLG and thought he remembered Graves' name as a poet.)

S. Cox will probably get professorship some day, though slow bec. of stirrer-upper inclinations. F thinks he has kept C to the *right*. But doesn't know whether he's been a good influence or a bad.

DeVoto met RF first in Fla. when D lecturing on Mark Twain. Got to talking NE farms, and RF surprised at someone who understood though he had never lived there.
D's eyes bulged when RF spoke of Harvard and CENorton Lectures:
   "What's come over Harvard?!" Etc.
D made rather a fool of self, and made it harder for F, at Harvard. D recently paid $20,000 for serial by Collier's under name August.
   Next will be $22,500 or $25,000.

P. Engle came to see RF in Fla.

E. Hemingway *can* score in stories, says RF, but seldom does, is content not to.

Hillyer and DeVoto neighbors across street. Hillyer nearly ruined, esp. by drink.

John Holmes an active promoter—of John Holmes. F recommended him to Holt's as one who might be useful to them in and around Boston.

WDHowells invited RF to call and F did. H sent F copy of *The Mother* uninscribed. F thinks WDH felt piqued—that he, WDH, had hit upon a blank verse similar to F's without recognition, and earlier. F likes A Boy's Town.

Best of S. Lanier is The Death of Hamish. Ought to be in his anthology.

Lindsay was mad, touched. Amy Lowell pretended it, showmanship. F thinks L killed self when L began to believe world's belief that he, L, was mad.

Lindsay would write, say, *cat*, then by other strokes to the handwriting would evolve a picture, maybe of a long boat with

shields, and then ("Can't you hear it coming?") a poem, maybe
of only two lines. L would give the manuscript picture and
poem, but would copy the poem into a notebook! "Two apples
rolled down a hill. / This one was named Jill." Or something
like that. L once talked whole afternoon to F, then went to NY
saying he had "converted" Frost!

F called on Amy Lowell. She dismissed a young central American poet, double-thumbing her nose and kicking toward his
tail—showing off.

When he called on her at hotel in Ann Arbor, she was changing
the beds, i. e. having the beds changed about. And stuffing pillows, instead of putting two into one case.

She had her special light and cord when she read at Ann Arbor,
and elsewhere.

RF spotted her authorship of the *Fable* from its tone and manner and content, not from biographical note in an English publication. I asked specifically about this point.

David McCord and Miss Parker, dau of former attorney-gen'l
may marry. McC apparently indifferent. But he's a smart man.
Talks too much, tho,—like his mother, to whose apron-strings
he's tied. Efficient office, secretary, etc. His poems are thin,
from the thinness of his living. Has never shown RF his books
of prose—Nature stuff.

MacLeish friendly, on board at Harvard, trying to get RF to play
ball.

Admires Meredith's *Melampus* as well as Love in a Valley.
Quoted, in some connection, "what a dusty answer. . . ."

Millay really false in recent magazine pieces, e.g. 'I have children to beget.' Women ought not 'beget' anything. Also in *Conversation at Midnight*—nine *men* talking! Or is it seven. . .

F stopped T. Morrison's DeVoto-like review of Recognition:
'Ted, are all these people wrong? Am I just a myth? Are you the
first to begin seeing me straight?'

To JCRansom F paid cordial tribute at Kenyon in acknowledging R's intro. Also spoke of him so at Cincinnati, so not just
front at Kenyon. But jested about JCR's "white slaves" to his

ideas. F complimented Roberta Schwartz Chalmers too, but afterwards, and condescendingly somewhat.

Professors regarded Untermeyer's lectures at Amherst as poor stuff, though audiences liked it. Profs thought RF paying off a debt.

Agreed that Yeats much like a weather-vane,—or MacLeish,— in responding to one influence after another.

Zorn turned King's man. Hastened to say, But you never were a professor. Cold to Louis Untermeyer. U called him a Nazi— pleased Z. Z moved RF from guest room to cubby-hole when son came home. Mrs. Z moved his clothes and soiled linen in the closet.

EDWIN ARLINGTON ROBINSON

Robinson the best of the moderns. Then Lindsay. Next Sand-burg,—not much or often. Finally, Millay, in early things.

See Stark Young's review of *Merlin* cir. 1916. Y talked with F, and at least half of the review reflects F's view.

R told F that at one time in his life he tried each day to drink himself to death before night. R said to F that it took a quart to get him up even with other people—and all after that was gravy.

R: You have a cold. You'd better have some bitters.
F: No, I haven't a cold.
R: Yes, you have!
· · · · · ·
R: Better have some more bitters.

Torrence told F that R's "fire was gone" 15 years ago.

At 40, R cried to Torrence about his lack of success. T laughed, EAR and RT never so close again.

One of the two questions Hagedorn says EAR asked him, F says he has no recollection. The second, says F, would be an imper-tinence. Who cares? As for himself, he didn't give a God-damn: he was *busy*!

Untermeyer used to give EAR whiskey when it was hard to get good stuff.

EAR sore at F on two counts:
1) "For God's sake, don't!"—when R seemed bent on Arthurian cycle, just after *Merlin*. "But I already have."
2) F not in 50th birthday tributes.

EAR and RF met often, in Boston and elsewhere. See Preface to King Jasper on the 'place of bitters.' RF liked R, well enough. R sent books for a while, but not after the Merlin business. And RF admired R: even in the later things, though RF says he only glanced at them, there were "touches."

R in letter to F said he was glad he came on *NoB* before *ABW*, or would have steered away.

F saw R last two times at home of Jas. Wells. W took Gage's wife Hilda. Then the sculptress, asking F to use "Sesame" as her middle name. W sold book inscribed by James Stephens to RF. Now at Charlottesville, Va. (?), in society.

LETTERS

F likes to receive letters. I observed this, and spoke of it. He admitted it freely. (And I recall his saying that Elinor had 25 years of excitement, that "every mail" brought something more or less exciting.)

But as for answering, he waits for the mood, for a similar sense of excitement, for something to say.

And he jolly well knows that some of his letters have *stuff*!

The U. of Michigan has asked Louis Untermeyer for his F letters. But RF doesn't think that the right place.

From England, wrote most to Cox and Bartlett.

LECTURES AND READINGS

At OSU, Literary Programs.
At Cleveland, Ruthlessness in Poetry.
At Cincinnati, Party Lines in Poetry Today.
Subjects elsewhere not announced.

Is hungry and thirsty afterwards, almost unnaturally so. Was grateful for steak "dinner" at Wesleyan.

Before-lecture eating:
2 raw eggs
Juice of a lemon, cut in half
Cup of tea, with lots of sugar
A few crackers
A dish of ice-cream, of which he's very fond

Wherever he went, much interested in local history, architecture, customs, etc. At Ohio U, int'd in early founding ( ), in the two old halls (and), remarking that the others would be better in the same style. and in the raised platforms for teachers in the old schoolrooms—remarking, "Why shouldn't a professor really occupy his chair?" And he sat down.

Was earlier at a Cincinnati girls' school on a very hot day, through John Erskine's arrangement. Stood in pool of own sweat. "Nothing worse?" asked New Yorkers afterwards.

At Cin., liked modernistic design and decorations of Station.

Amazed at size of Cin. Thinks depressions come from cities. Concentrations of population prosperous at whim of demand for products. "We'll have to go back and begin over on this flocking to cities." Maybe, almost surely, a small farm with small but steady income to be preferred.

Elinor never approved of his lecturing. She disliked to see RF go out into the world, though he never went more than 30 nights a year.

He knows how audiences grow. Perhaps 200 at OSU in 1922. Crowds turned away in 1936 and 1938.

He knows also relation of lectures and readings to book sales. Yet he hates the money-changers at the door, e. g. books for sale at the door in Cleveland. And as at Waco, Texas,—Armstrong a promoter kind of fellow.

Said Taeusch did good, "academic" introduction at Cleveland— biographical sketch. Taeusch had facts, yet the portrait seemed strange. RF said, since facts right—only three or four errors, and those all in his favor—he'd not complain. Afterwards Taeusch wanted to argue about his errors!—

Likes audiences of men—young or old, business or otherwise.

Uneasy with women likely in one way or another to grow hysterical.

Knows he can stir listeners, brand them, mark them for his own, make them his "slaves." There's a satisfaction in it.

Can explode, as in lectures, just so often. That's why too many, or too many at one place, bad.

Once when Frost left Elinor to lecture, she became very ill—of course for some other cause. But he didn't know she was going to be ill or he wouldn't have gone.

She was jealous, though he didn't use that word: she didn't like him to be out among women.

Kenyon topic: Knowledge, Wisdom, and Delight.
At Harvard Club, talked almost entirely about technique in a poem. At Ohio U, no "topic," but a hit,—and gave Items for or from "A Blue Ribbon at Amesbury."

Always had to screw himself up to lecture; always suffered exhaustion afterwards, and depression. Hard on family and friends. Works self up to sensitiveness and alertness, so it is that either compliments or jabs, however oblique, tell strongly on him.

Asked Cleveland audience, he told me, not to leave when he announced the last poem, as some of them started to do. Like leaving a football game when the home team behind: then they need support. So he needed their support when he had a poem in his mouth (that's the way he put it).

I observe that each talk is a hit, yet each talk is different; he says different things. Some repetition, i. e., some of same points made repeatedly, but very few of these. (He wanted to be reassured on this when I mentioned it.)

Precipitates of thinking, recombined, rephrased. Eg, at Kenyon, idea of Ph. D-ish boy like a "dessicated plum" (died), not able to be restored: "You can't back up into poetry from Aristotle."

At OSU, had approved of my introduction when described in full as long two or three sentences quoting Plutarch, etc., yet he made faces behind my back, the rascal. At Cin., I called him, in the intro., a "sinner-saint," and he mentioned it two or three times afterwards, liking it.

PORTRAITS, ETC.

Doesn't like Cartoto's silver-point at Amherst, esp. in photo. sent him by Green: eyes seem not on the same object.

This a defect of painting and other kinds of representational art as compared with photography. Camera gets everything at once; artist does it a bit at a time.

Has option to buy back Cartoto protrait at half price, and may exercise it.

Didn't like King's attitude of "It's that or nothing." As if his (F's) immortality depended on Amherst. . . .

Cartoto silver point of RF and EMF from passport photograph: $350.

RF wants Bishop to try an enlargement of the passport photo.

Blackington photographed Chapin's portrait of EMF and had it colored, but the coloring is wrong, in F's opinion.

F wants Bishop to try his skill at photographing that too. ?Passport of 1912 or of 1928? Probably the latter.

F promised me photograph of either Blackington's or Bishop's work on Chapin's portrait of Elinor.

RF intends to see DuChene to try to get the plaster head.

MISCELLANEOUS

Told Cleveland reporters he didn't mind them seeing him naked, but that he really wanted to sleep.

Pease offered RF a seminar in classics at Harvard, but spoiled it by offering to put a regular scholar with him, John Finley!

Not much for the old ballads, tho' Sir P. Spence. Less for Am'n ballads—cowboy, mountaineers, etc. Fond of the Waterboy by . . . ? Old Man River, too, by . . . Curran (Sp) Also "If ye will not when ye may, Ye may not when ye wold"—usually eviscerated in sung version.

Poems about England:
TO E.T.

IRIS BY NIGHT
NOT TO KEEP
THE THATCH
THE SOUND OF THE TREES
ENGLAND—This added to the list after reading let's to S. Cox.

Hon. A. M. at Amherst automatic: RF not given bid to stay for exercises at Com.

A. M. at Michigan: when he heard about it, F said he would take no pride in it; but Burton, even given time to reconsider, made no change. RF was minded to refuse, but accepted for appearance's sake.

Cox once began biography on basis of RF's seeking *him* out. RF bawled him out. Has done so repeatedly through the years.

F says he tells me many things chiefly so that I'll get deeper into the poetry. When I cap something he's said with a line or two from the poems themselves, he's pleased.

Irma would say Elinor got what she wanted out of life.

RF, like Dr. (Samuel) Johnson, demanded subjection wherever he went. Also like Dr. J., RF made a kind of confidant of nearly every one with whom he talked, and thereby flattered the listener into an exaggerated sense of the esteem in which the listener was held.

Gave me some closer data than before:

Poem about corn shocks or shooks in Bost. *Transcript* about Christmas time, 1891 or 1892.

Another poem about Graeco-Turkish War in Bost. *Transcript* under Charles Hurd's editorship, perhaps 1897.

Column for Lawrence *American* perhaps in 1894 under editor Jewett.

Editor, reporter, political commentator, etc., for Morrison family's Lawrence *Sentinel*, 1895 or 1896.

F says he can almost *see* "The Tuft of Flowers" in the *Derry News*, though the editor-owner didn't report it to Green! [Must search 1905–1911 thoroughly.]

SOME QUESTIONS ON THE CHRONOLOGY FOR THE YEARS
1892–1900

Which was the summer at *Canobie Lake,* 1892 or 1893 (and were there others)?

Did you spend any summer vacations after high school days *on farms* in southern New Hampshire?

When did you put in a spell as a *bobbin boy?*

Wasn't the *light-trimmer* experience around the turn of the year from 1893 into 1894?

When was the short period of your serving a Boston architect as a BLUE-PRINT BOY?

When was the experience as ADVANCE-AGENT-that-refused for the Shakesperian reader from Portland? And was it after this that you walked back to Lawrence?

. .You purchased THOMPSON's *Hound of Heaven* in Boston in 1893?

When did you make your walking sally into *the South?* Went down by boat (from Boston?), but where walk and how return?

Did you ever essay, as I have read, *shoe-making* in L?

When were you *paragrapher* for the *American?* 1894 or 1897?

When were you REPORTER-EDITOR for the *Sentinel,* the Morrison owned weekly?

After Ward published "My Butterfly" you called on him in NEW YORK: 1894 or 1895?

[*On* most of these points I have sufficient or abundant data, but I shall feel more secure as to footing with approximately correct dates in mind.—Of course the main line is apart from all this minute detail; but one can see over the fence.]

HARVARD, 1897–1899

Took English A under Sheffield, now at Wellesley. Got B on some poems now in his books!

Called on Sheffield once. Then *invited* to S's, and went, but S not home, so no later call. (See other notes on Sheffield.)

Took Harvard entrance examinations in Astronomy, English, Physics, and French—in addition to subjects studied in H. S.

Signed up for Kittredge's Milton as an elective. K read some the first time, "Fly, envious time," etc. S saw student's books, interleaved. Not for him! He stayed the hour, but he never went back. (This came after I told him of starting and dropping K's courses.)

(HARVARD—RECENT ASSOCIATIONS)

Is uncomfortable under the "respectability,"—and might do something to throw it off: Thad Stevens and marriage to Negress.

F relished what Chas. Curtis said to him, "Can't you feel it [respectability] crawling over you?" RF made appropriate gestures.

Is friends again with E. Sedgwick of *Atlantic* after brush of 1916. S. back from Spain, enthusiastic for Franco, another Overseer. At one meeting mumbled something to F about "losses" (he'd shortly lost his wife too) and dashed away overcome.

While he was here, received wire from Pres. Conant asking him to be guest at next meeting of Overseers, Nov. 20, 1938.

One board member said they were a *little* disappointed in Conant. Others said, A fine leader.

At first meeting RF attended, Lipmann talked most.

Murdock out by a nose as president of H.—by Chas. Curtis nose! Bec. of attention to a married woman? C himself out for that kind of trouble—divorce, etc.—resigned and it was accepted.

R. W. Emerson Chair of Poetry in prospect, he confided,—if it's created.

Dumas Malone, a southerner, of H. U. Press, and McCord, want F to do things:

Anthologies: H. U. Bk of Mod. Poetry, of Am. P., of Mod. Am. P.

Could do preface from memories of Norton lectures, and get that obligation cleared up too.

Income from job would be backlog for his estate.

HARVARD TERCENTENARY SONG

Never could write anything really to be sung. But note h.s. graduation song.

Harvard wanted something as singable as Fair Harvard, and F says it scared the liver out of him,—though he was joking when I called from Albany in 1936.

For a song, meaning should be spread thin. "I would always pack too much meaning in."

Got the shingles. McCord saw them, so RF released without prejudice.

Lamont got Masefield into the H. Tercentenary picture,—he who gave $500,000 for one of Conant's new cross-cut chairs. RF says he might have been able "to take it," but it would have been "a dose."

F has never met M. But a few letters have been exchanged.

McCord good at "occasional" things.

LAWRENCE, 1885–1900 (EXCEPT DARTMOUTH AND HARVARD)

One of the few things that he could talk of with his grandfather —Grover Cleveland, free trade, tariff.

First book he read: Porter's *Scottish Chiefs*

Then: *Tales of a Grandfather* by Hawthorne
      Verne's *Mysterious Island* (never did read *20 Leagues*)
      Hughes' *Tom Brown's School Days*

A year and a half in Lawrence schools: teachers disliked him, except Miss Chase.

Next year and a half before H. S. in Salem, under mother.

Two contacts with _____ Sanborn:

(1) Frost for a while a mill yard gatekeeper, S his boss.
(2) Later, S bec. a sea-captain. Called one day to ask F to go to sea. F, in stocking feet, reading a book. S, disgusted, left, without asking F to go.

F was regarded, and knew he was regarded, as an outcast, a pariah. His former teachers wouldn't speak to him.

Mother at Salem until 1890, at $9 a week for 36 weeks. Then in Methuen, at $11 a week for 40 weeks.

They lived in rooms,—or was it a room? No sitting room. F slept in room with m. and sister.

Yet his mother never complained at his worthlessness, never chided him, was "sporting," *never* said, 'I'm a widow, you're a responsibility," etc.

She was long dead when RF came to.

F himself teaching at Salem had 12 students, 4 from one family. Students ranged from 12 down. Mother indignant when F remarked their chronic lateness.

He could fire the students to learn, when he willed to.

Janitor work, sweeping once a week. Wood, small stuff for starting stove.

Saw Wolcott in his study once or twice on invitation, other times casually, once a year or so, on the street. Was not introduced to W's family. Could have been good friends with W, but W too busy.

F thinks he was always more honest because of his laziness!

F's fight in L. with _____ Parker, son of wealthy father. This P married dau. of brothel-keeper. The Fs rented upstairs, 3rd floor, to them. Mrs. P attacked F: he held her. Then F gave P a beating when P came home. Later F was fined in court—and paid gladly!

ON THE DERRY FARM, 1900–1911 (REALLY 1909)

Given no tools to start with! Just a fifty-dollar horse, a cart (too big for the horse), and a cow. Oh, yes, and a "helper"—Carl Burell!

Lazy, put-it-offish. Didn't put up curtains for Elinor at Derry for 6 mos.

Might have done so much so easily for her: e. g., dig a trench, lay a pipe (perhaps thirty feet), and bring pump indoors.

His puttering of course wasn't fair to Elinor.

He roused into life only at work-exchanging time—haying, etc.

Oatmeal, potatoes, ten-cent beef (round) for boiling. Some fruit. Chickens, but occasionally they'd go off, not lay—brood, or let down. [Berries, nuts.] Garden—grew up in weeds at the end of the summer.

Much reading. Whole poets. Many of them aloud. Many books read,—as many as five in one day, he recalls.

Before 1906, a few half-hearted moves to be "good"—to N. Y. etc.

About, he says, 33 when he came to. Saw children growing up, saw doctors' bills accumulating, etc.

———— Blanchette was the Manchester real estate man (or lawyer?) who helped Frost put through his farm mortgage. Facts in re mortgage in the records.

Wolcott got F job at Pinkerton by letter.

Salary at Pinkerton from $275 to $1100. See records.

To Bethlehem first time alone. Family next year, Lynches. Let them that set the fire put it out!

Xmas vacation, 1909, during first year of full-time teaching, suffered a nervous breakdown, prostration. Walked to Methuen, was given a lift to Lawrence, drank a beer, came home on the trolley, collapsed. Ached in stooping for a stone for ten years.

Grandfather left a trust fund. But it was a diminishing thing: it had no future. Frost saw this, Jeannie didn't.

IN SAN FRANCISCO: 1875–1885

Remembers teachers:

Fisher ("Chocolate")

Radford
Dudley
Principal (or Supt.): J. W. ("Cock-eyed") Anderson.

One classmate wrote RF in 1913: Wallington Hubbard.

Remembers picnics of Caledonian Club which parents joined.

Remembers Scotch friends: Adair, Boyd (f. died almost in his arms).

Lived a while at the Abbotsford, a family hotel.

Lived a while on Leavenworth St.

On beach, dragged out a 50-ft seaweed near Cliff House, long before it became a California Coney Island.

Was baptized in Presbyterian church; then attended Unitarian S. S., then Swedenborgian.

In schoolyard, up two bamboo poles by hands. (Girls had play yard in flower-garden place.) Of course saw small boy perversity.

All of his boyhood cuts and bruises seemed to become infected.

He remembers that as a boy he sometimes felt big, thick.

He remembers sitting in a chair, resolved on silence. Inside him there was a voice that mocked him when he spoke.

Mother told him of Wallace and Bruce, father of Lee.

She read much aloud, incl'g Edw. Bellamy's *Looking Bkwd*.

He told self stories—of a tribe of Indians in a deep valley surrounded by mountains, a race of little people making sure of security. (See Munson on this.)

Item 31:

Professor Sheffield's Recollection.

On April 27, 1939, Newdick wrote to Holmes:

Here's concrete evidence that I'm getting back to an even keel: the just completed first draft, subject to complete revision and the insertion of additional data of all kinds, of the chapter on Frost's two years at Harvard. Train your artillery on it and fire away! (I already have the reminiscences of Sheffield to insert; they came in the mail this afternoon, and will cause me to eliminate the bit in re the not-at-home and "the bearded lady." . . .)

On April 24, Professor Alfred D. Sheffield, had written from Cambridge that he was glad to hear of Newdick's biography: "His position in American letters makes due the kind of interpretation which you can give to his genius and to the impact of his career." He added this recollection, which Newdick realized would ameliorate the idea of their relationship when seen only through the eyes of RF:

My brief contact with young Frost in 1897 cannot have meant much to him in the ripening of his taste. It was my first year of teaching—as an assistant in English A—and Frost had already matured his own distinctive approach to writing. I remember very congenial talks with him in which he effectively contrasted the potent element of "sentence-tone" with the syntactic mechanisms in terms of which I tended to work for sentence-sense in the freshman group. I was myself at that time much influenced by Sidney Lanier, and by a discipline in the patterning of music which, I think, prevented me from appreciating the full importance of Frost's special sensitivity to the expressive cadences of speech. He was then, I recall, absorbed in reading the Odyssey, and his talk made it very evident that he was taking his own line as a writer, and could give any young teacher as good as he got.

Item 32:

The Selheimer Material.

On May 30, 1938, a descendant of students in the Lewistown Academy, of which William P. Frost, Jr., was principal and where Isabelle Moodie, his mother, met and married her husband, sent a longhand copy of the marriage notice of Frost's parents. From the Lewistown (Pa.) Gazette *of March 26, 1873, it reads: Married, Frost and Moodie / at the residence of Geo. W. Elder, on / Tuesday evening Mar. 18–1873 / by O. O. Mc-Clean, D.O. / Assisted by Rev. J. H. Brown / Prof. William P. Frost / to / Miss Belle Moodie / both of Lewistown Academy. This wording is almost identical to one later found in the* Lewistown Sentinel.

In thanking his informant, Miss Mary L. Selheimer, for the marriage information, Newdick voiced another query:

I wonder if Belle Moodie left behind her any Lewistown friends whom she might have told of her firstborn, with a resulting note in the newspaper? I'll tell you confidentially why I ask: Robert isn't sure whether he was born in 1874 or 1875, and all the San Francisco records were burned in the fire after the great earthquake. His birthday is March 26, and I should think word might have gotten back to Lewistown within a month or so.

Newdick's successor, Lawrance Thompson, has written that RF "admitted" that he had for most of his life thought he had been conceived out of wedlock, that marriage followed shortly after conception. He seems to have been able to believe the record of the marriage as well as that of his birth were destroyed in the San Francisco earthquake and fire of 1906. In spite of the fact that he gave 1874 as his birth year when he went to Dartmouth, he told Thompson that he gave 1875 as the year as soon as the public began to request information to protect himself against possible embarrassment on this score. Presumably the uncertainty about the birth-marriage situation did not bother him between 1892, when he entered Dartmouth, and November, 1900, when his mother died. Additionally, RF listed himself as being 21 years old when he was married in December 1895. The only certainty, of course, is that something made him start giving the year as 1875 and that Newdick had to go to great pains to establish the facts. On June 10, Newdick wrote to the California State Library for possible San Francisco birth record for Frost: "He isn't sure, and there is no family Bible that is known to survive."

Miss Selheimer also supplied a rare document, a receipt for fees paid for children attending the Lewistown Academy. It is dated January 25, 1873, and signed by Wm. P. Frost, Jr. (See Figure 5.)

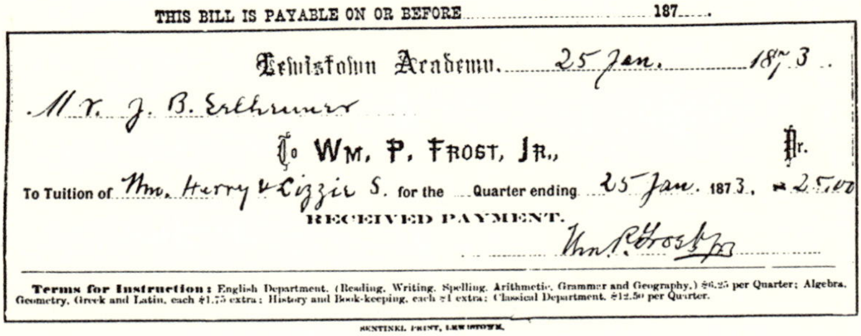

THIS BILL IS PAYABLE ON OR BEFORE _____ 187___ .

Lewistown Academy. 25 Jan. 187 3

M r. J. B. Selheimer

To WM. P. FROST, JR., Dr.

To Tuition of Wm. Harry & Lizzie S. for the Quarter ending 25 Jan. 1873 , $ 2 5.00

RECEIVED PAYMENT.

Wm. P. Frost Jr

Terms for Instruction : English Department, (Reading, Writing, Spelling, Arithmetic, Grammer and Geography,) $6.25 per Quarter; Algebra, Geometry, Greek and Latin, each $1.75 extra ; History and Book-keeping, each $1 extra ; Classical Department, $12.50 per Quarter.

SENTINEL PRINT, LEWISTOWN.

FIG. 5. *The Selheimer Receipt. (Supplied by Miss Mary L. Sel-heimer, Lewistown, Pa., May 30, 1938.)*

Item 33:

Frost Addresses in San Francisco

On June 30, 1939, Newdick wrote to the public library in San Francisco about "home addresses for William Prescott Frost, Jr., . . . for the years 1875–1885 inclusive. There may be one for 1874, too." The reply, which gives an address for each year, beginning with 1874, is of especial interest because of deviations from the official biography of Thompson. Thompson's list is given as from Langley's Directory. The list, compiled by R.S.F. of the library staff, is headed: "The following addresses for William P. Frost, Jr. appeared in the San Francisco directories for the years given." Substantially in agreement, the lists are different in two respects. The library gives no directory listing for 1877, but Thompson gives the Abbotsford House. In 1878 the library places the family in the Colonnade Hotel, but Thompson says there was no listing and supplies the Inglewood Hotel as given by RF.

Item 34:
Mrs. Hall's Map of the Derry Farm.

Thanks to his friendship with Miss Sylvia Clark, of Derry, N.H., Newdick had corresponded with Mrs. S. B. Hall, then living at the Magoon Farm, where Frost and his wife and children lived during the most significant period of his poetic development and the halcyon days of his family life. When Mr. Hall said that perhaps Mrs. Hall could "map out the place," Miss Clark supplied a stamped envelope. Accordingly Mrs. Nellie O. Hall wrote a note on June 19 to accompany her "very crude sketch," which she sent with her best wishes. Newdick put it with his recollections and photographs to prepare a finished map for his biography.

On June 23, Newdick sent his thanks for the map, acknowledging the way it improved upon the sketch he had. He sent six "relatively trifling questions" in the interest of being "absolutely accurate in regard to everything I say about the farm." After his signature he included "one more question": "Did you talk with Robert in the spring of last year when he came back to Derry to walk again over the farm, after the death of his wife?" The next day he sent his "new sketch-map," asking that any corrections be marked directly on it.

In the first part of a letter of June 29, Mrs. Hall commented on Newdick's map and answered all his questions:

To your sketch map I've added a window to back of the house, because Mr. Frost speaks of this in his poem. From this we can look eighteen miles to Hooksett N.H. and see the beacon for the mail air-way. Also I've added trees, maybe trees which surely were here when Mr. Frost lived here. They are tiny circles thus o, either side of the pump and on toward street, & up along beside the street to our barn which I have also added, one pair as I have just spoken of, another here near state road, corner of front small orchard. . . . Now as to the sketch. I do not see how that I can improve on it at all. . . .

The West-running brook. That is one half or more miles from here toward the North. Yes, I think it was the same brook Mr. Frost refers to in his poem. But do you know, I've always wondered why, it being so far away and seemingly has nothing to do with this place. Mr. Nat Head built this place and was the original owner of course, then sold it to Magoun (wonder if that is the correct way to spell that name) and from Magoun to Mr. Frost to Mr. Charles Senna to Stillman Hall, present owner when we bought. [On the] South Herman Webster, present owner, born there & about 60 years of age.

The field and pasture across State Rd is ours & covers 8½ acres. Over this side of the road there are 16 acres. Mr. Frost owned that too, the 8½ acres.

This brook you have mapped runs through our woods & meadow on to State Rd thru a conduit on thru mowing field and pasture across State Rd. From this conduit on up the grade & down, to next house below is Klein's hill, and small house at foot of this hill is where Kleins [same as Cline's Hill. W.A.S.] lived years ago.

To the casually inserted, but urgently interesting, question about Frost's visit to the farm, Mrs. Hall gave a very tantalizing answer. It will be recalled that Mrs. Frost's body was cremated and that the plan had long been for the couple to have their ashes scattered over the hallowed ground of the farm. His trip in the spring of 1938 was to make arrangements for the taking of Mrs. Frost's ashes to the farm. By all evidence, the Halls must have objected. In her reply, Mrs. Hall makes no suggestion of this.

In the spring of last year when Mr. Frost was here I did talk with him. We were very much pleased as always to see him & sincerely hope you and Mr. Frost may find it convenient to call again.

Item 35:
Burell Documents.

On May 20, 1939, Newdick had written to Carl Burell to say, "The more I get into the actual writing of the Frost biography, the more convinced I am that I need and must have your reminiscences of him as you knew him from 1887 on. He has told me, at length, of your botanizing with him in the 'nineties for instance, and even of your living a year with him and Elinor on the farm at Derry because his grandfather was afraid he didn't have gumption enough to get along alone."

On June 25, he got this astounding reply from the Executor of the Carl Burell Estate, along with the news that "Mr. Burell died June 13, 1938":

He left thousands of pages of prose and poetry unpublished.

He left diaries covering the period when he was living with Mr. Frost but of no value to you I believe.

Probably this letter was not answered by Newdick. On July 22, when he was no longer able to reply, a request was received that the six years' Lawrence High School Bulletin, *which Newdick had borrowed, be returned.*

Item 36:

Membership in the Society of the New Jerusalem (Swedenborgian).

As the month was ending, in a letter of June 26, 1938, from the Rev. Othmar Tobish, pastor of the two churches of the Swedenborgian San Francisco Society of the New Jerusalem, the following information, exceedingly important to speculations relating to RF's religious beliefs and not published before now:

I have searched the records of the old O'Farrell St. church in San Francisco, and ascertained the following data:

Robert Lee Frost, baptized July 10, 1881, no membership record.

Belle Frost, taken out membership, July 10, 1881.

The church record also mentioned the burial, for which there is ample other record, of "W. P. Frost" on May 11, 1885, at the age of 35 years, 4 months, and 6 days. The respondent thought there was "a slight chance" that Frost because he "was only 10" [actually 11] years old when he left San Francisco, might have joined in Massachusetts. He advised inquiry of the church's general secretary in Boston.

Appendix A

Newdick's "Suggested Regrouping of Frost's Selected Poems" (1928).

PROEM: Revelation, 207

AUTUMN: In the Home Stretch, 135–147; The Road Not Taken, 163; The Axe-Helve, 154–9; The Mountain, 86–92; Going for Water, 70–71; October, 171; Reluctance, 211–212; My November Guest, 168.

WINTER: The Onset, 169; The Runaway, 5–6; Dust of Snow, 15; An Old Man's Winter Night, 19–20 (indented); The Woodpile, 109–110; The Grindstone, 101–114; Stopping by Woods on a Snowy Evening, 12; Storm-Fear, 208; Snow, 113–134; Brown's Descent, 200–203; Birches, 81–83; To the Thawing Wind, 172; A Hillside Thaw, 107–8.

SPRING: Nothing Gold Can Stay, 11; The Pasture, 3; Putting in the Seed, 69; Flower-gathering, 210; Range-finding, 170 (in parentheses); The Self-seeker, 46–59 (indented); "Out, Out-", 64–65 (indented); Mending Wall, 96–98; Hyla Brook, 167.

SUMMER: Blueberries, 193–199; A Time to Talk, 175; A Tuft of Flowers, 93–95; Mowing, 72; The Code, 176–181; An Encounter, 105–6; The Need of Being Versed in Country Things, 73–4 (indented); The Hill Wife, 60–3 (indented); A Servant to Servants, 37–45 (indented); Home Burial, 21–7 (indented); Fire and Ice, 13 (indented and in parentheses); Two Look at Two, 77–8 (indented); A Hundred Collars, 182–192 (indented); The Gum Gatherer, 84–5; The Black Cottage, 148–153;

The Oven Bird, 164; The Sound of Trees, 166;
Into My Own, 213; A Vantage Point, 165; To
Earthward, 9–10; The Cow in Apple Time, 4.

AUTUMN: The Death of the Hired Man, 28–36 (indented);
After Apple-Picking, 79–80; Goodbye and Keep
Cold, 99–100.

CONCLUSION: Bond and Free, 209.

Note: The reader is reminded that Newdick had said in his letter of July 30,
1934, to which the "suggested regrouping" was attached, that lyrics which were
put in the organization on an "associational" basis were put in parentheses.
Those which rested "more on a basis of observation than on a basis of direct
experience" were indicated by indention.

Appendix B

Some Essential Questions for the Student of the Poetry of Robert Frost (as found in letter of October 14, 1934, from Robert S. Newdick to Robert Frost).

Sketch Frost's life.
> The question can be varied in a number of ways, e.g. Sketch Frost's rural experience, a variant which stresses the most important aspect of the poet's background, and also a variant involving facts necessary to a valid response to such a question as

Frost's poetry as the artist's expression of farm life.
> This question too can be much varied, e.g. The directness and accuracy of Frost's farming observations.

A comparative study of, on the one hand, Frost's poems growing out of rural experience and observation, and of, on the other hand, his other poems.
> (Is it too much, to expect students to be able to handle such a question successfully?)

The nature of Frost's realism stated and set forth by specific examples.
> (This question assumes that the instructor will have given the necessary critical material from Frost himself, will have read and discussed important poems not in the volume of Selections, e.g. New Hampshire, etc.)

Symbolism in Frost.
> (Certainly the instructor will have assisted beginning students to look beneath the surface of The Road Not Taken, Mending Wall, Misgiving, etc, etc.)

Frost's philosophy. (Nature, Science, People, Nations, Art—esp. Poetry)
> (If the instructor has performed this synthesis for his class, he should not ask this question on an examination, inasmuch as, in that instance, the answer would be no more than parrot work. If, however, the philosophical elements have been

merely indicated, the question will be an excellent one for sorting sheep from goats.)

The comparative strength of Frost in lyric, narrative, and dramatic verse.
Frost's verse as speech-rhythms caught and held fast.
Frost's vocabulary: simplicity, naturalness, colloquialness, etc.
Frost's subjects as further extensions of the field of poetic art.
Frost and Masefield compared as to . . . . . .
(The possibilities here are obviously numerous.)

Frost as a Greek. ("That course, they tell me, isn't offered this year.")
(Valid to some extent if the instructor has pursued the subject only far enough to whet the desire of specially curious students to learn more of all that is involved in Frost's own question, "How about being a good Greek, for instance?")

Appendix C
Bibliography Plan of March 27, 1935.

Part I lists Frost's poems, alphabetically, from 1894 through 1934, with full bibliographical notes . . . E.g.:

A Brook in the City
New Republic, XXVI.48 (March 9, 1921).
First collected in *American Poetry, 1922. A Miscellany*,
p. 37.
Included in *New Hampshire* and in *Collected Poems*

Cross-references are given for the same poem published under different titles. E.g.:

[Blood: see The Flood]

Part II lists Frost's separate publications through 1934,—from *Twilight* (1894) through *The Lone Striker* (1933). —the first editions completely described bibliographically, the points of the later editions or issues, etc., with pertinent notes, e.g., for the *Collected Poems*, the titles of the poems first collected therein, the titles of the poems omitted from it, etc.

Part III lists Frost's contributions to joint publications of one sort and another, e.g., his introduction to *Dartmouth Verse* (1925), his remarks at the dedication of the Wilfrid Davison Memorial Library, etc., etc.

Part IV lists the periodicals to which Frost has contributed, with reference to the particular volumes. (Reprints in such as the *Literary Digest* are of course ignored.)

Part V lists the biographical and critical material on Frost in books and periodicals from 1913 through 1934. Each year is treated separately, and in each year the material in books is separated from that in periodicals. For 1923, to take one year, there are seven entries under the heading Books and Reference Works, and twenty-six under Periodicals. Material appearing in both periodicals and books is cross-indexed. And each item is accompanied by a succinct description and evaluation, e.g.

(Anonymous,) Times Literary Supplement, March 29, 1923. p. 213. Ostensibly a review of *Selected Poems*; really a short critical essay. (a) condemning Frost's narratives as never rising to poetry and (b) praising his lyrics.

Part VI lists the likenesses of Frost that have been published: camera portraits, informal photographs, snapshots; drawings, caricatures, sketches; woodcuts, portraits; casts. (The seventy entries in this list are now arranged merely chronologically, for so they have a particular useful to students; but they might well be rearranged into groups.)

Part VII is a chronology of Frost's life, somewhat similar to Cushwa's for Conrad in the Doubleday-Doran *Introduction*.

Colleges and universities, belatedly making their adjustments to the post-War world, are coming more and more to discard their traditional courses for beginning students of literature (the old, too old, "survey" course; the even worse "types" course; etc.) and to substitute for them courses in contemporary literature. Their first hesitant moves were toward courses built around somebody-or-other's anthology. Now, I believe, they are courageously (courageously for them) picking groups of significant individual artists for closer study than is possible with an anthology. So we are doing, as you know, here at Ohio State.

The bibliography I am preparing will be useful, then, not only to collectors (that section or those sections will not bulk too large), but also to teachers who are working their way conscientiously into modern literature, and also to the dazed students who are called upon for "papers" on this or that aspect of this or that artist—in this instance Robert Frost.

If you, Frost's chief American publisher, are sufficiently interested, I shall be glad to send the nearly-but-not-quite-finally-prepared typescript for its first examination, for I am now far enough along with the work to be concerned with placing it with a strong publisher.

Very truly yours,
Robert S. Newdick

Appendix D

As Printed in American Literature, *VII (May, 1935)
181–7, "Some Early Verse of Robert Frost and Some
of His Revisions" by Robert S. Newdick.*

I

A springboard from which to dive into the subject of Robert
Frost's early verse and some of his revisions, is to be found in the
main portion of a sentence of Marguerite Wilkinson's concerning poets: "Some . . . like Robert Frost, write rapidly and make
few alterations, but they may make many, many poems which
they regard as mere practice-work and throw away."[1] General
report confirms Mrs. Wilkinson's assertion concerning Frost's
making and throwing away many poems; and Elizabeth Shepley
Sergeant, writing from intimate knowledge, declares that
Frost's "The Mountain" was written "with one stroke of the
pen," as were also "Birches," "Two Look at Two," and "Stopping by Woods on a Snowy Evening";[2] but regarding the few
alterations, at least in Frost's early poems, there is more to be
said. And the business of this paper is first to establish a list of
those early poems and second to examine the alterations that
the poet has made in them since their original publication.

II

The line between Frost's early and later poems may well be
drawn just before the appearance of *A Boy's Will* in 1913.[3] True,
the poet was then thirty-eight years old; but, as Harriet Monroe
put it, mindful of the title (from Longfellow), it was "as if, at
thirty-eight, he had just got around to the business of growing

1. *The Way of the Makers* (New York, 1925), p. 221.
2. *Fire Under the Andes* (New York, 1927), p. 300. This study, "Robert Frost,
A Good Greek Out of New England," appeared originally in *The New Republic*,
XLIV, 144–148 (Sept. 30, 1925).
3. London: David Nutt

up."[4] And of course a large part of his growing up, so far as the reading public could know, still lay ahead of him, for, as one of his friends phrases it, even *A Boy's Will* "represents only a small and scarcely typical part of Mr. Frost's literary personality."[5] Finally, while some of the reviewers welcomed Frost "unhesitatingly to the ranks of poets born,"[6] others felt his achievement to be "no great matter."[7] In short, the line taken as dividing the poet's early poems from his later ones is at once arbitrary and conservative.

Appended to *A Boy's Will* is this note: "Certain of these poems are reprinted by courteous permission from:—*The Forum, The Independent, The Companion.*" By *The Companion*, it may be observed incidentally, is meant *The Youth's Companion;* but surely, realizing that *A Boy's Will* was first published in England, no one will think it disingenuous in the poet to have simplified the title of that distinctly American periodical. And doubtless it was merely an oversight of the poet's that *The New England Magazine* was not listed, too. At all events, it was in these four periodicals that Frost published fourteen poems during the years 1894–1912.[8]

POEMS PUBLISHED IN PERIODICALS BEFORE 1913

"My Butterfly / An Elegy"
The Independent, XLVI, I (Nov. 8, 1894).

4. *Poets and Their Art* (New York, 1926), p. 56. This study, "Robert Frost," appeared originally in *Poetry, A Magazine of Verse*, XXV, 146–153 (Dec., 1924).
5. Sharon Brown, *Poetry of Our Times* (Chicago, etc., 1928), p. 139.
6. *The Academy*, LXXXV, 260 (Sept. 20, 1913): cf. *The English Review*, XIV, 505 (June 1913): "that *inevitable* response to nature which is the hallmark of true lyric feeling"; William M. Payne, *The Dial*, LV, 211–212 (Sept. 16, 1913): "His songs give us the sort of pleasure we have in those of . . . Mr. Housman."
7. Katherine Tynan, *The Bookman* (London), XLIV, 130 (June, 1913); cf. *The Nation* (London), XIII, 924 (Sept. 20, 1913): "more promise than is usual in a first venture."
8. In Part II of *The Colophon* for 1930 H. Boutell, following data supplied him by Vrest Orton, describes *Twilight*, a small five-poem volume privately printed by Frost in 1894 and containing, besides "My Butterfly," which had already appeared in *The Independent*, four other poems: "Twilight," "Summering," "The Falls," and "An Unhistoric Spot." Only two copies of this volume were printed. One was immediately inscribed to Miss Elinor Miriam White, soon thereafter Mrs. Frost, and remains a cherished private possession. The other was subsequently destroyed.

Twilight (1894); *A Boy's Will* (1913), with gloss "There are things that can never be the same"; Collected Poems (1930), without gloss.

"The Birds Do Thus"
The Independent, XLVIII, I (Aug. 20, 1896). Never reprinted.

"Caesar's Lost Transport Ships"
The Independent, XLIX, I (Jan. 14, 1897). Never reprinted.

"Warning"
The Independent, XLIX, I (Sept. 9, 1897). Never reprinted.

"The Quest of the Orchis"
The Independent, LIII, 1494 (June 27, 1901). Never reprinted.

"Ghost House"
The Youth's Companion, LXXX, 132 (March 15, 1906).
A Boy's Will (1913), with gloss, "He is happy in society of his choosing"; Collected Poems, (1930), without gloss.

"The Trial by Existence"
The Independent, LXI, 876 (Oct. 11, 1906).
A Boy's Will (1913), with gloss / He resolves . . . / "and to know definitely what he thinks about the soul"; *Collected Poems* (1930), without gloss.

"A Line-Storm Song"
The New England Magazine, XXXVII, 204 (Oct., 1907).
A Boy's Will (1913), with gloss "It is the autumnal mood with a difference"; Collected Poems (1930), without gloss.

"Across the Atlantic"
The Independent, LXIV, 676 (March 26, 1908). Never reprinted.

"Into Mine Own"
The New England Magazine, XL, 338 (May, 1909).
A Boy's Will (1913), as "Into My Own," and with gloss "The youth is persuaded that he will be rather more than less himself for having forsworn the world"; *Collected Poems* (1930), without gloss.

"The Flower Boat"
The Youth's Companion, LXXXIII, 248 (May 20, 1909).
West Running Brook (1928), with note "Very early," *Collected Poems* (1930), without note.

"October"
The Youth's Companion, LXXXVI, 512 (Oct. 3, 1912).
A Boy's Will (1913), with gloss "He sees days slipping from him that were the best for what they were"; *Collected Poems* (1930), without gloss.

"My November Guest"
The Forum, XLVIII, 612 (Nov., 1912).
A Boy's Will (1913), with gloss "He is in love with being misunderstood"; *Collected Poems* (1930), without gloss.

"Reluctance"
The Youth's Companion, LXXXVI, 612 (Nov. 7, 1912).
A Boy's Will (1913), unglossed; *Collected Poems* (1930).

It will be observed that of these fourteen poems, nine have survived into Frost's *Collected Poems* (1930), eight of them having been utilized in *A Boy's Will* (1913) and one of them first reappearing in *West-Running Brook* (1928). It will be observed further that of the poems not reprinted, four are among the first five that Frost was able to sell.

Happily, however, the very first poem that Frost sold is still among his *Collected Poems*. This fact is of some significance in view of his emphatic declaration that "The poet, as everyone knows, must strike his individual note sometime between the ages of fifteen and twenty-five."[9] Frost was but nineteen when William Hayes Ward bought "My Butterfly" for *The Independent*.

III

In not a single instance, however, has one of Frost's early poems survived in his Collected Poems wholly unchanged. It is generally true, as one would expect, that the later the poem the fewer the changes. And it should be noted at once that the vast majority of the changes are minor ones—changes in punctuation, spelling, capitalization, indentation, spacing, and so on. Such points as these are of course relatively trivial, although it is interesting, in making close comparisons, to see the poet

9. Introduction to *The Arts Anthology: Dartmouth Verse 1925* (Portland, Maine: The Mosher Press, 1924), p. viii.

change his mind. In "October," for instance, he prays the "morning mild" to

> Release one leaf at break of day;
> At noon release another leaf;
> One from our trees, one far away.

The semicolons at the end of the first two lines were originally commas, while the period at the end of the third line was originally a semicolon.

The significant changes are the revisions in thought and expression. And these alterations are invariably improvements. Here one sees no old and clumsy Wordsworth marring the "jeu d'esprit" of his youth, but, instead, a thoughtful artist skilfully touching up what already was well done, and making improvements that for the most part are to be realized as improvements only after the revisions are accomplished.

To begin at the beginning, turn in Frost's Collected Poems to "My Butterfly." Now the third strophe begins:

> When that was, the soft mist
> Of my regret hung not on all the land,

but originally the second line was marred by inappropriate detail:

> . . . . the soft mist
> Of my two tears hung not on all the fields[.]

The fourth strophe is the most changed of all, but the alterations in the fifth are even more noteworthy. At first Frost wrote:

> These were the unlearned things.
> It seemed God let thee flutter from his gentle clasp,
> Then, fearful he had let thee win
> Too far beyond him to be gathered in,
> Snatched thee, o'er-eager, with ungentle grasp,
> Jealous of immortality.

Dropping one line removes one thought altogether:

> And there were other things:
> It seemed God let thee flutter from his gentle clasp:
> Then fearful he had let thee win
> Too far beyond him to be gathered in,
> Snatched thee, o'er-eager, with ungentle grasp.

The alterations in the next three of the republished poems are relatively slight. In "Ghost House" the peculiarly Frostian touch comes through replacing *so* with *how* in the line,

> And yet, in view of how many things[.]

In "The Trial by Existence" the elided ta'en gives way to taken. In "A Line-Storm Song," in the verses:

> All song of the woods is crushed like some
> Wild, easily shattered rose[,]

crushed is an afterthought, substituted for the much weaker *hushed*.

Slight changes, however, may accomplish almost magical results. Perhaps the most generally acclaimed line in all of Frost's poetry is the last line of the second stanza of "Into My Own" (a later, simpler, and less conventionally poetical title for "Into Mine Own"), for it has an Homeric simplicity and dignity, and it has also a haunting quality akin to that of the "the slow smokeless burning of decay." Originally the line read:

> Or highway where the slow wheels pour the sand.

A few years afterwards, with two slightest changes, Frost made it perfect:

> Or highway where the slow wheel pours the sand.

"The Flower Boat," like "My Butterfly," waited nineteen years for republication in revised form. In the first stanza Frost found nothing at all to mend. In the second he simply reduced *a-growing* to *growing*. But behold the third:

> And I know from that Elysian freight
> She will brave but once more the Atlantic weather,
> When dory and fisherman sail by fate
> To seek for the Happy Isles together.

—with changes and improvements in three lines of the four:

> And I judge from that Elysian Freight
> That all they ask is rougher weather,
> And dory and master will sail by fate
> To seek for the Happy Isles together.

Similar revisions are to be found in the last three poems in the list, poems published here in America after Frost had sold his farm, quit his teaching, and embarked with his family for England in September, 1912, early in his thirty-eighth year.

In "Reluctance" the first line of the third stanza stood originally:

And the dead leaves are huddled and still,

but soon it stood amended, as still it stands:

And the dead leaves lie huddled and still,

strengthened through the replacement of the colorless copula *are* by the vivid verb *lie*.

One final instance of significant revision: In "My November Guest" Frost, speaking of his Sorrow, begins:

My Sorrow, when she's here with me
   Thinks these dark days of autumn rain
Are beautiful as days can be;

and in the second stanza he wrote, at first:

She's glad her simple worsted gray
Is silvered now with clinging mist.

But early in the next year, preparing manuscript copy to submit to Mrs. David Nutt for publication, he touched both lines lightly in alteration, the touch in the last line proving beyond the shadow of a doubt that he is a poet not only in the intense thoughtfulness of creation but also in the cool contemplation of revision. For as he changed them the lines read:

She's glad her simple worsted grey
Is silver now with clinging mist.

The revisions that Frost has made in his early poems are few indeed. But surely, too, they are significant. For they reveal the poet, who has always been slow to publish, as capable of rethinking, rephrasing, and even rehearing, his already most carefully wrought verses. Cutting out skilfully here a mere point of weakening detail and forthrightly there an entire thought that he is no longer sure of; now replacing already adequate words with subtly stronger and better ones, now deftly eliminating a harshness in a speech melody; on up to transmuting (in more ways than one) silvered to silver. Frost the artisan in revision is the peer of Frost the artist in creation.

Appendix E
Notebook Sent to Newdick by Frost in 1935.

On Front cover of Notebook sent to Newdick in 1935:

Bring all under the influence of *great* books as under a *spell*.
Teach all the satisfaction of successful speech. 1912.

Most of this goes back to earlier than the above date. R.F.
1935.

*On October 16, 1935, "Robert Frost / Amherst, Mass."
mailed to "Professor Robert Newdick / English Department /
Ohio State University / Columbus / Ohio" a large envelope
which contained a notebook, which, in a note on the upper
right margin of the first page, Robert Frost wrote was "For
Robert Newdick to keep and to get what he can out of
ingenious inference / Robert Frost 1935". The original was
bought by the Dartmouth College Library from the Newdick
Collection in 1966 or 1967. The following is the text of it:*

Page 1:

Disongiong [Approximated lettering of word not found
understandable].

Wherein is a teacher like a fireman.

Wherein not

If you grant me the friendly letter as / end and aim it is all I ask;
you grant / me everything

We wont [sic] assume that they are / all going to be written. Silly
to / teach as if we did.

Suppose they show a little vein of / humor a vein of mockery
as vein / of homely truth.

Page 2:

Against inquisitorial and exegetical reading. For devotional reading.

Part of literature is the education of the emotions. Superior to music here because better balanced.

Danger of taking away the pleasure of finding beauty for ourselves.

Danger of exhausting interest by overusing in / youth. Leave reading to the self-imposed labor.

In literature we come into the enjoyment of what we have gained in other subjects. Fructional.

Not prepared to labor hard in it till the fire of / joy turns a steady and unquenchable flame.

Page 3:

The Waiting Spirit
The spirit won't stand waiting for you till the mechanics of learning are mastered. It must be enlisted from the first or it will fly away to other things.
There are all sorts of zests to depend on—the zest even of spelling. A good deal [*Most* written above that phrase, as supplanting it.] of the / zest in everything comes from seeing what it / is for—in having the end in view. To[o] much / to ask children to go years without knowing / what their studies are all about.

Page 4:

[Evidently as an afterthought, these two lines were written in an upward slant in the top margin of the page:]

Like two circles one looks at with a partition between / the eyes and the circles. They float together.

Eclipsing circles of books they can enjoy and / books they ought to enjoy.

Convergence of the eyes to prevent image being / double.

Education depends on the number of times you have stirred a

right feeling. Number of times the fine / thrill has run your fiber.

Not a question of arguing anyone [written above: or correcting anyone] into the reading / of good books. The will should not be aroused / for or against till late in education.

How many books are available for the teacher's / library.

To be remembered that the thrill is launched / nowhere else as in simple poetry.

After the mechanical part of reading has been / required (and haste in everything here) nothing counts / but the spell I speak of.

Page 5:

[Just one line near the bottom of the page:] This rain is as dry as a sand storm.

Page 6:

[Written in top margin:]

(I seem not to have hated the word thrill as much as I do / now in 1935)

There are all sorts bad cheap good Aim is not *any thrill* [arrow connects to word *all* in line above] but only response to the fine / impulsion. The writing and reading converge on the point / of the conscious use of words sentence forms / intonations and figures (marks of personality) / in both pupil and author. The pupil / has to learn at last to equal himself in a way with / the great ones. Put himself in their place. This / is the culmination of both reading and writing and / where education should possibly leave those / who have done well in english [sic].

Figures of speech sentence forms etc should / be discriminated first and first named in their / accidental appearance in the ones [sic] own writing. They are taken in from the vernacular / rather than from literature.

Page 7:

[In three lines in top margin of this page:] (This must be some

afternotes on a talk I / called A Literary Moment. A Good
Teacher Knows One When He Sees It. R.F. 1935)

    Recurrence of the Moment
    Hanging round for the moment.

To know a moment when you see it—that is / to be a teacher.
"There there you are—You've said / it" is the most influencing
thing you can say / to a person. Or I know exactly—you get it /
just as I have felt it. Fellow feeling and / common experience.

Question of what the teacher shall address / himself to in theme
reading—handwriting / spelling grammar punctuation
paragraphing / imagination reality stories ideas.

You may say that what you care most for / is the idea but if you
never address yourself / in comment to anything but the
mechanics who / will believe you?

Page 8:

It is healthy and normal for things and objects to keep a child's
mind off words (spoken or written) till he is well along in years.

He is in little more use of being corrected in his early writing
than in his early speech. Why / speed the day of self-
consciousness?

Probably he first notices his speech with satisfaction when he
thinks he has given an antagonist his / answer "good and
plenty."

He will be aware of having acquitted himself well in speech
before ever he is in writing.
    In the writing it will / probably be a letter he is proud of as
giving his / enemy what he deserves.

Page 9:

The problem will be to show him that such moments are
literary and they must be repeated. They must be extended to
other feelings and brought into his writing.

He must be taught that the fun of being epigrammatic is a
legitimate form of literature.

Will he ever feel the satisfaction of being epigrammatic in an examination in history? / The question is crucial. Has he time?

Poverty and inertness are the result of our teaching thus far.

The mind must be induced to flow: to see that there is a plenty to say on a thousand / subjects.

Let the teach[er] threaten to use up all the ideas on

Page 10:

a given subject an[d] see how the child will beg for a chance to talk or write before it is too late.

From quantity quatity [accidental crossing of "l"] by selection. / Many random movements are more apt than / a few to contribute the right movement.

Care not to divert a mind from a thought on / which it is running free by much talk about the / way it is running.

Intonation possibilities of what they read and what they write should be noticed as early as anything.

Cultivate shame but dont [sic] try to before the instinct for it makes itself apparent.

Here we may all touch the artistic soonest and most directly.

Page 11:

"Aim low enough: As much as we can expect is to get them to write a good business letter." All right aim low enough but why not make it a good friendly letter?—and that lets in everything.

Recognition

Page 12:

Something of the artistic experience for all.

Make conscious of sentence forms the wrong way by present method.

The subject you know for yours assembles the scattering experience of years. [Is a gatherer] [RF's brackets, seemingly interpolated in 1935, before sending to Newdick.]

You be able to say "I am / forced to notice". "I am forced to think."

Things happen to you and things / occur to you, the latter with as little help from / you as the former.

It is the thing "given" from without that has substance. This is the age of the given. We look to see if we find patriotism given in our natures. We look to see if we can find any

Page 13:

modifying passion along with it.

What occurs to you must be given from without

Will say ten happenings make an occurence [sic].

What we call creation is at most the modifying influence of one actual thing or another / in the mind.

We are on safest ground with things remembered.

Every thing that is a thing is out there and there it stands waiting under your eye till some day you notice it.

Page 14:

Pursuit of the Spirit to its Source

Page 15:

Assigned subjects

Incentives to the spirit.

The right kind of subject as an example solely

the moment

Page 16:

Division of Nature.

Page 17:

Reading for pleasure, reading for improvement.

Families where the word improvement is never heard.

Movies in the name of improvement.

Page 18:

Your Doubts and Docility

Page 19:

The Better Part of Imagination

Page 20:

Efficiency in Reading

Page 21:

Composing in Things.

Page 22:

Recognition. How tell us something we dont [sic] know. Tell us something we know but haven't been told before. (heard before

Material you didnt [sic] know you had before

The Log Keepers

Rulers and Rule

The Wreck of the Raft

The Four Boys

Page 23:

The Moment

Page 24:

Care not to turn their nature all to seeking your approval. A little scorn of that wont [sic] hurt them. Not to have children remember you as having taught them anything in particular. May they remember you as an old friend. That is what it is to have been right with them in their good moments.

Page 25:

The Waiting Spirit
How long will the spirit be put off.

Evidence that the spirit is there in the first place in the bubbling of children.

Quantity copiousness is something / given in the child's nature. Something to keep. Manipulate it into something from quantity quality.

Practical help in what to address yourself to in theme reading. "I'd keep that if I were you." Let me have a copy of that

First

Taste the satisfaction of successful speech. When.

Page 26:

They like a game because it gets somewhere. The spirit is deedal. Ends real and false success with teachers. Success with the work in completion.

The Jumping Frog. Not what I can load you up with.
                    It is what do you say

Privation that the spirit may come [Above that: inappreciation helps].

Cheering the spirit on

Inappreciation. Near is dear. Someone far enough away to chastise.

Page 27:

[In three lines, surrounded by elongated parentheses, Robert Frost wrote across the top margin of this page: "Somebody angered me by saying About / as much as we can expect from them is a / correct business letter. R.F. 1935". See p. 11 of this notebook for another reference to the "aim low" remark.]

A Business Letter

Assuming a good deal to assume that writing can be taught— that anything can be taught.

Any writing that is to someone else as [sic] is speech. To not for. The less makebelieve the better. The best make believe is play.

As to the saying Dont [sic] write till you have something to say.

Appendix F

*"How a Columbus Mother Inspired Her Son to
Become The Dean of America's Living Poets."
As in* The Columbus Sunday Dispatch, *May 17, 1936,
Graphic Section, on p. 5.*

Columbus can rightfully claim some share in the rich and
varied background of Robert Frost, dean of America's living
poets, and when he steps up to the lectern to begin his reading
and talk on poetry, Thursday evening, May 21, in the chapel at
Ohio State University there will be in the audience a number of
local residents who are blood relatives of his through kinship
with his mother.

From lowland Scotland, in June, 1830, there came to America
and on out to Ohio, Thomas Moodie, a young barrister newly
graduated from the University of Edinburg. Not long thereafter
he sent to the homeland for his affianced bride, and soon they
were settled permanently in Columbus.

In the years that followed, he became a prosperous banker, an
elder in the First Presbyterian Church, and the father of seven
daughters and one son. The old Moodie home was on the southwest corner of State and Sixth streets.

Four of Thomas Moodie's daughters grew to womanhood.
Fannie married Thomas Baldwin and moved to the east; Jennie
married a Cincinnati Proctor and moved to the west. Euphelia
became the mother of Jeannie, Effie, and Katherine Duncan.
The last named, now a resident of Washington, D.C., for many
years was the secretary of President W. O. Thompson of Ohio
State University.

The youngest, Florence, married William G. Harrington,
jeweler, now retired from business and living at 2250 Bryden
Road. Three of his children now with children and grandchil-
dren of their own, still reside here: G. Dana Harrington, 2466
Bryden Road; Henry K. Harrington, 82 East Main Street; and
Mrs. Fred C. Walker, 53 Latta Avenue.

Back in lowland Scotland the Moodies were a seafaring family
and the sea had taken its toll of them. It had already taken
Thomas Moodie's nephew and namesake, now it took his sea-
captain brother, leaving his niece, Isabelle Moodie, an orphan.

So late in the 50's, accompanied by her grandmother who returned at once, rosy-cheeked, dark-haired immigrant Belle Moodie, about thirteen years old, came to America, and on to Columbus, to spend the remaining years of her youth with her uncle and his family.

       *   *   *

Here she resumed her education: graduating with the class of 1864 from Columbus High School, more recently known as the old Central High School, formerly at Sixth and Broad streets. Her part in the graduation exercises, an essay on Gas, was "received with great favor by the audience," according to an account in the press, and was "unsurpassed by any other effort of the evening." Her graduation picture shows her to have been a striking, beautiful girl.

Then from 1864 to 1872, save for one year, Miss Moodie taught in the public schools of the city, rising from primary teacher to intermediate teacher, high school teacher, and finally assistant principal of District No. 3.

Particular friends of Miss Moodie during those years were the Misses Jane and Elizabeth Sullivant, especially the former. When Frost visited Columbus in January, 1922, he called on these old friends of his mother and Miss Jane Sullivant. . . .

Appendix G

Undated Frost-Newdick Inscriptions.

1. An edition of *From Snow to Snow*, used as a pamphlet with a special title page honoring the twentieth anniversary of The Hampshire Bookshop (1916–1936). Under the two lines which indicated

Robert Frost
Guest of Honor

is Robert Frost's signature. This is followed by printed designation that the anniversary occurred

on the evening of
April 16, 1936

The third blank page has the following written on it:

My dear Miss Dodd:

You are one of
the few bookshops in the world
where books are sold in something
like the spirit they were written in.
You are a splendid exibition [sic] of
enterprise for a lot of college girls
to look on at. I should think some
of them, who hadn't just seen
what to do with and for themselves after
graduation, might be inspired by
your example to try to do in other
small towns what you have done
in Northampton. They couldnt [sic]
do better with and for themselves, or,
for that matter for the small towns,
or for publishers and authors. I know

publishers and authors who would
like to encourage them.

Sincerely yours [no comma]

Robert Frost

(Possibly acquired by Newdick directly from Miss Dodd
but included here for long Frost inscription.)

2. A 1934 edition of *A Boy's Will* has the last stanza of "Trial by
Existence" inscribed on the fly leaf. It is signed:

Robert Frost

To Robert Newdick

3. *Selected Poems*, March, 1923, has "The Silken Tent" written out sideways on the fly leaf. The fourteen lines of the
poem are word-perfect. No punctuation is used at the end of
any of the lines, thus omitting the comma at the end of lines
three, four, five, seven, eight, and eleven. The period of the
published version at the end of the last line is omitted in the
inscription. It is signed:

Robert Frost

For Robert Newdick

4. First edition of *West-Running Brook*, 1928, is inscribed with
couplet entitled "The Span of Life". It is signed:

Robert Frost
For Robert Newdick

5. *North of Boston*, Holt, 1915, Second Edition.
Title page is inscribed:

Robert Frost
To Robert Newdick

On fly leaf is modified version of first three stanzas of "All
Revelation." "By that Cyb'lean avenue" of published version
has been written: "By what eternal avenue" (fourth line of
first stanza).

The published version of the second stanza has for lines three and four:

> These things the mind has pondered on
> A moment and still asking gone.

Frost has written:

> Thus only mind has pondered on
> The head alone has asked and gone.

The third stanza has three changes. The published first line is "But the impervious geode."

In the second line, the comma between *entered* and *and* is omitted in the inscription.

In the fourth line, "At every point" of the published version has become "In every point" in the inscription.

The entire inscription is signed:

> Robert Frost
> For Robert Newdick

6. Marjorie Frost's *Franconia*, Spiral Press, 1936. Inscribed:

> To Robert Newdick
> from his friend
> Robert Frost

Picture of Marjorie and one of Amherst house are loose in the book.

7. *From Snow to Snow*, Holt, 1936, hard cover, 20 pp.

On blank page opposite first poem, "Storm Fear", the text of "To the Throwing Wind", third poem in the book, is written out with changes. "Come with rain, O loud Southwester!" is written as follows: "Come with rain oh Loud Southwester!" Lines 2, 3, 4, 5, 7, 8, 9, 10, and 11 have a period instead of a semi-colon at the end of each one. Line 6 has *tonight* with no punctuation instead of "to-night,".

8. On page 7 of *An Anthology of New Hampshire Poetry*, R. F. wrote:

> Robert Frost's thanks
> to Robert Newdick for
> the foregoing praises.

[This is undated, unsigned but certainly in Frost's hand.]

9. *A Boy's Will*, Holt, n.d.
   Inscribed on title page below author's name:

> The fact is the sweetest dream that labor knows,
> [Line 13 of "Mowing".]
>
> Robert Frost
>
> To Robert Newdick

Appendix H

Text of Robert Frost's Longhand Table of Contents for Recognition of Robert Frost, *September, 1937.*

Recognition of Robert Frost

I   The Permanence of R. F. Mark Van Doren The American Scholar

II   First Recognition   A letter in 1894 from the poet Maurice Thompson to William Hayes Ward, editor of the N.Y. Independent

III   Some First Reviews of A Boys [sic] Will
        Anonymous The Academy 1913
        *Norman Douglas The English Review 1913

IV   Some First Reviews of North of Boston
        Edward Thomas The English Review 1914
        Lascelles Abercrombie The English Nation 1914
        Edward Garnett The Atlantic Monthly 1915

V   First American Notice
        *William Dean Howells Harpers [sic] Monthly
        Amy Lowell The New Republic
        *Ezra Pound Poetry: A Magazine of Verse

[One line obliterated by scribbling.]

VI   Tribute in Verse
        The Golden Room Wilfred Gibson The Atlantic Monthly
        A Rhymed Review James Stephens London Times
        ? A Letter Robert Hillyer *Lit Supplement*

VI   [Actually VII] Home Places (Chronologically)

New Hampshire Cornelius Weygandt The White
   Hills
Pinkerton Academy Derry N. H. Robert Newdick
   New England Quarterly
England J. W. Haines (in What)
Amherst College George Whicher The Amherst
   Record
Vermont Dorothy Canfield Fisher The Bookman
*Michigan Bernice Stewart The Detroit Free Press
Harvard John Holmes The Boston Transcript
Harvard Anonymous The Harv[ard] Alumni Bulletin
Dark Woods J. McBride Dubbs The Yale Review

[End of first sheet.]

VIII Bibliographical

   a Robert Frost and His Books Frederick Melcher The
      Colophon
   b Preface to the Clymer-Green Bibliography David
      Lambuth

IX Portraits

   a A Good Greek Out of New England E. S. Sergeant
      Fire Under the Andes
   b Original Ordinary Man Sidney Cox
  *c R. F. Padraic Colum Book of the Month Club News
      May, 1936
  *d From the Spotlight John Farrar?

X The Idea

   a The Neighborliness of R. F. G. R. Elliott The Nation
      Whole
   b The Less Travelled Road Caroline Ford Part
   c Against the World in General Gorham B. Munson
      Part
   d Sketch from Modern Am[erican] Poetry Louis Unter-
      meyer Whole
   e Review of Further Range Whole

(The *order* here is *not* determined. [RSN])

f	Percy Boynton	Discretion
g	T. K. Whipple	Discretion
h	Ludwig Lewisohn	Discretion
i	John Freeman	Discretion
j	Russell Blankenship	Discretion
k	Rica Brenner	Discretion
*l	Alfred Kreymborg	Discretion
*m	James Southall Wilson	Whole
*n	Llewellyn Jones	Discretion
*o	Jessie Rittenhouse	Discretion
p	De Selincourt	Last part
q	Desmond McCarthy	Discretion
r	Christopher Morley	
s	A. C. Ward	

XI   Continental

    a Feuillerat
    *b Schwartz
    *c Chamaillard

XII   Four Prefaces to a Book
    a Auden
    b Lewis
    c Engle
    d Muir
*-new

Note: Unfortunately, Robert Frost's longhand script could not be reproduced in this book. The material and format of the *Recognition of Robert Frost*, the plan for which Newdick took with him to the office of Henry Holt and Co. in September of 1937, has here been reproduced as accurately as possible to allow study of the significance of Frost's choices. Frost's spacing and punctuation have been maintained.

Index

428 · *Index*

Frost, Robert
Lectures
"Education by Poetry" 61, 296
"Literary Programs" 370
"Monument to Afterthought Unveiled, A" (High School Commencement) 29
"Party Lines in Poetry Today" 370
"Ruthlessness in Poetry" 370
"What Became of New England?" 175, 178, 179, 188, 208
"Where Is the Place of Ideals and Who Are the Custodians of Them?" 292
Little Review, The 295
Living alone 250
Livy 60
Loafing 39
Local customs 371
Local history 371
London 264, 266, 282, 349
London Times 418
Loner 282
Longfellow, Henry Wadsworth 36, 58, 78
Longhand manuscript 99
Looking Backward 360, 380
Lord, Annie Barker 309
Lord Jeffrey Inn 331
Lost photographs 335
Love 51, 74, 78, 187, 216
Love in a Valley 368
Love of humanity 289
Love of literature 288
Love of Nature 289
Lowell, Amy 264, 273, 275, 283, 299, 367, 368
Lowell, James Russell 58, 292
Lowell, Robert 362
Lowes, John Livingston 270, 271, 276, 292, 294, 323
Loyalty 37, 337, 351
Luck 79
Lucretius 62
Lumber camp 335
Luncheon hospitality 230, 234
Lynch Family 265, 321, 379
Lynch Farm 271
Lyricism 82, 91
Lyric verse 394
Macaulay, Thomas Babington 60
MacKaye, Percy 269
MacLeish, Archibald 165, 362, 368, 369

Macmillan Company 263, 269, 282
MacPherson, Mary 290
MacVeagh, Lincoln 294, 313
Madness 367
Magoon Farm 387
Malone, Dumas 376
Manchester, N.H. 326, 379
Manchester reporter 336
Manhood 74
Mannerism 270, 317
Manthey-Zorn, Otto 322, 332, 337, 351, 358, 369
Manthey-Zorn, Mrs. Otto 333, 335
Manuscript 98, 112, 140
Manuscript approval 280
Manuscript authenticity 110, 111
Manuscript dereliction 202
Manuscript destruction 163
Manuscript procrastination 201
Manuscript poems 214
Manuscript reading 282
Manuscript re-copying 164
Map 387
Maramor 355
"Mark-sick" 322
Marlowe, Christopher 302
Marital dependence 165, 170
Marital problems 376
Marriage 53, 241, 307, 308, 354, 384
Marriage engagement 28, 49, 51, 356
Masefield, John 91, 266, 298, 313, 377, 394
Massachusetts General Hospital 358
Massachusetts State College 262
Masses, The 281
Masters, Edgar Lee 275
Masters' faults 275
Masters' manuscript 275
Mathematics 24, 35, 211
Maturation 60
Mayan sculpture 337
Mayflower 355
Mayflower Hotel 279
McAllister, Frank B. 309, 322
McCann, Thomas 334
McCarthy, Desmond 420
McClelland, ——— 335
McCord, David 325, 368, 376, 377
McQuestin, Nettie 349
Meaning 210, 363, 377
Meaning in poetry 362
Mechanics 407